THE ORWELL CONUNDRUM:

A Cry of Despair or Faith in the Spirit of Man?

THE ORWELL CONUNDRUM:

A Cry of Despair or Faith in the Spirit of Man?

Erika Gottlieb

> "No. I believe it. I *know* that
> you will fail. There is something
> in the universe — I don't know,
> some spirit, some principle — that
> you will never overcome."
> "Do you believe in God, Winston?"
> "No."
> "Then what is it, this principle that
> will defeat us?"
> "I don't know. The spirit of Man."
>
> (*Nineteen Eighty-Four* 232)

Carleton University Press
Ottawa — Canada
1992

ISBN   0-88629-175-5 (paperback)
ISBN   0-88629-174-7 (casebound)

Printed and bound in Canada

Carleton General List

Canadian Cataloguing in Publication Data
  Gottlieb, Erika
    The Orwell conundrum

    Includes bibliographical references and index.

  ISBN 0-88629-174-7 (bound)
  ISBN 0-88629-175-5 (pbk.)

1. Orwell, George, 1903–1950. *Nineteen Eighty-Four*.   I. Title.

PR6029.R8N53 1992   823′.912   C92-090138-7

Distributed by   Oxford University Press Canada,
                 70 Wynford Drive,
                 Don Mills, Ontario,
                 Canada. M3C 1J9
                 (416) 441-2941

Cover design: Aerographics Ottawa
Cover photo: George Orwell in the 1930s
                by courtesy of Mabel Fierz

Acknowledgements

Carleton University Press gratefully acknowledges the support
extended to its publishing programme by the Canada Council
and the Ontario Arts Council.

This book has been published with the help of a grant from
the Canadian Federation for the Humanities, using funds provided by the Social Sciences and Humanities Research Council
of Canada.

Acknowledgements

I wish to thank Professors Dennis Rohatyn (University of San Diego), Patrick Reilly (University of Iowa State), and William Christian (University of Guelph), for their helpful comments on earlier versions of this manuscript.

I am also grateful to Professor Michael Gnarowski from Carleton University Press and Mrs. Denise Lachance, Senior Officer of Aid to Publications for the Canadian Federation for the Humanities, for their help with the publication of this book.

Earlier versions of Chapters 4, 5, and 9 appeared in *George Orwell: A Reassessment*, ed. Peter Buitenhuise and Ira Nadel (London: Macmillan, 1988); and in *Utopian Studies II* and *Utopian Studies III*, ed. Michael Cummings and Nicolas Smith (Lanham, New York: American University Press, 1989 and 1990), respectively.

To
My Parents
and
Paul, Peter, and Julie

Contents

Part I

A Cry of Despair or
Faith in the "Spirit of Man"?

Chapter 1

The Orwell Conundrum

Was George Orwell a literary genius?

His major novel, *Nineteen Eighty-Four* has been compared to the satires of Huxley, Waugh (Greenblatt), and Swift (Reilly), to dystopias such as Golding's *Lord of the Flies* (Gulbin), Zamiatin's *We* (Beauchamp), and Koestler's *Darkness at Noon* (Calder, Fink). Orwell's stature as a writer has been measured against his contemporaries ranging from Sartre (Wilson) to T.S. Eliot (Good), as well as to various disillusioned Socialists in the late thirties and early forties, such as Koestler and Silone (Weintraub).

Lionel Trilling celebrates Orwell for "the virtue of not being a genius" (Introd. *HC* x); Koestler, however, suggests that we consider Orwell "the only writer of genius among the littérateurs of social revolt between the two wars" and the "missing link between Kafka and Swift" (Rebel's 4–5).

Is *Nineteen Eighty-Four* a major novel of this century? In spite of the exceptional coincidence between the high intensity of critical attention due only to major literary achievement, and the unabated public interest that turned it into an all-time bestseller, the majority of academic analysts argue that it is a flawed work — granted a "flawed masterpiece." This verdict has been upheld even in the novel's busy 'title year,' 1984, amidst the plethora of symposia and conferences on two continents paying tribute to Orwell. Thus, in a 1984 lecture on the novel, Leslie Fiedler refers to Orwell's "cardboard characters," echoing Cyrill Connolly's 1965 dismissal of the same characters as puppets (89–94). Although the 1984 conferences have re-examined Orwell in the light of Lacan, New Linguistics, Wittgenstein, the Deconstructionist and Feminist critical theory, they have kept on regurgitating many of the earlier charges about Orwell's literal mind that makes him a "slight artist" (George Elliott 152); that his novel is flawed because "there is no genuine tension, no struggle; the defeat is there from the beginning" (Dutsher 312), and that Orwell's obsession with the "real," the "process," allowed no time for the imagination to do its work — in short, that Orwell had a literal mind and was therefore a slight artist.

The problem is, if Orwell is not a genius and *Nineteen Eighty-Four* is not a great work, how can one explain the continued impact of the novel, the recognition extended to its central concepts, and Orwell's increasing international stature?

The first impulse may be to bypass this dilemma and turn to Bertrand Russell (5–7), George Woodcock (293), or more recently, Bernard Gorfman, all of whom suggest that *Animal Farm* and not *Nineteen Eighty-Four* is Orwell's greatest work. Naturally, there is no consensus on this point either. W.H. Auden argues that neither *Animal Farm* nor *Nineteen Eighty-Four* "quite comes off" (86) as a great work of fiction. Robert Lee considers *Coming Up for Air* as the central transitional work, while John Wain, in an influential study written in 1954, recommends that we ignore Orwell the novelist in favour of Orwell the essayist and pamphleteer, since "as a novelist [Orwell] was not particularly gifted but as a controversial critic and pamphleteer . . . [he] was superb, as good as any in English Literature" (71).

There are, of course, many who consider *Nineteen Eighty-Four* to be Orwell's crowning achievement. Philip Rahv, E.M. Forster, Peter Stansky, and among recent Orwell critics, William Steinhoff and Ian Slater, regard *Nineteen Eighty-Four* as the culmination of Orwell's work. Daphne Patai, in *The Orwell Mystique*, agrees with Steinhoff and Slater on the significance of *Nineteen Eighty-Four* among Orwell's works, but argues as well that Orwell's pessimism and final despair render it flawed.

Even Bernard Crick, who in his *Orwell: A Life* and "Critical Introduction and Annotations to *Nineteen Eighty-Four*" has come closer than any other critic to a consistent synthesis of Orwell's work, tends to subscribe to the popular "flawed masterpiece" theory. Although he admits that Orwell wrote "a masterpiece of political speculation [and that] *Nineteen Eighty-Four* is to the twentieth century what Thomas Hobbes's *Leviathan* was to the seventeenth," he nevertheless adds that "it is a flawed masterpiece of literature and of political thought" (*Life* 398–399).

Even Crick's fundamentally sympathetic assessment reveals the ongoing schism, the perpetual somersault in logic so characteristic of Orwell criticism. While one may easily understand this in the case of a biographer, Crick is by no means the only one whose reading reveals this strange anomaly. It is as if admiration for Orwell followed from something other than his stature as a writer. It is as if most critics would seem to agree that,

with all due respect, although this undeniably outstanding man
may have achieved his fame as a writer, the writing is unfor-
tunately devoid of something that ought to be there, but is,
unhappily, missing.[1] I suggest that the source of this schism, as
well as of the "flawed masterpiece" theory, is the widely shared
assumption that Orwell's last novel conveys a vision of despair.

Despair as Flaw in Literary Achievement

There are several political or ideological 'subtexts' underlying
the particular position of the individual critic who perceives
pessimism and despair in Orwell's work, and each contains an
implied reproach, often an accusation. Four of these critical
positions are worthy of closer examination.

One of the most intriguing areas of Orwell criticism is represented by the 'psychological critic.' However, psychological
critics of the Freudian persuasion take it as an article of faith
that the defeat experienced by the major character signifies the
despair of the author. Fiderer, Smith, even Paul Roazan, take
it for granted that Winston's defeat by Big Brother should be
seen as a reflection, first of the character's, and ultimately of the
writer's, neurosis. From the psychological critic's perspective,
defeat equals despair equals neurosis. The professional bias of
Freudian depth psychology, in spite of some brilliant insights,
leads to a diagnosis of Orwell that is too facile, and results in
a misconception of the novel.

In the second and largest school, the 'political critics' tend
to judge the merits of the novel according to what they see as
Orwell's political stance. Those reading Orwell's political views
sympathetically become "body snatchers" (Labedz 25), eager to
claim ownership of Orwell. In 1984, conservatives, liberals, neo-
conservatives, and the New Left battled over the possession of
Orwell's political legacy, often blithely oblivious to the literary
text, let alone aesthetic considerations.

However, when the critics of this school are not in sympathy with Orwell's politics, they return to the novel's aesthetic flaws resulting, they suggest, from the writer's despair.
Such influential political critics as Raymond Williams, Isaac
Deutscher, and more recently Gilbert Bonifas in France, have
reiterated that *Nineteen Eighty-Four* conveys despair; all of
them equate "flaw" in political thought with "flaw" in literary
achievement. According to Deutscher, Orwell's despair is the

typically irrational, hysterical reaction of the ex-Communist. Alas, Deutscher's criticism of Orwell tells us more about Deutscher than about Orwell. In his "The Ex-Communist's Conscience" (which appeared originally in his 1950 review of *The God that Failed*), Deutscher offers his diagnosis of the mental attitude that he applies equally to all disillusioned ex-Communists, such as Silone and Koestler. Significantly, Deutscher puts Orwell in the same category as these writers. Of course, Orwell had never been a member of any party, except the Independent Labour Party for a short period, and had always been critical of Stalin's regime. Deutscher misreads the novel because he misinterprets the politics of Orwell the man. Deutscher accuses all ex-Communists of an irrational emotionalism verging on hysteria,[2] "a characteristic incapacity for detachment . . . The picture of Communism and Stalinism he draws is that of a gigantic chamber of intellectual and moral horrors. Viewing it, the uninitiated are transferred from politics to pure demonology" ("Ex-Communist's" 13).

To recognize the reasons for Deutscher's verdict on *Nineteen Eighty-Four*, one should read his definition of *all* ex-Communist literary expression. He admits that "sometimes the artistic effect may be strong — horrors and demons do enter into many a poetic masterpiece," but argues that such works are "politically unreliable and even dangerous. Of course, the story of Stalinism abounds in horror. But this is only one of its elements; and even this, the demonic, has to be translated into terms of human motives and interests. The ex-Communist does not even attempt the translation" ("Ex-Communist's" 13).

When in his extremely influential 1955 article, "*1984* — The Mysticism of Cruelty," Deutscher identified the novel as a "piercing shriek" (49) of despair, he must have taken for granted that Orwell was an ex-Communist, a status, for Deutscher, tantamount to an incurable disease of the imagination. Clearly, it was Deutscher's preconceived (and misconceived) notion of the political position of Orwell the man, and not a close analysis of the novel, that gave rise to the legend of *Nineteen Eighty-Four* as a "cry from the abyss of despair" ("1984").

Although their motives may be quite different, both 'psychological' and 'political' critics tend to agree that Orwell's final vision is one of despair. When Orwell died at 46, very soon after the publication of the novel, the notion of his final despair became accepted as something of a commonplace, and was, therefore left unexamined for a long time. Another, even more regrettable assumption left unchallenged is that if the book ends in despair, this must surely be a sign of aesthetic failure.

This latter assumption seems to be very widespread. It also supports the third voice of Orwell criticism, that of the Feminist critic. In *The Orwell Mystique: A Study of Male Ideology*, Daphne Patai argues that Orwell's final position of despair is attributable to his traditional, even misogynist gender ideology. According to Patai, Orwell regards the drive for power as innate and incorrigible because of his androcentric view of humanity. Implied in Patai's criticism, I believe, is the assumption that it is the limitation of this androcentric view that causes Orwell to overlook the chance for a new kind of humanity, a new ego-ideal that would be enriched by the feminine components of the personality and thus no longer dominated by the drive for power.[3] Once again, the critic's verdict on Orwell's despair is tantamount to dismissal: how can Orwell be considered a major writer when his seminal novels end in despair?

The fourth critical strain charging Orwell with despair is that of the humanist, a voice potentially far more sympathetic to Orwell than those of the other three. This voice is best represented by Bertrand Russell, whose 1950 tribute to Orwell states: "I am grateful to men, who like Orwell, decorate Satan with the horns and hooves without which it remains an abstraction" (5). Although his tribute is no doubt genuine, in the closing words of his essay Russell reproaches Orwell for his pessimistic conclusion, his despair.[4] Here Russell takes a fellow-humanist to task for giving in to demons. Inevitably, Russell sees despair as a kind of betrayal, the giving up of the humanist's belief in man's perfectibility, the acceptance that the drive for power is permanent and hence incorrigible. This last comes dangerously close to accepting the theological position on the existence of radical evil — a stand that defies the entire creed of post-Enlightenment humanism.

However tempting it would be to respond here to each of these four critical voices, it will be more useful at this stage to look at the underlying assumption that, surprisingly, they all seem to share. While each critical school has a different strategy behind its condemnation of despair, they all take for granted that if the novel conveys despair, it must be classified as a "flawed masterpiece." Of course, Orwell is neither the first nor the only major writer in this century whose contemporaries were convinced that his work had been marred by despair. Nor is Orwell unique in feeling compelled to refute the accusation. Thus, Sartre protests that Existentialism "isn't trying to plunge man into despair at all. But if one calls every attitude of unbelief despair, like the Christians, then the word is not being used in its original sense" ("Existentialism" 84). Camus protests the same accusation: "By what right would a Communist or Christian . . . blame me for being a pessimist? I didn't invent human misery or the terrible formulas of divine malediction" (*Notebook* 123). Like others accused of despair, Orwell felt it necessary to publicly insist that *Nineteen-Eighty-Four* was not a prophecy, not the scenario of what *will* take place in a certain way, but something that *might* happen unless prevented (v. 4, 564).

Before determining whether a particular writer's vision conveys despair, we must answer the following questions. Does one particular philosophy lead to aesthetic excellence more than another? Is a vision of despair necessarily an aesthetic shortcoming? Is there an irreconcilable conflict between the metaphysical position of pessimism and artistic excellence? Clearly, these questions point to wider issues in criticism.

Even the vision of Kafka, long regarded as a synonym for despair, is being carefully repoliticized nowadays, no doubt to prevent his aesthetic downgrading. Significantly, it is often the critic with the highest regard for the writer who feels compelled to insist that deep down even Kafka must have believed in free will, the freedom of choice, and possibly in a hopeful future for mankind.[5] I believe that such a repoliticization denies the very essence of the author's message. Endemic to Kafka's vision is the confrontation of the individual and the gigantic, monstrous State; in this confrontation the individual is bound to lose everything that would make him human; he is dwarfed, loses specific gravity and significance. To interpret Kafka's message as more "optimistic" would be equal to removing its essence, passion, and character.

It seems as if most contemporary critics view the novelist's craft as a kind of game, played in an underground labyrinth, which, unbeknownst to the writer, has several exits, marked "Affirmation," "Acceptance," "Hope," "Scepticism," "Denial," and "Despair." The rules of this game state that the writer can enter at any point as long as he or she doesn't surface at the wrong exit. The writer's performance will then be judged

acceptable only if he or she finds an approved exit that leads towards a conclusion of hope, acceptance, or affirmation. But why
should not the game allow the writer to exit at *any* philosophical conclusion, providing it is a genuine, "earned" conclusion in
the context of the vision emerging from his journey? And what
of the sense of catharsis that follows from having confronted
the darkness, in both its social and psychological aspects, of
the tragic dimension of life?

My first point, then, is that even if Orwell had a tragic attitude to life, why should we assume that this would undercut
the validity, the magnitude, the degree of intensity, or the credibility of his vision as a writer? Whether *Nineteen Eighty-Four*
is a masterpiece should be determined by the uniqueness, the
intensity, the breadth, and the coherence of the vision it commu-
nicates. Critical assessment should focus on the writer's success
in integrating his vision and the work; on the appropriate relationship between genre, theme, structure, and texture; and in
the case of this particular novel, on the satirist's effectiveness
in conveying his message and hitting his targets. It is on the
basis of these issues that this study argues against the various
proponents of the "flawed masterpiece" theory.[6]

Does *Nineteen Eighty-Four* Convey Despair?

Having argued that neither despair, pessimism, nor indeed any
particular philosophical or metaphysical point of view provides
a basis for dismissing a literary work as "flawed," I would like to
address the question of whether Orwell's last work does indeed
convey despair, pessimism, or paranoia about human nature
and the future of humanity.

To examine Orwell's "despair" and "paranoia" from a political perspective, it would seem to me only fair to consider the
following three questions:

First, was Orwell's description of Oceania (the parody of the
totalitarian state he had ample opportunity to observe in the
Germany and Russia of the thirties and forties) an accurate
assessment of the essential features of totalitarianism?

The second question concerns the validity of Orwell's diagnosis. There is no doubt that Orwell diagnosed the workings
of the totalitarian state as a mechanism of terror, and its mentality a widely spreading and self-perpetrating contagion, but
was Orwell the only one or even the first in his time to diagnose

this? And, in comparison with other analysts of totalitarian terror, did Orwell mis-diagnose or exaggerate the seriousness of the disease?

Finally, the third question refers to Orwell's conclusion, the prognosis he made on the basis of the patient's condition in the late forties. Was there any indication in 1948, when Orwell wrote the book, that the trends of totalitarianism that had been so clear in the 1930s and the early 1940s were once more on the upsurge, that totalitarianism was going to embrace and paralyze more and more of the civilized world and the civilized mind in the future?

To answer the first question. If we examine historical documents from the period, many of them not at Orwell's disposal at the time, we find it increasingly obvious that Orwell was a most able diagnostician of the actual dynamics of totalitarianism, the mental state inducing and induced by terror. His diagnosis was confirmed not only by the political observers among his contemporaries in the West, but also by the survivors of terror in Hitler's Germany and Stalin's Russia.[7]

As for the second question, there is no doubt that some of the most significant ingredients of Orwell's diagnosis were also confirmed by later analysts of totalitarianism, such as the historian Hannah Arendt; political scientists Friedrich, Brzezinsky, and Schapiro; as well as psychologists and writers of the stature of Carl Jung, Thomas Mann, and Albert Camus. (Chapter 10 will discuss this question in more detail.)

Finally, we would do well to remember that at the time of the writing of *Nineteen Eighty-Four*, Orwell had good reason to be concerned about an upsurge of totalitarian thinking. He had watched the swallowing up of Eastern Europe by Soviet Russia with alarm and apprehension. He was one of the first to diagnose what was later defined as the "Stalingrad syndrome" (Devroey 140) — that is, Western intellectuals' condoning of Stalin's methods both in his foreign politics and in the treatment of his own people. The general sympathy with the tremendous sacrifices of the people of the Soviet Union in World War II blinded the intellectuals and rendered them unwilling to draw a distinction between the Soviet people and their leadership. Orwell had also commented with dismay on the increasing influence of the Comintern, and when that was dissolved, the international network of the Communist parties that had become the direct instrument of Russian foreign policy. Through this network the outlook was determined not only for Western Communist parties, but also for the growing number of "fellow travellers," and for the whole community of "progressive" intellectuals. He also had reason to be concerned about the fate of Western Socialism if the "progressive" intellectual was duped into accepting the "Soviet myth" — that is, considering Stalin's system as a viable model of Socialism.[8]

All this should indicate that the novel was not an hysterical diagnosis of a world in a normal state of health; it was, rather, an accurate diagnosis of the world in the throes of an hysterical disease. Nor was Orwell the only commentator to foresee the crisis of the Western world, even if he was among the first writers of fiction from the camp of Social Democrats to point out that not only the temporary policies, but also the very essence of Stalinism, went against the original ideals of Socialism. His position was by no means unique, even if it was very far from being a popular one in the Western Europe of the late 1940s; Camus followed suit in the early 1950s, while Sartre made his move after the Hungarian Revolution of 1956.

The Threat of Timelessness — Satirical Overstatement

The vision informing *Nineteen Eighty-Four* was far from being inspired by personal obsession. Nor did the ensuing years prove that Orwell had been driven by paranoia or demonic obsession. Why, then, do so many of the critics accept Deutscher's famous verdict of the "cry from the abyss of despair"?

To understand the nature of the Orwell conundrum, we have to recognize that the central conceit of the book is the threat of timelessness. The Inner Party is indestructible. This conceit is a significant feature in the political vision informing *Nineteen Eighty-Four*; it differs from the views of other commentators both in Orwell's lifetime and afterwards. It is at the very centre of the novel: once totalitarianism has been allowed to spread, it will indeed spread all over the world, and once it has conquered the world, it will become timeless, unchangeable. It is therefore legitimate to ask: even if Orwell's concern about the horrors and the spreading of totalitarianism was fully warranted, doesn't he succumb to despair and paranoia in his presentation of the demonic world of Oceania, Eastasia, and Eurasia as an eternally totalitarian world?

The major reason that *Nineteen Eighty-Four* is one of the most controversial dystopian satires, and that so many of its critics accept the verdict of despair, comes, ironically, from Orwell's success as a writer in the mode of psychological realism. In creating such a palpably "real" vision of the induced insanity and cruelty of the totalitarian mindset, by giving it global and eternal dimensions, the book presents us with superlative evil, and as Carl Jung points out, "everything that exceeds a certain human size evokes equally inhuman powers in man's unconscious" (*Civilization* 226).

Yet, it is precisely this characteristic of evil being larger than life that should give us pause before we come to a decision on the dilemma of Orwell's demonic vision, and his "cry from the abyss of despair."

I suggest that the virtually unprecedented impact of the novel as a satire comes precisely from the deeply felt horrors of contemporary reality projected on a worldwide screen, making them appear timeless and eternal, at least while we are engaged with Winston's personal story. As Orwell explains, his purpose in *Nineteen Eighty-Four* was "to indicate, by parodying them, the intellectual implications of totalitarianism" (v. 4, 520). We should recognize that, for Orwell, parody is a synonym for satire, and the genre requires the devices of reversal, overstatement, exaggeration. So, if Orwell the political commentator saw that totalitarianism was on the upsurge, it would be natural for Orwell the satirist to dramatically overstate this danger by giving it global dimensions. If as a political commentator he saw examples of totalitarian systems threatening, with unprecedented staying power, it was quite within the legitimate strategies of the satirist to pronounce them timeless and endless. Hitler's Third Reich was to last a thousand years, and in the early 1940s there were many who believed the claim. Stalin's regime, at the time of Orwell's diagnosis in 1948, had been going strong for over twenty years, and was extending its grip over the Party within, over the governments of Eastern Europe, and over the Communist parties all over the world. The very urgency of Orwell's prognosis (he gave the world less than forty years, between 1940 and 1948, to turn upside down), reveals the same satirical device of overstatement and acceleration. The strategy of making alarming current trends appear more striking and threatening is quite appropriate to classical satire. Consequently, the unspeakable horror of an evil system spreading over the world, setting in for an eternity, is to be contemplated in earnest, albeit within the context of satire.

Dark Prophecy or Powerful Satire?
Political Fluctuations in Orwell Criticism

It is true that from the time of the novel's publication there had been many critics who suggested that *Nineteen Eighty-Four* was a satire, and hence more of a warning than a prophecy of inevitable doom and despair. Yet even these critics would have difficulty in drawing a clear distinction between the vehicle and the target, unable to agree what exactly Orwell meant to be the butt of the satire. Due to the fluctuations in the political climate during the years between 1949 and the late 1980s, this disagreement contributed to the gradual de-emphasizing of the novel's satirical dimension to the point where the term 'political satire' almost disappeared from the critical vocabulary.[9]

At first, in the months immediately after publication, the Trillings, Golo Mann, Philip Rahv, and many others welcomed the book as satire. They also agreed that Stalin's Russia was the primary target — the most topical, even if not the only one. In the early fifties, however, the enthusiastic American reception of the novel as not only anti-Communist but also anti-Socialist changed this situation. Critics on the Left became concerned that if they emphasized the anti-Stalinist target of Orwell's satire, this might add to the red-baiting hysteria of the Mc-Carthy era. Increasingly, critics felt the need to de-emphasize the resemblance between Big Brother and Stalin. Naturally, they could not deny the resemblance altogether, but instead of dwelling on Stalin's system as the primary target, they would emphasize that the target was universal, dealing with totalitarianism in general. While there is nothing wrong in pointing out that the universal target of the satire *is* the nature of totalitarianism, one should not fail to point out also that the most vivid examples of totalitarianism at Orwell's disposal were the systems of Hitler and Stalin, and Ingsoc carries allusions to both. However, critics of the liberal Left were also somewhat uncomfortable with Orwell's emphasis on the essential similarity between the regimes of Hitler and Stalin and with his use of the double edge of satire to make it quite clear that, in spite of fundamentally different ideologies, both systems used terror as their method of government. The same critics might have been just as uncomfortable when reminded that when Orwell was defending "the freedom of the intellect" (v. 4, 84) in the West in 1948, he must have considered the lure of Fascism a far less active threat than the lure of Stalinism.[10] Then came the period that saw Orwell come under frontal attack; the Left of the late sixties and seventies began to argue that if Orwell's work lent itself as ammunition for the Right, the responsibility was Orwell's. Alexandr Zwerdling's 1974 study outlines the typical line of such an attack.

But to complete the changes in critical opinion concerning Orwell's target we should also take a look at the early 1980s. The mainstream of current Leftist liberal criticism is probably best represented by Bernard Crick. Crick and his followers emphasize that Orwell's target was the Western world, and allusions to the U.S.S.R. are secondary or coincidental. Not surprisingly, by underplaying the importance of Stalinism as Orwell's primary satirical target, Professor Crick finds that "the text seen as a projective model of totalitarian society actually works badly" ("Introduction" 15). Interestingly, the 1984 film version of the novel also follows this emphasis on the West;[11] consequently, as an interpretation of Orwell's work it indeed "works badly." In his article in *The New York Times*, Michael Billington quotes the director, Michael Radford, as saying that in "the book Orwell was offering an image of totalitarianism derived from the world he knew. The film mustn't be a pseudo-documentary about what might happen if the Soviets took over Britain" (19). Of course *Nineteen Eighty-Four* does not suggest that the Soviets took over Britain at any time. Orwell's concern is with the British intellectuals' tendency to regard Stalin's regime as a viable model for Western Socialism, a model to imitate. But in Radford's film the horrors of the totalitarian system in Oceania are seen as the direct consequence of the post-war economy in England in 1948. This interpretation entirely overlooks Orwell's statement that *Nineteen Eighty-Four* was intended as a "show up of the perversions to which a centralized economy is liable and which have already been *partly* realized in *Communism and Fascism*" (v. 4, 564, my italics).

Ironically, the Western liberal critic's tendency to wipe Stalin's picture out of *Nineteen Eighty-Four* happens to coincide with the 1984 "reclamation of Orwell by the Soviet press" (Labedz 16). After almost forty years of ignoring the novel's existence (while suppressing its circulation in Russia and in the Eastern

European countries), the Soviet press came forth to welcome the novel in the year 1984, declaring it a scathing satire of Capitalism in general, and of the United States of America in particular. The *Novoe Vremya* declared that "the tight suit of totalitarianism tailored by Orwell is just the right cut for capitalism" (1 Jan. 1984), and according to Melor Stunia in the *Izvestiya*, Oceania alludes to "the reality of the western world and primarily of the United States of America" (15 Jan. 1984).

Of course, there is no doubt that *Nineteen Eighty-Four* is addressed to the Western reader, but forgetting that the primary satirical target is Soviet Russia under Stalin's regime leads to a serious misunderstanding of the novel. To arrive at an appropriate reading of the satire, we should understand why Orwell felt that it was absolutely vital for the Western intellectual *to see the Soviet regime* in its true light.

The satirist's message is addressed to the intellectual who is sufficiently duped by the "Soviet myth" to contemplate that system as a viable model for Western Socialism. To overlook the vital role played by Orwell's allusions to Stalin's regime in his message to the Western leader leads to a serious misunderstanding of Orwell's achievement as the writer of a powerful work of fiction and (*pace* Professor Crick) a masterpiece of political satire.

The Satirist's Adversary

Like classical satire, *Nineteen Eighty-Four* reveals a concentric circle of targets. The most topical, that is, the primary target, is the betrayal of the originally humanistic goals of democratic Socialism by Stalin's totalitarian regime in the U.S.S.R., and the satire is addressed to the Leftist intellectual who had overlooked, ignored, or justified this betrayal. In fact, here I would like to introduce the idea that in *Nineteen Eighty-Four* this intellectual takes on the role, well known from classical satire, as the satirist's Adversary. Athough the Adversary is usually a silent auditor in the background, the role he plays is important: he "impels the Satirist to speech" (Robert Elliott "Satire" 738).[12] He is the opponent whom the satirist wants to persuade to change the course of his thinking, the course of his action. As we will see in the next chapter, Orwell's stance in relation to such an unnamed background presence should be quite familiar to us from his essays, where it is often the position of such a duped, self-deluded, or cynical Adversary that provides impetus for the unfolding argument. I believe we should remember this rhetorical situation when reading *Goldstein's Book*. In fact, *Goldstein's Book* will become a surprisingly effective key for the decoding of the entire satire, once we recognize that the satirist's voice is generated by a Socialist writer's intention to condemn, ridicule, or enlighten a particular type of opponent, an Adversary he disagrees with about the course of democratic Socialism in the Western world.

The next, more general, target of the satire is the totalitarian mentality, the "blackwhite" of deception and self-deception practised inevitably by anyone once forced into the intellectual strait-jacket of the totalitarian ideology.

At the most universal level of the satire, the target is the mentality of any orthodoxy — political or religious — that offers a sense of belonging at the price of the believer's abnegation of free emotional and intellectual expression — in other words, at the price of the believer's practice of deception and self-deception.

As we approach the wider and wider circumference on the dartboard of satirical targets, the satirist's Adversary also comes to assume the more and more universal attributes of Everyman or Everywoman, a representative of *our* common humanity so eminently capable of succumbing to folly, lies and self-delusion, but also and equally capable of Reason, or at least, capable of struggling against the temptations of Unreason.

The Mood of the Satire:
Comic Humour or Serious Wit

At this point it may be interesting to mention that some of Orwell's most recent critics argue for or against the genre of satire based on their interpretation of the mood created by the novel. In support of his claim that the novel is a parody, Professor Crick suggests we "consider the comic distancing of those two tell-tale gin-scented tears trickling down poor Winston's nose" ("Introduction" 55) in the last scene. Patrick Reilly, quite rightly I think, refuses to read this famous scene as comic. On the basis of this objection, however, Reilly concludes (203) that the book should not be read as a satire because it is lacking in comedy, or humour. I tend to disagree with both Crick and Reilly on this point, and in the concluding chapters shall turn

to some earlier examples of great satire to prove the point that
the mood of many of the finest works in the satirical genre is
not really comic; in fact, great satire often relies on serious wit,
even shocking, savage irony, to make us aware of the absurd,
the irrational. When Orwell presents us with the parody of
such well-observed rituals of power worship as the Two Minutes Hate and Hateweek, the bitter anger in the satirist's voice
is overpowering. Time and again *Goldstein's Book* makes us
think that what we hear is the "savage indignation" of Swiftian
satire, and the novel does, indeed, invite comparison with "A
Modest Proposal," as well as with *Gulliver's Travels*, not to
mention the bitter condemnation of non-Reason in Voltaire's
Candide and Kafka's *Penal Colony*.

But would it be fair to dismiss any of these examples of satire
as "flawed masterpieces" because they, in effect, convey despair?
Classical satire is by nature critical; the attack may be corrosive, the anger on the verge of savage indignation, and yet the
ultimate purpose is curative: our sense of the grotesque, the
topsy-turvy, leads us to the recognition of what is absurd, and
then to a moral-intellectual awareness that we need to "reverse
the reversal."

The Conflict between Psychological Realism and the Political Allegory of Dystopian Satire

There is, of course, one more good explanation for the difficulty
experienced by so many critics of widely differing political and
aesthetic persuasions in accepting *Nineteen Eighty-Four* as a
satire. I suggest that this difficulty is connected with the problems presented by the novel as a composite of genres,[13] containing the elements of what Orwell himself described as a "naturalistic novel" on the one hand, and a "fantasy," a "novel about
the future" (v. 4, 378) — what we would call today dystopian
fiction — on the other. It was also to be, at least to some extent,
a "thriller", a "love story" (v. 4, 519), and a "parody" of the
"intellectual implications of totalitarianism drawn out to their
conclusion" (v. 4, 520). The true difficulty, as I see it, lies in
the dichotomy between the genres conducive to allegory (that
is, the political parody, the satire of ideas, and the dystopian
satire) and the genres associated with the verisimilitude of psychological realism (thriller, romance, naturalist novel).

The mental exercise associated with the tradition of satire begins with a relatively clear-cut separation of the reader's mental and emotional responses. Having followed Candide's or Gulliver's journey, we are expected to recall our distance from the imaginary time and place and return to our own gardens from Eldorado, or to our "civilized" domestic circle from the world of the Houyhnhnms. We are expected, as well, to return with new intellectual insight but without much of an emotional upheaval. By contrast, in all modern novels of psychological realism, by and large, the readers are expected to identify with the central character, and part of Orwell's tremendous success with each of his individual readers is in making us identify with Winston Smith, a convincing representative of the anti-hero, the Everyman of the twentieth century. We are not at all tempted to laugh at Winston with his gin-scented tears at the end of the novel. Broken, brainwashed, mutilated, he is our brother; he represents us, even the best in us, although his courage and fundamental decency are inevitably broken by the indomitable power of that gigantic monster, the totalitarian State.

I suggest that one of the critical controversies leading to the Orwell conundrum is due to the contradictory demands of the two genres, the two kinds of demands Orwell has imposed on his reader. To begin with, there is the demand of intellectual distance and relative unemotionalism associated with the reading of satire; at the same time, the reader is also faced with the need for emotional identification and sympathy associated with the reading of a powerful work of psychological realism. Therefore, it is probably a legitimate question, and a question at the very heart of the conundrum of Orwell criticism, whether the exceptional achievement of Orwell the satirist is, indeed, not undercut by the exceptional achievement of Orwell the writer of realistic fiction in the powerful and sophisticated mode of psychological realism.

In an attempt to answer this question, in Chapter 4 we will examine the interaction between the various genres, with particular attention to the satirical mode of political allegory and the mode of psychological realism. I suggest that such an examination of the tributary genres and their hierarchy will show that satire is the dominant genre of *Nineteen Eighty-Four*. What is more, all other sub-genres are co-ordinated and subordinate to the central goal of the satire, which is to explore, parody, and condemn the totalitarian habit of mind.

The question that may come to mind at this point is, of course, why did Orwell find it necessary to complicate his task by the multi-dimensional difficulties of a complex genre? The answer is relatively simple and points to the very heart of Orwell's achievement. The central message of the satire is that totalitarianism inevitably destroys the individual, penetrates the very essence of his skull and the very core of the inner heart; hence, once it comes into being, totalitarianism leads irrevocably to the destruction of our humanity. Had we not found in Winston a convincing representative of that complex modern species, a "psychological man" we could readily identify with, the central message of the satire would leave us with nothing more than an intellectual abstraction. Orwell made both an aesthetic and a moral choice by combining the powerful allegorical weapons of political satire with the verisimilitude of psychological realism: only through such a combination of genres could he present us with the haunting picture of the destruction of *our* common humanity in the totalitarian system.

Despair or Tragic Humanism?
Orwell's Spiritual Position

But neither the fluctuations in the political climate that formed the background to Orwell criticism in the past forty years, nor the complex problems raised by the novel's composite genre, would be sufficient in themselves to explain all the elements of the Orwell conundrum that lie behind the various "flawed masterpiece" theories. The various indictments of Orwell's pathological pessimism, despair, and paranoia should at last be examined in their context, that is, in the framework of Orwell's religious-spiritual vision of the world. In spite of Valerie Simms's excellent 1974 article on the subject, neither the symposia of 1984 nor the critical studies in the last few years found it important to re-examine the long-standing assumption that Orwell was suddenly hit by despair at the end of his life. Orwell's well-articulated position on spiritual and religious matters in his essays reveals that this assumption is unfounded. From the essays written at the same time as *Nineteen Eighty-Four* and after, his position as a secular humanist with faith in the "spirit of Man" emerges clearly and consistently. Indeed, it is hard to explain why, in spite of the wide academic and media exposure of Orwell's politics in 1984 and in the years since, few critics have chosen to address the question of the novel's spiritual-religious dimensions directly.

There is, of course, a long list of those who did so before 1984, and by now we should not find it surprising that almost every one of them has come to a substantially different conclusion. Thus Anthony Burgess in *The Novel Now* classifies *Nineteen Eighty-Four* as a Utopia, while Richard Gerber finds it "too despairing for the [Utopian] genre." There are arguments that Orwell's stance is substantially Christian (Ashe 57–59;) that *Nineteen Eighty-Four* presents a version of Christianity but stripped of mysticism and hope (Beadle 51–63;) that it shows the bankruptcy of integrity that is divorced from spiritual belief (Birrell 49–65.) In an entirely different vein, W.H. Auden suggests that Orwell's "one blind spot was an essentially religious hatred of Christianity" (86–87), while in a thought-provoking comparison of Orwell, Huxley, and Pope, Irwin Ehrenpreiss (215–230) argues that Orwell's stance differs from that of Christianity because it dismisses original sin and follows the Enlightenment position proclaiming the essential goodness of man. In line with this position, Peter Faulkner argues that Orwell is an agnostic who sees religious values as antithetical, no proper concern for man. Chris Goodey goes even further by suggesting that Orwell simply refuses to cling to a dead tradition, while Christopher Small in his 1975 *The Road to Miniluv* works out Orwell's theological position as a kind of negative *Pilgrim's Progress*.

In one of the most recent studies, Patrick Reilly suggests that Orwell recognizes the vacuum left by the disappearance of religious belief in the twentieth century, and his despair is the direct result of this sense of loss (28, 293). I thoroughly agree with Reilly on the importance he attributes to Orwell's statements about the psychological vacuum left by the loss of religious belief. Nevertheless, in this book I wish to argue that Orwell's response to this vacuum is somewhat more complex than Reilly suggests.

There is no doubt that Orwell frequently registers a profound sense of spiritual loss. It is equally obvious that he returns to explore the emotional and intellectual connotations of this loss in several of his essays and works of fiction, most prominently in *A Clergyman's Daughter*.

Nevertheless, and this will be one of the central points of my conclusion, Orwell is a secular humanist who quite consistently resists the temptation to accept any religious structure, even though (or precisely because) the acceptance of such a structure could prove so soothing psychologically. In fact, as Chapters 2, 9, and 14 will demonstrate, Orwell the humanist is aware of and in sympathy with life's spiritual dimensions, yet he would like to see the universal values of good and evil emerge from an anthropocentric, humanist approach to morality, a morality that is not based on belief in heaven and hell, or belief in any given religious structure. What he is in search of is unmistakably the pursuit of the twentieth-century humanist, an affirmation of moral-spiritual values that does not follow from faith in religion but from a deep-seated faith in the "spirit of Man."

But even if Orwell's intention was to present the humanist's point of view, did he not in fact present us with a demonic world of superhuman evil? Even if he intended the novel as the humanist's warning against extreme forms of irrationality, did he not, unintentionally, commit the mistake of presenting us with the horrors of the future as if they were overpowering? In other words, isn't Orwell the humanist defeated by Orwell the visionary?

These questions are certainly worth exploring, the more so since Winston, who makes a passionate final plea for faith in the "spirit of Man" as the only power to overcome the deadly grip of the totalitarian mind, is forced to recant at the end of the novel. Part IV of this study addresses itself to this question, suggesting that even though Winston is made to relinquish faith in the "spirit of Man," Orwell's faith here does not waver. Winston's position, having been forced to accept at the end that the Party is eternal, is not equivalent to Orwell's position. The dominant genre of the novel is satire; at the end of Part 2, and then, once more, after we have followed Winston to the end of his tragic journey, Orwell introduces two devices to make us, as it were, pull back from Winston in time and register our distance from him. These two devices are *Goldstein's Book*, which tells us of Oceania's past, and the *Dictionary of Newspeak*, which hints at its future. Accepting the invitation to read these two works of expository prose, first in the middle and then at the very end of the moving personal story, we are called back to our own reality, our own timeplane, and are repeatedly reminded that the satire does not present our world "as is" but as it could be unless *we* assume responsibility and change our course of thinking, and our course of action.

The following chapter-by-chapter synopsis will outline the general direction and the individual stepping stones in my argument about the various causes for, and the possible solution to, the Orwell conundrum.

Part I. A Cry of Despair or Faith in the "Spirit of Man"?

Part I discusses the phenomenon of the Orwell conundrum: In spite of the substantial and self-renewing spiral of public and critical interest in *Nineteen Eighty-Four* in the past forty years, many of its academic critics argue that it is a work conceived in despair, conveying pathological pessimism, and that it is at best a "flawed masterpiece," if not even a "failed novel." My study intends to analyze the 'subtext' for this surprisingly uniform and negative verdict in the otherwise so widely divergent streams of Orwell criticism, and to argue against it. Propounding the view that *Nineteen Eighty-Four* is Orwell's crowning achievement — at once his most complex and most powerful work — I also believe it deserves to take its place among the literary masterpieces of twentieth-century humanism,[14] possibly for the same reasonsc critics now see as its 'flaws.' This study then sets out to offer a comprehensive reassessment of the novel, claiming that it is a complex, well-integrated aesthetic whole that brings to life a great humanist's mature vision of his deeply troubled times in its political, psychological, and spiritual dimensions.

More specifically, I argue that the novel is a successful composite of genres, with the genre of satire as its dominant, organizing principle. The primary target of the satire is the betrayal of the originally humanistic goals of Socialism in Stalin's totalitarian regime, and the satire is addressed to the satirist's Adversary, the Leftist intellectual in the West, who has fallen under the spell of the totalitarian mentality and therefore overlooks, condones, or justifies this betrayal. Chapter 2 illustrates the birth of the Adversary's persona through the course of Orwell's career as an essayist and polemicist; his commitment to democratic Socialism crystallizes in the activity of arguing against the misguided ideas and the intellectually dishonest attitudes of various representatives of the Leftist intelligentsia. Chapter 3 takes a brief look at Orwell's fiction through various themes, techniques, and genres leading to *Nineteen Eighty-Four*, arguing that the last novel is Orwell's most mature achievement. Through a close textual analysis of the climactic scene in Room 101, Chapter 4 discusses this achievement in terms of Orwell's unique combination of the political allegory of dystopian satire and psychological realism. It is through the combination of the two genres that Orwell gives expression to his profound discovery: the inseparable connection between psychological and political dimensions in the totalitarian system.

Part II. Goldstein's Book — The Key to the Decoding of the Satire: The "Secular Religion" of Totalitarianism

Part II suggests that *Goldstein's Book* is the powerhouse of the satirical devices essential to the decoding of Orwell's parody of the totalitarian mentality. Chapter 5 analyzes this mentality in its unique, antagonistic relationship to historical time. Chapter 6 suggests that *Goldstein's Book* is a bridge between what was our present in 1948 and the future, by pointing out the cause-effect relationship between "our" world and the 1984 world of Oceania. Chapter 7 explores the emergence and the various manifestations of the mental-psychological construct of Doublethink, the fundamental concept of Orwell's parody of the totalitarian mentality. Chapters 8 and 9 offer an analysis of Orwell's humanistic stance in his parody of totalitarianism as a "secular religion" that polarizes into the mystical adulation of the 'sacred' leader at one extreme and the persecution of the 'satanic' opponent at the other. *Goldstein's Book* makes clear that Orwell's consistent analogy between the Party and the Church of the Middle Ages constitutes a significant strategy in his humanist, Socialist critique of Stalin's regime, and in his argument with his 'progressive' Adversary.

Part III. Confronting the Demonic in Totalitarianism — Orwell and Contemporaries

Part III takes a new look at the critics' verdict on Orwell's ostensibly personal obsession with the demonic. Chapter 10 discusses Orwell's diagnosis of a dynamism one could describe as a demonic spiral, an obsessive-compulsive escalation of aggression endemic to the totalitarian mentality at work. Elements of this 'demonic spiral' have also been dealt with in other psycho-historical interpretations current today and in Orwell's day. Chapter 11 compares Orwell with such masters of psychological realism as Thomas Mann, Camus, and Sartre, by concentrating on a common theme dealing with the problem of evil: betrayal and self-betrayal in the totalitarian system. Chapter 12 examines Orwell's position on evil in the tradition of utopia and dystopia, by juxtaposing Huxley's terror of science in *Brave New World* and Orwell's science of terror in *Nineteen Eighty-Four*. These three chapters demonstrate how Orwell's position on the evil of totalitarianism significantly coincides with a wide range of humanist interpretations in his day; hence his diagnosis reflects the pathology of the phenomenon and not the pathology of the author's despair or demonic obsession, as has often been said.

Part IV. Tragic Humanism: Orwell's Answer to Marx, Freud, the Existentialists, and his "Religion of Humanity"

Chapter 13 delineates the various aspects of Orwell's faith in the "spirit of Man" by examining his characteristic response to the 'realism' of Marxist, Freudian, and Existentialist tributaries to twentieth-century thought. Chapter 14 explores Orwell's ties with the moral idealism rooted in the Romantic and Enlightenment tradition that inspired his faith in the "religion of humanity." To give an accurate picture of Orwell's tragic humanism, the chapter ends with a discussion of Orwell's synthesis of realism and idealism in his revealing definition of the spirit of tragedy.

Part IV concludes that Orwell's synthesis is a complex but coherent vision of a tragic humanism that celebrates the "spirit of Man" both for its capacity to affirm the process of life and for its unceasing will to struggle against overpowering forces.

Part V. Coming through the Other Side: The Metamorphosis of Tragic Irony into the Militant Wit of Satire — an Ultimate Faith in the "Spirit of Man"

Part V forms the conclusion of this argument. It demonstrates that Orwell's tragic humanism is powerfully integrated with and incorporated by the structural and thematic developments in the novel. Chapter 15 concentrates on the structural connection between the main narrative text and such 'documentary' inserts of expository prose as The Appendix of Newspeak. Chapter 16 offers a thematic interpretation of Newspeak as it leads to the particular catharsis appropriate to dystopian satire — intellectual illumination.

Like great tragedy, which liberates because it makes us confront the abyss of despair, great satire also compels us to confront the extreme, the limits of human existence. There is no doubt that Winston is trapped at the end of his journey in the Ministry of Love; however, it is through that very journey that the reader comes to identify and recognize the irreplaceable value of each intellectual and emotional attribute of the autonomous individual and of the political system that offers maximum protection for individuality. Far from denying the value of the human struggle for freedom, far from suggesting that we give up in despair, Orwell emerges upholding faith in the individual, faith in the "spirit of Man."

This faith also implies that in the intellectually challenging tradition of classical satire, Orwell has respect for his readers' ability to recognize, and confidence in their commitment to struggle against, the demonic, dehumanizing forces of the irrational.

Notes

* References to George Orwell's *Nineteen Eighty-Four* are to the novel's 1984 Penguin edition. Page references are indicated in brackets immediately after the quotation.

All my quotations from George Orwell's essays, articles, and letters refer to *The Collected Essays, Journalism and Letters of George Orwell* in 4 volumes, ed. Sonia Orwell and Ian Angus, Penguin Books, in association with Secker and Warburg, 1970. Page references are indicated in parentheses following the quotation, and include both volume and page number.

References to Orwell's other novels are from to the *Penguin Complete Novels of George Orwell*, 1983. Page references follow the abbreviation of the title, such as *CUFA* for *Coming Up for Air*, *BD* for *Burmese Days*, *CD* for *A Clergyman's Daughter*, *KAF* for *Keep the Aspidistra Flying*, and *AF* for *Animal Farm*.

References to *Homage to Catalonia* are to its 1952 edition by Beacon Press, Boston, with an introduction by Lionel Trilling. The abbreviation used is *HC*.

References to *Road to Wigan Pier* are to its 1952 Penguin edition. The abbreviation used is *RWP*.

[1] In *The Crystal Spirit: A Study of George Orwell*, Woodcock quotes, with approval, Julian Symons: "I have always believed that what Orwell wrote is less important than what he was" (293).

[2] In his 1988 *Orwell and the Politics of Despair*, Alok Rai returns to the term "hysterical" in his statement, "It is to such a hysterical world, or alternately, a world perceived in such hysterical terms, that the Orwell myth speaks, then as now" (162).

[3] In *The Orwell Mystique: A Study in Male Ideology*, Daphne Patai sees a clear connection between flawed gender ideology, ensuing despair, and intellectual and aesthetic shortcomings. "From mere ambivalence and then pessimism . . . Orwell moves to a position of despair, most forcefully expressed in his last novel, *Nineteen Eighty-Four*. This progression is . . . a logical consequence of Orwell's commitment to a not clearly articulated paradigm that polarizes human beings according to sex roles and gender identity and legitimizes male display of dominance and aggression" (17). Patai feels that "suppressing recognition of women's oppression and ignoring the issue of patriarchy lock Orwell in an insoluble doublebind, and the inability to express this contradiction and then think through it undermines his work" (266).

For a detailed rebuttal of Patai's view please see my review on *The Orwell Mystique: A Study in Male Ideology* in *Dalhousie Review* (Dalhousie, Halifax) 64, 4 (1984–1985); 807–811. Also see Arthur Eckstein's "Orwell, Masculinity, and Feminist Criticism" in *The Intercollegiate Review* 21.1 (Fall 1985), 47–54.

[4] Bertrand Russell concludes: "He preserved an impeccable love of truth, and allowed himself to learn even the most painful lessons. But he lost hope. This prevented him from being a prophet of our time" (7).

[5] Peter Heller, in his 1966 *Dialectics and Nihilism: Essays on Lessing, Nietzsche, Mann and Kafka*, takes the more traditional position: "Kafka said of himself that with his 'weakness' he had assimilated the negative element of his age which was so very close to him that he had the right never to fight it but rather to represent it. For he had inherited no part in its slight positive element nor in its negative extreme which could tip over or change dialectically into the positive" (250). Heller concludes that "Even in his most positive mood, even when he asserts a certainty that remains beyond reach, Kafka's central theme is despair" (266).

By contrast with this assessment, in his 1959 *Three Studies in Twentieth Century Obscurity*, Francis Russell points out, "after the war Kafka was canonized as a man of defiance who had dared to oppose his individual ego to the nihilistic universe" (46).

To give an example of this shift in critical emphasis, one should examine the Existentialist position in Kenneth Noble's interpretation of Kafka in his 1981 *Damascus and the Bodhi Tree: Ancient Wisdom and Modern Thought* (written with Robert Price). According to Noble: "In his writings . . . Kafka attempts to meet the cultural crisis. In an age in which man is questioning the traditional standards and the religion which supports those standards, Kafka endeavours to deliver his message: (1) our society is riddled with falsehood; (2) for those who are willing to "see," there is a true basis for life" (Price 101). Noble concludes that "one finds in the writings of Kafka a hope for the future" (Price 101).

[6] In his comprehensive study *George Orwell: A Life* (1980), Professor Crick asserts that *Nineteen Eighty-Four* is a "flawed masterpiece." In his *The Politics of Literary Reputation* (1988), John Rodden objects to the exclusion of Orwell's last two novels from the "high canon" of the "major author category" in American universities. Although both "masterpiece" and "canon" are terms to be used carefully, I believe both of them have their function in my argument. I intend to show that in this case Crick underrates Orwell's achievement, while Rodden comes closer to doing justice to it. In my exploration of the novel's merit in terms of its composite genre and its political and literary context, "masterpiece" refers to an outstanding work of integrity and power, of the calibre of Huxley's *Brave New World*, Camus's *The Plague*, or Thomas Mann's *Mario and the Magician*, for example.

[7] Milan Simecka writes in the Introduction to the Czech Samizdat edition of *1984*:
When I read the story of Winston Smith, I received a shock, because all of a sudden I realised that this was my own story I was reading. . . . Those living in Eastern Europe, and especially those who were born here and who have lived through all the "victories" and defeats of real socialism, are struck when reading *1984*, by many astounding similarities. . . . The similarity to our everyday lives comes as a physical shock, neither pleasant nor amusing. The prophetic accuracy of the book arouses in us feelings that are difficult to describe . . . a numbing sense of *déjà vu*. . . . I have grown up in a world of forbidden books, a world of omnipresent indoctrination, where the past was being rewritten all the time. . . . Can you wonder, given all this, that Winston Smith came to seem to me like my own brother? (4).

In his study of Orwell's literary reputation, John Rodden also points out that "among dissident Soviet and Eastern European intellectuals, Orwell has been admired as a brilliant satirist and a courageous artist in the mold of Pasternak, Solzhenitsyn and Milosz" (211).

[8] In his Preface to the Ukrainian edition of *Animal Farm* Orwell writes: "Indeed, in my opinion, nothing has contributed so much to the corruption of the original idea of Socialism as the belief that Russia is a socialist country and that every act of its rule must be

excused if not imitated. And so for the past ten years I have been convinced that the destruction of the Soviet myth was essential if we wanted a revival of the Socialist movement" (v. 3, 458).

[9] Ignoring the novel's satirical dimension, Mark Connelly's *The Diminished Self* of 1987, Alok Rai's *Orwell and the Politics of Despair* of 1988, and James Coomb's 1989 essay "Towards 2084" in *The Orwellian Moment* (ed. R.L. Savage, James Coombs, Dan Nimmo, Fayetteville, Univ. of Arkansas Press, 1989) all read *Nineteen Eighty-Four* as a work reflecting Orwell's final loss of hope, even pathological despair.

[10] Orwell makes this shift quite clear when he writes: "Fifteen years ago, when one defended the freedom of the intellect, one had to defend it against Conservatives, against Catholics, and to some extent — for they were not of great importance in England — against fascists. Today one has to defend it against Communists and 'fellow-travellers'" (v. 4, 84).

[11] The 1984 film version of the novel was directed by Michael Radford, produced by Simon Perry, and starred John Hurt and Richard Burton.

[12] In his essay on "Satire" in the *Princeton Encyclopedia of Poetry and Poetics*, Robert C. Elliott reminds us that "the formal satire is a quasi dramatic poem 'framed' by an encounter between the Satirist (or, more reasonably, his *persona*, the 'I' of the poem) and an Adversarius who impels the Satirist to speech" (738).

[13] Orwell hints at some of the difficulties posed by the multiple genre: "I don't like talking about books before they are written, but I will tell you that this is a novel about the future — that is, it is in a sense a fantasy, but in the form of a naturalistic novel. That is what makes it a difficult job" (v. 4, 378).

He acknowledges that, in the composite of genres, the novel also includes elements of the thriller and the love story. Yet, he points out, the blurb "makes the book sound as though it were a thriller mixed up with a love story, and I didn't intend it to be primarily that" (v. 4, 519–520). Orwell continues to explain that "What it is really meant to do is to discuss the implications of dividing the world up into 'Zones of influence' (I thought of it in 1944 as a result of the Teheran conference) & in addition to indicate by *parodying* them the intellectual implications of totalitarianism" (v. 4, 520).

[14] In his 1989 *The Politics of Literary Reputation*, John Rodden remarks on the "exclusion of *Animal Farm, Nineteen Eighty-Four*, and the essays from the 'high canon'" in the United States, so that for a Ph.D. examination in 1980 "Orwell was not an eligible choice for the major author's category" (396).

Chapter 2

Orwell's Essays:
The Birth of the Adversary

Nineteen Eighty-Four represents the cumulation of Orwell's major themes and concerns throughout his years as a book reviewer and political observer. His day-to-day responses to domestic and foreign affairs, and political, cultural and literary events in the course of twenty-odd years as a professional writer and reviewer inform the principal issues of *Nineteen Eighty-Four*. Yet the novel demonstrates that the whole is significantly more than the sum of its parts: the individual themes so consistently culled over the years gain new momentum as leitmotifs within the complex harmony of the novel.

In addition to their thematic relevance, Orwell's essays also prepare the reader of *Nineteen Eighty-Four* for the 'decoding' of a particular rhetorical situation that largely determines the relationship between the satirist, the reader, and the satirical target. Both the essays and *Nineteen Eighty-Four* assume the presence of an 'Ideal Reader,' the writer's contemporary, someone who picks up naturally Orwell's numerous allusions to the most specific details of contemporary cultural, literary, and political issues, and who feels personally affected by these issues. No doubt we as readers are expected to assume this role without further notice. But to decode the satire successfully, I suggest we listen to the satirist's pronouncements as if he were responding to an Adversary, a silent, invisible third party in the background, the same persona Orwell the polemicist has in mind when developing the various arguments in his essays. This persona is the Socialist writer's Adversary, ostensibly also an intellectual on the Left, but also a representative of those erroneous attitudes the writer finds dangerous for Western Socialism.

Naturally, in the course of the 1930s and 1940s both the Adversary's persona and Orwell's own position evolve through various stages. Gilbert Bonifas reminds us that if the 1920s were characterized by post-war disenchantment, the 1930s were characterized by "depression and unemployment at home, the rise of Fascism and the economic success of Russia abroad. The result was a literature of anxiety and revolt. Thus the writers of Auden and Spender's generation felt compelled by a new Messianism, the 'predicament of being obliged to save the world'" (13).

This compulsion defines the aesthetics of the Leftist writer of the period, who feels compelled to "draw his inspiration from reality . . . to stop contemplating formalism . . . [and in order to] convey a message, . . . write as simply as possible" (14). Even if Orwell had no personal sympathy with the "Auden-Spender group" (v. 1, 554), in "The Frontiers of Art and Propaganda" he makes clear that he was in agreement with their literary principles:

> The writers who have come up since 1930 have been living in a world in which not only one's life but one's whole scheme of values is constantly menaced. In such circumstances detachment is not possible. You cannot take a purely aesthetic interest in a disease you are dying from; you cannot feel dispassionately about a man who is about to cut your throat . . . literature had to become political because anything else would have entailed mental dishonesty (v. 2, 152).

The question is, why did Orwell feel that he had no common cause with the other Leftist writers between the two wars, when, "like them, [he was] . . . in rebellion against the environment of his origins . . . repudiated the values of his class, and . . . took a position on his country's situation that amounted to a conversion to progressive ideas?" (Bonifas 384). According to Bonifas, the conversion of Auden and his comrades was more like a "salon conversion" that took place within a relatively short period in the early 1930s, while Orwell's was gradual and based on facts he understood well. He had first-hand knowledge of colonialism and poverty, and his "conversion" was the slow process of a growing distaste for capitalism, concern about unemployment, an awareness of the Fascist danger and, finally, "commitment to socialism in his journey to Spain" (Bonifas 384). But in sharpest contrast with his "Adversary" in the 1930s, "Orwell was never duped by the nature of the Soviet regime, because he never closed his eyes to the Stalinist purges or was ready to find any kind of justification for them, and finally, because he never had the mentality of the cosmopolitan and hence uprooted intellectual, Orwell's Socialism can be called only a most heterodox form of Marxism" (Bonifas 390).

Orwell's argument with a politically orthodox Russophile Adversary became, if anything, even more pronounced and more dramatic after the Spanish Civil War. His statement, "Every line of serious work that I have written since 1936 has been written, directly or indirectly, *against* totalitarianism and *for* democratic Socialism, as I understand it" (v. 1, 28), becomes a forceful political manifesto, hardly reconcilable with an attitude of despair, apathy, or pessimism. The attempt to persuade his Adversary of the dangers inherent in following the totalitarian version of Socialism elicited from Orwell the polemicist a vast array of strategies, determined not only to diagnose the disease but also to name the cure. In his 1947 essay "Toward European Unity," Orwell outlines his greatest fears for Western civilization. What he sees as the first possibility of disastrous proportions is that "the Americans will decide to use the atomic bomb while they have it and the Russians haven't." The second alternative is "that the present 'cold war' will continue until the U.S.S.R. and several other countries have atomic bombs as well." But what he sees as most frightening is the third scenario:

> That the fear inspired by the *atomic bomb* and other weapons yet to come will be so great that everyone will refrain from using them. This seems to me the worst possibility of all. It would mean the division of the world among two or three vast super-states, unable to conquer one another and unable to be overthrown by an internal rebellion. In all probability their structure would be hierarchic, with a semi-divine caste at the top and outright slavery at the bottom, and *the crushing out of liberty would exceed anything that the world has yet seen*. Within each state the necessary psychological atmosphere would be kept up by complete severance from the outside world, and by a continuous phony war against rival states. Civilizations of this type might remain static for thousands of years" (v. 4, 424).

No reader of *Nineteen Eighty-Four* can fail to recognize that what Orwell describes here as the third scenario became the political structure of Oceania in the novel. However, far from signifying Orwell's final despair about the fate of our civilization, the same essay presents a detailed scenario for the way out, to make sure *none* of the three alternatives will be realized: "The only way of avoiding them that I can imagine is to present somewhere or other, on a large scale, the spectacle of a community where people are relatively free and happy and where the main motive of life is not the pursuit of money or power. In other words, *democratic Socialism must be made to work* throughout some large area" (v. 4, 425, my italics).

The enslavement of the masses and the crushing out of liberty are perceived as real threats. It is typical of Orwell that in trying to avert them, he dismisses the capitalist system of the U.S., the "oligarchical collectivism" of the U.S.S.R., and the "racial mysticism of the Asiatic national movements" (v. 4, 425) with equal vigour. His solution suggests that instead of going back and forth between various flawed systems, which in some respects can be seen as diametrical opposites, one should return to the original question: What is democratic Socialism? What are its original goals? How should one go about achieving these goals? In order to realize the Socialist United States of Europe, Orwell proposes, one has to work on public opinion, develop intellectual awareness; it has to start in countries with "a tradition of democratic Socialism," "to whom the word *Socialism* has some appeal and for whom it is bound up with liberty, equality and internationalism" (v. 4, 425).

Orwell's persistent argument with his Adversary here comes fully into focus. It is the duty of the intellectual to see clearly and to influence public opinion correctly. The chances for an economically fair and free society could become a reality only "if people really wanted it, and if there were ten or twenty years of assured peace to bring it about. And since the initiative would have to come in the first place from Britain, the important thing is that this idea should take root among British Socialists" (v. 4, 370).

No doubt, at the time of the writing of *Nineteen Eighty-Four*, Orwell saw that crisis was impending. Nevertheless, he advocates neither pessimism nor political apathy. On the contrary, his argument with his Adversary becomes more and more powerful, more and more specific. He is convinced that the Leftist intellectuals, most specifically the British Socialists, have an important part to play in creating a solution to the crisis. Precisely for this reason, they must recognize that Stalin's regime has not solved any of the moral and economic problems of our civilization, and its claim to have achieved the life-long dream of Socialism is a blatant lie.

The Psychological Reason for
the Adversary's Self-Deception

The first reason for the Adversary's reluctance to read the signs of totalitarian danger is that he is simply unable to imagine conditions in a totalitarian state. By now we have access to a great deal of information that was not readily available in Orwell's time. In his 1981 *Stalin's Secret War*, for example, Nikolai Tolstoy raises the issue of the millions of people in the U.S.S.R. who died during the years of World War II but were not killed in battle. He concludes that "millions of Russians killed at that time died in the invasion of Finland and in the subsequent war of the NKVD [Soviet Secret Police] *against the civil population of the USSR*" (278, my italics). Tolstoy finds it bitterly ironic that,

> It was this government and the political system it enforced which aroused the enthusiastic loyalty of so many in the West. Though much of what was going on in Soviet Russia was hidden from view, more than enough information was accessible to those who wished to know. The truth was available in countless books and articles written by fugitives from the USSR, from thousands of citizens and (after 1941) Poles in the West, from Western visitors such as Malcolm Muggeridge, Eugene Lyons and Andrew Smith, and even from published Soviet sources. What was glaringly obvious to Arthur Koestler and George Orwell might have been equally so to Louis Aragon, J.D. Bernal or Lillian Hellman (278).

Tolstoy goes on to raise the question: "How did it happen that thousands of intelligent people inveigled or encouraged millions less intellectually endowed into blind admiration of mass murder, torture and slavery?" (278) He finds the answer in a "quasi-religious emotion" in the war years when "millions of people came to elevate Stalin's Russia as a model to be admired and emulated" (278).

Decades before Tolstoy, Orwell turns to an exploration of the spiritual-psychological roots of this "quasi-religious emotion" in several of his essays. The modern intellectual has lost faith in personal immortality; this loss left a psychological vacuum:

> Western civilization, unlike some oriental civilizations, was founded partly on the belief in individual immortality. If one looks at the Christian religion from the outside this belief appears more important than the belief in God. The western conception of

good and evil is very difficult to separate from it. There is little doubt that the modern cult of power worship is bound up with the modern man's feeling that life here and now is the only life there is (v. 3, 126).

Orwell diagnoses this loss as very severe, comparable to "an amputation of the soul," where "the wound has a tendency to go septic" (v. 2, 31). At the same time, Orwell the humanist finds return to religious faith unthinkable: For the modern mind grounded in an empirical mode of thought, "religious belief, in the form in which we had known it, had to be abandoned. By the nineteenth century it was already in essence a lie" (v. 2, 30).

Orwell emphasizes that the appropriate attitude to our spiritual quandary is neither nostalgia nor despair, but the assertion of a new, secular moral code:

> I do not want the belief in life after death to return, and in any case it is not likely to return. What I do point out is that its *disappearance has left a big hole*, and that we ought to take notice of the fact. Reared for thousands of years on the notion that the individual survives, man has got to make a considerable psychological effort to get used to the notion that the individual perishes. He is not likely to salvage civilization unless he can evolve a system of good and evil which is *independent of heaven and hell* (v. 3, 127, my italics).

Having lost the security associated with religious faith, we are left with a psychological vacuum. If we are unaware of our own psychological need for security, the totalitarian dictator who inspires the "worship of power" may step in to fill that vacuum. Our loss of certitude, our loss of moral values make us susceptible to the dictator with his "secular religion" based on the worship of power. To the "progressive" intellectuals who have dismissed religion and have not faced in themselves the ensuing psychological vacuum, this "secular religion" becomes a dangerous substitute. In analyzing his Adversary's motives, Orwell arrives at the conclusion of his humanistic warning: we can free ourselves from the lure of ideology and power worship, modern substitutes for religion, only after we acknowledge our psychological need for religious certainties in the first place. Only by being willing to name and understand this need can we attempt to overcome it.

This should not mean that Orwell has forgotten that man
cannot live by bread alone: he emphasizes that our spiritual
well-being depends on our ability to create a system of universal moral values, a system of good and evil not based on
our relationship to the Supernatural, that is, a belief in heaven
and hell, but on an affirmation of what is indispensable to the
"spirit of Man." Orwell defines these indispensable attitudes
at various places in his writings, as respect for objective truth,
equal respect for the subjective truth of "psychological fact,"
and respect for the laws of "common decency" determining human conduct. But to be truthful to the "spirit of Man" is not
an easy task: it requires both an intellectual and a moral effort. By saying that "the intellectuals are more totalitarian in
outlook than the common people" (v. 3, 178), he reproaches his
Adversary for failure in this moral effort.

Wars, particularly drawn-out periods of war, Orwell points
out, are especially dangerous for the seduction of the intellectual. Exhaustion and fear propel him, without resistance, in
the direction of "secular religions." The more vulnerable because he is unaware of his weakened spiritual condition, he is
ready to indulge "his desire for power" and accept any ideology
personified by a "semi-divine fuehrer," becoming indifferent to
the lack of moral principles in "the unit [in which] he has chosen
to sink his own individuality" (v. 3, 411).

Orwell admits that in the turbulent age of the thirties and
forties it was impossible for "any modern intellectual to look
closely and honestly into his own mind without coming upon
nationalistic loyalties and hatreds of one kind or another. It is
the fact that he can feel the *emotional tug* of such things, and
yet see them *dispassionately* for what they are, that gives him
his status as an intellectual" (v. 3, 388, my italics).

Orwell reproaches his Adversary in the 1940s for being blind
to the psychological reasons informing his own "loyalties and
hatreds." Having renounced patriotism and religion as unbe-
coming to a modern man of a scientific, materialist world view,
the "progressive" Western intellectual fails to understand that
his feelings for the U.S.S.R. and Stalin are motivated by his
need to find a substitute for patriotism and religion. In fact,
Orwell speculates, it may be even less dangerous to give in to
the emotional appeal of monarchy than to the appeal of the
quasi-divine dictator. However, "if you point these facts out to
the average left-winger he gets angry, but only because he has

not examined the nature of his own feelings towards Stalin" (v. 3, 103). Through his feelings for Stalin as a "father" or "saviour" abroad,[1] the "average left winger" allows the "dislocated idols" of patriotism and religion to return, "not recognized for what they are," so that he may obtain emotional satisfaction without facing his intellectual regression. Ultimately, the intellectual's adherence to this particular form of nationalism is "power hunger tempered by self-deception." Repeatedly, Orwell castigates his Adversary for a slavish admiration of the U.S.S.R.:

> Among the intelligentsia . . . the dominant form of nationalism is Communism — using the word in a very loose sense, to include not merely Party members but 'fellow travellers' and russophiles generally . . . A Communist, for my purpose here, is one who looks upon the U.S.S.R. as his Fatherland and feels it his duty to justify Russian policy and advance Russian interests at all cost (v. 3, 414).

Orwell draws attention to the fact that by "justifying Russian policy" throughout the 1930s and 1940s, the Communist parties of Europe thwarted the original aspirations of Western Socialism more than the most Conservative "right-wing" opponents of Socialism. Consequently, Orwell is much less concerned about the power of Stalin to "take over" the Western world than he is about the Leftist intellectuals' "corruption of the original idea of Socialism . . . [through] the belief that Russia is a Socialist country and that every act of its rule must be excused if not *imitated*" (v. 3, 458).

To emphasize his intellectual Adversary's self-delusion, Orwell repeatedly points out the moral superiority of the working class. By refusing to accept "the western cult of power worship" and the principle "that might is right," the working class remained faithful to an old-fashioned " 'bourgeois morality' (i.e., common decency)" (v. 3, 22). As a result, it is far less vulnerable to the diseased totalitarian mentality than the self-deluded, amoral intelligentsia.

This is the main thrust of Orwell's ongoing argument with his Adversary in the 1940s, which by now has become a composite figure of such intellectuals as Joseph E. Davies (v. 4, 189), Professor J.D. Bernal (v. 4, 188–190), and Harold Laski, for example.

A Personal Representative of the Adversary

In fact, probably Orwell's attitude to Professor Harold Laski, "who exercised profound influence on several generations of students at the London School of Economics" (Caute 59) and was a member of the National Executive of the Labour Party between 1937 and 1949 (Deane 32), is a representative example of his attitude to all those Leftist intellectuals he reproaches for blindness to the crimes of Stalin's regime, a "protective stupidity" causing intense harm to the English Socialist movement.

David Caute's *Fellow Travellers*, published in 1973, once again confirms Orwell's attention to Laski as someone "symptomatic of a general pattern whereby the changing landscape of domestic and international politics could rapidly propel an intellectual into impassioned refutation of the very arguments he had previously propagated with equal passion . . . Laski was indeed a brilliant bird in perpetual migration, guided by the changing political climate and singing all the way" (159). Thus, in March 1938, Laski attributed "the remaining negative aspects of the Soviet system to hostile imperialist encirclement. Yet only a few months after the Nazi-Soviet Pact he attributed the corruption of the Soviet dictatorship to the corruption of Stalin and his associates by power" (161).

To understand Orwell's animosity to Laski, it should be remembered that between 1936 and 1950 the total number of deaths among the labour camp population of the U.S.S.R.

> would be in the region of twelve million. This does not include the executions . . . the three and a half million who died as a result of collectivization, plus others lost during the mass deportation of nationalities. . . . Granted that the present estimated figures could not have been accurately gauged then, . . . there was evidence enough for those who wished to see it (Caute 107).

In Orwell's words, from June 1938:

> The GPU are everywhere, everyone lives in constant terror of denunciations . . . there are periodical waves of terror, sometimes the "liquidation" of kulaks and "nepmen", sometimes some monstrous State trial at which people who had been in prison for months or years are suddenly dragged forth to make incredible confessions . . . meanwhile the invisible Stalin is worshipped in terms that would have made Nero blush (v. 1, 370).

What *Goldstein's Book* describes as the true believer's instinctive ability to blind himself to the truth by practising "crimestop" or "protective stupidity" could be well illustrated by Caute's account of Laski's lecture tour in Russia in 1934, where Laski met "the Bentham of Soviet legal reform," Andrei Vyshinsky. Vyshinsky "had been a Menshevik until 1921 and then forged a career . . . which culminated in his appointment as Procurator General. In this role he later exacted a terrible revenge on the GPU men who despised him, wringing confessions from them in purge after purge and executing the executioners." In a veritable feat of Doublethink, Laski gives a reverential account of the Procurator's unchecked power, whereby "the judge, the investigator, the advocate, even the police are all, in a real degree, under his jurisdiction." Rather naively Laski adds that "the public undoubtedly feels confidence in him; the stream of visitors to his office is evidence of that." As Caute points out,

> it is interesting that a system which puts judges under the authority of the public prosecutor should not have aroused Laski's distrust. . . . As for that 'stream of visitors' — where do people turn for news of arrested relatives except to the power that arrested them? . . . One night in the Lubianka would have taught this professor of politics more about politics, and perhaps about human nature, than ten thousand books read, lectures heard and officials interviewed. Even in 1940, when the Nazi-Soviet Pact had sharpened his awareness of the 'criminal blunders' of Soviet Russia, he still refused to believe that torture was practised there. Not that. Impossible (112).[2]

In Laski's case Orwell's anger against his Adversary takes an indirect expression. He singles out the following "entirely typical sentence" of Laski's prose to demonstrate that corrupt language represents corrupt thought: "As a whole, our system was a compromise between democracy in the political realm — itself a very recent development in our history — and an economic power oligarchically organized which was in its turn related to a certain aristocratic vestigia still able to influence profoundly the habits of our society" (v. 3, 164).

Orwell remarks that "this sentence, incidentally, comes from a reprinted lecture, so one must assume that Professor Laski actually stood up on a platform and spouted it forth, parenthesis and all" (v. 3, 164). What Orwell objects to in left-wing writing is the hypocrisy "that the louder people yap about the proletariat, the more they despise its language" (v. 3, 164). To draw attention to his Adversary's pretentious language is, of course, a successful strategy in discrediting his political orthodoxy: "Sometimes 'Freudian errors' are to blame, sometimes sheer mental incompetence, and sometimes an instinctive feeling that sheer thought is dangerous to orthodoxy. But there does seem to be a direct connection between acceptance of totalitarian doctrines and the writing of bad English, and we think that this should be pointed out" (v. 4, 190).

Orwell also reviewed Laski's *Faith, Reason and Civilization*; his review "should have appeared in the *Manchester Evening News*, 16 March 1944 [but it] was rejected by the editor." In his commentary in *Politics*, November 1944, Dwight Macdonald chooses this incident to show that "editors will print nothing anti-Russian because of the supposed russo-mania of the general public and also because of the complaints which the Soviet government is constantly raising about the British press" (v. 3, 169 footnote). At the same time, Orwell remains fair to Laski, both in the book review and later, when in his column "As I Please" he comments on Laski's libel case. According to Herbert Deane,

> although the electoral victory of Labour in 1945 was a great satisfaction to Laski, the triumph was marred for him by the growing tensions of the international scene, particularly between the United States and the Soviet Union, and by his failure to win a libel action that he had instituted during the 1945 campaign, when several newspapers reported that he had made a speech in which he advocated violent revolution in Great Britain (32).

In his column Orwell points out that "Professor Laski took ... action ... on behalf of the Labour Party," taking issue with "the anti-Red propaganda of part of the Conservative press. It will therefore be extremely unfair if he is left to pay the very heavy costs unaided." Orwell actually closes his column by asking for contributions to Laski's legal costs to be sent to the Secretary of the Labour Party (v. 4, 302).

At the same time, Orwell's personal suspicion of Laski is never allayed, as we shall see in the letter where he tells Koestler about the Ukrainian translation of *Animal Farm* to be distributed "among the Ukrainian D.P.s, who now seem to have printing outfits of their own going in the American Zone and Belgium" (v. 4, 433). The conflict between the D.P.s and the

"Soviet repatriation people" was evidently clear to Orwell, as he recounts that the American authorities in Munich "must have felt it their duty to seize and hand over 1,500 copies of the Ukrainian translation of *Animal Farm* to the 'Soviet repatriation people' but it appears about 2,000 copies got distributed among the D.P.s first" (v. 4, 434).

Orwell's sympathy for the D.P.s in this case is an indication of his awareness of their difficult position (v. 4, 84–85). In effect, as we know now, thousands of them were repatriated against their will, and the British press decided to suppress the news or minimize the importance of their unwillingness. Russophile intellectuals were undoubtedly responsible for this attitude of the press, and, as we find out from documents that have come to light since, they were also at least partially responsible for the policy of the British Foreign Office, which was willing to comply not only with Stalin's ruthless repatriation policy of Soviet prisoners of war, but also with his conspiracy to "repatriate," that is, forcefully abduct, former Russian émigrés who were no longer Soviet citizens. The Russophile intellectual simply refused to believe that repatriation was a euphemism for torture, execution, or deportation to forced labour camps for all those "repatriated."[3] This is the intellectual climate that explains Orwell's precaution when, at the time the Ukrainian D.P.s decided to publish a translation of *Animal Farm*, he felt it important to warn against Laski, who might, in effect, betray the underground publications to the Soviet authorities. Orwell describes the situation to Koestler:

> Sevcenko [the representative of the Ukrainian D.P.s] asked me simultaneously whether he thought *Laski* would agree to let them have some of his stuff (they are apparently trying to get hold of representative samples of western thought). I told him to have nothing to do with *Laski* and by no means let a person *of that type* know that illicit printing in Soviet languages is going on in the allied zones (v. 4, 434, my italics).

That Orwell was on the right track, as far as Laski was concerned, is borne out by Nikolai Tolstoy, who in *Stalin's Secret War* presents us not only with numerous examples of the Western intellectual's Russomania, but also shows how significant a role these intellectuals were to play in Stalin's future plans to weaken the Western bourgeois democracies from within:

Western Europe . . . Stalin believed to be racked by internal conflict. The enormous Communist Parties of France and Italy represented a sizable Trojan horse *within the citadel.* Their vociferous claims, together with those of fellow travellers and pacifists everywhere, suggested to the *Vozhd* that the masses would prefer Soviet domination to that of the United States. On 7 August, 1946 a British Labour Party delegation, opposed to what they saw as Foreign Secretary Bevin's anti-Soviet policy, had had an audience with Stalin in the Kremlin. Whilst the excited delegates were watching a film of life on a collective farm, Stalin left the darkened hall with the noted socialist ideologue, *Harold Laski.* A conspiratorial discussion followed, with Stalin explaining that a Soviet-dominated continent could still allow (within limitations) Britain to pursue her own brand of socialism. Before this, *Laski* expressed his conviction that in the event of a quarrel between the USSR and the USA, Britain would support the former" (360, my italics).

Orwell's suspicion of Laski and "persons of that type" was not unfounded. On the evidence recounted by Tolstoy above, they were quite willing to endanger Britain's "own brand of Socialism," that is, democratic Socialism,[4] and imitate the totalitarian example of the U.S.S.R. In Tolstoy's words,

> The fact that war was eventually averted is no mitigation of the conduct of *Laski* and other fellow-travellers in Western Europe and America. There has been much complacent condemnation of the motives of the guilty 'Men of Munich'. But Chamberlain and his colleagues, however naive their expectations and misguided their politics, were repelled by Nazi totalitarianism and desperately anxious to check its expansion. Laski and the majority of travellers and Communists, on the other hand, not only ardently supported Stalin's worst excesses, but acted in a way calculated to bring the world to the brink of war (361).

On the evidence of Tolstoy's account, then, Orwell's suspicion of the various representatives of his Adversary was not a sign of his paranoia. Nor was he wrong in diagnosing the imminence of a crisis. In the words of Nikolai Tolstoy: "That Stalin drew back from the brink was no thanks to them [that is, Laski and his like]. And what that war would have brought about was summed up pithily in a conversation . . . [by Red Army General] Klykov . . . 'If we intend to build communism seriously [in Western Europe] we'll have to send half the population to Siberia'" (360). Tolstoy concludes that "Europe was for the time being spared experiences Russians had undergone for more than thirty years. Stalin died on 5 March 1953, his project unfulfilled. It was his death that for a moment opened a terrifying vision of reality to his successors" (360–361).

The 'Laski episode' in Orwell's writing opens an interesting perspective on the relationship between Orwell the Satirist and his Adversary, the Leftist intellectual of the forties. Of course, we have to realize that this Adversary may appear in a wide variety of incarnations and the Persona may represent a whole range of attitudes, beginning with, at one end of the spectrum, naive faith in the only Socialist country and the censoring, the blocking out, the denial of facts that would go against this faith. At the other end of the spectrum, the Adversary represents cynical condonement of the worst excesses of Stalinism. Orwell's long-standing argument with this Adversary is important to keep in mind when we read *Nineteen Eighty-Four*, particularly *Goldstein's Book*, which explains how the intellectuals in the forties and early fifties opened the "citadel" of democracy to the totalitarian mentality.

Does Orwell's attitude to his Adversary offer illumination to our central dilemma, whether *Nineteen Eighty-Four* conveys despair or faith in the "spirit of Man"? If we approach the novel in the context of the Satirist's continuous argument with his Adversary, it should become clear that Orwell's intention to destroy the "Soviet myth" does not signify disillusionment with the Socialist ideal. On the contrary, he makes clear that it is precisely in the interests of the "revival of the Socialist movement" in the West that one has to destroy "the belief that Russia is a Socialist country" (v. 3, 458).

To 'decode' the satirist's target in *Nineteen Eighty-Four* with the help of Orwell's essays, we should recognize that *Goldstein's Book* holds up a mirror to Orwell's contemporaries, showing the potentially disastrous results of *their* self-deception and corrupted consciousness, which, by 1984, could lead to the triumph of the diseased totalitarian mentality all over the world. We will do well to remember, however, that when Orwell warns his Adversary against making the wrong choice, he implies that there is a right choice available as well, that of creating a society with "economic security without concentration camps," that is, the choice "to make democratic Socialism work" (v. 4, 370).

Notes

[1] In his *Fellow Travellers*, published in 1973, David Caute confirms Orwell's judgement by pointing out that "fellow travelling involves commitment at a distance which is not only geographical but also emotional and intellectual" (3). In other words, "it is remote-control radicalism. The fellow traveller prefers 'socialism in one country' — but not in his own." Caute also underlines Orwell's point about the fellow traveller's hypocrisy: "The fellow travellers cultivated a convenient schizophrenia: they scorned democracy at a distance; they invested their dreams of positivistic experimentation and moral regeneration — at a distance" (6–7).

[2] One is reminded here of a recent item by Bill Keller in *The Collapse of Communism* (1990), which appeared under the title, "The Soviets Proudly Present their Friendly K.G.B. Agent," giving an account of the screening of a "film, *The K.G.B. Today*, . . . intended to convince Soviet and foreign audiences that the agency long feared as an engine of repression has transformed itself into a rather likable law enforcement agency" (*Collapse* 151).

[3] On December 1, 1989, an article appeared in *The Toronto Star*, with the headline "British Lord Awarded Libel Damages," announcing that "Lord Aldington, 75, a decorated World War II officer and former deputy chairman of the Conservative Party, was awarded a record $2.75 million in libel damages . . . over a pamphlet accusing him of deliberately sending 70,000 Yugoslavs and Cossacks to their death." The pamphlet was written by historian Nikolai Tolstoy. The article ends by stating: "Aldington did not contest that the executions had taken place, but said he *did not realize that the victims — soldiers who had fought with the Germans, along with women and children — were going to their deaths*" (20, italics mine).

[4] In his *Politics of Literary Reputation*, John Rodden also confirms that Orwell "identified himself with Aneurin Bevan's and the *Tribune* writers' 'democratic' Socialism" (161).

Chapter 3

Orwell's Fiction:
From Psychological Realism to Political Satire

The First Four Novels

It has been generally accepted that none of Orwell's early novels — that is, *Burmese Days*, *A Clergyman's Daughter*, *Keep the Aspidistra Flying*, and *Coming Up for Air* — has achieved the stature of *Animal Farm* or *Nineteen Eighty-Four*, yet these early works of fiction are important signposts marking the course of Orwell's career. Interpretations of the course they mark, however, differ widely. A few of these are worth pondering:

Does Orwell's career describe an ideological curve on which the first four novels represent the author in search of an ideology, a curve reaching its peak in his commitment to Socialism in *Road to Wigan Pier*, followed by the falling off, the disillusionment with the cause of Socialism in his last two works, *Animal Farm* and *Nineteen Eighty-Four*, both of them "flawed" by despair? (Bonifas 308–377).

Do the four novels explore themes that lead to the peak of Orwell's career embodied by the masterpiece of *Animal Farm*, followed by the "flawed masterpiece" of *Nineteen Eighty-Four*? (Crick; Woodcock) Are they landmarks in the gradual unfolding of socio-political themes, showing how "the dangers inherent in those forms of hedonism endemic to industrialism" are finally "supplanted by an even greater threat emanating from a related but distinct phenomenon, the worship of power in all forms, but especially in politics? (Claeys 219)

Are they simply earlier variations of "the thematic centre of every Orwell novel" (Carter 28), the individual's search for authenticity?[1]

Are they landmarks in a chronological unravelling of themes in depth psychology, centring on the Oedipus complex, "primal crime," and "the sado-masochistic pattern of self-assertive aggressiveness and passive victimization" (Smyer 153)?

Probably most of the above patterns would be worth responding to. Yet, since this study concentrates on Orwell's final achievement in *Nineteen Eighty-Four* as a successful composite of genres, here I would like to discuss the first four novels only very briefly, and mainly to establish that they are all representatives, ranging from the relatively minor to the not-yet-major works, of the genre of psychological realism. I suggest *Animal Farm* is a significant new departure, showing a hitherto entirely unexpected dimension in Orwell's fiction: the visionary perspective of an original, imaginative structure finding its best embodiment in the sustained allegory of brilliant political satire. At this stage, however, he seems to have left behind the genre explored so painstakingly in his four earlier works. Finally, *Nineteen Eighty-Four* represents a composite of both genres, a masterpiece combining psychological realism and the visionary dimension of great political allegory.

Although this chapter discusses the first four novels by concentrating on their genre, it would be a mistake to ignore the strong sense of thematic continuity they reveal, because this continuity sheds light on the question central to the Orwell conundrum: Does the darkness of *Nineteen Eighty-Four* signal a sudden break in Orwell's vision due to a final stage of pathological despair, or does the last novel represent Orwell's crowning achievement because it brings into clear focus the mature vision of a tragic humanism, offering a coherent synthesis of the major themes, techniques, and genres he had worked on throughout his career?

The dilemma is not unlike the one created by the 'darkest' fourth book of *Gulliver's Travels* some critics have read as evidence of the insanity overtaking Swift in his old age.[2] Of course, today we know that Swift's insanity appeared biographically much later than the fourth book of Gulliver's journeys, and even more important, the third book was written *after* the fourth. Although Gulliver does go insane at the end, the darkness in the fourth book does not reflect the *writer's* insanity; it is the well-earned culmination of the gradually more and more savage satire dictated by the dynamism of the four-book structure of the work as a whole.

At this stage it would be also worthwhile to examine the interrelationship of Orwell's first four novels on the basis of a continuity between the two themes, the spiritual bankruptcy of hedonism and the worship of power (Claeys). There is no doubt that in *Keep the Aspidistra Flying* Gordon Comstock's

"Money God," representing the worship of success, is a precursor of O'Brien's "God of Power." It is equally true that *Coming Up for Air* exposes "the effects upon the majority of the hedonism of mass civilization which prepared the way for the totalitarian power worship by undermining traditional values and emphasizing those of brutality, strength, novelty and success for its own sake" (Claeys 220). Nevertheless, thematic continuity among the four works does not necessarily unfold gradually and chronologically. In fact, I believe that Orwell's first novel, *Burmese Days*, probably foreshadows the power worship in Oceania much more directly than the later three works. Thus Flory, privileged member of the upper class in colonial Burma, comments on the "Big Lie" that penetrates even the most intimate aspects of life in a tyrannical, exploitative system: "Why, of course, the lie that we're here to uplift our poor black brothers instead of to rob them. I suppose it's a natural enough lie. But it corrupts us, it corrupts us in ways you can't imagine" (94). An even 'Bigger Lie' in *Nineteen Eighty-Four* is the deceit integral to the totalitarian system: Big Brother who pretends to protect the people from the enemy *is* the enemy, and this lie necessitates an entire web of lies and corruption in Doublethink.

Like Winston (who, as a Party member also belongs to the privileged class of the oppressors), Flory knows that in a despotic system even the privileged class is unfree: "even friendship can hardly exist when every white man is a cog in the wheels of despotism. Free speech is unthinkable . . . you are a creature of despotism . . . tied tighter than a monk or savage by an unbreakable system of tabus" (213). Flory also knows that in such a system even the wish for resistance serves merely as "a safety valve: a little Black Mass on the sly" (97) or "the Lord's Prayer repeated backward" (95) — two concepts foreshadowing the 'Black Mass' and O'Brien's 'catechism' in the scene in which Winston joins the resistance movement.

However, *Burmese Days* foreshadows *Nineteen Eighty-Four* most directly in its central concern with achieving and maintaining political power. In U Po Kyin, a Machiavellian Burmese magistrate, we meet a local Big Brother on the ascendant. A clear precursor of the latter's cynicism, U Po Kyin admits that he is playing "*agent provocateur*, . . . raising [a] rebellion merely in order to crush it" (157). He also admits that in order to rise, he needs scapegoats. He anticipates both Big Brother and the carnivorous rats in his uncanny ability to find out where his victims are most vulnerable, a trait he shares with the crocodile, to whom he is repeatedly compared. In fact, with his "small perfect teeth, blood red from betel juice" (76) and with his body "swollen with the bodies of his enemies" (79), U Po Kyin is an early incarnation of Big Brother, a cannibalistic God of Power *preceding* both Gordon Comstock's Money God and the thematic connection between hedonism and power worship Orwell explores most fully in *Coming Up for Air*. Also, precisely because of its preoccupation with a social system that is more ruthless and oppressive than the societies of the next three novels, *Burmese Days* happens to be a 'darker' but also a richer, more ambitious, more interesting work than *A Clergyman's Daughter* or *Keep the Aspidistra Flying*.

Each of the four works can be shown to foreshadow aspects of central themes in *Nineteen Eighty-Four*. Each explores the struggle of a lonely individual exerting his or her energies to find the truth of the "inner heart" against a sense of spiritual emptiness, social restriction, and corruption. Yet precisely because the confinement, restriction, and corruption of Winston's society is so much more concrete and menacing, his struggle for the truth of the "inner heart" achieves a far more dramatic focus and an incomparably higher degree of suspense.

If this effect were a sign of Orwell's final despair, which allegedly struck him at the end of his life, how would one explain the fact that among the four first novels it is *Burmese Days*, Orwell's very first work of fiction, that comes closest to these qualities of *Nineteen Eighty-Four*?

My point is that Orwell, whose most highly regarded works are satires, obviously works best with political themes that are 'dark,' or rather, where the source of darkness is relatively easy to determine and criticize. The works in which Orwell hits his stride as a great writer are political satires, built on a dramatic contrast between darkness and light, between real and ideal, between the way things *are* and the way they *ought* to be.

Of course, satire never tells us explicitly the way things ought to be. All we see is the dark, insane, topsy-turvy world of the way things are, and it is up to us to 'decode' the message by searching for the satirist's norm, his standard for a 'straight' world both in terms of an ideal society and an ego-ideal. Among the first four novels, *Burmese Days* has the strongest political focus, but it lacks a vision of what Orwell the satirist will consider his 'norm' for a 'good place,' a good society. In fact, none of the novels before *Animal Farm* hints at such a social ideal. They offer, however, significant clues to Orwell's ego-ideal, to his personal 'norm' in its psychological and moral dimensions. Flory, Dorothy, Gordon, and George unanimously represent Orwell's determination to avoid what he considers the pitfall of the modern novelist, like Graham Greene, for example, who can feel empathy only with a protagonist who is a person of ideas (v. 4, 501). Although none of these four characters is as fully developed as Winston Smith, like him they all represent the decency of Everyman (or Everywoman) as the measure of our humanity.

At the beginning, just like Winston, all of these characters feel alienated, dissatisfied with themselves and with their society, yet, unlike Winston, they are unable to clearly define the source of their dissatisfaction. Each is driven by a feeling that life could and should become more worth living and each is capable of experiencing moments of true joy. Often these moments combine the feeling of being in love and being at one with nature, like the scene when Flory takes Elizabeth hunting into the jungle. But Dorothy's moment comes when she is alone, ready to do her chores, riding her bicycle along her neighbour's meadow. She experiences a "mystical joy in the beauty of the earth and the very nature of things that she recognized, perhaps mistakenly, as the love of God" (287).

George Bowling has a sense of this joy while driving in his car along a country road: "But I tell you I don't care. I don't want the women. I don't even want to be young again. I only want to be alive. And I was alive when I stood looking at the primroses and the red embers under the hedge. It's a feeling inside you, a kind of peaceful feeling, and yet it's like a flame" (528–529).

Gordon's feeling of elation at the sheer fact of being alive arrives when his pregnant wife tells him that she felt their baby move inside her: "A strange, almost terrible feeling, a sort of warm convulsion, stirred in his entrails. For a moment he felt as though he were sexually joined to her, but joined in some subtle way that he had never imagined. He had paused a step or two below her. He fell on his knees, pressed his ear to her belly, and listened" (737).

Yet, in spite of these rare moments of joy and celebration, in the overall journey each protagonist is invariably thwarted, or defeated. In *Burmese Days*, defeat take its extreme form: Flory commits suicide. In *A Clergyman's Daughter*, Dorothy is

resolved to accept a no-win situation with dignity. Having gone
through the spiritual struggle of "people who had lost their faith
without losing their need for faith" (424), she decides to live by
the moral code of the secular humanist, in which "faith and no
faith are very much the same provided that one is doing what
is customary, useful, and acceptable" (425). In *Keep the Aspidistra Flying*, Gordon Comstock, a frustrated poet, feels sti-
fled by the callous materialism of capitalist society, which com-
bats its spiritual emptiness by the mass worship of the "Money
God." By giving up his lucrative job in advertising, Gordon
is determined to defy this deity. When, however, his girlfriend
announces that she is pregnant with their child, Gordon gives
up his one-man resistance to capitalism and undertakes the re-
sponsibilities of father, husband, provider: he affirms a private
morality at the expense of a public one. George Bowling, in
Coming Up for Air, also has to accept defeat. He tries to break
out of his humdrum lower middle-class existence and his loveless
marriage by returning to his own version of the Golden Country, his birthplace. At the end he realizes that there is no way
of returning to the world of the past, except in memory. Yet
this recognition makes him feel a sense of renewal; he "came up
for air" for a sufficent time in order to gather strength for the
continued struggle of existence.

Once more, it is worth noting that if it is the first work that
offers the 'darkest' resolution, clearly this can have nothing to
do with that despair critics attribute to illness and political disillusionment *at the end* of Orwell's life. On the whole, critics
accept that suicide here is the literary expression of the 'dead-
end' of Flory's (and not Orwell's) political and and psychological struggle against the overpowering forces of his society.

Each of the four works gives us insight into the importance
Orwell attributes to our struggle against society as a process of
individuation. Anticipating *Nineteen Eighty-Four*, in each of
these four earlier works a fundamentally "decent" Everyman or
Everywoman undertakes to face this struggle with dignity, to
undertake the "hard work" (v. 4, 528) of finding love in a bond
with another human being, of reaching the knowledge of the
"inner heart." Yet, in spite of the social aspects of this struggle,
Orwell's attempts at social criticism or social satire are not fully
integrated with the characters' psychological development, at
least not till the fourth work, *Coming Up for Air*. In the earlier
works, especially in *A Clergyman's Daughter* and in *Keep the*

Aspidistra Flying, the characters' struggles seem occasionally chaotic, or lacking in focus; even when we may understand the social problem they are struggling against, we rarely see the social-political resolution they may be struggling for. I believe none of the first four works gives us an indication of what Orwell the satirist will come to consider the social 'norm,' the ideal for society.

Of course, no one would deny that the first four novels are recognizably 'Orwellian' in tone and texture: in their documentary, often rather journalistic sense of naturalism they are very much the works of the author of *Down and Out in Paris and London*, *The Road to Wigan Pier*, and *Homage to Catalonia*. The narrative technique combines an extremely sharp focus on the close observation of the environment and the revealing nuances of the individual's psychological response. Still, I believe they are, on the whole, the reliable, respectable works of a not-yet-major writer: the imagination is restrained, the vision is private, the insights and observations have a tendency towards not only the specific, but also the minuscule or the eccentric.

Finding the Voice of Satire

Then, in what appears to be a direct break with this whole 'documentary' stream of social and psychological realism, *Animal Farm* suddenly presents us with an entirely new aspect of Orwell's imagination. The satire bespeaks the intellectual and moral passion, the clear focus and conviction, of great political allegory — the universality and compelling vision of a major writer.

I believe this new development has much to do with the powerful *twofold* experience in the Spanish Civil War that compelled Orwell to write satire. The first aspect of this experience lies, undeniably, in Orwell's new-found commitment to Socialism. In *Down and Out in Paris and London* his sympathy with the downtrodden, the unemployed, did not have a political focus. Although involved in dialogue with his Marxist fellow-contributors at the *Adelphi* for years, like his Gordon Comstock, Orwell was not won over by theory. It was while doing research among the unemployed in preparing *Road to Wigan Pier* that he came to the intellectual conclusion that only a collective economy can overcome the two great evils of capitalist society: economic and social injustice and the continued threat of unemployment. But, as Gilbert Bonifas so succintly suggests, it was not before Spain that Orwell received emotional confirmation for this intellectual conclusion. For the first time, in the uprising of Barcelona he saw that Socialism as the highest form of democracy, a movement *against* any form of tyranny and *for* equality, brotherhood, and freedom, was suddenly becoming a viable movement. It was only at this point that he announced: "I have seen wonderful things and at last really believe in Socialism, which I never did before" (v. 1, 301).

It is in Spain that Orwell's long search for a moral-spiritual value system first finds its political focus; Socialism becomes the spiritual basis for his humanistic "faith," for his definition of the "spirit of Man." A poem he wrote at the time, one of his very few, gives us a hint of the emotional significance of this experience: "But the thing that I saw in your face/ No power can inherit./ No bomb that ever burst/ Shatters the crystal spirit" (v. 2, 306). Addressed to a working-class Italian soldier who came to fight for the freedom of his brothers in Spain, the poem celebrates the sacrificial struggle of the proletariat as the symbol of the immortal "spirit of Man" represented here in the purity, and hence permanence, of the crystal.

But we have to remember that the experience that made Orwell find his true voice in satire was twofold. His commitment to Socialism was co-instantaneous with his experience of seeing Socialism betrayed in Spain by the Stalinist faction, ostensibly the strongest guardian of Socialism. Orwell's personal experience of this betrayal (to be discussed in more detail in Chapter 15) was reinforced by his reading in the Western press about the atrocities of Stalin's purges, the rigged trials, torture, public confessions to phantasmagorical charges, mass denunciations, and executions in the U.S.S.R. (*HC*, 150–79; 230–31). But it was not only the Stalinist betrayal of the cause of Socialism in Spain and in Russia that aroused Orwell's indignation; what he was most alarmed by was the attitude of the Western intellectual who condoned these events complacently, equally willing to accept, and produce further distortions of, the truth according to the 'Party Line' determined by the Stalinists in the U.S.S.R. and spread by the Comintern all over the world. Observing how the fluctuations in the Party Line led to the numerous rewritings of the history of the Russian Revolution, with particular emphasis on the rewritings of the role and significance of Trotsky, Orwell's dismay turned into alarm when he detected the same process of directed falsification in the reports appearing in the Western press about the events in Spain.

It is this twofold experience of a deeply felt moral commitment to the cause of Socialism, and the bitter recognition that this cause is thwarted, deliberately betrayed by the Stalinists and their Western followers, that lends Orwell's voice the great satirist's powerfully focussed "generous anger." I suggest we look at this dynamic connection between deep moral commitment to an ideal and anger at its betrayal to explain the sharp focus and intellectual passion that appears, as it were, all of a sudden in Orwell's fiction, in his first great satire, *Animal Farm*.

I also think, however, that before giving expression to this dynamism, Orwell the polemicist had to find a genre that would allow for an ongoing argument with the persona of the Adversary, who becomes, in fact, the butt of the satire. The experience in Spain also provided Orwell with an ideal representative of this Adversary in the person of the duped Leftist intellectual whose quasi-religious faith in the "Fatherland of the proletariat" blinds him to the fact that the dream of Socialism has been cynically betrayed both in Spain and in the U.S.S.R.

One cannot overrate the importance of this betrayal in Orwell's development as a satirist and a humanist. It is this experience he is compelled to communicate, first in *Homage to Catalonia*, then in "Spilling the Spanish Beans," "Looking Back on the Spanish War," and with a greater dramatic impact than ever before, in *Animal Farm*.[3] It is also important to assert that the increasingly dramatic message about betrayal is not an expression of despair and apathy; it is more like a rallying cry to the duped Leftist intellectual — undoubtedly the satirist's Adversary, but only because he refuses to become a comrade in arms: "And so for the past ten years I have been convinced that the *destruction of the Soviet myth* was essential if *we* wanted a *revival of the Socialist movement*" (v. 3, 458, my italics).

This is a key consideration when we read *Animal Farm* and *Goldstein's Book* in *Nineteen Eighty-Four*: the target is not only the dictator's cynical betrayal of the goals of Socialism but also the Western intellectual's unwillingness to recognize this betrayal. "The whole point," Orwell explains, "is the effect of the Russian *mythos* on the Socialist movement here. . . . One cannot possibly build up a healthy Socialist movement

if one is obliged to condone no matter what crime when the
U.S.S.R. commits it" (v. 3, 443).

Orwell the humanist is inseparable from Orwell the satirist.
Critics who read his satires as expressions of despair or apathy
fail to see that Orwell's active commitment to the human struggle through Socialism is inseparable from his indignation when
he sees the betrayal of Socialism by the very Party declared its
greatest champion. In fact, it is Orwell's passionate response
to the paradigm endemic to the Utopian-satirical tradition, the
contrast between the way things *should be* and the way things
are, that crystallizes in the powerful, universally recognizable
vision of an unmistakably major writer.

The Search for the Central Metaphor
for *Animal Farm*

Yet it took Orwell several years after his return from Spain
in 1937 before he found the central conceit, the organizing
metaphor that led to the literary realization of his twofold experience in Spain. He came upon it, he tells us, quite inadvertently, when observing a little boy whipping a cart horse:

> On my return from Spain I thought of *exposing the Soviet myth*
> in a story that could be easily understood by almost everyone and
> which could be easily translated into other languages. However,
> the actual details of the story did not come to me for some time
> until one day (I was then living in a small village) I saw a little
> boy, perhaps ten years old, driving a huge cart-horse along a
> narrow path, *whipping* it whenever it tried to turn. It struck
> me that if only such animals became aware of their strength we
> should have no power over them, and that men *exploit* animals
> in much the same way as the rich exploit the proletariat (v. 3,
> 458–459, my italics).

In this incident Orwell describes the curious instance when the
writer becomes aware of the coming together of the tenor and
the vehicle of the metaphor, in this case also the target and the
vehicle of the satire. The target, of course, is the betrayal and
exploitation of the masses by the the same leaders who led them
to revolution. Introducing the conflict between exploited and
exploiter as the conflict between the starved and overworked
animals and a cruel, arrogant human master, the metaphor immediately establishes where our sympathies will lie. When the
cruel human master is first overthrown by the animals, only

to be supplanted by another animal, Napoleon, who begins to walk on his hind legs and carry a whip, this metaphor by itself could carry the full weight of "exposing the Soviet myth," that is, the "myth" that Stalin's U.S.S.R. is a Socialist country. The fortunate meeting between tenor and vehicle in this long-awaited central metaphor allows Orwell to harness that quality of a visual-visionary power we associate with the satire of Swift, or in a different frame of mind, with William Blake of the prophetic books.

Yet, although an unmistakably major work in the genre of political allegory, as an animal fable *Animal Farm* cannot embrace those accomplishments of Orwell that developed from his long and self-imposed apprenticeship as a naturalist in the mode of social and psychological realism. In other words, *Animal Farm* can be argued to represent a total and deliberate break with the overwhelmingly 'documentary,' 'journalistic' or 'naturalistic' approach of the entire stream of Orwell's earlier fiction. Then, in another sudden transposition in *Nineteen Eighty-Four*, the two streams finally come together: the allegorical approach of satirical vision and the painstakingly naturalistic approach of the 'realist' who builds his canvas through recognizable textures of sense impression and minutely observed nuances of human behaviour. In *Nineteen Eighty-Four* the vision of a whole world gone insane presented on a panoramic scale is combined with studies of the central character in extreme closeup: changing the perspective by looking at the world through both ends of the telescope contributes to the compellingly dramatic effect of *Nineteen Eighty-Four*, its suspense, and its convincing sense of verisimilitude.

Animal Farm in *Nineteen Eighty-Four*

And yet, in spite of the striking novelty of a new departure, there is a significant aspect of *Nineteen Eighty-Four* that either has not been perceived, or has not been found particularly important so far by Orwell's critics: in a sense *Nineteen Eighty-Four* is a perfect replica of *Animal Farm*. Certainly, in the later novel the scope of the political allegory is wider. Yet there is no doubt that *Nineteen Eighty-Four*, as it were, 'contains' *Animal Farm*. A look at the most significant points of comparison will illustrate this observation. Both Big Brother and Napoleon represent Stalin (although Big Brother also bears resemblance to Hitler, both in his physical and his political portrayal). Both Goldstein and Snowball represent Trotsky, at first Stalin's rival and then his ritual scapegoat. The role of the dictator's propaganda machine is fulfilled by Squealer in *Animal Farm* and by the Ministry of Truth in *Nineteen Eighty-Four*. Stalin's continuous rewriting of the history of the Revolution is represented by Squealer's changing of the seven commandments until he reverses the original meaning of each. A similar function is fulfilled by Winston and a crew of propaganda writers who rewrite former news items and make the original record disappear down the "memory hole."

The execution of the three pigs as traitors is paralleled by the trial and execution of Aaronson, Rutherford, and Jones in *Nineteen Eighty-Four*: both events are allusions to the showtrials during Stalin's purges, aimed at the elimination of Stalin's potential rivals among the Old Guard. The victim's public confession to the most phantasmagorical charges is an indispensable ritual in the systems satirized both in *Animal Farm* and *Nineteen Eighty-Four*: both novels demonstrate that the totalitarian dictator's popularity is based on the ritual public sacrifice of his scapegoats — a clear reference to the underlying cause behind Stalin's purges. To mention just one more of the numerous parallels, Napoleon's vacillation between Pilkington and Frederick as allies is a direct reference to the changes in alliances between Stalin, the bourgeois democracies, and Hitler during World War II. What was a matter of political expediency in history, the shifting of alliances, is developed into a principle in *Nineteen Eighty-Four*. Betraying one's ally and choosing a new one becomes a carefully choreographed minuet between Eastasia, Eurasia, and Oceania.

Such a close connection in satirical equipment between two works written within the span of only a few years (1944 and 1948) raises an interesting question. Why would a writer who had already been successful in conveying a satiric vision like *Animal Farm* decide to strike again in the same area; why would he want to repeat the *same* statement in another genre?

Even though *Nineteen Eighty-Four* 'contains' *Animal Farm*, is the second novel no more than a repetition in a different genre? This question leads inevitably to the significant differences between *Animal Farm* and *Nineteen Eighty-Four*.

Animal Farm vs. *Nineteen Eighty-Four*

To begin with, in spite of its close and convincingly detailed parallel between Oceania and Stalin's U.S.S.R., *Nineteen Eighty-Four* is quite clearly more than just a satire of the U.S.S.R. It is a satire of the totalitarian mentality in general; more specifically, it is a composite satire of both Hitler's and Stalin's regimes. The larger-than-life poster with Big Brother's face — the hypnotic eyes and the moustache, the shameless personality cult surrounding a "semi-divine fuehrer" — invites the reader to make a "double exposure" between Hitler's and Stalin's features. Each time Big Brother's face is being described, the reader is reminded that the personality cult was as characteristic a feature of Stalin's as of Hitler's dictatorship. In fact, in this case, it was Stalin who gave Hitler the idea:

> American correspondent Eugene Lyons, who was walking around Moscow on November 7, 1933, counted all the portraits of Lenin and Stalin in the windows along Gorky Street. The count was 103 to 52 in favour of Stalin. The "four-headed" portrait soon gained great popularity: the four profiles of Marx, Engels, Lenin, and Stalin looking to the future. Goebbels saw in this portrait an excellent propaganda device and immediately prepared a similar one for Germany; true, it had only three profiles: Frederick the Great, Bismarck, and Hitler. This trinity also looked resolutely to the future (Geller 266).

Incidentally, Michael Anderson, the director of the first film version of *Nineteen Eighty-Four*, was faced here with an interesting dilemma. Since he could not present us with Hitler's and Stalin's faces simultaneously, he opted for an ingenious solution. The face of Big Brother in the film is made to look quite obviously like a mask, a synthetic face, a composite portrait. Thus, without words, the personal existence of Big Brother is immediately called in doubt. This, of course, fits very well with the insight provided by *Goldstein's Book*, which explains that by 1984 Big Brother's face is used only as an icon; he is the guise, the mask through which the Party chooses to reveal itself to the people. The function of the icon is to appeal to the primitive, the childlike: if the people knew that they were controlled not by a demi-god but by the cold, impersonal intellect of a small ruling oligarchy, the Inner Party would be far less effective. If *Animal Farm* is the anatomy of betrayal, *Nineteen Eighty-Four* deals with the aftermath of a betrayed revolution.

Of course, the pain of the original betrayal is still there, witness the tearful old prole who keeps repeating "We didn't ought to 'ave trusted 'em" (33), as if putting into words the bitterness of Boxer, the representative of the revolutionary working class betrayed by the "pigs," the self-seeking intellectuals.

On the whole, in *Nineteen Eighty-Four* the target of the satire has become clearly universal: Orwell here re-scales the satire's political target from the miniature (the 'society' on Jones's farm) to a world-wide screen.

There is another significant difference: *Animal Farm* has already given a hint of the horrible efficiency of the totalitarian state machine, but the process was still contained in historical time. Although the name Napoleon suggests similar betrayals by leaders of earlier revolutions, the allusions to a specific time and place — Russia during the Revolution — are unmistakable. By contrast, by 1984, totalitarianism has become permanent, a world machine that can no longer be stopped, beyond the laws of historical change.

Deeply concerned with the consequences of our actions in time, *Nineteen Eighty-Four* also introduces a direct bridge, pointing out the cause-effect relationship between our 'present' (the time when the book is written) and the unchangeable, nightmarish world in *our* future. This bridge is *Goldstein's Book*, a satirical device that has no parallel in *Animal Farm*.

Finally, probably the most significant aesthetic and psychological difference between the two novels is the introduction in *Nineteen Eighty-Four* of the central eye, the central consciousness of Winston Smith as Everyman, a human consciousness we can readily identify with. The psychological distance between the reader and the character, appropriate to the animal fable, has been eliminated. Since we are expected to approach Oceania through the eyes of a human being, this also means that Orwell can call upon his mastery of texture, sense perception, and intimate detail. It is a mastery he had honed to perfection in the earlier novels. In other words, while *Nineteen Eighty-Four* maintains the visionary power and suspense of *Animal Farm* through the powerful structure of political allegory, Orwell could also re-introduce here the other aspects of his consummate skill as a master of detailed, closely observed texture. In *Nineteen Eighty-Four* Orwell the naturalist and Orwell the visionary finally come together.

These differences between two works so strikingly similar in satirical equipment draw attention to some important events between 1944 and 1948 that explain why in the second book the message has become more urgent, more dramatic, and more universal.

The first impetus for the novel came from Orwell's realization between 1943 and 1944 that regardless of Hitler's impending defeat, the totalitarian mentality was becoming condoned, was finding increasing acceptance all over the world:

> Hitler, no doubt, will soon disappear, but only at the expense of strengthening (a) Stalin, (b) the Anglo-American millionaires and (c) all sorts of petty fuehrers of the type of de Gaulle. All the national movements everywhere, even those that originate in resistance to German domination seem to take non-democratic forms, to group themselves round some superhuman fuehrer (Hitler, Stalin, Salazar, Franco, Gandhi, de Valera are all varying examples) and to adopt the theory that the end justifies the means (v. 3, 177).

Orwell sees signs of the abandoning of democratic aspirations, the emergence of a "caste system," the "horrors of emotional nationalism," and a "tendency to disbelieve in the existence of objective truth because all the facts have to fit in with the words and prophecies of some infallible fuehrer" (v. 3, 177). This tendency will become even more dangerous if "the sort of world that I am afraid of arrives, a world of two or three great superstates which are unable to conquer one another, two and two could become five if the fuehrer wished it" (v. 3, 177).

Three more political events that took place in the period in question add to the urgency of the satirist's message: the division of the world into "zones of influence," the dropping of the atom bomb, and the beginning of the Cold War. The bomb, Orwell speculates in his 1945 "You and the Atom Bomb," may be the last straw needed for the superpowers to perpetrate their "zones of influence" and enforce the totalitarian mentality already rampant all over the world. Since the atom bomb is extremely expensive to manufacture, only those few countries that emerged from World War II as superpowers will be able to afford it. Once these have the bomb, Orwell argues, they will have successfully circumvented smaller countries from ever again asserting their independence, and the world will stabilize into three large power blocks. Since each is in possession of the bomb, war as a means of changing the power structure will become useless between any smaller nation and the superpower, or among the superpowers themselves. A permanent deterrent of major warfare, the bomb could become the guarantee of an unbreakable *status quo* in terms of external affairs.

Further, since there can be no external change to be expected, the internal structure within each power block will also solidify, becoming virtually unchangeable. This is the idea that forms the backbone of the novel, as revealed in *Goldstein's Book*. With the beginning of the Cold War, Orwell becomes increasingly concerned about a potential crisis, particularly since the Western intellectuals' adulation of Stalin indicated their willingness to internalize the totalitarian mentality and be conquered from within. Therefore, Orwell feels, in the England of the mid-forties "the willingness to criticize Russia and Stalin is *the* test of intellectual honesty" (v. 3, 237). Orwell was not paranoid when he castigated Communists, fellow travellers, all the Russophile intellectuals who were "swept over" by an "extraordinary quasi-religious emotion" of adulation for Stalin that was "for the most part wholly uncritical and irrational" (Tolstoy 278). Nor was Orwell quite alone among his contemporaries in his opinion: We hear from Nikolai Tolstoy that "in 1942 Harold Nicolson remarked 'how sad it is that the British public are wholly unaware of the true state of Russia and imagine that it is some workers' Utopia. Anyone who makes even the slightest critical remark . . . is branded as an enemy of the Soviet.'" Tolstoy concludes: "Such was the atmosphere in Britain, where what George Orwell was to castigate as the 'Russian mythos' reigned almost unchallenged" (278).

As discussed in Chapter 2, by now historians agree with yet another aspect of Orwell's diagnosis: there was indeed a strong possibility of a crisis, especially since Stalin was quite cynically counting on the Leftist sympathizers to weaken the Western democracies from within (as we have just seen in the Laski episode). Orwell, then, is again on target when he foresees that if a choice is to be made "the question is whether capitalism, now obviously doomed, is to give way to oligarchy or to true democracy" (v. 4, 198). Orwell had good reason to fear that his Adversary would choose the Soviet model of a small ruling "oligarchy" and not the alternative Orwell had fought for, the "true democracy" of democratic Socialism.

The Search for the Central Metaphor
for *Nineteen Eighty-Four*

But to understand the growing urgency of impending crisis that informs the satirist's passionate plea for attention in *Nineteen Eighty-Four*, we should probably also recognize another, a more personal experience that usually draws little notice: Orwell's relatively brief sojourn as war correspondent in the post-war Europe of 1945. In his short but perceptive analysis of Orwell's marriage to Eileen O'Shaughnessy, Bernard Crick points out Orwell's insensitivity to his wife's final, fatal illness. Crick feels that Orwell's "adventuring" to Europe just at the time of Eileen's operation was unjustified, since he had started taking notes for the novel in 1943 and by 1945 would probably have had no vital need to gather more first-hand material for it. This, of course, acknowledges that for the type of writer Orwell was, first-hand material was vitally important. Thus, one cannot ignore the significance of Orwell's first-hand experience of Burma, Paris, and Spain in *Burmese Days*, *Down and Out in Paris and London*, and *Homage to Catalonia* respectively. Was Orwell's experience as a war correspondent in 1945 to add some absolutely essential, vital ingredient to the final version of *Nineteen Eighty-Four*? Wasn't he, in "adventuring" to Germany in 1945, also looking for some crucially important insight into the psycho-political dynamism of fascist terror, and by implication, the nature of terror in any totalitarian system?[4] Since we know that the idea, even the outline of the book, had been with him since 1943, wasn't he here, as in the case of *Animal Farm*, looking for an organizing metaphor, a central conceit that was to crystallize his vision and act as a structural principle for the novel?

In effect, several readers commented on his rather scanty and restrained accounts as a journalist when he visited the Nazi concentration camps in 1945, and on his restrained attitude when commenting on Nazi atrocities in general. Yet, I would argue that the entire concept of the Ministry of Love, the combination of the psychological with the physical torture, O'Brien's unabashed acknowledgement of the sadistic enjoyment of power, of the "boot in the face" in particular, could probably not have been conceived or executed with the same degree of passion and intensity if Orwell had not seen the devastations of post-war Europe and visited the camps, physical reminders of Nazi terror. Although it would be hard to confirm this by external evidence, it seems to me highly probable that it was Orwell's journey to the camps that inspired the organizing metaphor for *Nineteen Eighty-Four*: Room 101. (There is, by the way, no reference to Room 101 in his 1943 outline for the novel.) It has been pointed out since by several analysts of totalitarian regimes, but Orwell was among the first who recognized and communicated this central insight through Room 101, that in a totalitarian regime the torture chamber is not a temporary aberration of the dictatorship on its way to power. Camps, prisons, the chambers of interrogation are the experimental laboratory, the very core of the totalitarian regime, equally intent on the 'total' domination of the entire world and the 'total' domination of the human mind. In other words, the personal, first-hand experience of Germany in 1945 was very likely a significant factor in making Orwell arrive at his brilliant diagnosis of totalitarian regimes, his unique insight into the interpenetration of the public and the personal, the political and the psychological dimensions of totalitarianism — an insight that reaches full literary realization in the conceit of Room 101.

Nineteen Eighty-Four marries the two trends previously held separate in Orwell's writing: the imaginative structure of political allegory sustained by the unifying power of an organizing metaphor, and the close, reliable observation of individual psychology he developed through his long apprenticeship as a writer of naturalistic fiction. As noted in Chapter 1, critics to this day have trouble with the marriage of the two genres, in spite of the encouraging vital signs of the offspring: *Nineteen Eighty-Four* is an undeniably complex and 'highbrow,' but also an exceptionally readable and 'popular' book, unique in its combination[5] of psychological realism and political allegory. The next chapter will discuss the problems and the exceptional impact presented by such a combination.

Notes

[1] According to Michael Carter's *George Orwell and the Problem of Authentic Existence*, the search for authenticity "forms the thematic centre of every Orwell novel" (28). For my more detailed discussion of Orwell's ties with Existentialism, please see Chapter 13 of this study.

[2] The darkness of Swift's message, especially in Book IV of *Gulliver's Travels*, made critics underrate the literary merit of the work for two hundred years. See Louis Landa's introduction to *Gulliver's*

Travels (Houghton Mifflin, Riverside Editions, 1960), and the essays of John Traugott and Ernest Tuveson in *Swift: A Collection of Critical Essays* (20th Century Views, Prentice-Hall, 1961).

[3] Orwell's return to this important theme is similar to Huxley's return to the themes he introduced in *Brave New World*. He wrote *Brave New World* in 1930; wrote an interesting, probing foreword reconsidering the novel and its resolution in 1946; then returned to the same questions in even greater detail in *Brave New World Revisited* in 1958. Finally, in his last year, he wrote another novel examining the chances for Utopia in the modern world in *Island*, as if debating the inevitability of his prophecy to the very last.

[4] According to Michael Shelden's 1991 *Orwell, The Authorized Biography*, Orwell modelled Julia's character on Sonia Brownell: "Her outspokenness, her beauty, her apparent toughness, all had enormous appeal for him, and he was able to bring some of it to life in the novel which he began writing on Jura. In *Nineteen Eighty-Four*, Julia talks like Sonia, and even has a job which is the futuristic equivalent of editorial assistant at *Horizon* — she works on the novel-writing machines in the Fiction Department. . . . Like Sonia, Julia enjoys showing her disapproval of things by exclaiming, 'Oh, rubbish!'" (448).

Shelden seems to overlook, however, that at least as far as physical characteristics are concerned, the dark-haired Julia bears a closer resemblance to Eileen than to Sonia.

As for Julia's job in the Ministry of Truth, Professor Crick reminds us that, during the war, Eileen "worked in the Ministry of Food, preparing recipes and scripts for the 'Kitchen Front' . . . [and] many features of the Ministry of Truth owe as much to Eileen's experiences in the Ministry of Food, particularly the snappy slogans, as to George's in the B.B.C. Far Eastern Service" (*Life* 297).

On the whole, I believe that if we look for Julia's original, we should probably notice that she is, at best, a composite portrait. Her maternal, protective attitude when she covers Winston, horrified of the rats in the room over Mr. Charrington's shop, with her own body, is probably more characteristic of Eileen than of Sonia. According to Shelden and Muggeridge (Diaries, 268), Sonia was never particularly gentle or protective of Orwell's vulnerabilities even when Orwell was in the hospital, while Eileen had shown a great deal of truly exceptional courage and loyalty to Orwell. (She accepted his political loyalties as her own, followed him to Spain, and agreed to the adoption of a child because he wanted it so much.) Julia's loyalty to Winston when she takes the risk to join the Underground because he decided to do so, and her outcry not to separate from Winston under any circumstances, seem to me more closely inspired by Eileen than by Sonia. In fact, even if Julia reveals Sonia's "apparent toughness" at the beginning of the novel, she also undergoes a significant change in the course of her relationship with Winston. One may even speculate that her development in the novel parallels Orwell's hope that the independent, emotionally indifferent Sonia will, in time, somehow come to resemble the giving, nurturing, self-effacing Eileen in the course of their relationship. But, since Orwell and Sonia's relationship had no chance to develop, all this, of course, has to remain largely conjecture.

Yet there is an even more important factor that suggests the importance of Eileen's memory to Orwell when he was working on *Nineteen Eighty-Four*. Winston's sense of guilt upon betraying Julia is probably far closer to Orwell's own feeling of regret for having abandoned his wife at the time of her fatal operation than to his feelings for Sonia at the time he was writing the novel in Jura, (or indeed, at any time later).

But whether Julia reflects individual aspects of Eileen's or Sonia's personality, if we approach the novel as an independent symbolic structure, Julia's character assumes its independence from any individual woman in Orwell's life: For Winston, Julia becomes the triumphant enigma of the 'eternal feminine' in the world of Oceania, a world that intends to break the "spirit of Man" by denying beauty, romantic feeling, and sexual passion.

[5] Thus neither Huxley in *Brave New World* nor Camus in *The Plague* can come close to Orwell's intimate, psychologically credible portrayal of his central character, although they may have a similar urgency in their message as novels of ideas. Conversely, Koestler's *Darkness at Noon* may attempt psychological realism, but it falls short of the universality and the power of the vision of the political satirist. The scope of Koestler's novel, of course, is also quite deliberately limited to a political case study — by definition, less universal in its implications.

Chapter 4

Nineteen Eighty-Four:
The Reconciliation of Political Allegory
and Psychological Realism

As a political allegory directed against totalitarianism, *Nineteen Eighty-Four* is in the company of such great documents of twentieth-century humanism as Huxley's *Brave New World* and Camus's *The Plague.* Yet *Nineteen Eighty-Four* is unique in its achievement of what has rarely been attempted before, and not accomplished even by Camus or Huxley — the successful meshing of a consistent allegorical structure with a psychologically plausible, realistic texture.

We only have to recall the opening of the first chapter, indeed the first two pages, to recognize Orwell's unerring eye for detail: he makes us feel, touch, and smell the poverty and neglect as Winston ascends the ugly, run-down staircase of Victory Mansions, enters his barren, drab apartment, takes a gulp of foul-tasting Victory gin, and lights a poorly rolled Victory cigarette.

As the scene leads unobtrusively to Winston's overview of the sprawling gray city dominated by the overpowering structures of the four Ministries, we come face-to-face with the source, and the eventual explanation of, the ironic contrast between so many "Victories" and the conspicuous economic failure of Oceania. Guided by the convincingly realistic detail, we are scarcely aware of Orwell's mastery: by now the casually naturalistic description has imperceptibly turned into the scaffolding of the allegorical structure. Still on the same flight of stairs, we pick up Winston's growing sense of uneasiness as he observes the Party's incessant vigilance: the ever-watching eyes of Big Brother on the posters, the helicopters snooping through the windows, the omnipresence of the Thought Police, and the telescreen in the very centre of his own apartment. Without the use of explicit comment, we have been prepared to recognize the ironic contrast between Big Brother's World and the Word used to describe it. Having understood that Victory stands for failure, we can now proceed to solve the next puzzle: what is the true meaning of the Newspeak names "Minitrue, Minipax, Miniluv, and Miniplenty" (9)?

Within the space of the same two pages we get to know Winston, the middle-aged central character of the novel, not only in terms of his physical characteristics, but also in terms of his intellectual and psychological attitudes. As a result, the unfolding political allegory touches us with an intimacy unknown in novels of this genre. Through Winston we sense, as if on our own skin, what it is like to be living under the ever-watching eye of the Police State. (It seems to me that it is precisely this exceptionally convincing power of Orwell's vision right from the opening that may account for the initial reluctance of many a young reader today to 'enter' the novel.) That so few of the novel's critics show appreciation for the complexity and consistency of Orwell's literary achievement is due precisely to the fact that most critics have been unprepared for this kind of achievement: they approach the book *either* through the psychological *or* through the political perspective.

On the one hand, the 'political critic' concentrates exclusively on the interpretation of Orwell's political message, ignoring the psychological dimension of the book. (For the purposes of the generic dichotomy, the Feminist critics' preoccupation with sexual politics makes them also fit the description of the 'political' critic in this case).

On the other hand, critics who concentrate exclusively on the psychological analysis, tend to read the novel as a projection of the writer's or the character's paranoid or sado-masochistic tendencies (Sperber; Smith; Roazan; Smyer). They overlook an important factor: Freud's definition of the neurotic personality has been so influential that often it is accepted as axiomatic that the source of neurosis resides in the individual's failure to adjust to a societal standard, a commonly accepted 'norm' of sanity. Orwell's *Nineteen Eighty-Four* genuinely and systematically challenges this assumption. One cannot come to grips with the novel without understanding that Orwell here introduces a paradox of numbers: "Sanity is not statistical" (186). By juxtaposing the single individual's sanity and humanity with the insanity and inhumanity of an entire state, he proposes that in certain societies the exclusive norm of sanity may indeed reside in a "minority of one" (72). Totalitarian dictatorships can hold on to power only by convincing the masses that the unnatural, hate-filled, and topsy-turvy world created out of an insane obsession with power is normal. Orwell's political allegory contains the psychological warning: in a totalitarian state paranoia becomes the norm. Consequently, in a society based on suspicion, spying, fear, and hatred, Winston is not paranoid when he feels persecuted.

Therefore, it is really quite beside the point here whether *Nineteen Eighty-Four* reflects the writer's paranoia, or sado-masochistic tendencies related to an unhappy childhood (Sperber; Fyvel); what is essential is that we realize that the novel is based on the uncannily accurate analysis of the paranoid and sado-masochistic tendencies of dictatorship as exemplified by Stalin's Russia and Hitler's Germany. Many readers who have lived under totalitarian rule, such as Nobel Prize winner Czeslaw Milosz, for example, have expressed amazement "that a writer who never lived in Russia should have such a keen perception into its life" (qted. Edward Thomas 91), a perception more likely to come from Orwell's wide reading in contemporary history, including first-hand accounts of political prisoners in Germany and Russia (Steinhoff), than from the subconscious projections of his own psycho-pathological problems.

The Theme of Betrayal:
A Psycho-Political Phenomenon

Scrutinizing the impact of totalitarianism on the Western mind, in the major theme of *Nineteen Eighty-Four* Orwell presents us with a haunting demonstration of the psycho-dynamics of this particular political system. This theme is betrayal, a phenomenon endemic to the totalitarian system in both its political and psychological implications.

Betrayal is the major theme in Winston's story, and it puts the structure of Part 1 and Part 2 of the novel into an ironic perspective. At first glance, one would see this entire movement as Winston's ascent on the staircase (our first glimpse of him in the first scene) leading to self-understanding, liberation and moral regeneration. Yet, in the light of Part 3, which takes place in the Ministry of Love, it is clear that the whole ascending movement was mere illusion. Winston has been watched throughout: what he thought to be his liberation was part of a deliberate, systematic process leading to his defeat, his betrayal of Julia, his self-betrayal.

Various critics have been trying to come to terms with Winston's defeat. Some political interpretations define his goals as unrealistically Utopian, and blame Winston for being unaware of reality (Edward Thomas 91).[1] Others point out that as a member of the Underground, Winston was ready to become as ruthless as Big Brother himself; he would lose himself simply by entering political action. Psychological interpretations tend to blame various aspects of what these critics see as Winston's neurosis,[2] even his death-wish, for actually foreseeing, even provoking his own punishment (Fiderer).

Yet Winston is made to lose his battle neither because he is lacking in political judgement, nor because he is a personally flawed, neurotic human being. Throughout the book he is fighting for self-awareness, for an ability to detect and act upon the Truth. Purchasing the diary, buying the glass paperweight, renting the room that becomes his shelter with Julia — these acts should not be seen as expressions of a death-wish. On the contrary, these are the only means by which he can assert his will to live. It is only in a deadly, unnatural society that expressions of basic human instincts lead to death: in Oceania the wish to life is judged to be a death-wish.

When, in the same vein, Paul Roazan claims that it is "the tormenting capacity of memory [that] lends *Nineteen Eighty-Four* its nightmarish air" (690), he overlooks the fact that in a world with all reliable records eliminated, Truth must reside in the past; memory is Winston's only means of searching for historical Truth, his only means of breaking his bondage to his past and thereby ridding himself of his recurring nightmares.

The nightmarish air of the book actually comes from the opposite direction, from the collective nightmare imposed upon an entire civilization by totalitarian dictatorship. It is Big Brother who deliberately creates and maintains the nightmarish condition of confusion and mass hysteria intended to cover up for the one and only real betrayal in Oceania: it is the thief who cries "Thief" the loudest. It is his own crimes Big Brother blames on Goldstein and on all the other thought criminals; it is Big Brother who had originally betrayed the age-old dream of Socialism: human liberation through the Revolution.

The personal crisis Winston has to face in Room 101 is the dramatic climax and the symbolic centre of the novel, because here all the political and psychological dimensions of betrayal finally come together to bear their combined effect on the reader.

When in this scene Winston betrays Julia, he undergoes "the greatest horror that had lain embedded in the future," irrecoverable psychic disintegration. Intimately private as this experience may be, it is also the natural and inevitable consequence of all the other betrayals that constitute the system of totalitarianism.

Room 101: The Symbolic Centre
of Winston's Dreams and Nightmares

Critical assessment of the climactic scene in Room 101 springs from the same two, basically irreconcilable, schools of opinion that inform attitudes to the work as a whole. Critics concentrating on the political parable skim over this scene either by dismissing its importance or by admitting distaste for what they call the melodrama or the theatricality of Grand Guignol (Woodcock, 218), which to some verges on the ridiculous (Edward Thomas 94).

Critics who follow the assumptions of Freudian depth psychology tend to see the scene as crucial, but only insofar as it reveals the particular nature of Winston's neurosis — paranoia (Sperber 22), latent homosexuality and sado-masochistic tendencies (Fiderer 20), the wish to return to the womb (Smith) — all attributed to the Oedipal situation. What these psychological interpretations imply, and often explicitly state, is that Winston deliberately provokes his own punishment; that is, what happens to him in Room 101 is just what he has been subconsciously craving all along (Fiderer 20). These Freudian interpretations fail to see that although Winston's ordeal in Room 101 unmistakably follows from his inner life, it is also the ordeal of Everyman, of any individual's confrontation with the dehumanizing forces of totalitarianism.

Of course it would be wrong by dismissing certain kinds of psychological interpretations to altogether dismiss the psychological dimensions of this crucial scene. Should we decide to read it as political analysts only, we would miss the complexity and power of the entire novel as it brings to focus the struggles of the "psychological man," struggles mapped out by Winston's memories, dreams, nightmares — the world of his subconscious. It is worth noting here that Michael Anderson's otherwise well-intentioned film version of *Nineteen Eighty-Four* suffers from this flaw: in a film it may even be inevitable to ignore the character's inner life. But, as a result, when it comes to the scene in Room 101 — the climax in the film and in the novel — the film loses intensity. Not having been exposed to Winston's nightmares, to his dreams of the Golden Country, to the flashbacks to his past, the audience misses the very substance of Winston's psychodrama. Paradoxically, it is by concentrating exclusively on the political message that the director loses the focus of this message — its humanistic warning: the most dangerous threat facing us in a totalitarian system is the inevitable loss of the individual's inner world, and what is more, this loss is irrecoverable.

Looking for the motives for our actions, Orwell acknowledges the profound significance of the inner world of the subconscious, arguing that "the waking mind is not so different from the dreaming mind as it appears . . . Certainly the dream-thoughts take a hand even when we are trying to think verbally, they influence the verbal thoughts, and it is largely they that make our inner life valuable. . . . In a way this un-verbal part of your mind is even the most important part, for it is the source of nearly all *motives*" (v. 2, 18).

Although here Orwell echoes much of the terminology and concern of Freudian psychology, this does not mean that he is in full agreement with all the Freudian conclusions about personality. We must realize that, for Orwell, self, personality, and guilt assume a moral, ethical dimension. In effect, examining Orwell's method of characterization, one often gets a feeling that he must have regarded even the subconscious as somehow morally accountable. In Winston's case, for example, the "dreaming mind" is unmistakably a moral agent, performing much of the probing search for the Truth hidden in the past. It is with the assistance of the dream-mind, that is, through his numerous dreams and nightmares, that Winston succeeds in bringing to consciousness both his hopes and his fears, and succeeds in reaching self-understanding and moral re-integration by the end of Part 2.

Of course, Orwell's awareness of Freudian psychology is undeniable. Winston has carried the psychic burden of guilt for almost thirty years and his recurring nightmares are clearly expressions of a guilty conscience: somehow throughout this time he has been thinking that he was responsible for his mother's and sister's deaths. His guilt springs from a shameful memory he had buried in his subconscious: the events immediately preceding his mother's disappearance.

The first entry in Winston's diary is a record of irresistible excitement and, at the same time, of his resistance, as the hidden memory gradually comes to the surface. What he is trying to describe is a scene from a war film he has just seen, in which a Jewish mother holds a child, "screaming with fright," in her arms. In the face of inevitable disaster, she is shielding the child "as if she thought her arms could keep the bullets off him" (13). In describing this scene, Winston becomes so agitated that he is unable to express himself coherently: punctuation and sentence structure disappear; he is breathless, eager to blurt it out. Still, as the description approaches the forbidden, repressed memory, he is unable to handle his mounting excitement:

> . . . little boy screaming with fright and hiding his head between her breasts as if he was trying to burrow right into her and the woman putting her arms round him and comforting him although she was blue with fright herself . . . then the helicopter planted a 20 kilo bomb in among them terrific flash and the boat went all to matchwood . . . and there was a lot of applause from the party seats but a woman down in the prole part of the house suddenly started kicking up a fuss . . . until the police turned her turned her out i don't suppose anything happened to her nobody cares what the proles say typical prole reaction they never — (13).

The entry is interrupted in mid-sentence because at this point Winston is still torn between the Party's sniggering, inhuman attitude to personal love and loyalty and his own unfamiliar emotional reaction he cannot yet articulate.

The interrupted scene, however, will complete itself in Winston's subconscious mind, as if the dreaming mind had a will of its own, ready to "take a hand" in the process already started. It is quite obvious that it was the protecting, shielding gesture of the mother's arms in the film that triggered Winston's excited reaction, and that now works its way further in the dream-mind, in the form of a guilt-dream, a nightmare. "Winston was dreaming of his mother":

> At this moment his mother was sitting in some place deep down beneath him with his younger sister in her arms. He did not remember his sister at all, except as a tiny, feeble baby, always silent, with large, watchful eyes . . . he was out in the light and

air while they were being sucked down to death, and they were
down there *because* he was up here. He knew it and they knew it,
and he could see the knowledge in their faces . . . the knowledge
that they must die in order that he might remain alive, and that
this was part of the unavoidable order of things (30).

As the dream-mind probes deeper and deeper into the submerged memory of the past, Winston comes to understand
something about his guilt, and about the emotional and moral
significance of the mother's protective gesture, that he could not
have articulated earlier: "The thing that now suddenly struck
Winston was that his mother's death nearly thirty years ago
had been tragic and sorrowful in a way that was no longer possible. Tragedy, he perceived, belonged to the ancient time . . .
when there was still privacy, love and friendship" (31).

Winston's effort to articulate his thoughts in the diary leads
to more profound levels of mental activity in the dream-mind,
which, in turn, leads to increasingly higher levels of understanding, pointing to the liberation of the suppressed memory and
ultimately to the wish to liberate the self.

The second of Winston's recurring dreams, the wish-dream
of the Golden Country, is quite clearly a dream of liberation.
The importance of the sequence and the relationship of these
two dreams has so far gone unnoticed:

> All this he seemed to see in the large eyes of his mother and his
> sister, looking up at him through the green water, hundreds of
> fathoms down and still sinking.
> Suddenly he was standing on short springy turf on a summer
> evening when the slanting rays of the sun gilded the ground. . . .
> In his waking thoughts he called it the Golden Country (31).

What is important here is that it is the wish-dream that follows
the nightmare and that it does so abruptly; that is, there is no
gradual awakening, no transition between the two dreams. The
fact that the nightmare is overtaken by the wish-dream and that
it is in violent contrast to it in terms of kinetic, colour, and light
images seem to me unmistakable signs of the dreamer's wish
to escape, of what Orwell describes earlier in the book as the
"violent effort with which one wrenches one's head away from
the pillow in a nightmare" (18).

This "violent effort," this deliberate "wrenching away" is
quite consistent. Whenever the Golden Country appears it
manifests itself immediately after, and in sharp contrast to,

a nightmare; it is also there when the dream world turns into the world of reality. When Julia and Winston agree to become lovers, they meet on a crowded public square to discuss the way to their secret meeting place. They can talk to each other only by pretending that they are watching prisoners of war being led away to execution. Again, let's look at the juxtaposition, the relationship, between these two scenes:

> With hands locked together, invisible among the press of bodies, they stared steadily in front of them, and instead of the eyes of the girl, the eyes of the aged prisoner gazed mournfully at Winston out of nests of hair.
> Winston picked his way up the lane through dappled light and shade, stepping into pools of gold wherever the boughs parted (104–105).

As the drab, ominous urban scene is juxtaposed with the golden-green pastoral landscape, we experience the same sharp contrast, the same effect of a violent "wrenching away": Winston is trying to tear himself away from the world created by Big Brother. Then, with a "slow shock of recognition" (110), Winston realizes that the scene is the fulfilment of his wish-dream, as though it was the dream-mind that prepared him to find the Golden Country in reality. When the dark-haired girl appeared in the dream, with "what seemed a single movement she tore off her clothes and flung them disdainfully aside" (31). Julia comes close to fulfilling this dream: "And yes! it was almost as in his dream. Almost as swiftly as he had imagined it, she had torn her clothes off, and when she flung them aside, it was with the same magnificent gesture by which a whole civilization seemed to be annihilated" (111).

However, Orwell also shows the subtle difference between dream and reality. Although Julia and Winston's sexual encounter is a step towards liberation, at the moment of their first embrace they are still imprisoned by negative and primarily political emotions: "Their embrace had been a battle, the climax a victory. It was a blow struck against the Party" (112). Only through their repeated meetings in the room over the antique shop will their sexual-political conspiracy become a truly human commitment of personal love and loyalty. At this stage of their growth the glass paperweight will temporarily absorb the Golden Country, becoming their hope for a self-contained world together. Yet once it has become the centre of the lovers' world in miniature, the crystal suddenly expands to contain their whole cosmos (what John Donne would have described as making the lovers' world an "everywhere"). Appropriately, Winston comes to solve the puzzle of his personal existence after a dream in which he experiences a breakthrough that "had all occurred inside the glass paperweight, but the surface of the glass was the dome of the sky, and inside the dome everything was flooded with clear soft light in which one could see into interminable distances" (142).

In Julia's healing, liberating presence Winston no longer resists the shameful scene he had repressed for over thirty years. He recalls the last time he saw his mother and sister before they disappeared, after the starving family had been issued a small chocolate ration. He also recalls his selfishness in taking all the chocolate and fleeing for the door. This dream itself, and the discussion of its significance, mark the climactic moment of Winston's evolution, because it makes him recognize the source of his guilt: "Do you know," he asks, turning to Julia, "that until this moment I believed I had murdered my mother?" (142).

The searching, probing work of the "un-verbal dream-mind" has been successful in bringing the suppressed memory to the surface and in releasing Winston from his neurotic bondage to the past. What liberates him from his previous nightmares is his recognition that he had not murdered his mother, although he had acted selfishly and betrayed her love for him. He also recognizes that there is a way to redeem himself for that childhood betrayal — through forging a new bond with Julia. And determining that for the future "the object was not to stay alive but to stay human," he keeps dreaming about the Golden Country, about a world of the lovers' escape from the nightmare world of Oceania.

This dream of the Golden Country persists even after his arrest and through most of the long period of his torture and systematic degradation in the Ministry of Love. There is a point, for example, after he has been rendered intellectually harmless (he admitted 2 + 2 = 5), when he has a nightmare vision of becoming swallowed up by the big eyes, of becoming part of the brain-womb behind Big Brother's hypnotic eyes. "Suddenly he floated out of his seat, dived into the eyes and was swallowed up . . . the man in the white coat . . . was looking at the dials" (209–210).

Yet, even at this point, without waking out of this nightmare, the dream-mind wrests itself away from being swallowed up. Winston wrenches himself away; he escapes to the Golden Country, and with a hysterical sense of relief, "He was rolling down a mighty corridor, a kilometre wide, full of *glorious, golden light*, roaring with laughter and shouting confessions at the top of his voice" (210, my italics).

But the dream of liberation and escape has undergone a significant change by now. The original Golden Country was Paradise because it was the world belonging to two lovers in Nature, apart from society. In the recent version of the dream Julia is still present, but so are the guards, O'Brien, and Mr Charrington — Winston's torturers. Just as significant, the free, rolling countryside of the external landscape has shrunk, and turned into a corridor, albeit still a "kilometre wide." The golden-green world of Nature has changed into the corridor *within* the Ministry of Love. By now Winston is a captive of Oceania even in his dreams.

Yet the dream of the Golden Country, in progressively diminishing fragments, will recur several more times before Winston's last degradation, the decisive final transformation: "He was sitting among enormous *glorious, sunlit* ruins with his mother, with Julia, with O'Brien" (237), and then in a "flat desert *drenched with sunlight*." There is no doubt that the dream is waning, flickering, fading away. But even in its very last reminder, the Golden Country signifies that Winston still seeks a shelter because he has retained the basic ingredients of his selfhood. In spite of his loss of intellectual integrity and of emotional vitality (represented by the emptiness of the sunlit ruins and the barrenness of the sunlit desert), he has managed to preserve his humanity. He conjures up the image of Julia and she becomes a part of him, the focus of his inner self. Recognizing that his feeling of oneness is proof that his "inner heart is still inviolate," Winston experiences a sense of victory over his torturers. It is at this moment that O'Brien chooses to take up the challenge. Taking Winston to the "place where there is no darkness anymore," O'Brien forces him to go beyond the "wall of darkness," beyond the last boundaries of the self, of the inner heart.

Winston is made to enter Room 101.

Why Room 101?

To appreciate Orwell's unique achievement in combining credible psychology with the vision of political allegory, we should examine the following questions: Why in Room 101 does the Party require from Winston that he offer up Julia as human sacrifice to be devoured by the starved rats in their cage? And why are the rats the inevitable choice for Winston's final humiliation and annihilation?

Answers to these questions spring from the fact that the scene in Room 101 is, in effect, the re-enactment of a previous crisis; it relates to that significant "memory that [Winston] must have deliberately pushed out of his consciousness over many years" (142). After his breakthrough dream in the glass paperweight, Winston comes to remember and relive this scene in detail:

> In the end his mother broke off three-quarters of the chocolate and gave it to Winston, giving the other quarter to his sister. . . . Winston stood watching her for a moment. Then with a sudden swift spring he had snatched the piece of chocolate out of his sister's hand and was fleeing for the door. . . . His mother drew her arm round the child and pressed its face against her breast. Something in the gesture told him that his sister was dying. He turned and fled down the stairs, with the chocolate growing sticky in his hand.
> He never saw his mother again (144–145).

Winston had been haunted by the mother's protecting, shielding, sacrificial gesture for so many years because he feels that he betrayed her love. And as his mother had actually disappeared after this critical scene, the child Winston developed what we would today call 'survivor's guilt,' making him feel, incorrectly, responsible for her death. Neither Julia nor the reader has any difficulty finding an acceptable excuse for the child Winston's behaviour. Yet Winston himself feels that in his childhood crisis something about his deepest self was revealed. His recurring nightmares indicate that his horror of the "dreadful thing beyond the wall of darkness" relates to something he finds unendurable, something too dreadful to be faced about himself. The horror must relate to the self, since "in the dream his deepest feeling was always one of self-deception, because he did in fact *know* what was behind the wall of darkness" (128). He feels that if he had enough courage, "with a deadly effort, like wrenching a piece out of his own brain, he could even have dragged the thing into the open" (128).

In its omniscience, the Party is aware of the breaking point of the protective walls of the self, the specific kind of shame a particular individual can no longer tolerate. Consequently, O'Brien will shed light on the indescribable "horror which altered nothing . . . [yet had to] lie embedded in future time" (91). When O'Brien completes Winston's thoughts it is as if he were dragging to light the "dreadful thing" Winston had been unable to face: "It was the rats that were on the other side of the wall" (245). O'Brien has good reason for assuming that there is something in the hungry murderous beast crouching beyond the walls of darkness that Winston finds "unendurable." "The rat . . . although a rodent, is carnivorous" (246), O'Brien reminds us. When it is starved, it changes its nature, devouring, destroying anything.

The humiliation of hunger is a strong motif throughout the novel. Starved, the child Winston and his companions are reduced to scavenging beasts "scrounging round dustbins and rubbish heaps, picking out the ribs of cabbage leaves, potato peelings, sometimes even scraps of stale breadcrust from which they carefully scraped away the cinders" (143).

Hunger as a device for breaking down the personality is well known to the Inner Party. (In his "The Politics of Starvation," Orwell points at the politics of starving countries in order to force them to their knees [v. 4, 106–110].) As Winston enters the Ministry of Love, he gets a hint of the kind of fate Room 101 holds for him, seeing two victims being dragged in there; a man with a "tormented, skull-like face" who in full view of the other prisoners "was dying of starvation" and a "chinless man" who offers his last crumb of bread to the starving one (203). To punish this act of rebellion, the guard "let free a frightful blow . . . full in the chinless man's mouth" (203) — the part of the face already shattered and therefore the most vulnerable. One can assume that in Room 101 the man with the skull-like face will also be subjected to the suffering to which he is most vulnerable: his gnawing and unbearable hunger.

Both the chinless man and the one with the skull-like face are appropriate characters in the naturalistic description of the torture chambers. Just as important, they represent facets of Winston's own personality: they are externalizations of his own unbearable hunger, of the 'chinless' weakness of his own broken will, and the resulting 'loss of face.'

The scene between the chinless man and the starving man is significant in yet another way: it foreshadows the kind of supreme sacrifice expected from Winston in the end. The starved man's "eyes seemed filled with a murderous, unappeasable hatred of somebody or something" (202). He is willing to denounce, to betray anyone, beginning with the chinless man, his benefactor, including his own young children, and he gives them up to the most cruel forms of death imaginable. That starvation induces "murderous, unappeasable hatred" is hinted at again when in Room 101 we see that "the rats were fighting; they were trying to get at each other through the partition" in the rat cage (246). In their insane hunger the rats are ready to devour each other, to destroy their own species.

Let us now take a closer look at Winston's personal phobia of the rats. When Julia describes how the rats "attack children. . . . In some of these streets a woman daren't leave a baby alone for two minutes. . . . And the nasty thing is that the brutes always —" (128), Winston finds the story so unbearable that he begs her not to finish the sentence. Once more, the sentence will be completed for Winston by O'Brien in the Ministry of Love: "In some streets a woman dare not leave her baby alone in the house, . . . They also attack sick and dying people. They show astonishing intelligence in knowing when a human being is helpless" (246).

Through the repeated flashbacks we know that when the child Winston "snatched" away the last piece of chocolate, his baby sister was dying and his mother was also sick and helpless. As demonstrated by the episode he has repressed in his memory for thirty years, all the characteristics of the rats Winston is repelled by apply to Winston himself. His childhood crisis haunts him because he senses that in the ultimate trial the walls of the personality melt away and he will turn into what he is most ashamed of.

Various psychological interpretations have related Winston's phobia of the rats to Freud's study of the Ratman's case (Sperber 22; Smith 426). In this famous case study the source of the grown man's phobia is traced back to the child's Oedipal hatred of the father, and to his ensuing fear that he will be castrated by the rats as punishment.

There are, however, fundamental differences between Freud's and Orwell's handling of this phobia. It should be recognized that Freud describes the child's original offence as having taken place in the Oedipal situation, at the subconscious level in early childhood, that is *before* the awakening of moral consciousness. Young Winston's offence, on the other hand, is not related to the Oedipal drama. It takes place when he is between ten and twelve, and contrary to Freud's interpretation, young Winston's original offence is already a moral drama. He is tested through his feelings of love and loyalty to the only people who love him.

It is significant that his mother had already given him most of the chocolate willingly. "Snatching away" and "devouring" the rest, Winston allows his hunger, like uncontrollable fear or pain, to overpower the self until he becomes nothing but the living need to satisfy hunger. It is as if he were saying: "I don't care whether you live or die: my hunger is unendurable, stronger than my love for you." Going even further, devouring the food of the starving, he symbolically devours them alive. This symbolic act destroys something in Winston, and his sense of guilt literally 'gnaws' at him for nearly thirty years.

There is a moral and psychological paradox here essential to the understanding of the Orwellian definition of guilt, moral will, subconscious, and self: Winston feels guilty because he *did* have a concept of love, loyalty, and self-sacrifice which he was forced to deny in the moment of crisis. As he describes the scene to Julia, he realizes that although he could not have caused his mother's death — it was the Party that had vaporized her — he was nonetheless guilty: in the moment of crisis he willed her death.

Just as important, he realizes that with Julia he has a new chance to forge another emotional and spiritual bond based on loyalty, devotion, and the mutual willingness to sacrifice. To liberate himself from the past and expiate the guilt, this is his second chance. By entering the world of adult love, he can redeem his childhood fall. Hence the first nightmare (in which his mother and sister sink to their death so that he may survive) is followed immediately by the dream of liberation. The lost Paradise of childhood can be regained by entering Paradise with Julia in the Golden Country.

Julia is not much of a character in her own right.[3] We don't even know her last name. Neither do we know a great deal about her inner life, the limits of her personality, the nature of *her* Room 101. What we do know about her is that she brings back to Winston the almost forgotten smells and tastes of real chocolate (108), "real sugar," "real coffee" (125), the sensual, emotional "reality" of a world he had once known as a child through his mother's love.

Julia, then, allows Winston to return to this love, but in a new form, with a new hope. The glass paperweight, emblem of their life together, enforces this almost magical connection between past and future, because the mysterious pink coral, the memento of the past, is also like a rosebud. It is an embryo, a small but distinct hope that the two lovers may have a chance for futurity. "How small it always was!" (198), thinks Winston regretfully when the Thought Police shatters the crystal on "the hearth stone" of what could have been their home, and "the fragment of coral, a tiny crinkle of pink like a sugar rosebud from a cake, rolled across on the mat" (190). And instead of heralding the birth of the child they are not allowed to have, Julia's convulsions of pain (she was "doubling up like a pocket ruler" and was "thrashing about on the floor" (190)), anticipate Winston's grotesque birth trauma in the Ministry of Love.

Julia shows some of the characteristics of the nurturing, sheltering mother. Not only does she bring coffee, sugar, and chocolate to their meetings, she also covers Winston with her limbs when he is frightened by the rats in their room. Yet her gesture of love is uniquely her own. The repeatedly "magnificent gesture by which a whole civilization seemed to be annihilated" (111) bespeaks liberation rather than protection. In its "carelessness," the "splendid movement of the arm" (31) offers Winston liberation from sexual and political anxiety; in its "grace" (31) it offers Winston a chance for the liberation of the self, for acting out the original test again. In spite of all his humiliations in the Ministry, as long as he is able to stay loyal to her, he feels that he is still human, that the "dreadful thing which had lain embedded in the future had somehow been skipped over" (210). Should he, however, fail in his second chance, he would no longer have the excuse of the child's immaturity or insufficient control over the self; the "dreadful thing" he is forced to face in Room 101 is a final, irreversible destruction.

Murray Sperber rightly points out that Winston's phobia of the rats takes the form of "a body destruction phantasy" (226). Yet I believe this fantasy here is quite different from Freud's concept of the fear of castration. Winston's deep fear of mutilation by the rats refers to the "wrenching a piece out of his own brain" (128), an image more characteristic of lobotomy than sexual mutilation. What is at stake in Room 101 is not

Winston's potency or manhood. It is his loss of face. The rats' cage is mask-like. They will devour his face from within. And it is not the Oedipal-sexual offence that he is guilty of. He is guilty of denying the fundamental values of the private self. In his selfish and uncontrollable hunger he denied his mother and tore himself away from the primary bond of belonging, loyalty, and love. Now, in his uncontrollable fear of the rats, he re-enacts this first act of betrayal: he offers up the body of the only person he loves, as a surrogate for his own. When he screams, "Do it to Julia!" he offers her as a human sacrifice to the hungry rats. Once again, symbolically, he devours the one he loves.

In Room 101 he can no longer stay "in front of the wall of darkness": he is forced to get over to "the other side" (245). And as the walls of the private self are being destroyed, he feels that he is falling "through the floor, through the walls of the building, through the earth, through the oceans, through the atmosphere, into outer space, into the gulfs between the stars — always away, away, away from the rats" (247). The irony is, of course, that having broken through the walls of darkness, he can no longer get away. Exposed to the cage of "starving brutes" (246), in Room 101 Winston hears *himself* become "insane, a screaming animal" (246). By allowing himself to be degraded to the level of the starved rats, he has become what he had been most afraid of. O'Brien did successfully conclude his experiment: the "inner heart" of loyalty and self-sacrifice is only sentimental illusion. Ultimately human beings are nothing but beasts, and like beasts can be degraded until they become obedient instruments in the hands of the Party.

At this point we should realize that Orwell's strategies lead to conclusions significantly different from those of the Freudian critic. The starved rats, just like the child Winston, were themselves the victims of the Party's brutality. Ultimately the real face behind the mask-like cage of the rats is the face of Big Brother himself. It is Big Brother who turns his subjects into ferocious, hate-filled beings like himself, forcing them to act out the ritual of his own "prime betrayal" as human sacrifice. Winston's own final, crucial act of betrayal is some kind of horrible *imitatio dei*: in the moment he betrays his loved one, he becomes one with the godhead, acting out the inevitable yet horrible mystery, the loving union between victim and victimizer.

In effect, all the citizens of Oceania are kept in their cage, systematically starved, deprived of food, love, sexual and emotional satisfaction, so that the Party may channel all their pent-up energy into the hysterical quest for new victims, leading to the equally hysterical worship of their leader. All the people of Oceania become instruments in the hands of the Party, ready to denounce one another in order to assure their own survival. Yet there is a tragic irony in this process: as the victim's last bond of personal loyalty is broken, he becomes the agent of his own enslavement, and ultimately of his own extinction.

Room 101 is the dramatic centre of the novel because it both repeats and reverses two previous crises. It is the reversal of the breakthrough scene in which Winston liberates himself from the long repressed guilt by pledging loyalty to Julia: "only feelings matter. If they could make me stop loving you — that would be the real betrayal" (147). The scene is also the re-enactment of his childhood crisis. Forced to revisit the crucial trial of his childhood, in Room 101 Winston fails again. The failure destroys his hard-won liberation, the maturity of his selfhood, and pushes him into another far more terrifying infancy. The private self is enslaved, wiped out by the collective self. He becomes the image of his Maker, the prodigal son returning to the "loving breast" (256) of his parent.

Politically, Winston's capitulation was pre-ordained by the dynamic of totalitarianism. Thus a sense of personal responsibility, guilt, or shame would be quite out of order. Yet the moral paradox here puts Orwell in a category quite distinct both from the Freudian critic and the critic studying the novel only in terms of the political spectrum. For thirty years Winston's sense of guilt has been a burden, but it has also served as a reminder that he still had a sense of personal loyalty and could feel shame. In fact, it was this mysterious sense of guilt or shame that made him start his search for the Truth in the past, the search that led ultimately to moral regeneration. Significantly, once he repeats his act of betrayal, he no longer carries the burden of guilt. Of course, he is also free of his sense of humanity, of the basic moral attitudes defining the private self. Once reborn, united with the collective self of Oceania, he is no longer capable of regret or guilt because he has no further claim to a private conscience.

Room 101 is the climactic scene in the novel, bringing together all the betrayals in a series of symbolic reversals. Visually, "101" suggests two parts of the self, face to face through zero: reduced to nothingness through fear and shame, Winston is forced to face the rats in himself. The number "101" also suggests repetition after a reversal: repeating the childhood trial, Winston reverts to another state of childhood.

In yet another visual allusion, "101" suggests links of a chain — that is, not only one, but a whole series of continuous, repeated reversals. Room 101 is at the heart of the novel because it is the centre of the mythical, the political, and the psychological drama of betrayal. It is here that each citizen of Oceania can be turned into the victimizer of others by giving up, betraying his bond of private loyalty. Paradoxically, it is precisely at this point that he or she will be finally trapped, 'chained' to become a true victim, willing to stay in the cage forever. Ironically, it is by adjusting to the norm of the majority that Winston has now become, finally, insane. Having joined in the collective insanity imposed upon the population by Big Brother, Winston now willingly joins the other rats in the cage.

The Aftermath of Room 101

To see the effect of this psychic devastation — that is, the changes between private and collective self — we should take a last quick look at Winston's inner world, a look at his dream country after his "rebirth" in the Ministry of Love.

In the last scene Winston is sitting in the Chestnut Café, the haunt of released traitors and thought criminals: "He had grown fatter since they released him, and had regained his old colour — indeed more than regained it. His features had thickened, the skin on nose and cheekbones was coarsely red, even the bald scalp was too deep a pink" (249).

Guzzling his Victory gin and belching occasionally, with his bald pink scalp and thickened, expressionless features, he is like a grotesque reminder of a new-born infant (or a well-fed rat?). Then, we hear, suddenly, "uncalled, a memory floated into his mind. He saw a candle-lit room" (255). In a reverie he recalls his home before his childhood crisis, the last happy moments before his mother's disappearance. But according to the Party, there could have been no happiness in the past, especially not in the private bond between parent and child. As a result, the new-born Winston who would no longer acknowledge any private bond, dismisses the happy scene as a "false memory" (255).

And now, as he wrenches himself away from the memory of private happiness, the loudspeaker announces Big Brother's newest victory. Winston undergoes the communal experience of the hysterical hatred of the freshly appointed enemy, followed by the ecstatic worship of the leader. Then, in the midst of this communal ecstasy, we catch a last glimpse of Winston's familiar dream. In this final reverie he sees himself "walking down the white-tiled corridor, with the feeling of walking in sunlight, and an armed guard at his back. The long-hoped-for bullet was entering his brain" (256).

The earlier change from the golden-green landscape to the golden-white interior should remind us that in this sun-flooded white-tiled corridor we have caught yet another glimpse of the diminishing Golden Country. But what happened to the originally wide and free landscape? Once it was swallowed up by the corridor in the Ministry of Love (210), it had kept on shrinking and shrinking. But there is something else, still unexpected, in the form and the sequence of these last two dreams. What we would call the 'good dream' appears first and Winston rejects it, while what we would call the 'bad dream' comes after, and now this is the one he craves. What is more, the Golden Country has undergone a total reversal.

Originally the wish-dream of the Golden Country represented Winston's violent effort to wrench himself away from the nightmare — first to find freedom away from Oceania, then to rescue whatever was left of the inner self, within. By the end of the novel Winston is totally enslaved: nothing remains of the former self to compel him to get away or seek shelter. He dismisses his past as a "false memory" and wishes to return to the torture chamber. Not only does he accept, he anticipates and celebrates the bullet in the back. It is the nightmare world of Oceania that has taken the place of his dream of Paradise.

It is only at the moment when Winston comes to celebrate the latest victory that his conversion has become complete: "He had won the victory over himself. He loved Big Brother" (256). To celebrate this victory is to celebrate a world born out of the madness of hatred, to celebrate the bullet in the back of the head. It is by giving up the private world of memories, of dreams and nightmares, that he is submerged in the collective insanity of Oceania, drowned by the waves of madness and self-destruction.

It is characteristic of Orwell's definition of the self that Winston is subjected to a series of tests leading towards his final disintegration. It is as if Orwell had set a series of rigorous examinations to define the indispensable ingredients, the last boundaries of our humanity. Are these fundamental ingredients to be found in the definition of the man of reason: "I think, therefore I am"? But Winston remains human after his intelligence has surrendered to the Party. Is it, then, the Romantic definition of "I feel, therefore I am"? But Winston is still human after his inner world is reduced to the barrenness of a desert. Winston's breakdown becomes total only when he loses his ability to dream. In *Nineteen Eighty-Four* Orwell's final definition of our humanity seems to be "I dream, therefore I am."

Changes in Winston's character are indeed inseparable from changes in his dream-life. As a matter of fact, one could delineate the structure of the plot simply by concentrating on the dream sequence. Parts 1 and 2 outline the rising action of Winston's search for self, for psychic liberation. To liberate himself from his nightmare, the dreamer reaches out to the wish-dream of the Golden Country. Eventually he is able to translate the wish-dream into reality, and then he is also able to rid himself of his nightmares. Part 3 describes descent, the systematic breakdown of the self in the Ministry of Love. The gradual diminishing of the landscape of the Golden Country is tantamount to the gradual diminishing of Winston as a human being. Finally, after the climactic scene in Room 101, the dream emerges once more, but now it takes an entirely new form, assuming a significance diametrically opposite to that of the original wish-dream.

Having been forced to betray himself — as everyone must in Room 101 — the last man of Europe has survived, but he is no longer human. He is mutilated, lobotomized; he is no longer able even to dream, even to wish for an escape.

The psychological dimension of the novel does not contradict but gives vital support to the political allegory and is indispensable to the humanistic warning: since totalitarianism is built on a series of self-perpetuating lies, and on the unstoppable 'chain-reaction' of betrayals in the political arena, it also leads to the irreversible disintegration of the inner self, to the irrecoverable loss of our humanity.

Notes

[1] Edward M. Thomas discusses Orwell's comments on Koestler's Utopian tendencies. Thomas argues that in Winston's character Orwell points at the flaws of Koestler's unrealistic, Utopian expectations — hence Winston's defeat (91).

[2] In "Gazing into the Glass Paperweight," Murray Sperber, for example, focuses on Winston's paranoia (22). Gerald Fiderer in "Masochism as Literary Strategy," concentrates on Winston's masochism and his "homosexual resolution of the Oedipus triangle" (20). Finally, Marcus Smith in "The Walls of Blackness" considers Winston's phobia of the rats the conclusion of a fixation on the mother. Since Winston also feels that he had offended against his mother, he seeks his punishment through the rats as a condition to be allowed to return to the womb (423–433).

[3] Here I agree with Daphne Patai's "Gamesmanship and Androcentrism in Orwell's *Nineteen Eighty-Four*" when she discusses Orwell's tendency to use feminine stereotypes in the novel. Nevertheless, I believe this tendency has little to do with "sexism" or the writer's overt or covert tendency for misogyny, as she suggests. Orwell's strategies in *Nineteen Eighty-Four* are directed to the emphasis of the difference between private and public personality, and he uses the family, with the woman in the centre, as a focus of private values. Also, the story deals with Winston's development — all the other characters are subordinated to his point of view.

Part II

Goldstein's Book:
The Key to the Decoding of the Satire:
The "Secular Religion" of Totalitarianism

As a naturalistic novel (v. 4, 378) in the mode of psychological realism, the novel makes its appeal to the readers on the basis of our almost unconditional identification with the central character. At the same time, it was also intended as a fantasy of the future (v. 4, 378, 536), what we call today dystopian satire. As such, Orwell tells us, it is a parody — a word he uses as a synonym for satire — about the splitting up of the world by the superpowers (v. 4, 520), the effect of the atom bomb on the divided world, and the perversions of a centralized economy (v. 4, 564). But more important than any of these individual targets, it is a parody of the "intellectual implications of totalitarianism," the totalitarian mentality (v. 4, 520, 564). The next five chapters will concentrate on the central function of *Goldstein's Book* as a distancing mechanism essential to our more cerebral contemplation of the political satire, and demonstrate that *Goldstein's Book* is our key to the 'decoding' of Orwell's parody of the totalitarian mentality as a state religion, a "secular religion."

Chapter 5

Time as Theme and Structure
in Dystopian Satire

Orwell has been taken to task by his publishers and critics for interrupting the narrative flow of *Nineteen Eighty-Four* by the insertion of a 'book within a book,' a lengthy historical treatise that slows down the action. Orwell, however, was adamant, insisting that *Goldstein's Book* was indispensable and must be kept at its present place and length (v. 4, 544–545, 548–549). In the light of the complex strategies of *Nineteen Eighty-Four* as a composite of genres, this decision was absolutely correct.

At first glance it may indeed appear that *Goldstein's Book* slows down the action, especially if we approach the novel as a political-psychological thriller. Upon closer reading, however, it becomes obvious that 'the book within the book' is in fact the powerhouse of the intricate machinery of political satire. By its very presence it provides us with some emotional distance to decode the complex of ideas indispensable to the more cerebral, intellectual genre of classical satire. More specifically, it is *Goldstein's Book* that determines the focus of *Nineteen Eighty-Four* as a dystopian satire based on the interaction between two timeplanes. It is by reading "the Book" (17) that the 'ideal reader' is challenged to recognize those alarming trends in the 'present' of the 1940s that might lead to the absurd, nightmarish future of the 1980s. It is *Goldstein's Book* that crystallizes the major themes of Orwell's satire as it concerns that complex target, the totalitarian mentality, with particular emphasis on its unique relationship to Time.

Historical and Mythical Time

The antagonism between the totalitarian state and the concept of historical time had been a theme on Orwell's mind for many years, but it is in *Nineteen Eighty-Four* that this theme finds full literary expression in Winston's passionate search for reliable records and in the State's consistent effort to annihilate history.

It is remarkable how carefully Orwell works on the integration of *Goldstein's Book* with the rest of the novel, which is also a work of suspense, a political and psychological thriller. Thus the excitement of *Goldstein's Book* builds up gradually. At first, Winston hears a rumour about the Conspiracy, an underground resistance movement called the Brotherhood, and about the existence of the forbidden "Book" attributed to Goldstein. Winston's irresistible compulsion to find out about his personal past, the past of Oceania, and to read the Book, are inextricably intertwined right from the beginning.

Since Winston works in the Ministry of Truth and his job is to falsify records, he is well aware of the tremendous effort expended by Big Brother to destroy the past. Winston also comes to sense, almost by instinct, that his only way of resisting mental control and the threat of insanity is to find a fixed point in the ocean of lies. This is why he starts his diary. This is why, when he joins the Underground and O'Brien asks him what he would like to drink to, he answers, "To the past" (156). Winston finds it quite natural that in Oceania the only resistance imaginable should be connected with a book of history. Long before he gets hold of *Goldstein's Book*, it comes to represent to him history as the World of Truth and the Truth of the Word.

The moment in which Winston receives the Book is highly significant. It has been arranged that he should be standing in the throng of a cheering crowd, celebrating Hateweek against Eurasia. Suddenly, at this very moment, the Party announces that Eurasia, which had been the enemy only a moment ago, was actually an ally, while the ally of yesterday, Eastasia, had been the enemy all along. The scene represents the most outrageous attack on the sanity and common sense one would usually associate with the perception of the majority. Yet everyone seems to accept not only the change, but also the outright denial that a change has taken place at all. The greater is Winston's need to find reassurance that, although he must be a "minority of one" when he sees this world topsy-turvy, he is not insane. This is the reassurance to be provided by *Goldstein's Book*, which offers a rational historical explanation for the seemingly irrational machinery of the State system.

Goldstein's Book, also called simply "the Book," with an obvious reference to the Scripture — represents the Genesis of Oceania, giving an account of how the world of 1984 was born from the world of the 1940s. To understand the Party's attitude to history, we should juxtapose this account in *Goldstein's*

Book with the propaganda version of the same process in the *Children's History Book* Winston borrows from Mrs. Parsons.

According to the *Children's History Book*, Big Brother came to power to save the people from the Capitalist Exploiters "who owned everything in the world and everyone was their slave. . . . The chief of the capitalists was called the King" (67). In the thirty-odd years since the Revolution of the 1950s, the personification of the Capitalist Exploiter with his hard hat and his indispensable fat cigar has become interchangeable not only with the King, but also with the feudal lord of the Middle Ages, exercising his seigniorial rights of the *jus primae noctis* (67). This double and triple exposure of stereotypes and the hopeless confusion about different stages in history is Orwell's parody of the crude, childish oversimplifications of Marxist interpretations current among his contemporaries, interpretations found acceptable not only in the U.S.S.R. but also among his Adversaries in the West. But the satire goes deeper. When the *Children's History Book* introduces the Capitalist Exploiter, it introduces him as the first 'demon' in the popular mythology of Ingsoc. Should the masses be allowed to realize that when Big Brother came to power he was already determined to become a far more ruthless oppressor than any exploiter before him, the entire myth about Big Brother as the Saviour of the people would collapse immediately. Hence, from the Party's point of view, the only real 'demon' is the past itself, the kind of historical consciousness that insists on the objective scrutiny of the past based on reliable records.

The contrast between the *Children's History Book* and *Goldstein's Book* is a poignant demonstration of the Party's slogan: "Who controls the past controls the future." By controlling the past —that is, by representing the masses with a grossly distorted version of history — the Party takes full control of human consciousness; it controls both the past and the future.

But like most paradoxes in Oceania, the slogan can also be turned backwards, and then we get: "Who controls the future, controls the past." Here Orwell's satire points to the role of prediction in the ideologies embraced by totalitarian systems. As much as Communism and Fascism differ from each other in terms of their major premises and their desired end result, they have two significant common features. First, since they predict the end result of the historical process as inevitable, they tend to interpret facts in a peculiar way. The diversity of events and characters, the whole amorphous world of reality is forced into the strait-jacket of the particular logic of the given ideology (Arendt 471). In this sense, whoever "controls" the future — that is, whoever has power to enforce belief in the predicted end — will also have power to interpret and falsify, that is, to "control" the past. The past will be *made* to fit the ideological premise and its prediction. Second, both ideologies insist on a strictly scientific basis and methodology, yet they also reveal undeniably eschatological dimensions. They predict the goal of the historical process as some kind of Paradise Regained.

Orwell shows that in spite of its allegedly scientific basis, ideological thinking leads back to the barbaric, the primitive, the diabolism of long bygone eras (v. 4, 547). And here we arrive at one of the most subtle points of the satire: the Party's power to change, to falsify the past so that it will fit the ideology, will also have a significant effect on the present. In fact, our concept of a spontaneous, changeable present is the kernel of our sense of freedom. Therefore, when the Party exerts control over past and future, this control is equivalent to their abolition of our present, and thus of our sense of freedom. A somewhat similar phenomenon is also characteristic of primitive civilizations. It has been noted that

> for primitives history is not connected with the mysterious and evasive "now" which continuously passes away, but with primordial time and the primordial event that occurred in the beginning. Primitive people abolish continuous history and give meaning to it only in connection with archetypal events, usually the happenings of gods and their deeds (Moreno 160).

Orwell points out the significant connection between the Party's abolition of History and its insistence on a primordial, mythical time. The best illustration of this concept is the Two Minutes Hate. Anyone familiar with Stalin's era in the U.S.S.R. or in Eastern Europe could identify the Two Minutes Hate as the daily enforced discussion of official news at the work place. Yet, in the novel, this mundane event also gains the unmistakable significance of religious ritual. Well may the news concern Eastasia or Eurasia, whichever may be designated the enemy of the day, but what the people relive in the unchanging ritual of the Two Minutes Hate is the *primordial* clash between the hosts of Big Brother and the hosts of Goldstein, the daily ritual acting out the victory of the archetypal forces of the 'sacred' over the archetypal forces of the 'satanic'.

At this point we come to the second 'demon' established by the official myth, the undying Enemy and Traitor whose importance surpasses that of the Capitalist Exploiter laid to rest by the Revolution. This second demon is the equally grotesque stereotype of Goldstein the Traitor who, for reasons never quite clarified, betrayed Big Brother, the people's hero and Saviour in the course of the glorious Revolution (68). Like everyone else around him, Winston knows that "Goldstein was the renegade and backslider who once, long ago (how long ago, nobody quite remembered) had been one of the leading figures of the Party, almost on a level with Big Brother himself, and then had engaged in counter-revolutionary activities and had been condemned to death, and had mysteriously escaped and disappeared" (15).

Orwell describes the oscillation in Winston's consciousness due to the fog created by official history, where public figures keep appearing and disappearing, finally to assume their appointed position with the larger-than-life definition of mythical characters. In this process the natural framework of our mental lives — the specific time and place that delineates individual existence — is blurred and transformed into something mythical, supernatural. Although a great deal of time has elapsed since Goldstein has been discovered as the "primal traitor, the earliest defiler of the Party's purity," people still believe that "somewhere or other he was still alive and hatching his conspiracies, perhaps somewhere beyond the sea, under the protection of his foreign paymasters, perhaps even — it was occasionally rumoured — in some hiding place in Oceania itself" (15).

Capable of being at several places at the same time, Goldstein is able to "seduce spies, saboteurs" and a "vast shadowy army of conspirators," very much like Satan, whose powers are self-renewing: "What was strange was that although Goldstein was hated and despised by everybody, although every day, and a thousand times a day, on platforms, on the telescreen, in newspapers, in books, his theories were refuted, smashed, ridiculed, held up to the general gaze for the pitiful rubbish they were — in spite of all this, his influence never seemed to grow less" (16).

A constant object of hatred, Goldstein is the perfect foil to Big Brother, the constant object of adoration. *Goldstein's Book* shows us their synchronized graduation from the arena of history to mythology. It is the superhuman stature established for the satanic Goldstein that is the precondition for Big Brother's apotheosis: "Nobody has ever seen Big Brother. He is a face on the hoardings, a voice on the telescreen. We may be reasonably sure that he will never die, and there is already considerable doubt as to when he was born" (179).

All these trappings of the personality cult and the fanatical worship of the semi-divine leader are part of the popular mythos the Inner Party has created for the benefit of the masses, because such a mythos had worked wonders in Hitler's Germany and in Stalin's Russia in the 1930s and 1940s. However, by the 1980s, the Inner Party is fully aware that whatever Big Brother's role might have been at the beginning, by now he is merely an icon, a mask, a guise in which the Party chooses to reveal itself to the masses. The benevolent, smiling face on the posters all around the streets is there merely to appeal to the uninitiated: it is in sharp contrast to the ferocious deity, the God of Power worshipped by its priesthood, the Inner Party. Of course, the Party might have a good practical reason to destroy the documents of the past so that it could protect the semblance of its infallibility on a day-to-day basis. But this infallibility itself relates to its wider promise of omniscience, an attribute of the superhuman. In the long run, what the Party insists on is the demonization of historical time so that it can create a sense of its own timelessness.

This concept of timelessness is one of the central conceits of the novel, and it is worthwhile to examine here Orwell's keen sense of satire. By pointing out the Party's continuous rewriting of history, he is directly satirical of Stalin's numerous rewritings of the role of Trotsky (v. 4, 143–144, 189) in the Revolution;[1] of the numerous rewritings of history by the Comintern after each of the various policy changes in Moscow (v. 1, 563); and of his Adversary, the Leftist intellectual who accepted and perpetuated all these 'rewritten' versions of history. Yet, in addition to these specific targets, the satire is concerned with the general characteristics of ideological thinking in a totalitarian system. The totalitarian state, Orwell points out, functions like a theocracy (v. 4, 86), a primitive state religion that can exert its power over the faithful only because of their initial need to find a framework for human continuity in the face of death.

In a study written more than twenty years after Orwell's novel, Robert Jay Lifton defines psycho-political themes that characterize a totalistic environment, "each theme . . . based on an absolute philosophical assumption — an extreme image —

that is in turn an expression of an exclusive and incontestable claim to the symbolization of immortality" (214). It is this promise of immortality that explains the Inner Party's tremendous hostility against History as recorded Time. "Totalistic programs," Lifton observes, "seek a once-and-for-all resolution of dilemmas around death imagery as human continuity. Their impulse is not merely to stop time (in the order of obsessive compulsive behaviour) but to stop history. The immortalizing system insists upon its own permanence and immutability" (215).

As we come to this second theme related to Time, we have arrived at one of Orwell's most original insights. It is the concept of the Party's immortality which is inextricably connected with its need for unending and self-perpetuating victimization. It is worth pointing out how carefully Orwell prepares this double revelation, which forms the intellectual climax of the novel, the disclosure of the Party's central secret. It is *Goldstein's Book* which prepares for and sets up this double revelation: "God is Power" and "Freedom is Slavery."

While reading *Goldstein's Book*, Winston comes to understand that the "mutability of the past is the central tenet of Ingsoc" (182) and he also comes to understand a great deal about Doublethink, the elaborate system of mental cheating indispensable to the totalitarian mind. Yet, before Winston can come to a full understanding of this concept, he interrupts his reading, and Orwell seems hard put to find a natural explanation for this interruption. It is true that Winston has reason to be tired, yet he has been propelled so far by his compulsion to find out the Party's secret ("I understand How: I don't understand Why"), and this is exactly what the last two paragraphs in his reading promise to reveal to him.

According to French critic Jean Pierre Devroey, Orwell left the final secret unrevealed either because he was too careless to notice that he had left a riddle unsolved, or because he was simply unable to offer a solution (190). Devroey does not notice that Orwell prepares the revelation of this secret most carefully. As a matter of fact, he must have found it necessary to make Winston stop his reading of *Goldstein's Book* on the note of a cliffhanger, so that he could create greater suspense before revealing the Party's central secret some forty pages later. Here are the last words Winston reads in *Goldstein's Book*:

But there is one question which until this moment we have almost ignored. It is *why* should human equality be averted? Supposing that the mechanics of the process have been rightly described, what is the *motive* for this huge, accurately planned effort to freeze history at a particular moment in time?

Here we reach the *central secret*. As we have seen, the mystique of the Party, and above all of the Inner Party, depends on doublethink. But deeper than that lies the original *motive*, the never questioned instinct that first led to the seizure of power and brought doublethink, the Thought Police, continuous warfare, and all other necessary paraphernalia into existence afterwards. This *motive really consists . . .*" (185, my italics).

Clearly the two key words here are *motive* and *why*. Neatly, Orwell picks up these two key words when, about forty pages later, O'Brien announces to Winston in the Ministry of Love that he had passed from Learning to the stage of Understanding:

"As you lie there," said O'Brien, "you have often wondered — you have even asked me — *why* the Ministry of Love should expend so much time and trouble on you. And when you were free, you were puzzled by what was essentially the same question. You could grasp the mechanics of the Society you lived in, but not its underlying *motives*. Do you remember writing in your diary, 'I understand how: I don't understand why'? . . . Now tell me *why* we cling to power. What is our *motive*? Why should we want power?" (225, my italics).

Then, after Winston's false starts, O'Brien answers his own question: "Now I tell you the answer to my question. The Party seeks power entirely for its own sake" (227). O'Brien now reveals that the morale of the Inner Party depends entirely on the worship of God as Power, which means the ability to make another suffer: "This drama I have played out with you during seven years will be played out over and over again, generation after generation. . . . That is the world we are preparing, Winston. A world of victory after victory, triumph after triumph after triumph: an endless pressing, pressing, pressing upon the nerve of power" (231).

It is significant that in the same paragraph where O'Brien defines God as Power (227), he also introduces the Party's definition of its own immortality in "Freedom is Slavery." Only when the individual is willing to "make complete and utter submission" to "merge himself in the Party so that he *is* the Party, can he become "all powerful and immortal" (228) through the Party. As Lifton points out, in a totalitarian system "there is an overall assumption that there is just one valid mode of being — just one authentic avenue of immortality — so that an arbitrary line is drawn between those who do and those who do not possess such rights" (215). O'Brien's words confirm Lifton's observation that "collective relationship to immortality depends upon its collective denial to others" (219). Only those who belong to the collective body of the Party can hope to achieve the privilege of immortality, in contradistinction to the proles and other outsiders.

Here the entire concept of immortality is related to exclusion, the branding, the eventual scapegoating, of the outsider. As also noted by Mircea Eliade, early cultures made a sharp distinction between "sacred space" and "unknown and undetermined space," which they saw inhabited by "demons, ghosts, and foreigners" (219). Totalitarianism goes back to this fundamentally primitive distinction between the in-group and the outsider. What is more, as Orwell demonstrates in the novel, the entire concept of the Party's immortality is dependent on the demonization of the outsider, the foreigner, the enemy, the traitor. In Lifton's words, "Totalism *requires* victimization, the claim to ultimate virtue requires the contrasting image — and too often an embodiment — of absolute evil" (216).

We could find no better demonstration of this dynamism than in *Nineteen Eighty-Four*. Of course, Orwell was not the first to notice this connection between totalitarianism and victimization, but he is probably the first great writer to express this dynamism in all its horrible consequences not only as a psychopolitical theory, but also in its full personal impact. Going even further, Orwell contributes another significant area of exploration: What is it in the psychology of the victim that allows the victimizer to assume his dangerous power? What is the dynamism that drives a modern human being into the arms of institutions offering collective immortality?

Orwell considers it one of the greatest traumas of our civilization that the modern individual has lost faith in personal immortality (v. 1, 564; v. 3, 387–388). As a result, we are left with a vacuum, a psychological need that may be easily filled by the totalitarian ideology's promise of collective immortality. Should we fail to recognize this psychic need to begin with, we should become easy prey to deception. Originally, the deceiver himself might have been driven to the system offering immortality, by the same psychic need. This possibility is hinted at in the scene in the Ministry of Love when Winston is first confronted with O'Brien:

> The boots were approaching again. The door opened. O'Brien came in.
>
> Winston started to his feet. The shock of the sight had driven all caution out of him. For the first time in many years he forgot the presence of the telescreen.
>
> "They've got you too!" he cried.
>
> "They got me a long time ago," said O'Brien with a mild, almost regretful irony (206).

No doubt, O'Brien is making fun of Winston; at the same time, his "regretful irony" also implies that originally, a long time ago, he himself may have been caught by the lure implied in the Party's promise of collective immortality.

Winston himself is not immune to the security offered by a sense of belonging. He is haunted by his isolation from others, but he suffers even more from being cut off from the past and the future, from the sense of continuity granted to the human being as a member of the human species. This is why he wants to leave behind a record in his diary, a testament to the future. As long as he is allowed to remain human, Winston clings to his right of the individual's historical consciousness. It is the sign of his utter degradation when, in the last scene, he gives up his right to personal memory. Only after the sacrifice of declaring his personal past a "false memory" (255) can he finally join in the celebration, the public immortalization of Big Brother.

As we have now reached the third concept related to time, we are able to define the central function of *Goldstein's Book* in the dystopian satire. By the very existence of the Book as a record of the past Winston was so eager to get hold of, we are alerted to the significance of historical time. As Orwell's 'ideal readers,' we are alerted to a gap of nearly forty years between Winston's world and ours. *Goldstein's Book* is a bridge between these two time planes, showing Winston how 'our' world of the 1940s has led to his world of the 1980s. As such, it emphasizes that Winston can no longer stop the totalitarian state machine: his world in 1984 embodies the inevitable consequence of a past he can no longer return to.

We, however, frozen in the world of the 1940s, the world of the 'present' that the satirist shares with his 'ideal reader,' are still in a markedly different situation from Winston's. In fact, in a sense, Winston is our victim: his fate is the consequence of our action or inaction in the 1940s. And yet, it may be fairer to say that he is our "pharmakos," the sacrificial hero of tragedy. The fact that he is enslaved by the cause-effect relationship between his past and his present may be the key to *our* liberation. The time gap between Winston's world and ours should work in our favour. Indeed, the very urgency of the crisis — there are *only* forty years between his world and ours — is also a reminder of the significant difference between present and future. We still have a chance to prevent Oceania from coming into being. By its clear analysis of the trends of the 1940s, *Goldstein's Book* makes us accept the likelihood of Oceania as a distinct possibility, a threat. At the same time, the Book is also a reminder that 1984 has not come about yet — hence as a true record of History, *Goldstein's Book* may become the readers' guide for action. A valuable bridge between the satirist and the readers, *Goldstein's Book* exemplifies that characteristically Orwellian concept that clear thinking is in itself an act of moral dimensions (v. 4, 59–60).

Offering a crystallization of what the satirist considers the harmful trends in the 'present,' *Goldstein's Book* makes an appeal to us, 'ideal readers,' to conside the possible consequences of these trends in the future: Once the atom bomb has become a deterrent of all-out war, it might also act as a stabilizer that guarantees the invincible power of a particular Superstate within its own "zone of influence"; there are authoritarian trends in the Socialist movement that distort and might ultimately deny its originally humanitarian ideals; deprived of faith in personal immortality, human beings in the twentieth century have become susceptible to the immortality promised by the "secular religion" of ideology; they are easily drawn to worship God as Power. When choosing to ignore or even condone these harmful trends today, we fall victim to the mental cheating, the schizophrenia of Doublethink, and as a consequence 'our' world of the late 1940s could turn into the world of Oceania in a very short time.

At the same time, *Goldstein's Book* also implies that this picture is not inevitable. Witness how the Inner Party came to power. Having been conscious of the recurring cycle, the ongoing struggle between the Middle and the Upper classes, the Inner Party was determined to achieve power and then to arrest the cycle. The Party's first real advantage was its knowledge of how historical forces operate. By extension of this thought, the proper exercise of historical consciousness is our antidote to the threat of totalitarian ideologies. We can arrest the growth of the immortalizing and victimizing system of the totalitarian mentality only by insisting on reading History and trying to read History well.

It is *Goldstein's Book* that defines what Orwell sees as the signals of our impending political-spiritual crisis. At the same time, it is also *Goldstein's Book* that offers us a bridge, a reminder that we may still avert the crisis. Hence it has an indispensable function in the novel as dystopian satire.

Note

[1] Orwell was deeply concerned about the various rewritings of history and the series of false allegations against Trotsky, particularly the charges about his association with the Nazi government. Once the "Gestapo records [were] in the hands of the Allied Power, and Hess — the only Nazi named in the Moscow indictment — [was] available at Nuremberg for public questioning," Orwell decided, in the company of Arthur Koestler, Julian Symons, H.G. Wells, and ten others, to circulate a letter to the British press, asking for an "investigation aimed at the establishment of historical truth and bearing upon the political integrity of figures and tendencies of international standing." The letter asked that "Hess be interrogated at Nuremberg in regard to his alleged meeting with Trotsky," that Trotsky's widow "be invited . . . to cross-examine the accused and witnesses," and that "the Allied experts examining Gestapo records be instructed to state whether there are any documents proving or disproving liaison between the Nazi Party or State and Trotsky or the other old Bolshevik leaders indicted at the Moscow trials and if so, to make them available for publication." The letter was signed February 25, 1946, and appeared in *Forward* on March 16, 1946 (v. 4, 143–144). Orwell returns to the topic "to counter totalitarian propaganda" and find out about historical truth several more times in his letters (v. 4, 229, 231).

Chapter 6

Proles, Intellectuals, and
the Betrayal of Socialism:
Orwell's Satirical Devices

Much of the grim humour of *Goldstein's Book* derives from the readers' gradual recognition that the grotesque reign of conspicuous dishonesty and gratuitous cruelty in 1984 is ultimately the logical consequence of the dishonesty and cruelty we accept and even justify as normal in our own 'present' world of 1948. The satirist's purpose is to convince his contemporaries — his 'ideal readers' — that there is a clear cause-effect relationship between these two worlds. Consequently, *Goldstein's Book* is essential to the 'decoding' of Orwell's satirical devices — irony, allusion, the reversal between cause-effect relationships, apposition, overstatement, the carrying of an assumption to its absurd conclusion — all of them barbs aimed at *us* from the topsy-turvy world of Oceania.

Our first bridge between these two worlds is the first sentence of the chapter entitled "War is Peace" in *Goldstein's Book*. It points out that "the splitting up of the world into three great superstates was an event which could be *and indeed was foreseen* before the middle of the twentieth century" (163, my italics). This is a clear allusion to the emergence of the superstates after World War II, a development the satirist considers such a serious threat to human freedom that he declares "what [*Nineteen Eighty-Four*] is really meant to do is to discuss the implications of dividing the world up into 'Zones of influence' (I thought of it in 1944 as a result of the Teheran Conference)" (v. 4, 520). If this fatal disaster "could be foreseen" and the satirist's contemporaries failed to do so, they were misguided and foolish; if it "was indeed foreseen" and yet they did nothing to prevent it, they failed morally.

The second sentence in the same chapter is a relatively mild joke stating that, as could have been expected, the British Empire became absorbed by the United States (163) — a satirical overstatement of the increasing American influence on British culture and politics in the late 1940s. The 'joke' is set up at the beginning of the novel when the satirist innocently mentions the dollar as the established form of currency in London (11). At this point it is important to note that Orwell does not carry this joke of England's Americanization any further, in spite of what some of Orwell's more recent critics, including the 1984 article in the *Izvestiya*, might lead us to expect.[1] The transformation of Trafalgar Square into Victory Square with its telescreens and loudspeakers has an element of the comic, as it superimposes London over Moscow and Berlin. But it certainly does not suggest the superimposition of London over Washington or New York. Had Orwell wanted to develop his satire into a sharp criticism of the expansionist or totalitarian trends in the United States, he would have had ample opportunity here to do so; instead, the rest of *Goldstein's Book* proceeds as a recognizable parody of an England that has become a totalitarian state modelled on Hitler's Germany, and even more on Stalin's regime in Russia. *Goldstein's Book* also implies that both Great Britain and the United States must have *chosen* the same model, since Oceania is not conquered by external powers: it exists parallel to Eurasia (the "zone" designated as the U.S.S.R. after it absorbed the rest of Europe).

Another typically Orwellian device is the reversal between cause and effect, or means and ends. Waste and devastation have always been accepted as the effects of war. Since war was waged to accomplish certain ends (those of defence or expansion), rulers in the past had accepted waste and devastation as side-effects, admittedly unpleasant means to their ends. All this is turned upside down in Oceania: here it has become the *aim* "to use up the products of the machine without raising the general standard of living" (166). War is used as a *means* to accomplish this end; it is a strategy.

As part of this strategy, the Inner Party seals off Oceania from the other two superstates, and periodically declares *one* of the two its enemy of irreconcilable ideological differences. Yet, in spite of ferocious Party propaganda against the enemy of the moment, the unending series of hostilities constitutes "a warfare of limited aims between combatants who are unable to destroy one another, have no material cause for fighting and are *not divided by any genuine ideological difference*" (164, my italics).

Why does the satirist draw attention to the fact that the ideologies of "Ingsoc," "Neo-Bolshevism," and "Death-Worship

. . . [also called] the Obliteration of the Self" are "barely distinguishable" (171)? Of course, the point is that the Ingsoc of 1984 is the orthodox Adversary's intellectual position brought to its conclusion, and as such it is a form of Death Worship — the unconditional adherence to an ideology that emerged from the conditions of the nineteenth century. It is part of the same joke that the Adversary's ostensibly 'progressive' and 'scientific' position demands the virtual "obliteration" of the private self at the altar of the collective, a notion reminiscent of ancient Oriental religions.

Readers of Orwell's essay on "Nationalism" may also be reminded here of another startlingly Swiftian example of apposition that shocks us into recognizing the analogy between two things hitherto considered not only different but also diametrically opposite: "Nationalism, in the extended sense in which I am using the word, includes such movements and tendencies as Communism, political Catholicism, Zionism, Anti-Semitism, Trotskyism and Pacifism" (v. 3, 411–412). Orwell's juxtaposition of such obvious opposites as Communism and Catholicism, Zionism and anti-semitism, Communism and Trotskyism, as manifestations of the same phenomenon underscores his point that their contrast is illusory. All of them are symptoms of the *same* disease and fulfil the same psychological need; each is a form of nationalism that gives free reign to the worship of power, and as such each functions as a substitute for religion, a "secular religion." By the same token, *Goldstein's Book* reveals that the seemingly different ideologies of the three superstates in the future are essentially identical, since each state is governed by terror (a state of affairs prepared by *our* generation's acceptance of "secular religions" based on power worship).

Does *Goldstein's Book* confirm the claim of some critics that pessimism impaired Orwell's vision at the end of his life? To begin with, we should recognize that Orwell's analysis of the psychology of power, the "impulse to bully others," does not indicate much of a change from one period of his life to another. Quite consistently, Orwell the essayist returns to the thought that the modern mind is diseased by power worship, yet

> one must continue the political struggle, just as a doctor must try to save the life of a patient who is probably going to die. But I do suggest that we shall get nowhere unless we start by recognizing that political behaviour is largely non-rational, that

the world is suffering from some kind of mental disease which must be diagnosed before it can be cured (v. 4, 289).

Goldstein's Book is a summation of Orwell's position on the power worship of his age, consistent with his characteristic concern that "it is not easy to find a direct economic explanation of the behaviour of the people who now rule the world. The desire for pure power seems to be much more dominant than the desire for wealth" (v. 4, 289).

Orwell's diagnosis of Big Brother's irrational destructiveness, aimed at his own people, agrees with other diagnoses of totalitarianism. Hannah Arendt, for example, points out that the "Nazis behaved like foreign conquerors in Germany" (417), ruthlessly exploiting and willing to destroy the resources of their own land, their own people.[2] In *Stalin's Secret War*, Nikolai Tolstoy also argues that the strange quirks in Stalin's foreign policy should be re-examined in the framework of his secret war against his own people. Many of Solzhenitsyn's revelations in *The Gulag Archipelago* give further evidence of the dictator's paranoid fear of, and hostility against, his own subjects.

Years before Arendt, Tolstoy, and Solzhenitsyn, in *Goldstein's Book* Orwell draws attention to the fact that he modern dictator's ruthless drive for 'total' domination can no longer be sufficiently accounted for by Marx's "direct economic explanation" (v. 4, 289) of imperialism.

The Proles

Goldstein's Book also flies in the face of another Marxist assumption — namely, that revolution will become inevitable when the economic oppression of the proletariat reaches its worst stage. On the contrary, *Goldstein's Book* explains, the Inner Party succeeded in securing its position precisely *because* it succeeded in keeping the masses permanently deprived of food, leisure, and education. "From the moment the machine first made its appearance it was clear to all thinking people that the need for human drudgery, and therefore to a great extent for human inequality, had disappeared. If the machine were used deliberately for that end, hunger, overwork, dirt, illiteracy, and disease could be eliminated within a few generations" (153).

Here Orwell's analysis of the proles' condition gains particular poignancy in the light of our increasing access to information about Stalin's policy on slave labour: it has been estimated that in the period starting with the mid-thirties up to his death in 1953, approximately one-tenth of the whole population of the U.S.S.R. was engaged in slave labour in the camps, and among conditions deliberately designed to maximize "drudgery . . . hunger, overwork, and disease," aiming for the deliberate dehumanization of the worker. Underlying Orwell's indignation in the description of the proles' condition in Oceania is his conviction that the rational use of technology in the twentieth century could easily bring fulfilment to the age-old dream of economic and political equality. That such a natural process is so forcefully hindered must be attributed to an irrationality verging on insanity, and this is the mentality of those we allow to rule the world: "For if leisure and security were enjoyed by all alike, the great mass of human beings who are normally stupefied by poverty would become literate and would learn to think for themselves; and once they had done this, they would sooner or later realize that the privileged minority had no function, and they would sweep it away" (154).

The very crux of the satirist's message here — and this is the hidden standard, the norm of sanity implicit in the whole satire — is that a society based on equality would be the natural consequence of the blessings of the machine. Increase in production could be naturally followed by the equitable distribution of goods produced and by equal opportunity for education. *Goldstein's Book* emphasizes how unnatural it is for a small oligarchy like the Inner Party to rule the majority. They would be swept away without the "imposture" of war because only war can effectively reduce the population to poverty and ignorance, and "in the long run, a hierarchical society was only possible on a basis of poverty and ignorance" (167). By recognizing the satirical device of ironic reversal, we should be able to determine Orwell's message: to prevent the realization of a world like Oceania we should dedicate ourselves to the elimination of poverty and ignorance.

According to Bernard Crick, Orwell mis-diagnoses the role of the proles in a totalitarian system when he makes the Inner Party announce that "proles and animals are free" (66). Professor Crick also suggests that the condition of the proles in Oceania is "to serve as a satire of what the mass media, poor schools, and the selfishness of the intelligentsia were doing to the *actual working class of Orwell's time* ("Introduction" 30, my italics).

By assuming that the proles' condition in 1984 simply follows from the flaws of the capitalist system in 1948, Professor Crick overlooks the mainspring of the satire. This assumption, I believe, also goes hand in hand with his overlooking of the significance of Orwell's consistent allusions to the practices in the U.S.S.R., where the Party came to power ostensibly to liberate the masses, but proceeded to set up a class system that introduced the degradation of the working class in a way "unexampled for centuries past" (184). The Party's contempt for the masses is superseded only by its hypocrisy in asserting that the collectivization of private property is tantamount to equality. Orwell points out repeatedly that "the so called collectivist systems now existing . . . are a sham covering a new form of class privilege" (v. 3, 365). In spite of the Marxist platitudes in the *Children's History Book* about the rule of the proletariat (67), the Party knows that should the proles be allowed to fulfill their human potential, Big Brother would be rendered powerless. Hence the Party removes all books from the prole quarters (65), and "proletarians, in practice, are not allowed to graduate into the Party. The most gifted among them, who might possibly become nuclei of discontent, are simply marked down by the Thought Police and eliminated" (180). The threat implicit in allowing the proles to reach consciousness is amply registered by the Party: the central goal of introducing a war economy and inducing war hysteria is to reduce the masses to a bestial, subhuman level. This is the true meaning of the Party slogan that animals and proles are "free." The aptness of Orwell's analysis is also endorsed by Hannah Arendt: in Hitler's Germany the masses were controlled more by terror and deprivation than by propaganda or indoctrination. As for the masses in the U.S.S.R. of the 1940s, in *The Yogi and the Commissar* Koestler points out that, paralysed by fear and confused by contradictory propaganda campaigns, the "masses resign themselves to the fact that the mysteries of politics are impenetrable . . . [They] unconditionally surrender their critical faculties to their leaders and fall back into the mental state from which they started twenty-five years ago" (136).[3]

On the whole, the purpose of the Inner Party is to achieve economic deprivation as a means: the end is the proles' intellectual, spiritual deprivation. Deprived of leisure, comfort and education, they are compensated by the drugs of "cheap sex, pornography, and gambling" that become further deterrents to developing political consciousness.

But the major ingredient of the totalitarian "opium of the masses" is the circus of Hateweek and the public executions — trappings of the state religion based on worship of power. At this point we may take issue with another of Professor Crick's suggestions, that "little Miss Parsons'" anxiety to see a hanging suggests a throwback to the barbaric eighteenth- and early nineteenth-century time of public executions in London ("Introduction" 434). If this were the case, Orwell's allusion would indeed weaken the focus of *Nineteen Eighty-Four* as a satire of totalitarianism. But once more, Orwell's essays indicate that the Parsons children's interest in public hangings is another allusion to practices in the U.S.S.R., most specifically to the public execution of German war criminals in Kharkov. Orwell regarded such public scenes typical of the state's brutalization of the masses: "Recently another newspaper published photographs of the dangling corpses of Germans hanged by the Russians in Kharkov, and carefully informed the readers that the execution had been filmed and that the public would shortly be able to witness them at the theatres. (Were children admitted, I wonder?)" (v. 3, 266–267).

It should also be noted that Orwell reviewed *The Yogi and the Commissar* and was a personal friend of Koestler, whose insights often find their way into *Nineteen Eighty-Four* quite naturally. A case in point is Koestler's essay on the Kharkov trials, explaining that in a totalitarian system the 'circus' of public executions is one of the

> emotional compensations for the masses. Deprived of the right to judge, they are encouraged to condemn; scapegoats are provided to canalise unease and discontent. . . . A crowd of thirty to forty thousand people watched the hangings after the Kharkov trial; the proceedings were filmed in detail including close-ups of the actual process of strangulation, and shown all over Russia and abroad (136–137).

Both Orwell and Koestler express concern that this repugnant aspect of the totalitarian mentality is taken over by the Western papers. Koestler condemns the "Special Correspondent of *The Times* [for expressing] obvious approval and sympathy" (136), while Orwell comments on "the disgusting gloating in the British press over the spectacle of dangling corpses" (v. 4, 192).[4]

Kept hungry and compensated by circuses, the proles in Oceania are to demonstrate to the satirist's contemporaries what might happen to the working class in England, should the intellectuals decide to model Western Socialism upon the example of Soviet Russia. Professor Crick's interpretation overlooks Orwell's consistent allusions to practices in Stalin's Russia. Yet these allusions are essential to an understanding of the satirist's warning that Stalin's regime should not be condoned or imitated. I believe Professor Crick is reluctant to acknowledge that Orwell's determination to destroy the "Soviet myth" in England is central to his satirical message. It is probably this reluctance that makes him conclude that "the text seen as a projective model of totalitarian society actually works badly" and therefore *Nineteen Eighty-Four* "is not [Orwell's] clearest model of the totalitarian society" ("Introduction" 15).

There may also be an additional reason for Professor Crick's conclusion, and it is his assumption that the proles' condition in 1984 is the *uninterrupted* continuation of their existence under capitalism. He argues that "one of the satirist rages that moved Orwell was plainly bitter disappointment that a hundred years of mass education had not realized the dream of the nineteenth-century reformers. . . . Instead, he saw a largely passive population glued to the radio, the cinema seat, and the sporting page" ("Introduction" 14). I believe it is important to point out here that the proles in Oceania are not simply *left* in the position they occupied in Orwell's time. Their condition in 1984 is not simply the further development of the 1948 flaws of capitalism. Rather, their fate is the consequence of England's reaction to a crisis Orwell believed the capitalist system was to face in the fifties and the sixties (178). *Goldstein's Book* suggests that Big Brother came to power after a nuclear war followed by a revolutionary period in these decades, and that he came to power with the promise of fulfilling the Marxist prediction about Socialism. Of course, he knew that "one does not establish a dictatorship in order to safeguard a revolution; one makes a revolution in order to establish a dictatorship" (227). Together with the tearful old prole's self-reproach, "We didn't ought to 'ave trusted 'em" (33), all this indicates that during the "crucial years" (180) of a crisis, the Western world was tricked into accepting, condoning and *imitating* the previous models of totalitarianism. (A sense of an absurdly slavish imitation of the Soviet experience is also hinted at in the 1960s conflict between Big Brother and Goldstein, after which "Goldstein had fled," an event followed by "Big Brother's great purges in which the original leaders of the Revolution were wiped out" (68). In fact, the novel here makes us feel a grotesque sense of *déjà vu*, as if the Western world decided on the re-enactment of Stalin's rivalry with Trotsky, followed by Stalin's great purges beginning in the 1930s. This sense of ritualistic imitation is further enhanced by the acting out of the original Stalin-Trotsky conflict in the Two Minutes Hate daily.)

It is also important to recall once more that Oceania is not ruled by Eurasia: the chances for democratic Socialism were not destroyed by conquest. The Western world created a system based on the imitation of the totalitarian model out of its own free will.

At this point it is also worthwhile to look at the critical comments suggesting that the hopeless position of the proles in Oceania is a sign of a sudden loss of political hope at the end of Orwell's life. Indeed, *Goldstein's Book* describes history as a cyclical movement.

> A struggle which is the same in its main outlines recurs over and over again. For long periods the High seem to be securely in power, but sooner or later they are . . . overthrown by the Middle, who enlist the Low on their side by *pretending* to them that they are fighting for liberty and justice. As soon as they have reached their objective, the Middle thrust the Low back into their old position of servitude and themselves become the High. Of the three groups, only the Low are never even temporarily successful in achieving their aims (175).

Undeniably, this passage is a pessimistic assessment of the proles' hope for advancement in Oceania. What is more, for greater emphasis, Winston looks at it briefly before turning to another chapter (163), and at the end reads it again in full (175). But even if the emotional weight of the passage is undeniable, neither the tone nor the insight appears all of a sudden at the end of Orwell's life. In fact, he expresses very much the same ideas in a review published on June 16, 1938, in the *English Weekly*:

> It would seem that what you get over and over again is a movement of the proletariat which is promptly canalized and betrayed

by astute people at the top, and then the growth of a new gov-
erning class. The one thing that never arrives is equality. The
mass of the people never gets the chance to bring their innate de-
cency into the control of affairs so that one is almost driven to the
cynical thought that men are only decent when they are powerless
(v. 1, 372).

But even if one may be driven to such a "cynical thought"
based on the past, the future defeat of the proletariat is not
inevitable. If between the 1940s and 1984 the proles moved so
much closer to a position of utter powerlessness, it is so only
because at the time of the crisis in the fifties, the "progressive"
intellectual, the satirist's Adversary, rejected the genuinely Socialist tradition in favour of the Russian model of totalitarianism.

Orwell recognizes the significant difference between the working class in Russia and the working class in the West. In the
words of Borkenau, one of the writers whose works Orwell reviewed and respected, in Russia "the Bolshevik Party has really been a . . . select community, a sort of religious order of
professional revolutionaries" (346). Hence, Borkenau explains,
Lenin's basic assumption was that "the revolutionary Party
must not be an agent of the proletariat, but a separate group,
only knitted with it by its convictions. The Western labour
parties are the labour movement itself, are identical with it"
(348).

Orwell echoes Borkenau's observations by stating that

> placed as they were, the Russian Communists necessarily devel-
> oped into a permanent ruling caste, or oligarchy, recruited not
> by birth but by adoption. Since they could not risk genuine crit-
> icism, they often made avoidable mistakes; then, because they
> could not admit that the mistakes were their own, they had to
> find scapegoats, sometimes on an enormous scale (v. 4, 515).

By contrast, in the Labour Party the British working class had
its own voice and managed to maintain the structure of democracy. Hence, Orwell asserts, "My recent novel is not intended
as an attack on Socialism or the British Labour Party (of which
I am a supporter)" (v. 4, 564).

What the Inner Party represents is the totalitarian mentality
put into practice. Orwell does not see the 1948 social landscape
of England, including the condition of the working class in this
landscape, as hopeless. *Goldstein's Book* points out that the

nightmare world of Oceania evolved as a result of some wrong decisions made in the "crucial years" of an international crisis in the 1950s.[5] This crisis is yet to be confronted by Orwell and his contemporaries in 1948.

Intellectuals

Goldstein's Book makes clear that due to the advantages of the machine, the ruling class no longer has a justifiable function; it can maintain itself in power only if it induces and sustains a state of imbecility in itself and in the masses around. When the Book suggests, ironically, that "the mentality" of the Oceanian intellectual is "appropriate to a state of war," this means that it is appropriate to the induced insanity of a "credulous and ignorant fanatic whose prevailing moods are fear, hatred, adulation and orgiastic triumph" (168). Just as Orwell did not invent the irrational self-destructiveness of totalitarianism, he did not invent or even exaggerate the mental state of the fanatical Party member who is "supposed to live in a continuous frenzy of hatred of foreign enemies and internal traitors, triumph over victories, and self-abasement before the power and wisdom of the Party" (181). All these characteristics form a realistic assessment of the Party cadres in Hitler's Germany or in Stalin's Russia. Stalin's personality cult in the U.S.S.R. offers some particularly telling examples of this uncritical "adulation": for over a decade all the intellectuals, writers, musicians, philosophers, botanists, and geneticists regarded Stalin as an all-round genius, a universal authority to pontificate on the most diverse issues that emerged from any of the intellectual disciplines, an authority eligible to set trends for absolutely every branch of the arts, the humanities, and the natural sciences.[6] That intellectuals were also expected to demonstrate "self-abasement" before his more than human wisdom is illustrated by the case of Soviet philosopher Deborin, for a long time the most eminent authority in his field. When in 1929 Deborin was suddenly reprimanded by the Party for his "abstract" philosophical views, he recanted and publicly thanked Comrade Stalin for "having restrained him just in time" (Edwards, v. 2, 164–165). Orwell captures the spirit of this adulation and self-abasement in the scene where Parsons contemplates what he is going to say before the Party tribunal: " 'Thank you,' I am going to say, 'thank you for saving me before it was too late' " (201).

Having asserted that Oceania is an accurate description of totalitarian systems that existed before, or were still in existence at the time of, the writing of the novel, the 'ideal readers' of the 1990s may still legitimately question the timeliness or universality of Orwell's message today. Does Orwell suggest what *we* should do or avoid doing to prevent the further development of the totalitarian mentality in our world? An answer to this question will be found if we look at one particular characteristic of the satirist's Adversary, his intellectual dishonesty based on moral callousness.

Orwell is convinced that there is a powerful connection between the proliferation of atrocities and the moral callousness of the general public, particularly the intellectuals, who tend to condone atrocities committed on "our side." *Goldstein's Book* points out that probably the most significant of the intellectuals' 'sins' in the 1940s was their refusal to take a fair moral stand: "Such acts as raping, looting, the slaughter of children, the reduction of whole populations to slavery, and reprisals against prisoners which extend even to boiling and burying alive are looked upon as normal, and when they are committed by one's own side and not the enemy, *meritorious*" (164, my italics).

The Swiftian understatement of "meritorious" should alert the reader to Orwell's "savage indignation" not only against the perpetrators of brutality, but also against the callousness of the onlooker:

> And in the general hardening of outlook that set in round about 1930, practices which had been long abandoned, in some cases for hundreds of years — imprisonment without trial, the use of prisoners as slaves, public executions, the use of hostages, and the deportation of whole populations — not only became common again, but were tolerated and even defended by people who considered themselves enlightened and progressive (177).

The atrocities Orwell describes have been committed both in Hitler's Germany and in Stalin's Russia. But here the target is the "enlightened and progressive" Western bystander who "tolerated" and even "defended" these practices. It is by condoning such practices as a means to an end that the satirist's Adversary — indeed his 'ideal reader' of any time and any place — may prepare a world to be ruled by the God of Power.

The Betrayal of Socialism

Goldstein's Book demonstrates that it was precisely such callousness and lack of moral insight that led to the gradual distortion of the original goals of Socialism in the 1930s and the 1940s.

In the first decade of the twentieth century the promise of scientific advancement introduced an "imaginary future to which the people of the period looked forward." This promise consisted of a Wellsian vision of "a future society unbelievably rich, leisured, orderly, and efficient — a glittering antiseptic world of glass and snow-white concrete [which was] part of the consciousness of every literate person" (166). This vision of benevolent science and technology also coincided with the age-old Utopian dream of Socialism. It is this dream, the combination of high living standards and equality, that was betrayed by the rulers of the new world who deliberately made our civilization regress to the primitive world of starvation and human sacrifice.

Goldstein's Book describes the process "from about 1900 onwards" whereby the "aim of establishing liberty and genuine social and economic equality was more and more openly abandoned" (176), until, "by the *fourth* decade of the twentieth-century all the main currents of political thought were authoritarian. The earthly paradise had been discredited at exactly the moment when it became realizable. Every new political theory, whatever name it called itself, led back to hierarchy and regimentation" (177).

What Orwell attacks here is the willingness of his own fellow Socialists in the "fourth decade" to condone the hierarchy and regimentation so clearly evident in Stalin's Russia, while insisting that Stalin still followed the principles of Socialism. The old-fashioned Socialist is often misled by allowing Marxist slogans to blind him to the actual developments of the twentieth century. For example, because

> he had been trained to fight against something called "class privilege," [he] assumed that what is not hereditary cannot be permanent. He did not see that . . . hereditary aristocracies have always been shortlived, whereas adoptive organizations, such as the Catholic Church, have sometimes lasted for hundreds or thousands of years (180).

What the old-fashioned Socialist also failed to realize was that the Inner Party has actually assumed the kind of centralized control that rules out any chance for equality: "Collectively, the Party owns everything in Oceania, because it controls everything, and disposes of the products as it sees fit" (178). The satirist's 'joke' derives from the reversal of a predicted cause-effect relationship. Ironically, it was by abolishing private property (in order to abolish inequality) that the Inner Party made sure "economic inequality has been made permanent" (178). This, of course, is a clear allusion to developments in the U.S.S.R.: instead of demonstrating a tendency to "wither away," the Soviet state came to assume absolute power. Here Orwell comes close to the position of Rudolf Hilferding, a European Social Democrat who pointed out that it was precisely the "managed economy which was to replace capitalism" that allowed the Soviet State to move towards "unrestrained absolutism" (338).[7] This explanation also illuminates Orwell's otherwise rather obscure statement that the aim of *Nineteen Eighty-Four* was to parody "the perversions to which a centralized economy was liable" (v. 4, 564). Like Orwell, Hilferding also objected to the "simplified and schematic" applications of Marx's nineteenth-century theory to events in the twentieth century, but still continued to use Marxist terminology when analyzing these events.

Whether Orwell was fundamentally critical of Marxist thought or only of its schematic application, *Goldstein's Book* makes clear that the original promise of Socialism had been betrayed by the Inner Party who came to power "after a decade of national wars, civil wars, revolutions and counter-revolutions" with an ideology that "had been foreshadowed by the various systems, generally called totalitarian" (177). As it becomes clear from the *Children's History Book* (67), the Inner Party must have come to power with an ideology resembling Marxism, but by 1984 the Marxist concepts are presented in such a schematic, over-simplified manner that they become barely recognizable. Describing the betrayal of Socialism in Winston's past, in the 1940s and 1950s, Orwell here points a finger at those among his own contemporaries whom he suspects of the desire to turn into the ruling oligarchy of the future. "The new aristocracy was made up for the most part of bureaucrats, scientists, technicians, trade-union organizers, publicity experts, sociologists, teachers, journalists and professional politicians . . .

shaped and brought together by the barren world of monopoly industry and centralized government" (177).

Even if one does not turn to the essays for further confirmation, from Orwell's tone it becomes obvious that he cannot hold the bureaucrats, trade union organizers, publicity experts, journalists, and politicians of his time in high esteem. As a matter of fact, we should once more recognize here the satirical device of apposition, reminiscent of Swift's juxtaposition and implied equation between "a Lawyer, a Pickpocket, a Colonel, a Fool, a Lord, a Gamester, a Politician, a Whore-master, a Physician, an Evidence, a Suborner, an Attorney, a Traitor or the like." Suggestive of an angry tirade, this sentence of Swift inspired Orwell's remark that "one has the feeling that personal animosity is at work" (v. 4, 253). In Orwell's own use of such Swiftian apposition, we become aware of Orwell's "personal animosity" against all those among his contemporaries who aspire for power. Yet, his animosity notwithstanding, Orwell acknowledges that "as compared with their opposite numbers in past ages, [members of this new class] were less avaricious, less tempted by luxury, hungrier for pure power, and, above all, were conscious of what they were doing and were intent on crushing opposition" (177). Also, even though their tyranny was foreshadowed by the Inquisition and by the totalitarian regimes of Hitler and Stalin, the new ruling class of Oceania is more competent than its predecessors because it has access to the most advanced techniques of the media, able to "keep [the] citizens under constant surveillance" and "in the sound of official propaganda, with all other channels of communication closed." As a result, "the possibility of enforcing not only complete obedience to the will of the state but complete uniformity of opinion on all subjects, now existed for the first time" (177). Of course, what *Goldstein's Book* describes as developments in the 1950s, Orwell in 1948 regards as a threat in the near future. This is to draw attention to the potential new oligarchy's aspiration as extremely dangerous, particularly because of its unprecedented opportunity to keep the population under 'total' control, including control over thoughts and feelings.

At this point we have arrived at the topic central to the first chapter in *Goldstein's Book*, entitled "Ignorance is Strength." This slogan refers to the complex mental control implied by Doublethink (also called "mental cheating," "protective stupidity," "blackwhite," "controlled insanity," and a "schizophrenic way of thinking"). As we have seen, Winston is not allowed to *read* the entire chapter because he has to explore what Doublethink means through experience. His conversion to Ingsoc is not regarded as complete, until in the last scene he also learns to *practise* Doublethink. Consequently, we realize that Doublethink is the single most important concept in *Goldstein's Book*, a concept at the very heart of Orwell's satire about the "intellectual implications of totalitarianism" (v. 4, 520).

Notes

[1] For the attitude of the Soviet press to *Nineteen Eighty-Four*, please see L. Labedz's 1984 "Will George Orwell Survive 1984?" in *Encounter*, which quotes a review written by Melor Stunia in *Izvestiya*, 15 Jan. 1984, and another one that appeared in *Novoe Vremya* 1 Jan. 1984. See also "'Enemy of Mankind?': The Soviet Union's Orwell," in John Rodden's *The Politics of Literary Reputation* (200–210).

[2] Hannah Arendt points out that "If the totalitarian conqueror conducts himself everywhere as though he were at home, by the same token he must treat his own population as though he were a foreign conqueror." She gives several examples to prove that the "Nazis behaved like foreign conquerors in Germany" (416–417).

[3] Koestler's view probably had a direct influence on Orwell when he determined the position of the proles in Oceania. Says Koestler in *The Yogi and the Commissar* in 1945:

Admittedly political education is a basic requirement for the realisation of socialism. Admittedly the Russian masses are so backward that propaganda for home consumption must be couched in over-simplified terms. What effect then can be expected from a succession of all-out propaganda campaigns each in total contradiction to the previous one? Obviously this: that the masses, bewildered by the contradictions vaguely sensed behind the fiery exhortations, resign themselves to the fact that the mysteries of politics are impenetrable, unconditionally surrender their critical faculties to their leaders and fall back into the mental state from which they started twenty-five years ago (136).

As for Aleksandr Solzhenitsyn, he insists that Stalin relied on terror, the constant fear inculcated by the purges, to make the people "believe" — that is, accept the propaganda without question, and without criticism.

[4] Clearly, Koestler saw the Bolshevik Party as intent on brutalizing the masses as a means to keep them under its domination. As he points out,

There are, however, emotional compensations for the masses. Deprived of the right to judge, they are encouraged to condemn; scapegoats are provided to canalise unease and discontent; a new and unique political vocabulary, including 'mad dogs', 'devils', 'hyenas' and 'syphilitics', replaces the distinctions for political dissent of former days. The apotheosis of this process of socialist re-education was reached in the revival of public hangings as a mass festival. A crowd of thirty to forty thousand people watched the hangings after the Kharkov trial; the proceedings were filmed in detail, including close-ups of the actual process of strangulation, and shown all over Russia and even abroad. The event was described by the Special Correspondent of *The Times* (December 31, 1943) in terms of obvious approval and sympathy which are worth quoting:

> The trial itself was an important phase in the educational process. It not only satisfied a burning desire for justice in its sternest form, but revealed to the huge crowds that thronged the market-place — the centre of the German-inspired speculation and corruption — and to the country people, who for three days after the execution saw the swinging bodies, the vulnerability of the enemy and the fundamental weakness of the Fascist character . . . There were some who showed their scorn of the dying men by adding whistles to the sound of their gasps. Others applauded. (*The Yogi and the Commissar*, 136–137).

This is the background to Orwell's savage satire on Syme, who proudly admits that he likes "to see them kicking . . . [with] the tongue sticking out and blue — a quite bright blue. That's the detail that appeals to me" (47).

[5] In *Stalin's Secret War*, Nikolai Tolstoy presents a convincing picture of Stalin's last plan to strike at the edifice of the Western democracies through the "sizable Trojan horse within the citadel," that is, the Western Communists, sympathizers, and fellow travellers. In Tolstoy's analysis, Stalin intended to take advantage of the sympathizers, and then, according to formula, get rid of them (360–361). Tolstoy also refers to documents that indicate Stalin planned for a decisive move in 1946, and then he postponed it to 1951.

[6] See Mikhail Geller and Aleksandr Nekrich's *Utopia in Power*, 266–267. For examples of Parsons-like public self-abasement, we should read in detail the case of philosopher A.M. Deborin who, in the late 1920s, became head of a group of philosophers who strongly opposed the school of Mechanism led by Bukharin: "the deborinists emphasized the importance and integrity of the philosophy of dialectical materialism, basing their view to a considerable extent on the work

of Plekhanov." However, on September 27, 1929, Deborin was suddenly "accused of being 'abstract', of divorcing theory from practice, philosophy from politics . . . Deborin recanted and publicly thanked the Party and especially Comrade Stalin for having 'restrained him just in time!'" (*The Encyclopedia of Philosophy*, ed. Paul Edwards 2, 164–165).

As for that curious mixture of fear, self-abasement, and adulation Orwell alludes to, Solzhenitsyn gives us a representative example in the case of Yagoda, formerly the head of the NKVD and in charge of the camps. When his turn came to be arrested,

> This murderer of millions simply could not imagine that this superior Murderer, up top, would not, at the last moment, stand up for him and protect him. Just as though Stalin had been sitting right there in the hall, Yagoda confidently and insistently begged him directly for mercy: "I appeal to you. *For you* I built two great canals." And a witness reports that at just that moment a match flared in the shadows behind a window on the second floor of the hall, apparently behind a muslin curtain, and while it lasted, the outline of a pipe could be seen. Whoever has been in Bakchisarai may remember that Oriental trick. The second-floor windows in the Hall of Sessions of the State Council are covered with iron sheets pierced by small holes, and behind them is an unlit gallery. It is never possible to guess down in the hall itself whether someone is up there or not. The Khan remained invisible, and the Council always met as if in his presence. Given Stalin's out-and-out Oriental character, I can readily believe that he watched the comedies in the October Hall. I cannot imagine that he would have denied himself this spectacle, this satisfaction" (411).

[7] Among others, Rudolf Hilferding, in a 1947 article "State Capitalism or Totalitarian State Economy," which appeared in *The Modern Review*, discusses this question in detail (338–339).

Chapter 7

Doublethink

It is in the concept of Doublethink that the satirist's argument with his Adversary, the Western intellectual, reaches its climax, the peak of its persuasive power. At the stage of its full maturity, Doublethink is a form of controlled schizophrenia practised by a ruling class that no longer has a legitimate function, trying to convince others, but most of all itself, of its own importance. But Doublethink represents the methodical "falsification" (172) of an entire thought system, designed to perpetrate the "false view of the world" (172) implied in the totalitarian mentality. Originally designed "to sustain the mystique of the Party and prevent the true nature of present-day society from being perceived" (180), Doublethink embodies the very essence of "the intellectual implications of totalitarianism" (v. 4, 520), "any perversion of thought" (172) that is endemic to the totalitarian mentality. Therefore, at various levels of sophistication Doublethink is to be practised by everyone in Oceania, by both the Deceived and the Deceiver.

In Doublethink Orwell offers a multidimensional parody of the cerebral and psychological dimensions of the corrupted consciousness practised in Hitler's Germany and in Stalin's Russia, but even more significantly, of the corrupted consciousness in the Western world that condoned or justified the emerging totalitarian systems in their coming to power and maintaining themselves in power. In fact, *Goldstein's Book* implies, it is in the self-deception practised by the satirist's Adversary, the Western intellectual, when faced with the rising tide of the totalitarian mentality throughout the 1930s and the 1940s, that the Doublethink of Oceania was conceived.

Like a monstrous child that carries visible reminders of the various phases of the evolutionary process it passed through during its gestation, in its "vast system of mental cheating" (184) Doublethink is a full-blown incarnation of all the different stages and the entire spectrum of intellectual dishonesty Orwell the political commentator had observed in the body politic of the 1930s and 1940s.

The Minuet of Alliances and Betrayals

To understand Orwell's point behind the grotesque minuet of alliances and betrayals acted out by Oceania, Eastasia, and Eurasia in 1984, we should recall the wild swings of "realpolitik" in the years between 1933 and 1945. Readers familiar with the subject will recall these major shifts in the relationship between Hitler, Stalin, and the Western democracies in the following five phases:

1. In the period between 1924 and 1933 Stalin advocates the world revolution of the proletariat, and in the meantime rejects the idea of any interaction between the U.S.S.R. and the capitalist democracies. The latter are declared 'evil' in the U.S.S.R. and the Leftist press in the West.
2. 1933–1939. As Hitler comes to regard Russia and the Western democracies his obvious targets, Stalin contemplates forging an alliance with the latter. This is the period of the Popular Front, which was gaining momentum at the time of the Spanish Civil War, emphasizing co-operation between Russia and the West *against* Fascism. Naturally, Fascism is declared evil by the U.S.S.R. and the Leftist press in the West.
3. 1939. By signing a Non-Aggression Pact, Hitler and Stalin suddenly become allies *against* the Western democracies. Stalin does, in fact, aid Hitler in his campaign against France. Naturally, the evils of Fascism are no longer considered a subject fit for contemplation in the U.S.S.R. or in the Western Leftist press.
4. 1941. Hitler attacks Russia. Stalin and the Western democracies become allies *against* Hitler. Once more, Fascism is declared evil in the U.S.S.R. and in the Western Leftist press, and remains so until the end of World War II in 1945.
5. Once the common enemy is defeated, the allies turn against one another again: a Cold War, accompanied by mutual name calling, commences between the U.S.S.R. and the Western democracies. (On occasion both parties call each other Fascist.)

No doubt History could not have obliged the satirist's pen, poised for the depiction of deceit, treachery, and the outrageous power of the irrational, with a more irresistible scenario. But the satirist in Orwell is less interested in the actual shifts dictated by power politics than in the effect of these changes on the minds of his contemporaries. *Nineteen Eighty-Four* reveals the satirist's genuine fascination with the way the human mind reacts, first to the sharp polarization between black and white, and then to the frequent reversals between black and white. We see the ultimate result in Oceania: The mind simply denies that the black of today is in contrast to the white of yesterday; ultimately all distinctions disappear, not only between black and white, but also between today and yesterday. In Russia, of course, the loss of memory was aided by terror: people who dared to remember that the enemy of today happened to be the ally of yesterday were given ten-year prison terms for not controlling their memory. But Orwell's attention, both in his essays and in his novels, was focused on the effect of these shifts on the mind of the Western intellectual.

Doublethink and Political Realism

It is to be noted that, originally, Orwell shows equal interest in the corruption of consciousness in Communist and in Fascist sympathizers. In 1943 he reproaches the latter for their self-delusion in denying the threat of Fascism in the late 1930s:

> When one thinks of the lies and betrayals of those years, the cynical abandonment of one ally after another, the imbecile optimism of the Tory press, the flat refusal to believe that dictators meant war, even when they shouted it from the housetops, the inability of the moneyed class to see anything wrong whatever in concentration camps, ghettos, massacres and undeclared wars, one is driven to feel that moral decadence played its part as well as mere stupidity (v. 2, 366).

Orwell blames this blindness on the self-interest of the "moneyed class," the "lords of property," since "by 1937 or thereabouts it was not possible to be in doubt about the nature of the Fascist regime. But the lords of property had decided that Fascism was on their side and they were willing to swallow the most stinking evils as long as their property remained secure" (v. 2, 366).

However, by 1943 Orwell is getting increasingly concerned about the dangers implied by the 'progressive' intellectuals' uncritical sympathy with Stalin whom they consider to be the most obvious enemy of Fascism. In a typically Orwellian balancing act, he points out that the "attitude of the Left towards the Russian regime has been distinctly similar to the attitudes of the Tories towards Fascism. There has been the same tendency to excuse almost anything 'because they are on our side' " (v. 2, 367).

Condoning the betrayal of allies and justifying atrocities against the enemy, against those 'not on our side,' is the very essence of the disease Orwell the satirist-physician is so concerned about: " 'Realism' (it used to be called dishonesty) is part of the general political atmosphere of our time," he declares, and makes it clear that this kind of "realism" is not only immoral but ultimately also ineffective, 'unrealistic':

> If there is a way out of the moral pigsty we are living in, the first step towards it is probably to grasp that "realism" does *not* pay, and that to sell out your friends and sit rubbing your hands while they are being destroyed is not the last word in political wisdom (v. 2, 367).

Repeatedly, Orwell the essayist sets out to convince his Adversary that mental dishonesty has "real" consequences; the self-delusion of Fascist sympathizers in the late 1930s aided and abetted Hitler's rise to world power; the self-delusion of the Russophile Left in the late 1940s translates into the increasing power of Stalin and Stalinism, through the increasing power of the Communist Parties over fellow travellers and progressive intellectuals all over the Western world.[1] Orwell's essays reveal his humanistic conviction that to deny the moral dimension of our actions, private or public, is insane, that ultimately this denial leads to self-destruction. In this instance the Adversary assumes the voice of the Machiavellian cynic, arguing that ideals and morality don't really matter; it is the number of tanks and the amount of ammunition, in other words, the "realities" of war, that are decisive. By contrast, Orwell's point is that underrating the importance of moral responsibility goes hand in hand with overrating the opponent's power — it is a form of defeatism more perilous than the enemy's actual material power. Therefore, "from the point of view of survival [it is better] to fight and be conquered than to surrender without fighting" (v. 2, 302).

Orwell suggests that underlying his Adversary's "realism" is his lack of imagination. Coming from the liberal tradition of democracy, he simply cannot imagine what it means to live under "total" control. Here Orwell's recent experience of Hitler's threat to the survival of democracy in the early 1940s gives his voice particular urgency in dealing with the threat of Stalinism in the late 1940s. In this respect, he is not unlike a general who fights the last war during the current conflict. When he is engaged in argument with the Adversary about the consequences of a Communist dictatorship in the late 1940s, he still addresses the same Adversary who at one point debated whether or not to stand up against Hitler, and claimed that there was no substantial difference between Fascism and a flawed bourgeois democracy. It was the same Adversary who later debated whether it was better to capitulate than to fight Hitler to the death, a "defeatism" based on the assumption that if worst comes to worst, human beings can always adjust to external circumstances and remain "free inside" (v. 3, 159). Orwell ridicules such notions as "false ideas": "Out in the streets the loudspeakers bellow, the flags flutter from the rooftops, the police with their tommy-guns prowl to and fro, the face of the Leader, four feet wide, glares from every hoarding; but up in the attics the secret enemies of the regime can record their thoughts in perfect freedom — that is the idea, more or less" (v. 3, 159).

In *Nineteen Eighty-Four* Orwell refutes this idea with unforgettable impact. Winston's most harrowing discovery consists of the recognition that in a totalitarian system one can no longer be "free inside," that there is absolutely no hiding place for the inner self; bit by bit he has to give up the freedom of keeping a diary, of "the few cubic centimetres within his skull," of his "inner heart," and finally, even the freedom implied in having his last hiding place, his dreams.

In a way, then, Doublethink in Oceania has its roots in that kind of mental dishonesty that goes with the argument of political "realism," that kind of "mental cheating" that seeks expression in the Machiavellian excuse that might is right, in the tendency to justify power in any form, especially when exercised on "our side."

Doublethink and Ideological Thinking

Revealing the general attributes of "mental cheating," Doublethink can be narrowed down further by looking at a particular kind of intellectual dishonesty required by any orthodoxy, any ideology. Narrowing it down even further, Doublethink represents the particular *"system* of mental cheating" (184) characteristic of a totalitarian ideology.

In her seminal work on *The Origins of Totalitarianism*, Hannah Arendt names three attributes that may make a particular ideology fit for a totalitarian system: first, the "claim for total explanation . . . the tendency to explain not what is, but what becomes, what is born and passes away" (10); second, the inevitable "iron logic" of the applications of this prediction to the present; and third, the ultimate denial of reality in favour of the fictitious world of the ideology.

As discussed in Chapter 5, it is the claim to a "reliable prediction of the future" that allows the Party to take control over both the past and the future, a thought expressed succinctly in the Party slogan, "Who controls the past controls the future; who controls the present controls the past" (213).

What follows from the same claim for "reliable prediction" is the "iron logic" of ideology, which insists that any event in the present must be seen in the framework of, and illustrative of, a reality 'higher' or 'truer' than the reality we may perceive through our senses. Thus ideological thinking "becomes . . . emancipated from the reality that we perceive with our five senses, and insists on a 'truer' reality concealed behind all perceptible things . . . [and on a] *sixth sense* that enables us to be aware of it" (Arendt 471).

What Arendt calls the "sixth sense" of the ideologue is described in *Goldstein's Book* as the Party member's "right instincts":

> A Party member is required to have not only the right opinion but the *right instincts*. Many of the beliefs and attitudes demanded of him are never plainly stated, and could not be stated without laying bare the contradictions inherent in Ingsoc. If he is a person naturally orthodox (in Newspeak *goodthinker*), he will in all circumstances know, without taking thought, what is the true belief or the desirable emotion. But in any case an elaborate mental training, undergone in childhood and grouping itself round the Newspeak words *crimestop blackwhite*, and *doublethink*, makes him unwilling and unable to think too deeply on any subject whatever" (169).

It is interesting to note that Arendt also explains that there is a special "mental training" for this "sixth sense" to be provided by "ideological indoctrination . . . by the educational institutions . . . in the Ordensburgen of the Nazis or the schools of the Comintern or the Cominform" (471). It is such an indoctrinated belief in a "truer" reality, which does, in effect, deny the evidence of our senses, that Orwell calls interchangeably "goodthinking," "crimestop," and "blackwhite," each of them signifying particular aspects of Doublethink as "protective stupidity." In Orwell's depiction of the kind of stupidity implied in "crimestop," one may still detect a personal note of exasperation with a particularly trying conversational partner, a politically orthodox Adversary whose unswerving commitment to the Party Line illustrates to Orwell

> the faculty of stopping short, as though by instinct, at the threshold of any dangerous thought. It includes the power of not grasping analogies, of failing to perceive logical errors, of misunderstanding the simplest arguments if they are inimical to Ingsoc, and of being bored and repelled by any train of thought which is capable of leading in a heretical direction. "Crimestop", in short, means *protective stupidity* (181).

Orwell had given several examples of this "protective stupidity" among his contemporaries: the Tories used it when refusing to see Hitler's true colours for a long time because they expected him to protect them from Communism, and hence protect their property; the politician, indeed any writer working for any Party, has to use such protective stupidity to exercise self-censorship, to stop short at any thought that is heretical to the political orthodoxy he is writing for (v. 4, 90). But Orwell's most frequent target of "protective stupidity" is, undeniably, his Adversary, the Leftist intelligentsia.

Once again, Orwell is not alone in diagnosing the syndrome of their "reality control" (184), what Arendt describes as the ultimate denial of reality in favour of the fictional world of the ideology. Among others, Susan Labin in *Stalin's Russia*, published in the same year as *Nineteen Eighty-Four*, addresses an impassioned plea to her fellow Socialists, emphasizing that Western civilization faces a crisis. The Western intellectuals, Labin argues, fail to see the danger of Russian expansionism. In love with the fictitious world of ideology, they choose to remain ignorant of true conditions *in* Russia, in spite of the evidence of published material about slave labour, torture, and the ruthless oppression of freedom.

In his Foreword to Labin's book, Arthur Koestler suggests an ironic solution to punish and cure this "protective-ignorance": The Russophile intellectual should be condemned to "one year of forced reading" (Labin 1948), to do nothing else but read Soviet newspapers, Soviet works of fiction, Soviet documents relating to labour and criminal law, and the Party directives addressed to the Soviet population. Earlier, in *The Yogi and the Commissar*, Koestler made the same point, supported by an impressive selection of the documents in question (118–134, 202–204).

Both Koestler and Labin would agree with Orwell that the intellectuals practise self-deception, they use "protective stupidity," because they want to remain committed to the Cause. The example of Jean-Paul Sartre, cited by Tolstoy, may be an illustrative case here:

> Jean-Paul Sartre . . . believed that "To keep hope alive one must, in spite of all mistakes, horrors and crimes, recognize the obvious superiority of the socialist [i.e. Soviet] camp". Setting aside his unfortunate closing phrase, this declaration can only imply that it is better for millions of Russians to suffer "horrors and crimes" than that he, Sartre, and his friends should have to abandon their illusions (287).

Orwell is clearly aware of the emotional security offered by any Cause, any "ism," the fictitious world of any ideology. This is why he is so concerned about our self-censorship and self-delusion, the price we pay for such security:

> To accept an orthodoxy is always to inherit unresolved contradictions. . . . In every case there is a conclusion which is perfectly plain but which can be only drawn if one is privately disloyal to the official ideology. The normal response is to push the question, unanswered, into a corner of one's mind, and then continue repeating contradictory catchwords (v. 4, 467).

The Consistency of the Ideology's "Iron Logic"

Orwell's observation on the self-censorship demanded by any orthodoxy coincides with Arendt's analysis of the "iron logic" of ideological thinking, which "proceeds with a consistency that exists nowhere in the realm of reality" (471). Orwell explores the impact of this iron consistency in psychological terms in his novel. Hence the irresistible power of O'Brien's argument that overpowers Winston, an iron logic that has the same kind of impact as physical torture. In fact, Winston feels that his interrogators' "real weapon was the merciless questioning that went on and on, hour after hour, tripping him up, laying traps for him, twisting everything that he said, convicting him at every step of lies and self-contradiction" (208).

As Arendt points out, the impact of this iron logic is unique, because "once it has established its premise, its point of departure, experiences no longer interfere with ideological thinking, nor can it be taught by reality" (471). Had Arendt published these criteria of ideological thinking *before* 1949, one would be tempted to say that Orwell's novel simply gives a manifold illustration of her definition. When, for example, O'Brien makes the claim that the power of the Party simply transcends the laws of physical reality, that should he wish to do so, he could levitate because even the laws of gravity are irrelevant, or rather, they too, are under the Party's control (228), he demonstrates the ideological thinker's outrageous confidence that the iron logic of ideology transcends the laws of physical reality. But since *Nineteen Eighty-Four* was published *before* Arendt's book, one has to recognize that Orwell's Doublethink coincided with all these seminal insights to the psycho-dynamics of totalitarian ideologies.[2]

The Marxist Dialectic

Time and again Orwell emphasizes that he is not "suggesting that mental dishonesty is peculiar to Socialism and left-wingers generally, or is commonest among them" (v. 4, 468). There are, nevertheless, two significant reasons why *Goldstein's Book* parodies the particular version of "protective stupidity" exercised by the Adversary, the Leftist intellectual in Orwell's time. First, Orwell feels that the Left is misguided on a decisive question, that "nearly the whole of the English Left has been driven to accept the Russian regime as 'Socialist' in this country. Hence there has arisen a sort of schizophrenic manner of thinking, in which words like 'democracy' can bear two irreconcilable meanings, and such things as concentration camps and mass deportations can be right and wrong simultaneously" (v. 4, 466). Also, I suggest, there is something in the "blackwhite" pattern of Marxist dialectic the way it is practised in his time that captures Orwell's satirical imagination. It is with angry fascination that he follows the twists and turns of Marxist dialectic, a principle that Stalin had declared the 'scientific' foundation of Soviet philosophy and political thought in 1931. As a result of this declaration, the application of dialectical materialism became an essential feature in the various communications of the Comintern and in the political literature published by and for the progressive intellectual of the period.

Arendt explains "dialectical logic" as a process that moves "from thesis through antithesis to synthesis which in turn becomes the thesis of the next dialectical movement. . . . The first thesis becomes the premise and its advantage for ideological explanation is that this dialectical device can explain away *factual contradictions as stages of one identical, consistent movement*" (469, my italics).

Many times in the 1930s Orwell's writing has shown signs of his irritation with the Marxist theoretician for forgetting about the working man's plight in favour of the theory. In *The Road to Wigan Pier* he singles out the theoretician's preoccupation with dialectical materialism with particular gusto: "As for the philosophic side of Marxism, the pea-and-thimble trick with those three *mysterious entities, thesis, antithesis, and synthesis*, I have never met a working man who had the faintest interest in it" (*RWP* 176, my italics). In the same work he argues that, instead of concentrating on "thesis, antithesis and synthesis," the Leftist intellectual should concentrate on the alleviation of misery:

> The Socialist movement has no time to be a league of dialectical materialists; it has got to be a league of the oppressed against the oppressors . . . Less about "class consciousness," "expropriation of the expropriators," "bourgeois ideology," and "proletarian solidarity," not to mention the *sacred sisters, thesis, antithesis and synthesis*, and more about justice, liberty, and the plight of the unemployed (*RWP* 220, 229, my italics).

Orwell's irritation with dialectical materialism is, no doubt, connected with his mistrust of abstractions and the rigidity of theoretical thinking in general. But going even further, he regards the entire process of setting up contradictions and then showing their "interpenetration," the turning of one opposite into the other, as "a pea and thimble trick," or "blackwhite," a trick performed by the intellectual to deceive others and himself. Like Orwell, Camus also condemns what he calls the

"dialectic miracle . . . the decision to call total servitude freedom" ("Prophecy" 230).

In its more everyday manifestations, Orwell illustrates the
"blackwhite" of dialectical materialism as a device used by the
Comintern to vindicate the abrupt contradictions in Russian
foreign policy. Because, Orwell points out with characteristic
understatement, the U.S.S.R. was "*no more* scrupulous in its
foreign policy than the rest of the Great Powers," the Comintern was faced with the frequent task of demonstrating how
each zig-zag in Stalin's foreign policy was part of the *same* dialectic process, part of the *same* relentless march towards Socialism:

> Alliances, changes of front, etc. which only make sense as part of
> the game of power politics have to be explained and justified in
> terms of international Socialism. *Every time Stalin swaps part-*
> *ners "Marxism" has to be hammered into a new shape.* This en-
> tails sudden and violent changes of "line," purges, denunciations,
> systematic destruction of Party literature, etc. (v. 1, 563).

As an illustration, Orwell points out the abrupt changes in
Comintern propaganda regarding the relationship between the
U.S.S.R. and the West between 1930 and 1935:

> As Hitler's three targets of attack were, to all appearances, Great
> Britain, France and the U.S.S.R., the three countries were forced
> into an uneasy rapprochement. This meant that the English and
> French Communist was obliged to become a good patriot and im-
> perialist — that is, to defend the very thing he had been attacking
> for the past fifteen years. The Comintern slogans suddenly faded
> from red to pink. "World revolution" and "Social fascism" gave
> way to "Defence of democracy" and "Stop Hitler!" (v. 1, 563).

Obviously, what irritates Orwell more than the actual changes
in alliances is the denial by the Comintern that a change has
taken place at all, the pretence that factual changes notwithstanding, Stalin's foreign policy should be regarded as "one
identical, consistent movement" in the direction of Socialism.

After three more drastic shifts in history and in the Party
Line, in 1946 Orwell returns to this point with an even greater
urgency. By this time he emphasizes that what the Party
presents as "dialectic" is an outrage against the thinking process, leading to the blocking out of honest, creative thought:

> What is new in totalitarianism is that its doctrines are not only unchallengeable but also unstable. They have to be accepted on pain of damnation, but on the other hand they are always liable to be altered at a moment's notice. . . . Now it is easy for a politician to make such changes: for a writer the case is somewhat different. If he has to change his allegiance at exactly the right moment, he must either tell lies about his most subjective feelings, or else suppress them altogether. In either case he had destroyed his dynamo (v. 4, 89).

In fact, Orwell feels, the "dialectic" leads to the insanity of "blackwhite," since it implies that "we must alter our conception from year to year, and if necessary from minute to minute" (v. 4, 186). Moral decadence and mental imbalance are simultaneous, when "any virtue can become a vice, and any vice a virtue, according to the political needs of the moment" (v. 4, 186).

Psychological Defence Mechanisms

Discussing the unique characteristics of the totalitarian mentality, Orwell draws attention to the psychological aspects of Doublethink. In the past the 'true believer' was to pass "his whole life in the same framework of thought. . . . Now, with totalitarianism, exactly the opposite is true. The peculiarity of the totalitarian state is that though it controls thought, it does not fix it. It sets up unquestionable dogmas and it alters them from day to day." As a result, the 'true believer's' "emotional life, his loves and hatreds, are expected, when necessary, to reverse themselves overnight" (v. 3, 163).

At this point Orwell's parody of the totalitarian mentality reaches its next dimension: Doublethink also demonstrates the unique psychology of the 'true believer' who, to cope with the anxiety created by his intellectual confusion, has to develop a variety of psychological defence mechanisms, such as repression and overcompensation.

Probably quite independently from Orwell, Carl Jung also offers a similar diagnosis of the totalitarian mentality. To begin with, Jung defines totalitarianism as the dislocation of the religious instinct where "the State takes the place of God: this is why . . . Socialist dictatorships are religions and State slavery is a form of worship" ("Undiscovered" 360). But, Jung feels, the religious function cannot be dislocated and falsified this way without giving rise to *secret doubts, which are immediately repressed* — so as to avoid conflict with the prevailing trend of mass mindedness. The result, as always in such cases, is *overcompensation* in the form of fanaticism, which in turn is used as a weapon for stamping out the last flicker of opposition ("Undiscovered" 360, my italics).

In his illustration of the psychological effects of Doublethink, Orwell describes this connection between "secret doubts," "repression," and "overcompensation," through the case of a minor character, Tom Parsons. This most fanatical of all true believers, Parsons is denounced by his daughter for having uttered "Down with Big Brother!" in his sleep. The incident points to the ambivalent feelings at the core of the true believer's heart. In order to "love" Big Brother, he has to repress his consciousness of the Ministry of Love, poignant reminder of Big Brother's cruelty. Since he knows he is observed and could be punished at any moment for unorthodox thoughts, his hatred and fear of Big Brother has to be repressed, camouflaged even from himself. As a result, he also overcompensates, repeating the Party slogans to convince himself of his love for Big Brother.

In his analysis of Hitler's methods of creating anxiety and of the defence mechanisms developed by the German people to cope with anxiety, Bruno Bettelheim offers further insight into the psychological dynamism of Parsons' Doublethink. Bettelheim's illuminating analysis also allows us to appreciate Orwell's power of compression — in the Parsons episode he demonstrates a complex psycho-political phenomenon by means of the naturalistic description of a minor character.

To heighten anxiety, Bettelheim explains, the Nazis introduced the element of the unknown. While "newspaper notices had long made everyone aware of the concentration camp and its punitive character, . . . no detailed knowledge was available. . . . This may explain why the concentration camp was threatening not just to those who opposed the regime but even those who never violated the smallest regulations" (278).

The State further heightened anxiety in that punitive " 'actions' . . . nearly always punished something that was not yet forbidden by law. It would have been easy for the state to pass any laws it wished to. But that was not the purpose of the 'actions'. They were intended less to punish transgressions than to force all citizens to do as the State wished and to do it of their

own volition" (Bettelheim 279). Orwell is on target here also:
when Winston opens his diary, his anxiety is heightened by doing something that is not forbidden by law yet can be punished
by death (10). Also, Parsons' misery is heightened by his uncertainty as to whether his 'crime' deserves the death penalty.
Bettelheim points out that it was part of the Fascist State's
strategy to keep the people in uncertainty, so that they would
be forced to "anticipate" what might happen by going through
a "total identification with the State" (379), an identification
with the aggressor. This is to say, the State's success in totally
dominating the population depended on keeping them in a state
of unresolvable anxiety, which they could cope with only by the
various forms of psychological defence mechanisms, those forms
of "protective stupidity" and "crimestop" that Orwell defines
in Doublethink.

Although Parsons is a most fanatical representative of the
"crimestop" of the true believer, in his sleep even he may reveal some of the repressed fear and hatred for the idol of his
worship. Of course, we cannot really tell whether Parsons committed the 'crime' he is accused of, because we happen to know
that his daughter, an ambitious member of the Spy Movement,
has previously denounced innocent people in order to attest
to her vigilance. But whether or not he actually uttered the
words "Down with Big Brother!" in his sleep (when the inner
censor relaxed its vigilance), he is certainly familiar with the
temptation to do so. Consequently, true believer that he is, he
now wants to be cleansed. He declares, "Of course I'm guilty"
(201), and willingly undergoes his punishment, to be purged of
the "secret doubt": "I am glad they got me before it went any
further. Do you know what I'm going to say to them when I go
up before the tribunal? 'Thank you', I am going to say, 'thank
you for saving me before it was too late'" (201).

The Psychology of Religious and Political Fanaticism

But is the "secret doubt" of the true believer the consequence of
the "dislocation" of the religious instinct, as Carl Jung suggests,
or does Orwell regard such a secret doubt as the very root of
religious experience?

At its psychological foundation, Orwell defines Doublethink
to be based on a fundamental ambivalence, a psychological state
that may make the reader of the Essays recall a significant

incident from Orwell's account of his school years in "Such, Such Were the Joys." Here Orwell describes his childhood feelings for the tyrannical authority he saw represented by his schoolmaster and his wife at St. Cyprian's. He recalls having been dominated by anxiety and then the need to identify with the aggressor. He describes his confrontation with the tyrannical authority he saw represented by God in very much the same terms. To begin with, he describes the ambivalence caused by the conflict between "moral obligation" and "psychological fact," resulting in a strange emotional reversal that both Freud and Jung would describe as "overcompensation," a psychological defence mechanism where "one's hatred turned into a sort of cringing love" (v. 4, 401):

> Always at the centre of my heart the inner self seemed to be awake, pointing at the difference between the *moral obligation* and the *psychological fact*. It was the same in all matters, worldly or other worldly. Take religion, for instance. You were supposed to love God, and I did not question this. Till the age of about fourteen I believed in God, and believed that the accounts given of him were true. But I was well aware that I did not love him. On the contrary, I hated him (v. 4, 412).

We know that when Orwell wrote his recollections of his childhood, he had already written *Animal Farm*, and the process of thinking and preparing for the writing of *Nineteen Eighty-Four* was well under way. This is to say, the question isn't whether the child Orwell had indeed such an early insight into the "dual state" (Bracher 30),[3] the ambivalence of Doublethink; it is sufficient that the Orwell of 1947, at the time of writing *Nineteen Eighty-Four*, sees the psychological ambivalence in connection with religion in this light. If God is a tyrant who has to be feared, how can he be loved at the same time? To pretend love for the object of one's fear is, for Orwell, sheer hypocrisy. Therefore, he explains, as a child he had sympathy with Cain, Jezebel, Haman, and all the others who were considered rebels and who were given, as it were, bad press in the Old Testament. Whether or not Orwell's recollection of his childhood is accurate in this instance, it is important that to the Orwell of 1947 "the whole business of religion seemed to be strewn with psychological impossibilities. The Prayer Book told you, for example, to love God and fear him; but how could you love someone whom you feared?" (v. 4, 412).

Orwell's articulation of this "psychological impossibility" is essential to our understanding of the mental state he calls Doublethink in Oceania. Since you cannot love the person you fear, you have to lie about your feelings, even to yourself. The "psychological fact" of Orwell's deep ambivalence when asked to love and fear God at the same time shows that for him the source of this ambivalence is significantly different from what it is for Carl Jung. Jung diagnoses the root of this ambivalence in the "dislocation" of the religious instinct, that is, in the worship of a human being, or the State, in the place of God. By contrast, for Orwell Doublethink reflects the ambivalence *at the root* of the religious experience itself.

At this point, then, Orwell is significantly closer to Freud, who introduced the idea that it is precisely such an ambivalence between love and hate that characterizes our childhood feelings for a powerful father, and, consequently, our religious feelings for God the Father (Freud v. 20, 68).

Doublethink and the Satirist's Adversary

In fact, Orwell's most ironic argument against the 'progressive' Adversary is his point about the uncomfortably close resemblance between the Marxist dialectic and the thought pattern of the religious mysticism of a long-bygone era. Stalin's decree of January 25, 1931, was a turning point in the history of Soviet philosophy and political thought, because it announced dialectical materialism as the central principle of "scientific" thinking, a way of reasoning that was to become paramount not only in the natural sciences but also in literature, music, painting, philosophy, and, of course, political thought. In this decree "the law of the *conflict and interpenetration of opposites* was maintained as a fundamental law of dialectics, distinguishing 'true' Marxist philosophy from vulgar mechanistic materialism" (Edwards 164–165). To deviate from the Party's definition of the dialectic was tantamount to being accused of "idealism," of following religious belief, belief in the Supernatural, that is, belief in superstition — the gravest of offences against the Party's scientific principles. In its repeated references to the Party's "tricks with consciousness" (183), to "its peculiar linking together of opposites" (184), to its ability of "holding two contradictory beliefs in one's mind simultaneously, and accepting both of them" (183), *Goldstein's Book* alludes to the Marxist dialectic.

However, by defining the operating principle of the dialectic as the polarization of opposites followed by their coalescence — "For it is only by reconciling contradictions that power can be retained indefinitely" (185) — Orwell presents a striking analogy: Dialectic materialism is the method of thought forcibly advocated by the Party as the incarnation of the "scientific" method that is to wipe out that dangerous opponent, "idealism," once and for all. Yet, the pattern of the Party's dialectic, the polarization of opposites and their coalescence in the "Coincidentia oppositorum," is also at the very heart of religious mysticism, the pattern of the mystical dialectic. What is more, Orwell ironically points out, the religious fervour in the Party member's application of the "blackwhite" of Marxist dialectic is indeed a return to the mystical faith of the Middle Ages.

Once more, Camus confirms Orwell's point here by arguing that the true believer's faith in the Party plays the same role as "faith ... defined in the Spiritual exercises of Saint Ignatius: 'We should always be prepared so as never to err, to believe that *what I see as white is black*, if the hierarchical Church defines it thus'" ("Prophecy" 238). Another interesting illustration of Orwell's concept of "blackwhite" comes from one of Stalin's victims, Yury Patakov, who was first expelled from the Party, "then 'exiled' . . . after capitulating to Stalin, and finally executed by Stalin in 1938" (Geller 289). Before his execution, Patakov gave a definition of his intellectual position that confirms the connection pointed out by Orwell and Camus between the "blackwhite" of dialectical materialism and the "blackwhite" of religious mysticism: "Yes," admitted Patakov, "I will see black where I thought I saw white, or may still see it, because for me there is no life outside the Party or apart from agreement with it" (Geller 289). This is the process *Goldstein's Book* defines as the "blackwhite" aspect of Doublethink: "Applied to a Party member, it means loyal willingness to say that black is white when Party discipline demands it. But it means also the ability to *believe* that black is white, and more to *know* that black is white, and to forget that one has ever believed the contrary" (182).

Occasionally a satirist may perform a somersault in logic to demonstrate to the readers how far *they* have departed from the realm of logic and reason in their behaviour or intellectual attitude. A masterstroke of Menippean satire, the concept of Doublethink represents the skills of a satirical virtuoso: the double somersault, the double satirical twist. The Doublethink practised in Oceania shows to the 'true believer,' the satirist's Adversary, the disastrous consequence of his "mental cheating" in condoning the zig-zags, the abrupt fluctuations of power politics, as one uninterrupted journey towards Socialism. This self-deception of the 1940s has turned into a "vast system of mental cheating" (184), a schizophrenic system of "controlled insanity" (185), the frightening rule of Unreason in 1984. *Goldstein's Book* also makes fun of the "mental cheating" implied in the principle of "blackwhite" that allows the ostensibly enlightened, progressive intellectual to abnegate Reason and the moral integrity of the autonomous individual, to give up the critical, empirical attributes of the modern spirit, and return to a fanatical, mediaeval obedience to dogma — all in the name of the Party's "scientific" principles.

But Orwell here is not satisfied with the single satirical twist of demonstrating how the Adversary's misguided attitudes find their conclusion in the rule of Unreason. The double somersault, the satirical double twist, becomes apparent if we realize that the Party does not really rule entirely through Unreason, that there is method in its madness. While in the beginning, during the 1940s, the twists and turns of "mental cheating" were necessitated by the fluctuations in power politics, by 1984 the world is frozen into its post-historical shape in the form of three unchangeable power blocks, and there is no more excuse for power politics, let alone for their quick fluctuation. At this point the Party deliberately introduces the "imposture" of war, *so that* it can 'invent' changes in power politics, *so that* it can continue to lie about them. In fact, all events are choreographed in the interest of perpetrating a process of ritualized lying, the acceptance of unresolved contradiction, in order to confuse the inhabitants, to "dislocate [their] sense of reality" (184), to emphasize their need to have faith in the Party as their collective Reason, memory, and conscience. This is why "the official ideology abounds with contradictions even when there is no practical reason for them" (184). A gifted pupil of Stalin, Hitler, and the Inquisition, the Inner Party in Oceania supersedes them all in applying the insight already practised in the 1940s on a smaller scale: the stronger the abnegation of Reason and common sense the Party demands, the stronger the faith this abnegation generates. Ultimately, beyond the practical, political reasons for enslaving the population, this is the most important reason for the Party's insistence on the "imposture" of war and the choreographed changes and shifts between enemies and allies. The Party introduces changes artificially in order to be able to *deny* them. By participating in the self-perpetuating ritual of lies and contradictions, the true believers of the Party are expected to deny their memory, common sense, and Reason — denials that turn into self-perpetuating, self-renewing acts of faith. The purpose of Doublethink, this most sophisticated system of thinking, is to make people give up thinking altogether. To practise "double" thinking means repeatedly to give up the prerogative of thinking at all, and in the process generate more and more fervent faith in falsehood.

Orwell's analogy between the Adversary's faith in the Party and the mediaeval true believer's faith in the Church has a significant satirical function. The memorable image of Oceania as a demonic world brought to life by a fervent "secular religion" is predicated on this analogy.

Notes

[1] According to Nikolai Tolstoy,

However favourably the British and Americans came to regard the wartime Soviet Union, Stalin did not feel he could afford to allow the grass grow under his feet. He did not trust his Allies, Churchill in particular, and must in any case have been well aware that his post-war ambitions would arouse Western antagonism when their extent became clear. Left-wing sympathy was very useful. Indeed, in some ways a crypto-Communist or fellow-traveller could be more valuable than a card-carrying Party member. But the Communist fifth column in the West was far too important a weapon in Beria's arsenal to be left idle, nor did Stalin ever wholly trust foreign Communists living freely outside his domain" (328).

According to Tolstoy, Stalin displayed a most cynical attitude here:

The Soviet Union had now to collect its strength for the final struggle, achieve its own atomic bomb, and maintain iron discipline among its population. As Beria's deputy, Minister of State Security Victor Abakumov, explained to an audience of SMERSH officers at NKVD Headquarters in occupied Europe near Vienna in the summer of 1945, "Comrade Stalin once said that if we don't manage to do all these things very quickly the British and Americans will crush us. After all, they have the atom bomb and an enormous industrial advantage over us. . . . It is our good fortune . . . that the *British and Americans* in their attitudes towards us, have still not emerged from the *post-war state of calf-love*. They dream of lasting peace and building a democratic world for all men. They don't seem to realize that we are the ones who are going to build a new world, and that we shall do it without their liberal-democratic recipes. All their slobber plays right into our hands, and we shall thank them for this, in the next world with coals of fire. We shall drive them into such dead ends as they've never dreamed of. We shall disrupt them and corrupt them from within" (329 my italics).

Tolstoy also provides massive documentation on the human and financial resources deployed by the NKVD particularly in Britain and the United States to find intellectuals willing to act as agents of the Soviet Union: "The aims generally were to undermine Western morale and will to resist, to obtain military and industrial information, and to subvert high-ranking or key governmental personnel" (329).

[2] I am grateful to Professor Dennis Rohatyn for pointing out to me that Orwell could have read some of Arendt's chapters in *The Partisan Review* in 1948. Of course, we have no evidence whether he actually did so. It seems to me that the concept of Doublethink, a brilliant satirical device, is most likely the fruit of mature reflection, the distillation of Orwell's observations about the intellectual dishonesty inherent in the political language he had been so fascinated by throughout the 30s and the 40s. That many of his insights on Doublethink coincide with the various observations of Arendt, Talmon, Karl Popper and Arthur Koestler confirm rather than detract from Orwell's satirical *tour de force*. Doublethink compresses the various aspects of a complex political-psychological phenomenon into a literary conceit immediately accessible to the general reader.

[3] Historical analyses of Hitler's and Stalin's methods often comment on the strange mixture of law and lawlessness. As Karl Dietrich Bracher observes,

> The coincidence of radically arbitrary acts and apparent due process, manifested also in the facade of the legitimate constitutional state, is characteristic both of Hitlerism and Stalinism. Order and chaos, stability and revolution, are joined in the totalitarian 'dual state'" (30).

As a matter of fact, Orwell's analysis of his school years at St. Cyprians is quite obviously influenced by his analysis of totalitarian regimes. Thus he describes his floating anxiety and guilt "which was perhaps all the stronger because I did not know what I have done" (v. 4, 403).

Of course, this state of mind also foreshadows Winston's anxiety at the time he purchased his diary, an act that could be punished by forced labour or death. This "dual state" Orwell describes so well is a salient characteristic of totalitarian systems aiming at mind control.

Chapter 8

The Demonic World of Oceania:
The Persecution of the
'Satanic' Opponent

The conspicuous presence of religious allusions and imagery has been remarked on by many a reader of *Nineteen Eighty-Four*. It is another telling manifestation of the Orwell conundrum that different critics attribute entirely different significance to this phenomenon. Bernard Crick, for example, finds that the religious allusions may actually confuse the reader, because the "direct satire of the Catholic Church blurs the focus" of the satire of totalitarianism. "The Church may have some totalitarian tendencies but Orwell is saying that *it is* totalitarian. So the satire of total power moves ambivalently between totalitarian power and autocracy, with the Catholic Church singled out for special mention in the latter category" ("Introduction" 30). When analyzing O'Brien's statement that "we are the priests of power," Crick returns to his objection: "Somewhat confusingly, the example of power and hierarchy — the Church — which was certainly not the most important example in the modern world to Orwell, keeps surfacing in his imagery" ("Introduction" 52).

Undoubtedly, the Church is not the best modern example of totalitarianism. It is not Orwell's target: it is the vehicle, the means of the satirical attack. The analogy between the Party and the Catholic Church is used consistently throughout Orwell's essays as a strategy to discredit the 'scientific' and 'rationalist' pretence of the 'true believers' of the Party: "Between 1935 and 1938 the Communist Party had an almost irresistible fascination for any writer under forty. It became as normal to hear that so-and-so had 'joined' as it had been a few years earlier, when Roman Catholicism was fashionable, to hear that so-and-so had been 'received'" (v. 1, 562). It is in argument with this Adversary whose adulation of the Party parallels the feeling of the 'true believer' towards the Church that Orwell chooses to demonstrate analogies between the methods of Communist Russia, Nazi Germany, and the Mediaeval Church (with particular reminders of the practices of the Inquisition).

We are accustomed to seeing the great practitioners of the genre wield the two-edged sword of satire with grace and wit. When, for example, Gulliver wants to impress his Houyhnhnm Master with the sophistication of eighteenth-century civilization, he boasts of the miracles of modern warfare, able to create pain and devastation at an unprecedented rate. The Master simply cannot believe the atrocities Gulliver describes, and concludes that he must be saying "the thing that is not." How are the readers to respond to these two opponents? Of course, we are expected to smile at both. Gulliver is obviously proud of the wrong thing, and the Master is obviously superior to Gulliver when he abhors man's sophisticated methods of destruction. At the same time, by denying the existence of anything he had not seen simply because he had not seen it, the Master also reveals his own naiveté and his lack of imagination. What the seasoned reader of Swift's satire will gradually realize is that the fact that Gulliver's position is wrong does not yet mean that his opponent's is right.

Orwell's satirical thrusts, however, often move not in two, but in three directions simultaneously. By making repeated analogies between such 'opposites' as Stalin's Russia, Hitler's Germany, and the Mediaeval Church, Orwell creates a situation where sparks fly in all directions. For entirely different reasons, each of the *three* opponents here mentioned would have been ashamed to be caught in the company of, let alone be compared to, one of the others. Thus the satirist has activated a whole array of barbs; yet, the central thrust of the satire remains quite clear if we remember the underlying rhetorical situation. The point of the satirist's analogies is to get his Adversary to admit that when he condones the methods of Stalin, he also condones the terrors of Hitler's Germany and of the Inquisition. In fact, *Goldstein's Book* points out, "the Russians persecuted heresy *more* cruelly than the Inquisition had done" (218, my italics). It is interesting why Professor Crick would take exception to Orwell's analogy between the Church and the Communist Party, when this analogy is used quite widely in the period. For example, in his 1950 "The Failing of the Prophecy," Camus points out that when the quick changes in the Party Line assume the power of dogma overnight, the Party practises a mental tyranny comparable only to that of the Church in the Middle Ages, even if "the Church never went as far as to decide that a divine manifestation was embodied in two, then in four, or in three, and then again in two persons" (233). Camus's analogy, like Orwell's, is quite detailed, and when he describes the orthodox Marxist who "takes refuge in the permanence of the Party in the same way he formerly prostrated himself before the altar" (230), even the ironic tone is reminiscent of Orwell.

In the context of *Nineteen Eighty-Four* as a parody of the totalitarian mentality, Orwell's references to the Church as an institution are quite consistent with various satirical points he wants to make about the *Party*, namely, (1) its frightening potential for longevity, (2) its hypocrisy, (3) its aspiration for mental tyranny, and (4) its propensity to make the people regress to the mediaeval mass psychoses of persecuting 'satanic' opponents in the form of witch-hunts and witch trials.

1. Longevity

This analogy is important to help explain one of the central conceits of the satire. O'Brien insists that the system of Ingsoc is here to stay, Oceania will exist forever, Winston is the "last man," the last "guardian of the human spirit" (233).

The thought that the "Russian Communists," like the Church, "necessarily developed into a permanent ruling caste, or oligarchy, recruited not by birth but by adoption" (v. 4, 515) has been pointed out several times in Orwell's essays. The same idea is reiterated with great persuasive force in *Goldstein's Book*: "*adoptive organizations* such as the Catholic Church have sometimes lasted hundreds or thousands of years.... A ruling group is a ruling group so long as it can name its successors. The Party is not concerned with perpetuating its blood, but with perpetuating itself" (180).

By "perpetuating itself," the Party of today exercises mind control over the Party of tomorrow; in this sense both the Church and the Party can be said to represent the control "imposed by the dead upon the living" (180). If the Church's reign means the hierarchy's continuous control over the heretic, the "Protestant" who may question religious dogma, the Party's reign means the control of the dead 'letter' of Marxist dogma over the live 'spirit' of Socialism.

As noted in Chapter 6, Orwell's equation of Ingsoc, Neo-Bolshevism, and Death-Worship is yet another gibe at the Adversary, the doctrinaire Marxist, for allowing dead dogma to impose control over the living. I suggest we also interpret

Winston and Julia's admission, "We are the dead" (188), in this context. They see themselves "dead" because they belong to the Party and can never escape the mental control "imposed by the dead upon the living," in contrast to the prole woman singing in the yard, who is obviously vital, fertile, fully alive.

The Party's "worship of the dead" has, of course, another and equally obvious connotation in the novel if we recall that the principle behind the self-perpetuating terror in 1984 is the principle of *planned* waste and devastation, the principle of a death-bound, death-worshipping civilization. Undoubtedly Orwell considered the Church an example of longevity and, in its orthodox adherence to dogma, a paralyzing force that stifles free inquiry. Hence he found it an appropriate vehicle for his satirical target: the paralyzing force of the Party that stifles the critical intellect and denies the "process of life" (230).

2. Hypocrisy

The analogy between the Church and the Party also becomes an important vehicle for the satire's thrust at the Party's hypocrisy. Orwell describes an object of art that epitomizes for him the Church's hypocrisy: "It was not at first sight a particularly interesting work of art. But it turned out that the real point was that the *crucifix* took to pieces & inside it was concealed a *stiletto*. What a perfect symbol of the Christian religion" (v. 4, 574, my italics). For Orwell the Church's emphasis on spiritual and mystical symbols to camouflage its unswerving power drive is encapsulated in this vignette in which the crucifix conceals the stiletto.

By analogy, the Communist Party and the Comintern reveal the same hypocrisy when advocating international brotherhood to camouflage Stalin's aspiration for unlimited power. Most significantly, as *Goldstein's Book* points out,

> the Party rejects and vilifies every principle for which the Social-
> ist movement originally stood, and it chooses to do this in the
> name of Socialism. It preaches a contempt for the working class
> unexampled for centuries past, and it dresses its members in a
> uniform which was at one time peculiar to manual workers and
> was adopted for that reason. It systematically undermines the
> solidarity of the family, and it calls its leader by a name which is
> a direct appeal to family loyalty (184).

(Orwell's point about the leader's name is a reference to the frequent appellation of Stalin as "Father" to his people, in the Party literature of the period.)

3. The Mental Tyranny of the Inquisition

The third satirical point refers to the mental tyranny designed to uphold the hierarchy of the institution, and Orwell consistently points out the analogy between the methods of Stalin's Secret Police and those of the Inquisition. When, in *Goldstein's Book* (177) and in the torture scenes (218) Orwell mentions the Inquisition, Hitler's Germany, and Stalin's Russia in the same breath, he makes this point unmistakably clear. All three have been used as examples by the Inner Party, which set out to imitate and surpass them all in tyranny. Thus O'Brien takes pride in pointing out that "even the Catholic Church of the Middle Ages was tolerant by modern standards" (177).

The analogy between the Inquisition and Stalin's Secret Police is necessary to our understanding of that important scene where Winston is interrogated about his belief in the "spirit of Man" (229–232). Winston argues, like Galileo, that the earth is round and it revolves around the sun. O'Brien, who fulfils the role of Inquisitor, albeit an Inquisitor aided and abetted by the most advanced science of modern psychology (169), insists that it is in the power of the Party to determine whether the earth is round or flat, and whether it is the centre of the universe (229). Like Galileo, Winston has to recant at the end. Unlike Galileo, he is in no position to renege on his recantation; not even in private, not even within the "few cubic centimetres of his skull" is he allowed to maintain intellectual doubt, independence from the dictates of the Party. Of course, in this scene Orwell's contemporaries would also recognize allusion to Stalin's direct 'inquisitorial' control over all the scientific, biological, and genetic theories propounded in the U.S.S.R. in his day.[1]

Should any reader miss this analogy, Orwell makes O'Brien point it out several more times: "You have read of the religious persecution of the past. In the Middle Ages there was the Inquisition" (218). Then he confirms and extends his point: "Later, in the twentieth century . . . there were the German Nazis and the Russian Communists. The Russians persecuted heresy more cruelly than the Inquisition had done" (204).

Orwell's 'joke' here (and not all jokes are necessarily funny or light-hearted) is central to the satirist's argument with his Adversary. Although the Communist Party in Russia is based on a 'scientifically' based ideology that originally set out to liberate the mind from the shackles of religious tyranny, this ideology turned into a religion more intolerant, tyrannical, and hostile to free inquiry than any religion in the past. Although this point has an exceptionally powerful impact in the context of Winston's predicament, in itself it is not particularly original. Camus, for example, also observed the irony that "Historical thought was to deliver man from subjection to a divinity; but this liberation demanded of him the most absolute subjection to historical evolution. . . . The era which dares to claim that it is the most rebellious that ever existed only offers a choice of various types of conformity" ("Prophecy").

4. Regression to the Mass Psychosis of Witch-hunts

Finally, Orwell's consistent analogy between the Party and the Mediaeval Church gains full momentum in his pointing out of the way in which each creates an obsession with the satanic by demonizing its opponents. Once more, the satirist's intent is to ridicule his 'progressive' Adversary who, by condoning Stalin's purges, condones a "military despotism enlivened by witchcraft trials" (v. 2, 170).

Here Orwell's parallels between the Party and the Mediaeval Church are quite consistent. In periods when the Church was most consciously striving for power, witch-hunts became popular to promote fear of the 'satanic,' and consequently, uncritical obedience to Church authority. To promote fear and awe of the Party is the purpose of the incessant witch-hunts for 'satanic' traitors, thought criminals, and foreigners in Oceania — an allusion to the function of Stalin's recurring purges and show trials.

Winston's discovery in the Ministry of Truth that Aaronson, Rutherford, and Jones had been falsely accused, and forced to publicly confess to these accusations, is a direct reference to the false accusations against Trotsky and the various members of the Old Guard that Stalin set out to eliminate by labelling them Trotskyites. Regardless of their actual situation, these scapegoats would be accused of conspiring with the enemy of the moment. Thus Trotsky and the so-called Trotskyites were accused, in the early 1930s, of conspiring with the Capitalist enemy; at the time of the Popular Front, with the Fascists; after the 1939 Russo-German Pact, once again with the Capitalists. Needless to say, both the elaborate accusations and the forced public confessions were fictitious, a fact, Orwell implies, should have been quite obvious for all impartial observers.[2]

It is noteworthy that the purges of, for example, 1937 and 1938, did not "consist chiefly of the arrests of big Communists — and virtually no one else. . . . Out of the millions arrested at that time, important Party and state officials could not possibly have represented more than 10 percent" (Solzhenitsyn 70). Consequently, the hysteria of fear and denunciations was extremely widespread — The incident of the Parsons children denouncing someone with unusual shoes as a foreign spy exemplifies the absurdity of the mass psychosis (53). We also hear that the children set fire to the skirt of a market-woman because she had wrapped her sausages in a poster with Big Brother's picture on it (58). In these incidents Orwell suggests an analogy between the mass hysteria created by Stalin's purges and the mass psychosis of witch burnings in the Middle Ages.

Pointing out the analogy between Stalin's purges and the mediaeval witch trials is indispensable for the satirist when drawing attention to the compulsive scapegoating endemic to the totalitarian mentality. In fact, Orwell's analysis demonstrates that this seemingly modern phenomenon has all the following attributes of a mediaeval mass psychosis: (1) the accused are branded traitors; (2) the 'witch' is never acquitted; (3) the interrogators justify torture in the name of giving shape to a 'new man'; (4) the model of the 'new man' includes the demonization of sexuality; (5) the forced confessions create a sense of phantasmagoria; (6) any opposition to the tyrannical authority of the 'sacred' becomes branded as a 'satanic' denial of the dominant creed.

1.   Since in the Middle Ages witches and heretics were regarded as "traitors to God" (Robbins 415), under torture they were "constrained to name [their] accomplice. Thus one trial gave birth to a hundred. It was a satanic *perpetuum mobile*" (Seligman 185). The trial of traitors in the totalitarian system shows the same dynamics, with the exception that in Stalin's regime even the *perpetuum mobile* of terror was expected to function on the principles of a centrally planned economy. The

NKVD was given a strict quota of 'traitors' and confessions to round up in a given period in a particular region (Solzhenitsyn 71).[3] The intellectual revelation Winston receives in the Ministry of Love describes this "perpetuum mobile" of terror as the very principle of the worship of God as Power: "The heretic, the enemy of society, will always be there, *so that* he can be defeated and humiliated over again" (231, my italics). Winston's experience in Room 101 also teaches him, existentially, how this machine works. The moment he screams "Do it to Julia!", he has become a part of the chain-reaction of denunciations and betrayals.

2. It follows from the premise that the witch is a "traitor to God" that a person accused of being a witch can never be acquitted. Evidence from the NKVD files indicates that "there has never been acquittal of a political defendant in the U.S.S.R. . . . [and] no defendant before 1945 had yet pleaded 'not guilty'" (qtd. in Tolstoy 306).[4] Orwell makes this point quite clear in the case of Aaronson, Rutherford, and Jones: after their public confessions they are released, only to be re-arrested and shot "with a bullet in the back" in private. At the end, after his release from the Ministry of Love, Winston awaits his own execution; his last vision is walking down the corridor "with an armed guard at his back," receiving "the long-hoped-for bullet" (256).

3. There is no doubt that as a "priest of power" O'Brien feels no compunction about "curing" Winston's mind by torturing his body. His attitude mirrors the "missionary thrust of religious reformers [which] was crucial to the advent of witch trials on a massive scale" (Klaits 4) during the conflict between Protestant Reformation and Counter Reformation — also comparable to the 'mission' of the interrogators during Stalin's purges, intent on creating the "new Socialist man."[5]

4. The demonization of sexuality coincided with the introduction of this new ideal. It was in the name of opposition to 'satanic' deviations that the interrogators in the sixteenth century "tried to change behaviour and redefine standards of morality . . . [becoming] particularly concerned with prohibited sexual activity" (Klaits 4). As a matter of fact, sexual deviation from the Party norm is also one of the surest signs of heresy in Oceania. Although O'Brien barely needs any evidence at all for getting Winston into the Ministry of Love, as any "thoughtcrime" is tantamount to heresy, he keeps a record

of all the minute details of Julia and Winston's relationship, including films of their meetings and love-making. Obviously, the heretic's attitude to sexuality is the most telling sign of his or her spiritual standing, just as it had been in the eyes of the Church in the Middle Ages, when, due to the "Judeo-Christian demonization of sexuality," any type of forbidden sexual activity "was considered Satanic and consequently a sacrilege, deserving the harshest punishment" (Eliade 90). Describing the Church's repressive attitude to sexuality, Eliade makes another point that readers of *Nineteen Eighty-Four* may find illuminating to Orwell's strategies: In spite of persecution, Eliade points out, "the sacrality of sexual life could not be radically extirpated. For ritual nudity and ceremonial intercourse were not only powerful magic-religious forces, they also expressed the nostalgia for a beatific human existence, which . . . corresponded to the paradisiac state before the fall" (20). By making Winston and Julia's relationship the centre of the human drama in the novel, in their first meeting in the Golden Country Orwell taps all these associations.

Professor Crick questions Orwell's inclusion of the "antics of the Anti-Sex League or O'Brien's plans to abolish the orgasm" in a satire on the totalitarian system. He suggests that "these subjects are part of [Orwell's] satire on sexual Puritanism in our own society, and only indirectly relevant to the criticism of totalitarian society" ("Introduction" 120). This objection overlooks Orwell's consistent allusions to his totalitarian models. Of course he acknowledges the English origins of Puritanism, but the sexual puritanism in Oceania is clearly a reference to Nazi and Bolshevik approaches to sexuality. He explores this theme earlier in his essays, pointing out, for example, that "the English Puritans, the Bolsheviks and the Nazis all attempted to discourage cosmetics" (v. 3, 161), and observing that "Hitler's 'ideal woman', an exceedingly plain specimen in a mackintosh, was to be exhibited all over Germany and much of the rest of the world but inspired few imitators" (v. 3, 161).

In fact, both Hitler and Stalin insisted on close control over their subjects' sexuality, even if the nature of this control may have changed according to the different interests of the State at different times.[6] As Koestler points out in *The Yogi and the Commissar*, when in the mid-thirties "Nazi Germany began its birth-rate drive . . . with bachelor tax, money premiums and all the rest, the Soviet press echoed with justified derision about the 'debasement of womanhood to the role of prize brood-mares'" (159). Then between 1934 and 1936 Stalin went ahead to imitate the German example. He made divorce practically unobtainable, introduced a most restrictive policy on abortions, discouraged birth control, introduced taxation for families with fewer than three children, and handed out medals for "heroes of motherhood" (Carrère d'Encausse 78). Also, both Hitler and Stalin made the family legally responsible for all its members, encouraging children to denounce parents, and spouses to denounce each other, in the interest of the State. Orwell's Oceania offers an accurate description of the totalitarian system[7] intent on breaking the primacy of the sexual and the family bond, determined to reduce sexuality to the duty of bearing children to the State, to doing one's "duty to the Party" (62).

The powerful connection between political or religious tyranny and a puritanical denial of sexuality has also been observed by psychologists and political thinkers before and since Orwell. In *The Mass Psychology of Fascism*, Wilhelm Reich points out that "both religion and tyrannical political systems . . . provide excitement that is both anti-sexual and a substitution for sexuality," and he returns to Freud's point to explain that "every inhibition of genital gratification intensifies the sadistic impulse" (168). Both Winston and Julia understand the Party's purpose in demonizing sexuality, the "direct, intimate connection between chastity and political orthodoxy. For how could the fear, the hatred, and the lunatic credulity which the Party needed in its members be kept at the right pitch, except by bottling down some powerful instinct and using it as a driving force?" (118). The Party deliberately uses "sexual privation [to induce] hysteria which was desirable because it could be transformed into war-fever and leader worship" (118). This is why "the aim of the Party was not merely to prevent men and women from forming loyalties which it might not be able to control. Its real, undeclared purpose was to remove all pleasure from the sexual act . . . eroticism was the enemy inside marriage as well as outside it" (60).

Whether the sexual accusations against the witches or the traitors were based on real transgression, both accused and accuser acknowledged the fact that a free attitude to sexuality expressed a rebellion against the ego-ideal of the Church or the Party respectively. Hence Winston's delight when he finds out that Julia had been promiscuous (112).

5. In the forced confessions we find another significant characteristic of the witch trials Orwell alludes to when satirizing
Stalin's purges. Because of the nature of the confessions, it is
extremely difficult to distinguish truth from fiction. The interrogators expected the witches to perform a perfect act of contri-
tion, to internalize the accusations and to believe in their own
confession: "Outward conformity to the rulers' spiritual and
social standards was not sufficient. A true inner birth, mani-
fested by formal confessions and declaration of repentance, was
the goal of most judges in witchcraft cases" (Klaits 5).

By the same token, O'Brien explains to Winston that Aaronson, Rutherford, and Jones have repented, "whimpering, grovelling, weeping — and in the end it was not with pain or fear,
only with penitence. . . . There was nothing left in them except sorrow for what they have done, and love of Big Brother"
(220). O'Brien is like the interrogator at a witch trial, "able
to justify the most terrible kinds of violence in the name of a
supposed higher good." Consequently, just like "many a witch
suspect [who] was led to believe that he or she was guilty as
charged," both Winston and Parsons come to internalize what
they are accused of. Parsons admits, "Of course I am guilty!"
immediately (201). In Winston's case the process takes longer,
but O'Brien does not stop until Winston also gives "witness to
[his] internalization of the required values" (Klaits 151). In the
scene in Room 101 Winston is no longer told what is expected
from him. His anguished cry, "Do it to Julia!", has to come
from within; it has to be felt, willed, in earnest.

Orwell's allusion to the air of phantasmagoria surrounding
the witches' confessions is another important feature in his parody of the totalitarian mentality. Mircea Eliade draws attention to some clichés recurring throughout Western Europe in
the witches' confessions, references to some subterranean place,
to a place in the darkness, pointing at the "importance of that
mysterious sur-réalité revealed by an imaginary universe" (88).

The traitors' confessions in Oceania reveal the same clichés,
the same blatant disregard for the physical rules of the natural
world, the same sense of phantasmagoria. Such recurring clichés
are the betrayal of one's country to the enemy and the corrupting of the women in the Party. Even the old cliché of being at
several places at the same time and flying on a broomstick is
hinted at in the trial when Aaronson, Rutherford, and Jones
"confessed that on that date they had been on Eurasian soil.

They had flown from a secret airfield in Canada to a rendezvous somewhere in Siberia, and had conferred with members of the Eurasian General Staff, to whom they had betrayed important military secrets" (71). Winston observes that "very likely the confessions had been rewritten until the original facts and dates no longer had the smallest significance." In the same way, the "crime [of] promiscuity between Party members . . . that the accused in the great purges invariably confessed to . . . was difficult to imagine . . . actually happening" (60).

When Winston wants to terminate his own torture, he repeats all the same grotesque clichés he knows to be associated with deviation: "He confessed to the assassination of eminent Party members, the distribution of seditious pamphlets, embezzlement of public funds, sale of military secrets, sabotage of every kind. He confessed that he was a religious believer, an admirer of capitalism, a sexual pervert" (209).

All these crimes are regarded as equally sinful and are equally unlikely to have been committed by anyone in Oceania. Similar confessions, showing an alarming sense of consistency, were characteristic of Stalin's show trials, and, ironically, it was the very consistency of these fabrications that the masses found so impressive. In her analysis of totalitarianism, Hannah Arendt points out this irony:

> If . . . all the "confessions" of political opponents in the Soviet Union are phrased in the same language and admit the same motives, the consistency-hungry masses will accept the fiction as supreme proof of their truthfulness; whereas common sense tells us that it is precisely their consistency which is out of this world and proves that they are a fabrication (352).

By drawing attention to the fact that in Oceania all the recurring clichés in the traitors' confessions are fabrications, Orwell scores another point against his Adversary who, by condoning or justifying Stalin's purges, has regressed to the mass psychosis of mediaeval witch-hunts and witch trials.

6. Due to the torture-induced confessions in the mediaeval witch trials and in Stalin's purges, it is difficult to determine whether resistance to the 'sacred' authority did indeed exist, and if so, what the nature of this resistance was. Orwell picks up on this point also: one never finds out for sure whether the Brotherhood, the resistance movement against the 'sacred' authority of the Party, does indeed exist. But whether the

Brotherhood is a powerful movement or simply a figment of the oppressed people's imagination, Orwell demonstrates that in a world so sharply polarized, even resistance against the established orthodoxy will mirror the same attitudes the rebel wants to get away from. As Orwell points out in another context, to take fanatical revenge upon evil leads to a mirror image of that same evil, a thought he finds most memorably expressed by Nietzsche: "He who fights too long against dragons becomes a dragon himself; and if thou gaze too long into the abyss, the abyss will gaze into thee" (v. 3, 267).

The best example to illustrate this point is the scene where Julia and Winston visit O'Brien's apartment to join the Brotherhood. A sense of ritual with religious connotations is emphasized by O'Brien's "expressionless voice, as though this were a routine, a sort of catechism, most of whose answers were known to him already" (153):

> "You are prepared to give your lives?"
> "Yes."
> "You are prepared to commit murder?"
> "Yes."
> "To commit acts of sabotage, which may cause the death of hundreds of innocent people?"
> "Yes."
> "To betray your country to foreign powers?"
> "Yes."
> "You are prepared to cheat, to forge, to blackmail, to corrupt the minds of *children*, to distribute habit-forming drugs, to encourage prostitution, to disseminate venereal diseases — to do anything which is likely to cause demoralization and weaken the power of the Party?"
> "Yes."
> "If, for example, it would somehow serve our interest *to throw sulphuric acid in a child's face* — are you prepared to do that?"
> "Yes" (153, my italics).

Orwell's allusions to the 'black mass' of a satanic cult are unmistakable. Winston and Julia, clandestine lovers, go together to a forbidden assembly to participate in a ceremony to swear allegiance to the 'satanic' Goldstein, the arch-enemy of the 'sacred' in Oceania. They are offered a glass of wine and a wafer by O'Brien — allusion to the ritual feast of forbidden drink and food, a feast culminating in sacrificing innocent victims, usually children. Its restrained, 'naturalistic' tone notwithstanding, the scene is a reminder of rituals confessed to by some witches, attesting to their desire "to *claim* all the crimes and horrible ceremonies cited *ad nauseam* in the Western European witch trials" (Eliade 71).

Undoubtedly, when at the beginning of their visit Julia and Winston are offered that rare commodity, wine, and to cover up for the wine on their breath, at the end each is offered a wafer, we are made to realize that the scene is a 'black mass' — the reversal, the parody, of the Christian ritual. But the scene in O'Brien's apartment has a more complex function. The ritual begins with the 'prayer' "Down with Big Brother!" and culminates in the catechism expressing the conspirators' commitment to overthrowing Big Brother in the name of the satanic Goldstein. Hence the scene is also the reversal, the parody, of another ritual we have witnessed earlier in the novel, the ritual of the Two Minutes Hate, which celebrates Big Brother's victory over the satanic Goldstein and culminates in the fervent prayer "Long Live Big Brother!" (At the Hate Winston overhears a "little sandy-haired woman's . . . tremulous murmur that sounded like 'My Saviour!'. . . . It was apparent she was uttering a prayer" [19].)

But if the scene in O'Brien's apartment is a black mass, a satanic parody of religious worship, and at the same time the reversal of the State worship of Big Brother (itself a parody of the mass), the reader might wonder about the satirist's strategies in presenting us with these multiple reversals. Is the conspiratorial scene a parody of the religious ritual, or is it a parody of its inversion in the daily ritual of the State religion? Can it be intended as a parody of both? If so, what is Orwell's point in parodying *both* the religious ritual and its inversion in the "secular religion" of totalitarianism?

To answer this question, we should look for the attributes that the three rituals have in common. The answer lies in the habit of mind we have seen Orwell exploring both in his novel and in his essays; it is a mentality that sets up a sharp polarization between the 'sacred' and the 'satanic,' offering a fanatical condemnation of everything connected with "them" — the outsider, the satanic opponent, the heretic, the traitor.

The fact that the scene in O'Brien's apartment is a parody of two rituals usually considered diametrically opposite allows us to catch a glimpse, indirectly, of the satirist's 'norm' of human

conduct. Orwell's 'norm' is that of the secular humanist sceptical of any form of fanaticism, deeply reluctant to translate right
and wrong into the sacred and the satanic.

More specifically, Orwell presents us with the contrast between the "Long Live Big Brother" at the Two Minutes Hate
and the "Down with Big Brother" at the black mass in O'Brien's
apartment to make us aware that these two scenes are in a
sense mirror images. Orwell's point becomes clear when we
realize that there is no fundamental difference between these
two assemblies in their tenor and dominating emotion. Both
groups meet in the spirit of ritualized hatred, and both accept
Machiavelli's "realist" doctrine that the end justifies the means,
that the atrocities committed by our side can be accepted as
a matter of course. Most significantly, human beings in both
scenes define themselves in relation to a Cause, a transcendental Other, and not in relation to other human beings based on
the moral values dictated by common decency.

The scene in O'Brien's apartment makes clear Orwell's point:
fanatical adherence to an orthodoxy and fanatical adherence to
a counter-orthodoxy, its 'satanic' inversion, are both inhuman
and immoral. To join the Brotherhood was a trap for Winston
not only politically, but also internally, in terms of his inner life.
When in the Ministry of Love he is made to listen to the taped
version of his catechism, he realizes that he has deeply offended
against the "spirit of Man": in the scene in O'Brien's apartment
he was also trapped spiritually; he succumbed to the temptation
to fight fanaticism with fanaticism, to fight hate with hate, to
fight the dragon by becoming a dragon.

The true believer's fanatical loyalty to *Big Brother* and the
rebel's fanatical loyalty to the *Brotherhood* are, in effect, mirror
images; both the fanatical believer in the orthodoxy and the
fanatical heretic fighting the orthodoxy would "throw sulphuric
acid in a child's face" if their Cause required it. Both have
departed from the "spirit of Man" which depends on love and
decency among human beings, on the universal *Brotherhood of
Man*. (It is important to point out that Julia does not succumb
to this tempting logic of polarization. The only time she speaks
in the scene is to tell O'Brien that she refuses to separate from
Winston even in the name of the Brotherhood [153]). Through
this scene and its aftermath, Orwell presents us with a humanist
condemnation of the "secular religion" of totalitarianism that
is predicated upon a hate-filled obsession with the satanic.

Notes

[1] Hannah Arendt, *The Origins of Totalitarianism*, 345; Aleksandr Solzhenitsyn, *The Gulag Archipelago*, 90.

[2] For Orwell's comments on this subject see the following references in his *Collected Essays*: v. 1, 583; v. 3, 457; v. 4, 188, 425.

[3] Aleksandr Solzhenitsyn in *The Gulag Archipelago* emphasizes that it is a serious mistake to believe that "the history of 1937 and 1938 consisted chiefly of the arrests of big Communists." There were "*millions* arrested at that time" (70). He also offers documentation for the entirely arbitrary quotas that the Secret Police was to fulfill:

> The former Chekist Aleksandr Kalganov recalls that a telegram arrived in Tashkent: "Send 200!" They had just finished one clean-out, and it seemed there was "no one else" to take. Well, true, they had just brought in about fifty more from the districts. And then they had an idea! They would reclassify as 58's all the non-political offenders being held by the police. No sooner said than done. But despite that, they had still not filled the quota. At that precise moment the police reported that a gypsy band had impudently encamped on one of the city squares and asked what to do with them. Someone had a bright idea! They surrounded the encampment and raked all the gypsy men from seventeen to sixty as 58's! They had fulfilled the plan! This could happen another way as well: according to Chief of Police Zabolovsky, the Chekists of Ossetia were given a quota of five hundred to be shot in the Republic. They asked to have it increased, and they were permitted another 250" (71).

[4] Nikolai Tolstoy documents the fact that those accused in the course of the purges, just like the witches at witch trials, were never acquitted:

> In this context it is superfluous to note that, according to an Amnesty International Report, 'there has never been an acquittal of a political defendant in the USSR' (*Prisoners of Conscience of the USSR: Their Treatment and Conditions* [London, 1975], p.32). This is very nearly true (three Poles were acquitted in 1945 in [the] face of exceptional British and American concern: Z. Stypulkovski, *Invitation to Moscow* [London, 1951, 333]). But even more effective testimony to the efficiency of Soviet justice was the claim of State Prosecutor Rudenko that no defendant before 1945 had yet pleaded 'not guilty' (306).

[5] For an account of Stalin's purges see Solzhenitsyn's *The Gulag Archipelago* and Mikhail Geller and Aleksandr Nekrich's *Utopia in Power*.

[6] In his 1945 *The Yogi and the Commissar*, Koestler draws a parallel between Hitler's and Stalin's family law. There are many works from the 1930s that echo his concern about the position of women in Germany. Alice Hamilton, in her 1934 "The Enslavement of Woman," points out that in Nazi Germany "the State is all-important, not the individual child nor the mother: the State needs children, therefore not to bear children is treason to the State" (79). Stephen Roberts, in his 1937 *The House that Hitler Built*, describes some of the outstanding features of Hitler's New Penal Code dealing with the family: "Abortion is an offense, campaigns for birth-control are forbidden, and anybody who sneers at motherhood is liable to heavy penalties." He also comments on marriage loans "to assist marriages and to take young women off the labour market," explaining that the "debtor is released from a quarter of his obligations with every child he has" (232).

In his 1939 work on *Hitler's Germany*, Karl Loewenstein describes the "Spartan life" led by the Hitler Youth, engaged in military training from an early age (82), and comments that the "codes of domestic relations [are] revolutionized," including sexual relationships, to emphasize the subordination of the individual to the State. Thus, "couples intending to marry must submit to the registrar a certificate for the public health officer showing that they are not afflicted with any mental or physical disease which would prevent them having healthy offspring" (105). Loewenstein also describes the practice of enforced sterilization and castration of individuals the health tribunals find unfit for parenting healthy offspring (105).

In describing the Nazi campaign for a higher birth rate, in his 1935 book on *The Nazi Dictatorship* Frederick Schuman offers a memorable example of the State's "total" control over sexual relationships: "In November 1933 the Mayor of Frankfurt am Main ordered 1500 unmarried municipal officers to find wives or lose their jobs" (385).

[7] Also, we should not forget that Orwell reviewed Koestler's *The Yogi and the Commissar* which gave ample documentation on "the abolition of divorce for all but the privileged upper stratum" and on the various demonstrations of the sexual puritanism advocated by the Party ("Soviet Myth and Reality" in *The Yogi and the Commissar*, 122–180). For a more detailed treatment of this question, please see Chapter 12 of this study.

Chapter 9

The Demonic World of Oceania:
The Mystical Adulation of the 'Sacred' Leader

Unlike Bernard Crick, Richard Rees finds Orwell's consistent analogy between the Church and the Party essential to the satire in *Nineteen Eighty-Four*, but he does not contemplate the possibility that Orwell may be parodying the "secular religion" of totalitarianism from the point of view of the secular humanist. According to Rees, in creating analogy between political and religious concepts, "Orwell's purpose is satirical. He infuses religious metaphors into a completely secular context to suggest the corruption of the system, the perversion of eternal values by the ephemeral demands of politics. The transference of belief to Big Brother is profane — but inevitable in a world in which no sacred equivalents remain" (148).

Of course, Rees is right in pointing out the perversions of the religious ideal in Oceania, where it is a human being who demands to be worshipped as Divinity and who rules quite openly through Hate and not through Love. Rees assumes, however, that the topsy-turvy world of Oceania, the inverted world of parody, would reveal the satirist's hidden standard, if only we could turn this world back straight, right side up again. But would Orwell want to return to what Rees calls the eternal values of the sacred, the values of Christianity, the values of religion?

There is actually a far more interesting question here that Rees seems to overlook entirely. By juxtaposing religious and political spheres so consistently, does Orwell use religion to make fun of totalitarianism, or does he use totalitarianism to make fun of religion?[1] My suggestion based on the 'Catechism scene' is that Orwell the secular humanist parodies aspects of a mentality he sees as common to both. At the most universal level of the satire, in "blackwhite" Orwell sets out to parody three characteristics of this mentality: first, an insistent tendency towards polarization, towards splitting the entire world into the opposites of "them" and "us," black and white; second, the projecting of our "shadow" upon "them," the mutual name

calling that Orwell shows to be absurd and confusing; and finally, the tendency for all distinctions to collapse in a 'mystical'
oneness, a coalescence or coincidence of opposites.

The Two Minutes Hate, the daily ritual of public worship, is
clearly predicated on such polarization. It is by attributing satanic powers to Goldstein, the Prime Enemy, that Big Brother,
who admittedly had started his career as a mere mortal, could
imperceptibly arrogate to himself the power of supernatural
goodness, the power of the Sacred. "All that is needed is that
a state of war should exist," states *Goldstein's Book* (168), revealing the meaning of the paradox "War is Peace."

But the "imposture" of war (173) the Party engineers in the
political arena is also corollary to the psychic battle it engineers
between 'sacred' and 'satanic,' so that Big Brother may continually reveal his more than human power by scoring new victories
over the inexhaustible supply of invariably satanic opponents.
Thus who or what belongs to the satanic at any given moment
may change, but the category of the satanic is unchangeable,
indispensable to the psychological apparatus of totalitarianism.
(It is due to the experience of the communal ecstasy of hate
directed at the satanic Goldstein, that the true believer is "uttering a prayer" to Big Brother, the "Saviour!" (19).)

So far Orwell's parody implies a direct parallel between the
Party and the Church Militant. But as Chapter 7 on Doublethink indicates, there is a point where the Party goes beyond
the Church: to add to the tension of polarizing the entire world
in terms of 'sacred' and 'satanic,' the Party arrogates to itself
the power to switch the enemy at will, and then to deny that a
switch has taken place. The people of Oceania are trained from
childhood to be vigilant in detecting and persecuting evil, yet
they are also prevented from relying on their own judgement or
memory in identifying evil: As a result, they succumb to a state
of mind the Party chooses to call the "love" of Big Brother, the
same state of mind *Goldstein's Book* defines as "controlled insanity" or Doublethink. To have any sense of good and evil, the
people of Oceania have to be ruled by, indeed become one with,
the will of Big Brother, and Big Brother chooses to reveal his
will through the Law of Contradiction: "War is Peace, Freedom
is Slavery, Ignorance is Strength" (92). The cadence is a convenient reminder of both the obscure, paradoxical language of religious revelation and the oracular pronouncements of dialectical
materialism. (Orwell shows obvious irritation, when referring

to the paradox "the expropriation of the expropriators" [*RWP* 229], or to thesis, antithesis, and synthesis as those "mysterious entities" [*RWP* 176], or "the *sacred* sisters" [*RWP* 229].) What is just as important to note, for the majority of Oceania the triple slogan, which they accept as the very essence of Big Brother's Being, remains the language of *unresolved* paradox, unresolved contradiction.

In his analysis of "Triplethink," Professor Rohatyn raises the interesting questions of whether it is possible to believe in the Law of Contradiction, to act upon it, to elevate it to the level of an abstract principle (3). My answer would be yes on all three counts. It is possible to make people *believe* in contradiction if the purpose is to emphasize belief as a psychological state perceived to be the opposite, contrary to Reason. This kind of language and this kind of emphasis is familiar from the accounts of mediaeval mystics when they want to draw attention to the fact that their ecstasy, the peak experience of their spiritual journey, is inexpressible through the classical logic of the language of communication. Using the mystical logic of the "coincidentia oppositorum" embodied in the language of oxymoron and paradox — a code in itself — the Inner Party attempts to draw attention to a power beyond the realm of Reason, and to generate faith in this power. In effect, the greater the logical dichotomy, the greater the psychological intensity of faith.

Making the people abnegate Reason by accepting the unresolved triple paradox is just as effective in generating fervour of faith as exposing them to the omnipresent icon with the hypnotic eyes — indeed, the Party uses both strategies interchangeably, or simultaneously.

In the first scene of the book, when we meet Winston, he feels he is being watched by Big Brother's eyes from every direction, showing the sense of what scholars of mysticism call the mysterium, the tremendum, and the fascinans that a human being experiences when faced with the numinous, the more than human (Otto). The tremendum: Winston is in awe and fear; the fascinans: he is drawn to it, like a magnet; the mystery: he is intrigued by the secret behind Big Brother's expression.

Appropriately, in Part 1 Winston raises three questions. In stating that he understands "how" but not "why," he questions the motivating force behind the Party's unceasing scapegoat hunts and witch trials. His second question deals with a nameless horror awaiting him in the future. That he will be captured, tortured, and executed he accepts as inevitable. "Why then," he asks, "did that horror which altered nothing, have to lie embedded in future time?" (92). Part 1 ends with his third question. Both the political puzzle of "why" and the personal puzzle of the "nameless horror" are intertwined with the puzzle proposed by Big Brother's mask, the essential, hidden nature of the Godhead: "The face gazed up on him, heavy, calm, protecting: but what kind of a smile was hidden beneath the dark moustache?" (92).

At the end of Part 1 we leave Winston contemplating his future, musing over the baffling riddle of the triple paradox, which echoes his own three questions: "Like a leaden knell the words came back to him: WAR IS PEACE   FREEDOM IS SLAVERY IGNORANCE IS STRENGTH" (92). Winston's questions are triple aspects of the same mystery, and he will find his answer by probing into the triple paradox, the Word through which Big Brother chooses to reveal himself.[2]

In effect, one may approach the structure of the novel in terms of the three paradoxes Winston is compelled to understand one by one and in the right sequence. Exploring these riddles forms a spiritual journey O'Brien describes to Winston as "Learning, Understanding and Acceptance," which I suggest is Orwell's parody of the spiritual journey undertaken by many a mediaeval mystic, consisting of the three stages of Purgation, Illumination, and Union.

The stage of Learning for Winston begins with his reading about the first paradox in *Goldstein's Book*: War is Peace. This, by the way, is the only paradox he will begin to understand by reading about it. The next phase of his learning takes place in the Ministry of Love, where, to begin with, he is made to deny that he remembers the photograph of Aaronson, Rutherford, and Jones — clearly an allusion to what the mystics describe as "purgation through recollection" (Underhill 310). Next, Winston is made to admit that two and two make five; this is a parody of the mystic's "purgation through the senses" — that is, "the cleansing of the self to reach humility and perfect intention" (Price 73). Winston reaches this stage when he no longer wants to deceive O'Brien, but genuinely *wants* to see the four fingers as if they were five (216).

After his Purgation (O'Brien calls it Learning), Winston is ready to achieve Understanding, a stage bearing resemblance to the mystic's Enlightenment or Illumination. Winston's first moment of "luminous certainty" is his first glimpse at the "absolute truth" that "two and two could have been three as easily as five" (222). This stage culminates in O'Brien's revelation that explains the mystery of "why" the Party engineers its scapegoat rituals: "The Party seeks power entirely for its own sake. . . . The object of persecution is persecution. The object of torture is torture. The object of power is power" (227). This is the ultimate intellectual revelation in Winston's journey, offering explanation for the "why," the motivation behind the "perpetuum mobile" of terror, the self-perpetuating witch-hunts, denunciations, trials, and executions. This revelation is also a prerequisite for his understanding of the second paradox: Freedom is Slavery. Since God is the Eternal power of the Party, and the individual is powerless because he is mortal, he may "free" himself of the burden of mortality and powerlessness by becoming a "slave" to the Party — that is, by giving up the freedom of the autonomous individual in order to become a mere cell in the collective. This is as far as Winston is allowed to go in what the mystics have called the accumulating of knowledge about God, which comes through reason and study (Price 46).

The last stage, according to accounts of mysticism, involves both knowing and loving God perfectly, until the soul experiences "total self-abandonment" (Underhill 388), a sense of oneness in which, according to the mystic, "My *me* is God: nor do I know my selfhood except in God" (Underhill 396). It is this stage O'Brien calls Acceptance and it is clearly concerned with Winston's ability to love. The climactic scene here takes place in Room 101, where Winston is expected, though never told so directly, to break his emotional bond with Julia: To "love" Big Brother, to become one with him, is tantamount to betraying any human bond. Although Room 101 is the climactic scene in the novel, Winston's conversion is not complete until "the final, indispensable, healing change" (256) takes place in the last scene, when, like the prodigal son, Winston is ready to return from the individual's "self-willed exile from the loving breast" (256) in the spirit of repentance. To "love" Big Brother in the spirit of true Acceptance means to become one with the essential nature of the Godhead revealed as the brutal, treacherous God of Power. It is the God of Power that was hiding in "the smile . . . beneath the dark moustache" (92). Returning to the "loving breast," Winston is ready to admit this Divinity into his own breast and loses the "spirit of Man" irretrievably.

By the end of the novel, Winston has explored the meaning of the triple paradox. He has learned that War is Peace — the machinery of unceasing wars is an imposture to allow the world dictators to have absolute power over their own enslaved populations. Yet now, when listening to the war bulletin, Winston undergoes the same sense of orgiastic triumph as the rest of the people around him. He has also learned the meaning of "Freedom is Slavery"; yet now, he joins the masses, his individuality enslaved like everyone else's. Then, when for the last time he is haunted by a scene of his childhood, a memory of his old self, he learns to reject the scene as a "false memory" (255).

War is Peace, Freedom is Slavery, Ignorance is Strength — he has learned it all, but only now does he learn that Acceptance, the final stage after Learning and Understanding, is the ability to ignore, to forget, to *unlearn* all the knowledge he has accumulated throughout his journey. It is only now that he can practise the most mysterious third paradox for which he could have received no explanation: his new "strength" to become part of the cheering masses depends on his self-imposed "ignorance" of his old self, of the world of reality. Like all the others around him, finally he has learned to practise Doublethink. It is only now that, in the words of the mystic, "the individual drop had reached the ocean"[3] (Price 45): the heretic's atonement is complete; he is truly *at one* with Big Brother.

Orwell's allusions to the concepts of mysticism are surprisingly detailed and consistent;[4] indeed, I would like to suggest that these allusions form one of the most significant satirical undercurrents to the naturalistic texture. Winston's journey in the Ministry of Love through Learning, Understanding, and Acceptance is worked out in fine detail to parallel the religious mystic's journey towards Divine Love through Purgation, Illumination, and Union. Orwell also makes several allusions to the pervasive light imagery associated with mystics' accounts of their experience ("a blinding flash of light"; "luminous certainty"; "the place where there is no darkness"; etc.), and to the imagery of Pilgrimage, Spiritual Alchemy, and Spiritual Marriage scholars identify as the most important symbols in describing the mystic's journey (Underhill).

When O'Brien announces that "we shall squeeze you empty, and then we shall fill you with ourselves" (220), there is more

than an echo here from " 'Solve et coagula' — break down that
you may build up," the principle of "the Spiritual Alchemist
. . . who is to burn away the dross before he can reach the
Perfection of alchemical gold from which comes the Magnum
Opus: deified or spiritual man" (Underhill 146).

Images of the Pilgrimage and Spiritual Marriage are even
more readily recognizable: Winston's feeling for O'Brien right
from the beginning is an allusion to the mysterious attraction
that Underhill describes as a fundamental doctrine of mysticism, where the symbol of mutual desire is often mingled with
the images of pilgrimage. And if we keep in mind that the attraction between the human soul — traditionally represented
as female — and the Absolute — traditionally represented as
the pursuing male — is mutual, we may see the hide-and-seek
between O'Brien and Winston in an entirely new light.

Winston and O'Brien's relationship is a problematic and controversial one, often approached by Freudian critics as paranoid
(Sperber), homosexual or sado-masochistic (Fiderer). More recently Feminist critics have approached it as a sign of Winston's
preference for the male bond, and hence an expression of Winston's — or Orwell's — latent misogyny (Patai). What both
the Freudian and the Feminist critic overlook, however, is that
in the novel O'Brien is the representative of Big Brother, the
cold, cruel intelligence behind the smiling icon. In terms of
Orwell's consistent allusion to mystical symbols, the hide-and-
seek between Winston and O'Brien is like the mystical "Game
of Love," described, for example, by Francis Thomson in the
Hound of Heaven, which "shows to us the inexorable onward
sweep" of God, this "tremendous Lover . . . hunting the sep-
arated spirit rushing in terror from the overpowering presence
of God, but followed, sought, conquered in the end" (Underhill
135). Such a description is quite appropriate to Winston's journey both in the course and in the concluding scene of his "tour
aboli," his torture pilgrimage leading to the "love union" with
O'Brien. (In *Keep the Aspidistra Flying* Orwell draws a similar
analogy between God pursuing the human soul and the Money
God pursuing Gordon Comstock: "Sometimes your salvation
hunts you down like the Hound of Heaven," Gordon remarks
ironically [719].)

To read Winston and O'Brien's mutual attraction in terms
of the mystical symbol of Spiritual Marriage does not fly in
the face of the naturalistic level of the novel. As discussed

in Chapter 8, Orwell makes it quite clear that by depriving the people of sexual fulfilment the Party provokes hysteria, an emotional energy it will channel first into the fanatical hatred of the enemy and then into the equally fanatical worship of the leader.

But where Orwell makes most effective use of the mystical symbol is in the image of the pervasive eye, a fundamental concept of mysticism being that the human Soul is always in the presence of God. Big Brother's hypnotic gaze, which penetrates all minds of Oceania, is a parody of this concept, and it points to the greatest danger inherent in the totalitarian mentality. At the beginning Winston is horrified by the all-seeing eye and would like to hide from it. Looking at a coin with Big Brother's face on it, he feels that "even from the coin the eyes pursued you" (27). At the end of Part 1, "just as he had done a few days earlier, he slid a coin out of his pocket and looked at it. The face *gazed up at him*, heavy, calm, protecting" (92, my italics). Then, in the Ministry of Love, after he is broken intellectually, he feels "swallowed up" (209), absorbed by the mysterious eye. Finally, in the last scene, "*he gazed up* at the enormous face . . . [and] loved Big Brother" (256). By now he emerges with a new consciousness so that he could say with the mediaeval mystic: "The eye by which I see . . . is the same as the eye by which God sees me." Not satisfied with mere obedience, the Party makes the individual internalize the censoring eye of the punitive authority; by the end Big Brother has penetrated Winston's Superego, and the Thought Police has taken internal — that is, total — command over the Self.

Reading Orwell's essays, it becomes clear that he was sceptical of the mystic's search for confrontation with the sacred and associated the self-abandonment of mysticism with the relinquishing of personality, judgement, and responsibility — the prerogatives of the autonomous individual.[5] It is no wonder that what Orwell presents as Winston's "union" with the Godhead is equivalent to a psychotic breakdown, the disintegration of the personality. Winston's journey in the Ministry of Love — both a bureaucratic Ministry and the Ministry of Priesthood where he is taught to love and 'minister to' the ruling Divinity — is a cruel, bitter parody of the mysticism inherent both in the religious and in the totalitarian mentalities — ultimately a savagely bitter comment on man's miscarried search for the sacred.

This does not mean, however, that Orwell would take the materialist's contemptuous or condescending attitude to the human being's search for the spiritual. We feel great sympathy for Winston, who is a seeker, a pilgrim on the journey to Truth, a man with an undeniably spiritual dimension. As a matter of fact, Winston is doing well as long as he is in search of the "good" on his own terms, through his relationship to other human beings. When we meet him in the first chapter, he is on his way up a staircase, and throughout Parts 1 and 2 we should picture him ascending the 'ladder' of love, self-expression, and liberation. Part 3, which takes place almost entirely in the Ministry of Love, is the parody, the reversal of this process. He is broken down step by step, until in Room 101 he has reached "as deep down as it was possible to go" (244). In the hands of O'Brien he undergoes the spiritual experience of conversion, until he is re-made into the image of Big Brother, and made to live up to the Party's superhuman, and therefore inevitably *inhuman*, standard of the "good." In his essays, and indirectly in *Goldstein's Book*, Orwell reproaches his contemporaries, particularly his Adversary, the Leftist intellectual, for making a ludicrous mistake. Trying to get away from the 'non-scientific' ideals of religion, he is unaware of the psychological vacuum left behind, and falls into the trap of fanaticism and mysticism while giving his soul to the political dictator.[6] Orwell would therefore insist that what Richard Rees called the eternal values of the sacred should be re-defined as human, anthropo-centred values, depending on the human being's relationship to another human being, and not to a standard that is transcendent, superhuman — whether this standard is Hitler's Law of Nature, Stalin's Law of History (Berger 86–87), or what the Church has defined as the transcendental realm of the sacred.

Orwell's "Spirit of Man" and the "Human Form Divine"

As a parody of the totalitarian mentality, *Nineteen Eighty-Four* is also a warning against a system based on the mystical adoration of the 'sacred' leader and the fanatical hatred of the 'satanic' enemy. But in addition to this warning, has the satirist anything positive to suggest about our attitude to good and evil? Unlike his Existentialist confrères, Orwell feels we are

in need of spiritual, moral values that are universally acceptable, that Man "is not likely to salvage civilization unless he
can evolve a system of good and evil which is independent of
heaven and hell" (v. 3, 127).

The question remains as to how Orwell would define the spiritual without recourse to the religious dimension. I believe there
is a sequence of three significant scenes in the novel that allude
to the biblical concept of Man being created in the image of his
Maker, where Orwell the secular humanist explores the spiritual
dimension in relation to the "spirit of Man," a force in us capable of creating an image of God according to what is highest
in the human being, the ideal of the highest self. In this context, Orwell's concept of "the inner heart, whose workings were
mysterious even to yourself, [and that] remained impregnable"
(148) to external forces, is not unlike Blake's "Divine Image"
that resides in our heart, in "the human form divine."

In the first of these three scenes Winston ponders the connection between three mysteries to be revealed in the future:
his own essential self, the meaning of the Party slogans, and
Big Brother's essential nature, so far concealed by the "smile
. . . beneath the dark moustache" (92).

> The past was dead, the future was unimaginable. What certainty
> had he that a single human creature now living was on his side?
> And what way of knowing that the dominion of the Party would
> not endure *for ever*? Like an answer, the three slogans on the
> white face of the Ministry of Truth came back to him:
>
> > War is Peace
> > Freedom is Slavery
> > Ignorance is Strength
>
> He took a twenty-five cent coin out of his pocket. There too, in
> tiny clear lettering, the same slogans were inscribed, and on the
> other face of the coin the head of Big Brother. Even from the
> coin the eyes pursued you (27).

The second scene exploring this image is the one at the end
of Part 1, where Winston repeats the same gesture: "just as he
had done a few days earlier, he slid a coin out of his pocket and
looked at it. The face gazed up at him, heavy, calm, protecting:
but what kind of smile was hidden beneath the dark moustache?
Like a leaden knell the words came back at him: War is Peace

Freedom is Slavery   Ignorance is Strength" (92). What is implied in these two scenes with the coin is the concept of Man being created in the image of his Maker, an allusion to the parable where Christ explains the difference between worldly and spiritual powers to his disciples: "Shew me a penny. Whose image and subscription hath it? They answered and said, Caesar's. And he said unto them, Render therefore unto Caesar the things which be Caesar's, and unto God the things which be God's" (Luke 20: 21–25). While the coin has the "image and subscription" of Caesar, Man, being created in the image of his Maker, has the "image and subscription" of God. Therefore Man's first allegiance is to God, to his spiritual self, and not to the worldly powers of Caesar.

The image Winston sees on the coin is the image of Big Brother, a Caesar who demands to be worshipped both as a worldly and a spiritual authority. In order to remain true to the "spirit of Man," Winston should be able to pay his dues to Caesar and keep his "incorruptible inner self" (v. 4, 402), his "inner heart" (148) that is the core of his spiritual being, intact. The point in these two scenes is that when Winston ponders his essential being in relation to the image of his Maker, he does, in fact, ponder about Man making God in his own image, his choice of the highest good he is going to model himself upon. The perversion of Oceania derives from humanity's mistaken choice to accept God as Power (a divinity who shows remarkable resemblance to Carl Jung's "God of Terror which [also] dwells in the human soul" [*Civilization* 235]). In the second scene with the coin Winston still resists the image of Caesar gazing at him from the coin: he refuses to admit into his heart the God of Power because his own essential, highest self, his "inner heart," is still intact.

Finally, in the third scene in this sequence, which is also the last scene in the novel, Winston comes to the recognition that he has been made over into the image of Caesar, that he is unable to maintain his inner self. We realize that this was the "nameless horror . . . embedded in the future," a loss that follows from the essential nature of Big Brother, revealed as the cruelty and treachery of the God of Power. In the last scene Orwell brings to a conclusion Winston's original questions about his essential self and its reflection in the Divine Image in his breast, as Winston gazed up at the enormous face. Forty years it had taken him to learn what kind of smile was hidden beneath the dark moustache. O cruel, needless misunderstanding. O stubborn, self-willed exile from the loving breast! Two gin-scented tears trickled down the sides of his nose. But it was all right, everything was all right, the struggle was finished. He had won the victory over himself. He loved Big Brother (256).

To "love" Big Brother means to admit Caesar, who demands to be worshipped as the God of Power, into the "inner heart": Winston's "victory" over his old self is tantamount to the defeat of the "human form divine," of his highest self which made him "the last guardian of the human spirit," of the "spirit of Man."

In his essays Orwell warns repeatedly that the modern world's worship of the God of Power leads to the breakdown of all the moral values essential for the salvaging of our civilization. But how would Orwell define these universal values, without recourse to an absolute good or the sacred? It is probably in his delightful essay on Gandhi that he comes closest to revealing the norm or standard often hinted at, yet left hidden, in works of satire. Here he emphasizes that the "other worldly" and the "humanistic ideal" are incompatible. As a humanist, he is suspicious of Gandhi's "non-attachment" as merely "a desire to escape from the pain of living, and above all from love, which sexual or non-sexual is hard work" (v. 4, 528). Like Camus at the end of *The Plague*,[7] Orwell concludes that it takes greater courage to attempt to be human by participating in the "process of life" than to give it all up by aspiring to sainthood: "Many people genuinely do not wish to be saints, and it is probable that some who achieve or aspire to sainthood never felt the temptation to be human beings" (v. 4, 528). Although Orwell expresses personal appreciation for Gandhi, he is ironic about Gandhi's pursuit of the sacred: "No doubt, alcohol, tobacco and so forth are things a saint must avoid, but sainthood is also something human beings should avoid" (v. 4, 527).

A study of Orwell's essays and fiction should indicate that he was far from being obsessed by the demonic. In *Nineteen Eighty-Four* he parodies the totalitarian mentality precisely for *setting up* the category of the 'satanic' for the opponent in order that it could set up the category of the 'sacred' for the leader. Isaac Deutscher is quite off the mark, then, when blaming Orwell for presenting the world in terms of black and white and frightening the reader with the bogeyman of a demonic enemy ("*1984*"). Orwell in effect parodies Big Brother for doing so. *Goldstein's Book* reveals that Orwell, the secular humanist, condemns the "secular religion" of the totalitarian mentality because surreptitiously it re-introduced the categories for sacred and satanic. Having set out to "indicate by parodying them, the intellectual implications of totalitarianism (v. 4, 520), Orwell presents us with an unforgettable image of a world that assumes its demonic dimensions through a system where the mystical adulation of the 'sacred' is balanced by the cruel persecution of the 'satanic.' Orwell's image of the demonic world of Oceania contains a secular humanist's acute analysis and forceful condemnation of the totalitarian mentality.

Notes

[1] Christopher Small, in *The Road to Miniluv*, touches upon this problem when he raises the question "what actually is being parodied: Is it a parody of religion in terms of the totalitarian State, or of the State in terms of religion?" (165).

[2] According to the seventeenth-century Protestant mystic, Jacob Boehme, "From God flows his will which is revealed through the Word and God is made known to us as the Trinity . . ." (qtd. in Price 73).

[3] Orwell's attitude to this image of the "oceanic" is similar to Freud's, who acknowledges that the "oceanic feeling . . . of something limitless, unbounded" is the "source of religious energy which is seized upon by the various Churches and religious systems." He concludes, however: "I cannot discover this feeling in myself" (v. 21, 64).

[4] In spite of his admission that he was no theologian, Orwell was familiar with the images associated with mysticism. For example, in his book review of Karl Adam's *The Spirit of Catholicisim*, Orwell juxtaposes Adam's open emphasis on the mystical aspects of religious faith with the more rational emphasis advocated by Father Martindale's *The Roman Faith* (v. 1, 102–105, 109).

That the one-to-one relationship between the human soul and the Infinite occupied Orwell's mind is witnessed by *A Clergyman's Daughter*, where the narrative culminates in the heroine's loss of religious faith. In previous scenes Dorothy discusses mysticism with her father's assistant (292) and ponders over the difference between religious worship and the pantheistic "nature mysticism" her clergyman father frowns upon.

Orwell's perception of the mystical is also illustrated in his book review discussing Edith Sitwell's approach to Pope's poetry. Orwell

expresses surprise that "Miss Sitwell comes to Pope for the same enchantment as one finds in people like Francis Thomson or Gerald
Manley Hopkins" (v. 1, 45). There is a clear sense of Orwell's own
position; he would regard Pope's classicist sensibilities dictated by
the Age of Reason as diametrically opposed to the religious-mystical
sensibilities of Thomson or Hopkins. That Orwell admired the enchantment offered by the latter is made clear in his BBC broadcast of
1941, when he offered careful exegesis of a poem by Hopkins, based
on the poet's religious vision of reality (v. 2, 157–161). As for Francis
Thomson, the other poet he associates here with mysticism, Orwell
was undoubtedly familiar with *The Hound of Heaven* (which describes
man's relationship to the Infinite as a love chase — one of the best
examples of mystical poetry for the imagery of Spiritual Marriage).
Gordon Comstock, for example, refers to the Hound of Heaven ironically (*KAF* 719).

[5] Orwell's essays offer evidence that he considered the relinquishing
of the self in mysticism reprehensible. He says, for example, that
Henry Miller "performed the essential Jonah act of allowing himself
to be swallowed, remaining passive, accepting . . . . It is a species of
quietism, implying either complete unbelief or else a *degree of belief
amounting to mysticism*" (v. 1, 572). He also blames his Adversary
for relinquishing his freedom as "an autonomous individual" when
identifying with a "nation or other unit in which he has chosen to
sink his own individuality" (v. 3, 411).

[6] Orwell comments on this several times in his essays: "All the
loyalties and superstitions that the intellect had seemingly banished
could come rushing back under the thinnest disguises. Patriotism,
religion, Empire, military glory — all in one word, Russia. . . . God
— Stalin. The devil — Hitler. Heaven — Moscow. Hell — Berlin"
(v. 1, 565). He also points out that the Communist Party was "simply
something to believe in. Here was a Church, an army, an orthodoxy,
a discipline" (v. 1, 565).

[7] In *The Plague* Camus compares Taroux's ambition to become
a saint and Rieux's desire for "simply being a man." He concludes
that "heroism and sanctity" are indeed "less ambitious" than "simply
being a man" (209).

Part III

Confronting the Demonic in Totalitarianism — Orwell and Contemporaries

If we recognize that *Goldstein's Book* is a key to Orwell's satire, it becomes clear that his diagnosis of the evils of the "secular religion" of Oceania reflects the point of view of the secular humanist who condemns and ridicules the totalitarian system for surreptitiously re-introducing the categories of the sacred and the demonic. Nevertheless, when Orwell so convincingly portrays the gratuitous, self-perpetuating spiral of destructiveness and cruelty in Oceania, and when through the clearly recognizable network of allusions he so forcefully reminds us that this spiral was endemic to the systems that serve as the historical models for Oceania, he presents us with a curious dilemma. Do we have terms to deal with this spiral in the post-Enlightenment humanists' modern, scientific, secular vocabulary? Could we define and confront the unprecedented scale and intensity of cruelty produced by the totalitarian superstates without recourse to the concept of radical evil, a concept that carries traditional association with the demonic realm of the superhuman? Or could the twentieth-century humanists hold on to the Enlightenment philosophers' secular denial of the superhuman only by also denying that the unstoppable destruction and victimization endemic to the practice of the totalitarian superstates *are* radically evil? In other words, should we seek for the definition of the complex and alarming phenomenon before us in such a way that it can be accommodated within the parameters of our conceptual framework, or do we begin with the acute analysis of the phenomenon even if it forces us to rethink or reformulate our inherited conceptual framework?

Although reading many of Orwell's literary critics may sometimes make us think that Orwell must be the only twentieth-century writer on totalitarianism who feels compelled to struggle with this dilemma, such is really not quite the case. Nor does the sheer fact of struggling with this dilemma need to lead to cosmic despair and political apathy. But to address these assumptions so very central to the conundrum in Orwell criticism, we should examine Orwell's diagnosis of totalitarianism, not in isolation as many of his critics have done so far, but in its broader context of the twentieth-century humanist's dilemma in the intellectual landscape of his time. This context may be viewed from three perspectives.

1. How do Orwell's contemporaries — Hannah Arendt, Carl Jung, Wilhelm Reich, Nathan Leites, William Golding — articulate and explain the unprecedented scale and intensity of terror in the totalitarian superstates from the perspectives of political science, history, psychology, or psycho-history? How do the more recent interpretations of totalitarianism by Friedrich and Brzezinsky, Jeane Kirkpatrick, and Daphne Patai compare with Orwell's diagnosis?

2. How does Orwell's literary expression of the totalitarian state's attempt to achieve total control over the individual psyche compare with works on the same theme by Thomas Mann, Camus, and Sartre — writers in the mainstream of twentieth-century fiction in the mode of psychological realism?

3. How does Orwell's position on the transformation of human beings into cogs in the totalitarian state machine compare with the views of Huxley in the framework of the Utopian-dystopian tradition?

Part III will examine these three questions in Chapters 10, 11, and 12 respectively.

Chapter 10

The Demonic —
Psycho-Historical Interpretations

The Demonic:
Psychological and Theological Connotations

Charges of hysteria[1] and demonic obsession appear over and over in Orwell criticism (Deutscher, Bertrand Russell, Rai). It is a salient manifestation of the Orwell conundrum that a secular humanist who so consistently condemns the application of "other worldly" standards to politics or literature (v. 4, 344), a writer who so assiduously attacks those who give in to pessimism and despair (v. 3, 82, 282), is reproached by his critics for being preoccupied, even obsessed, with the demonic, and for giving in to cosmic despair and political apathy at the end of his life (Bonifas, Patai, Reilly, Connelly). Implied in this reproach is the charge that as a result of despair Orwell ended up with a flawed, inconsistent, or fragmented vision of politics, human nature, and our position in the universe. What makes this aspect of the conundrum even more puzzling is that in spite of their divergence on other issues, the majority of his critics agree on these accusations in connection with Orwell's last and deservedly most famous work, *Nineteen Eighty-Four*. That so many also pass a negative aesthetic judgement on the novel based on their assumption of Orwell's diseased, inconsistent, or fragmented vision of the world is the final consequence of a series of unexamined or mistaken assumptions.

If we are ready to examine Orwell's position not in isolation but in the context of the intellectual landscape of his time, it will become evident that his diagnosis of the evils of totalitarianism is not inspired by his personal obsessions. Confronted with the events of two world wars, the hopes and disappointments evoked by the Russian Revolution and the Spanish Civil War, the emergence of the monstrous totalitarian systems, and, by 1945, the introduction of the possibility of a nuclear holocaust, Orwell is certainly not alone among his contemporaries in making us contemplate evil as potentially overpowering: The question is, does his conclusion reflect the apathy of despair, or a determination to struggle for "faith" in the "spirit of Man" by trying to find a language to describe, analyze, and diagnose the disease of totalitarianism as the central crisis of our civilization?

In addressing this question, we have to remember that we are not necessarily compelled to accept the theologian's position on radical evil in order to discuss the phenomenon of the demonic. In his case study on "Demonic Possession in the 17th Century," Freud explains that what to the pre-scientific mind appeared as "demons are bad and reprehensible wishes, derivatives of instinctual impulses that have been repudiated and repressed" (v. 19, 72). Freud also points out that in the Middle Ages these mental entities were projected upon the external world, upon someone "possessed" or upon Satan himself. Freud's position in this instance comes remarkably close to the Jungian explanation of the demonic through the Shadow, that aspect of the personality we are unaware of, or are unwilling to claim, and therefore project on our enemy. Especially in times of wars or crises, "we let loose all [our] destructive impulses in the name and cause of victory for our side. . . . We fight our shadow by fighting our neighbours, on whom we project the *demonic* element" (Ulanov 143). Orwell shows this demonic projection to be central to the various state rituals in the Two Minutes Hate and in Hateweek, where Big Brother projects his own cruelty upon Goldstein or the enemy (17). Orwell also reproaches his Adversary for practising this projection inherent in the "black-white," "we-them" split characteristic of the Doublethink of the 1940s (182).

Although modern psychology may admit that the eruption of aggression may at times be overwhelming, it denies that the tendency for destructiveness or cruelty is endemic to human nature, that human nature is incorrigible. The psychologist's scientific, secular definition of the demonic follows from the Enlightenment philosophers' denial of radical evil, their denial of original sin, and their denial of the entire realm of the supernatural, including the dimensions of both the sacred and the satanic. Grounded in the scientific mindset of modern psychology, the twentieth-century secular humanist's position implies that the sources of the demonic are within the human being exclusively, and consequently not beyond the reach of our consciousness, will, and reason.

By contrast, in a recent fourfold summation of the theologian's position, Arthur McGill describes the demonic as "an agency of superhuman powerfulness, intent on doing evil" (116), (1) characterized by acts that are anti-human, resulting in eruptions of "excessive cruelty, destructiveness or waste." (2) It is also important that these acts are not committed at random, but by "deliberately malicious intent" and (3) their effect is anti-human and superhuman. (4) Finally, in the theologian's definition, the agency of evil reveals its connection with a realm that is the diametric opposite of the absolute good or the sacred (116–124).

The question to be considered is: does Orwell's analysis of the demonic world of Oceania fit the psychologist's or the theologian's interpretation? Admittedly, to draw a clear distinction between theological and psychological connotations is not always simple. One of the difficulties is that, faced with the phenomenon of the totalitarian superstate, the language of writers, even psychologists of Orwell's generation, shows an ambiguity, as if they are unable to remain within the boundaries of the humanist's vocabulary. In his *Civilization in Transition*, Carl Jung, for example, defines the "political mass movements of our time" as either "psychic epidemics" or "mass psychoses." As implied by this medical terminology, Jung does assure us that "the psychopathology of the masses is rooted in the psychopathology of the individual" (*Civilization* 218) — and hence, one would assume, also subject to the same kind of cure. At the same time, he refers to the forces of this disease as "demons," "devilish engines of destruction," in their collective name the powers of "the God of Terror" (*Civilization* 235). Clearly, there is a tension between the humanist's medical terminology that implies the disease is only temporary and subject to cure, and the religious-theological connotations of radical evil as something innate to our nature and ultimately beyond humanist therapy.

Orwell's *Nineteen Eighty-Four* is certainly not unique among the works of its time in making the reader perceive that in their effect and scope totalitarian forces stay continuously on the verge of the overpowering, the more-than-human. Nevertheless, he never questions his responsibility to struggle against these forces, precisely by drawing attention to their undeniably demonic power:

On the whole the English intelligentsia have opposed Hitler, but only at the price of accepting Stalin. Most of them are perfectly ready for dictatorial methods, secret police, systematic falsifications of history, etc., so long as they feel that it is on "our" side. . . . One can't be sure . . . that the common people won't think ten years hence as the intellectuals do now. I *hope* they won't, I even trust they won't, but if so it will be at the cost of a *struggle*. If one simply proclaims that all is for the best and doesn't point to the *sinister symptoms*, one is merely helping to bring totalitarianism along (v. 3, 178).

In fact, Orwell's medical-humanistic imagery is quite consistent, even when describing the "sinister" power of the "non-rational" in a world that is "suffering from some kind of mental disease which must be diagnosed before it can be cured," a situation where "one must continue to struggle" (v. 4, 289).

Oceania in the Light of Political Science

That Orwell's Oceania is an accurate picture of totalitarianism[2] is borne out not only by first-hand accounts of terror in Hitler's Germany (Bettelheim), or by the many "dissident Soviet and Eastern European intellectuals' . . . [astonishment] that an Englishman who never set foot in Eastern Europe could describe with such accuracy the climate of terror" (Rodden 211), but also by a good number of scholarly works in political science. Friedrich and Brzezinsky's paradigm, for example, seems to be tailor-made for Oceania when it defines a totalitarian system as having 4 elements: (1) a totalist ideology (in *Nineteen Eighty-Four* Ingsoc); (2) a single Party committed to this ideology, led by one man, the dictator (the Party led by Big Brother); (3) a fully developed secret police (the Thought Police); and (4) monopolistic control over mass communication, weapons, and every aspect of a centralized, planned economy (3–10) (in *Nineteen Eighty-Four* these three controls are represented by the Ministry of Truth, the Ministry of Peace, and the Ministry of Plenty).

Political scientist Jeane Kirkpatrick defines yet another characteristic of a totalitarian government: it "is prepared to use all the government's coercive power to transform economic and social relations, beliefs, values and psychological predispositions," making clear that according to their new ideal, "people matter only as members of a collectivity" (101). Undoubtedly both definitions of the political scientists coincide with Orwell's picture of Oceania. Going even further, the paradigms suggested by the political scientists could have been derived exclusively from *Nineteen Eighty-Four*, had they decided to demonstrate their paradigm through nothing else but Orwell's novel, and to use the novel as nothing else but a case study, a sourcebook for the key phenomena of totalitarianism. Why, then, do so many of Orwell's literary critics feel that his diagnosis is out of place? Why do critics otherwise as widely divergent in their positions as Bertrand Russell and William Deutscher agree that Orwell's diagnosis reveals a preoccupation with, and despair in the face of, the demonic?

To understand this aspect of the Orwell conundrum, we should point out that although the paradigm suggested by Friedrich, Brzezinsky, and Kirkpatrick could well have been derived from *Nineteen Eighty-Four*, for obvious reasons, what *Nineteen Eighty-Four* tells us about totalitarian systems could not have been derived exclusively from the political scientists' paradigm. Such paradigms, quite naturally, lack not only the emotional charge of a great work of fiction, but also the excitement of discovery characteristic of the first-hand observers of totalitarian terror, the passionate curiosity driving the first diagnosticians, who, together with Winston Smith, were propelled by the desire to find out not only "how," but also "why." Significantly, Camus's *The Plague*, Golding's *Lord of the Flies*, as well as psycho-historical interpretations of totalitarianism provided by Carl Jung, Wilhelm Reich, Nathan Leites, and Hannah Arendt agree with Orwell's *Nineteen Eighty-Four* in describing totalitarian terror as an escalating, self-perpetrating dynamism, spelled out in the spiral images of "explosion," "chain reaction," "avalanche" — images of the "overpowering forces" of physical and mental illness. In fact, what many literary critics of *Nineteen Eighty-Four* overlook is that Orwell is very much a man of his times when he describes the terror and destructiveness of the totalitarian system as a demonic spiral. The plot of the novel is a case in point.

The Demonic Spiral:
Orwell, Arendt, Jung, Reich, Leites, Golding

Although in the political satire Winston's journey carries the allegorical significance of a "tour aboli," the torture pilgrimage of the religious conversion experience acted out in the "secular religion" of totalitarianism, this journey also offers the suspense, the surprise, the unexpected reversal of the psychological and political thriller, a genre associated with the verisimilitude of psychological realism.   Nevertheless, the plot of *Nineteen Eighty-Four* has been seriously questioned by critics who argue that the motivation of O'Brien, the Masterplotter, is not credible psychologically.[3] Indeed, the reader does not need to be a professional critic to ask, as does Winston himself, why O'Brien, who had been fully aware of Winston's every move and thought over the past seven years, did not arrest him at his first act of deviation, or indeed at the first thoughtcrime that signified the wish for such deviation. Winston knows, the moment he opens his diary, that for this single act he could be condemned to forced labour for any number of years, even for life (11). In a society without fixed laws, any act of deviation can be punished with utmost severity. What is more, 'culprits' could be chosen entirely at random.[4] Why then, does O'Brien deem it important to play the seven-year-long cat and mouse game with Winston?

O'Brien answers this question at the time he reveals the secret Winston has been searching for all his life. In a state where God is worshipped as Power, what used to be the means has now become the end: the "object of power is power" (227) and to assert power you have to make another suffer (229). There is no doubt that the diabolic motivation of O'Brien, the mastermind behind the intrigue, is shockingly unexpected and that it would be found less than acceptable as a character's psychological motivation in the framework of a modern work in the mode of psychological realism. But, even though Winston could have been eliminated without any greater effort right at the beginning of the "plot," in the framework of the dystopian satire it is essential for the satirist to establish that Winston has been nursed, as it were fattened for the kill, by the State. Only by letting Winston first fulfill his human potential can O'Brien have the full satisfaction of conducting his gradual, programmed breakdown in the Ministry of Love, which is the State's experimental laboratory in total domination. This controversial, 'unmotivated' plot takes us to the very heart of the satirist's target: the *perpetuum mobile* of 'unmotivated,' compulsive victimization, the gratuitous and escalating evil that spells out a demonic spiral, the movement Orwell shows to be endemic to the totalitarian system. The controversial plot also takes us back to the two issues central to the Orwell conundrum: First, is the 'unmotivated' plot an expression of oversight, Orwell's uneven skill as a literary artist? Second, is his diagnosis of the demonic element in totalitarianism the expression of his unique, pathological obsession?

In addressing the first question, we should realize that images that spell out this demonic spiral are central to the totalitarian mentality delineated by the novel as a whole, and they naturally reinforce the plot predicated on the Party's gratuitous destructiveness and cruelty. The drama O'Brien enacted with Winston, with the grinding "boot stamping on the human face — for ever" (230), finds its complement in the "chain reaction" in Room 101 where each victim is to betray new and new victims. This movement also coincides with the compulsive spiral of the abnegation of Reason in Doublethink (the greater the abnegation, the greater the faith; the greater the faith, the greater is the demand for further abnegation, and so the spiral goes *ad infinitum*). The principle of the *reductio ad absurdum* of the vocabulary in Newspeak suggests the spiral of entropy. (The more diminished the vocabulary, the more limited the consciousness becomes. The more curtailed the consciousness becomes, the more it will encourage the diminishing, the ultimate elimination, of the vocabulary). The combined effect of all these images suggests the unravelling of the organic structure into its own ingredients, the self-perpetuating series of implosions at the very centre of the atom, aiming at the destruction of the nucleus, "the inner heart," the "incorruptible inner self" of the already 'atomized,' isolated individual (Winston has sensations "like wrenching a piece out of his own brain" [128], "his body being wrenched out of shape" [196], and of "a devastating explosion, or what seemed like an explosion, though it was not certain whether there was any noise" [221]). In fact, one may argue that the combined effect of all these movements — images of grinding, wrenching, explosion, implosion, chain reaction — acts out, on a symbolic level, a demonic spiral of the unstoppable destructiveness of the atom bomb. Although apparently restrained, the bomb's destructive force makes its presence felt throughout the totalitarian world system that was set up under its aegis as a form of "Death Worship."

Of course, the consistency and evocative power of Orwell's literary effects do not settle the second question at the heart

of the Orwell conundrum, the charge that his vision is pathological, expressive of a personal obsession with the demonic. In
order to refute this charge, we should simply take a look at
the diagnosis of the same phenomenon by his contemporaries,
also trying to come to terms with the compulsive-demonic spiral
they see as endemic to the totalitarian system. Thus, according
to Carl Jung, "the madman and the mob are both moved by
impersonal, *overpowering* forces." Consequently, "the gigantic
catastrophes that threaten us today are . . . *psychic events.* . . .
Instead of being at the mercy of wild beasts, earthquakes, land-
slides and inundations, modern man is battered by the elemental forces of his own psyche. This is the World power that
vastly exceeds all other powers on earth" (*Civilization* 235).
When Orwell locates this potential psychic catastrophe in the
loss of faith that makes us worship the cruel God of Power, he
is remarkably close to Jung, who argues that "The Age of Enlightenment, which stripped nature and human institutions of
gods, overlooked the *God of Terror* which dwells in the human
soul" (*Civilization* 235, my italics).

As for the eruption and escalation of these "impersonal, overpowering forces," a number of Orwell's contemporaries describe
their effect in terms similar to Orwell's demonic spiral. In his
influential *Mass Psychology of Fascism*, Wilhelm Reich defines
this spiral in Freudian terms. Since tyrannical political systems
repress sexuality and introduce a quasi-religious substitute for
sexual excitement, Reich points out that there is a strange "co-
hesion of sadistic brutality and mystical sentiments" (137) in
the fascist personality. When he attributes the sadistic urges to
the repression of the sexual instinct, he also returns to Freud's
concept of the relationship between renunciation and guilt as a
spiral movement: each time Ego renounces an instinctual drive,
Superego gets more and more demanding, inducing a greater
and greater sense of guilt, and, in turn, a need for greater and
greater renunciation.

In his study of the fascist personality in the *Psychology of
Political Attitudes*, Nathan Leites offers another psychological
approach to such a spiral. In accounting for the fascist victimizer's excessive and escalating aggressiveness towards his victim,
Leites draws attention to the authoritarian spirit in German
education where childhood aggressive acts "against powerful
father objects have been severely interfered with" (288). Consequently, the fascist personality developed a "compulsive

character," expressed in the "insatiability" of aggression towards those who are weaker. Leites cites the example of prison or concentration camp guards picking upon the least likely offender among their victims. He notes that in the camps "the completed acts of aggression against relatively powerless objects were far more frequent" and that "the SS committed atrocities against unduly exhausted members." The spiral delineates the "insatiability" of aggression, because "as each successful aggression diminishes the power of the target, it increases the probability of subsequent acts of aggression against it" (288–289).

It is a similar *perpetuum mobile* of escalating and self-perpetuating aggression against increasingly more powerless victims that Hannah Arendt points to as the central characteristic of Hitler's and Stalin's regimes, where terror is no longer a means to an end:

> The extraordinarily bloody terror during the initial stage of totalitarian rule serves indeed the exclusive purpose of defeating the opponent and rendering all further opposition impossible; *but total terror is launched only after this initial stage has been overcome* and the regime no longer has anything to fear from the opposition. In this context it has been frequently remarked that in such a case the means have become the end, but this is after all only an admission, in paradoxical disguise, that the category "the end justifies the means" no longer applies, that terror has lost its "purpose," that it is no longer the means to frighten people (440, my italics).

Both Arendt and Orwell demonstrate that in the hands of the totalitarian dictator the means *becomes* the end. Arendt's analysis is also in accord with Orwell's "plot" in the novel. Winston and the other scapegoats are not being victimized to punish them for a past transgression, or even to prevent a possible transgression in the future. The object of terror is terror. And the expression of power is to make others suffer. Neither the gratuitous, self-perpetuating aggression, nor its mechanism in the Ministry of Love and Room 101, is indicative of the satirist's pathological, nightmarish imagination: rather, they give powerful literary expression to Orwell's brilliant insight into the totalitarian system's "real secret, the concentration camps, [and torture chambers that fulfill the function of] laboratories in the experiment of total domination" (Arendt 436). (Once more Orwell's insight coincides with Arendt's seminal 1950 study on the origins of totalitarianism.)

Entropy as the Reverse of the Demonic Spiral

Arendt uses copious documentation from Hitler's and Stalin's archives to show that each time a dictator established and entrenched his position, outsiders accustomed to looking for enlightened self-interest in every political action expected the cessation of acts of terror against victims. In fact, it was precisely at such times that the dictator would escalate the terror. Thus, it was *after* Hitler had vanquished his political opponents within that he turned to the persecution of the Jews by setting up concentration camps; had he been able to complete his "final solution," there is evidence he was ready to turn to the persecution of other scapegoats: the mentally ill and the terminally ill were next on his agenda. In Stalin's case, after eliminating the bourgeoisie, he singled out the kulaks; at his death it was found he had an agenda of persecuting, deporting, and gradually eliminating one national minority after another. Arendt concludes that terror is the style, "the very essence of [the totalitarian] form of government" (344). In full accordance with O'Brien's crucial revelation, Arendt asserts that "Terror continues to be used by totalitarian regimes even when its psychological aims are achieved: its real horror is that it reigns over a completely subdued population" (344).

In her more recent study, Daphne Patai introduces the game theory as a clue to Winston and O'Brien's relationship. She points out, accurately, that "mastery and domination over another human being cannot be permanent; rather, these must be continually reestablished. It is in the exercise of power that power comes into being" (235). Yet, Patai also argues, even if "Orwell can successfully evoke the inescapable oppressiveness of Airstrip One . . . he cannot convincingly explain Oceania's inner dynamics, which tend toward entropy" (237). When suggesting that Orwell's diagnosis is inaccurate, Patai overlooks the fact that the principle of entropy, the tendency of a system towards disintegration, is, in fact, endemic to both the Fascist and the Stalinist models of Orwell's satire. Indeed, domination is a process that carries the seeds of its own failure: ultimately, when the victimizer has fulfilled his aims by breaking the will of the victim, he no longer has any outlet for his energies. As M. Grieffenhager points out, "totalitarianism, unlike other dictatorships, by its nature aims at self-disintegration. It carries within itself the germ of self-destruction" (56). One may even speculate that here the principle of entropy, the unstoppable tendency of the system to disintegrate, is simply the reverse phase of the demonic spiral.

The cause-effect relationship between the spiralling of aggression and the unstoppable unravelling of the system that has gained its definition through such a spiral, is demonstrated most memorably in another work of fiction of the period, William Golding's *Lord of the Flies*. In it, Golding offers the classical paradigm for this two-way process, acted out by a group of schoolboys shipwrecked on a southern island. Jack, the dictator, comes to power because he is the only one who finds an answer to his companions' dilemma: the boys' night-time fear and insecurity, or, more precisely, their unnamed fear of death. Jack recognizes that the only time he is not afraid is in the moment of aggression. Hence, he wins over the majority of the boys, who join him to hunt, first for animals, then for those members of the group who are, one by one, becoming designated "outsiders." Unable to find escape from their own fear of getting hurt except in the moment of hurting someone else, the boys' original fear is by now aggravated by their sense of guilt, which can be relieved only, and even then only temporarily, by repeated acts of aggression. Therefore Jack, the dictator, has no choice but to make the boys go on killing one another, until they 'burn up' their island, in reality their own psyche, destroying their individuality and their community at the same time.

An incisive diagnostician of Hitler's and Stalin's versions of totalitarianism, Carl Jung also draws attention to the presence of the demonic in the collective self: "If people crowd together and form a mob, the dynamisms of collective man are let loose — beasts or *demons* that lie dormant in every person until he is part of the mob" (*Civilization* 231). Also, just like Orwell, Jung sees the essence of the demonic as an unstoppable "chain reaction" of aggression: "For the group, because of its unconscious, has no freedom of choice, and so psychic activity runs on in it like an uncontrolled force of nature. There is thus set going a *chain reaction* that comes to stop only in a catastrophe" (*Civilization* 236, my italics).

The Source of the Demonic Spiral

The works of Orwell's contemporaries confirm his diagnosis that the scope and effect of the terror endemic to totalitarian systems assumes demonic proportions, even that, at a casual glance it displays what the theologian defined as the first attribute of the demonic, the eruption of excessive and gratuitous destructiveness and cruelty. But to determine the source of this eruption, we should take a closer look at the meeting between mob and leader. Does the dictator represent the theologian's "agency of superhuman powerfulness, intent on doing evil," not at random but by deliberately malicious design (116)?

Central to Jung's analysis of how the leader of mass movements comes to power is his concept of the Shadow, that aspect of our personality we deny or dare not face in ourselves. He also points out that "in Hitler every German should have seen his own worst danger . . . the overwhelming power drive of the shadow" (*Civilization* 221). According to Jung, among patients in an asylum none are more dangerous than those experiencing fear and insecurity, since the diseased, weakened psyche is particularly liable to compensate through acts of aggression, or through identifying with an aggressive leader. Hence it was "defeat and social disaster that increased the herd instinct of Germany" (219) and it was the "individual's feeling of weakness, indeed of nonexistence" that was "compensated by the eruption of hitherto unknown desire for power" (*Civilization* 223).

So far Jung's explanation coincides with some fundamental insights expressed in *Goldstein's Book*, explaining how the Inner Party was able to come to power. Already rendered weak by their loss of religious faith and the concomitant loss of moral values, the masses were to experience fear and insecurity induced by the protracted wars in the 1950s (170). By then they were ready to compensate for their sense of powerlessness by worshipping power and aggression personified in the dictator and his cohorts, who came to the top by borrowing the insights and methods of earlier totalitarian systems. Orwell makes clear that the slogans themselves were borrowed from Stalin: the methods of terror and persecution from *both* Hitler and Stalin: "Fascism is often loosely equated with sadism, but nearly always by people who see nothing wrong in the most slavish worship of

Stalin. . . . All of them are worshipping power and successful cruelty" (v. 3, 257).

In a 1940 essay Orwell also remarks on the charismatic fascist dictator who makes a direct appeal to the people's irrational, religious forces by demanding from them adulation and self-sacrifice: "All the great dictators have enhanced their power by imposing intolerable burdens on their peoples. Whereas Socialism and even capitalism in a more grudging way, have said to the people, 'I offer you a good time', Hitler said to them, 'I offer you struggle, danger and death', and as a result, a whole nation flings itself at his feet" (v. 2, 29). Jung also notes that "the dictator State has one great advantage over bourgeois reason: along with the individual it swallows up his religious forces" (*Civilization* 218) and in "the deification of the State and the dictator" it is religion that "reappears — evilly distorted" (*Civilization* 259).

Still in agreement with Orwell's analysis, Jung points out that the idol who is worshipped for his "successful cruelty" represents the mirror image of the worshippers in their own obsession with fear and powerlessness. Jung, however, also feels that in comparison to his followers, the leader is the one who has the "*least resistance*, the least sense of responsibility and, because of his inferiority, the greatest will to power. He will let loose everything that is ready to burst forth, and the mob will follow with the irresistible force of an *avalanche*" (*Civilization* 259, my italics). Ann Ulanov, a follower of Jung, confirms that "the person who is made leader . . . is the weakest of the group . . . because he lacks an ego of sufficient strength" (143).

At this point, it seems that Orwell's Big Brother parts company with the weak Jungian leader. While Jung presents the great dictators of his time as psychological weaklings who have risen to power by responding spontaneously to the irrational fears and needs of the mob, Orwell presents Big Brother as a systematic thinker who has studied the totalitarian systems of the 1940s, and, based on this study, made reasonable preparations for the future. Significantly, he is also far more horrifying than Jung's dictator because he is not alone. If he has a physical existence at all, he is one of the Inner Party, a group of faceless "executives" who use his image as an icon to be worshipped by the masses. In the person of O'Brien, Jung's "God of Terror" stokes the diabolic furnace of the state machine with the cold impersonality of the contemporary efficiency expert.

Human Source — Superhuman Effect?

Of course, the 'sane,' scientifically minded psychologist would now immediately point out that all the members of the Inner Party are simply insane, that they are a coven worshipping naked, brutal power institutionalized and elevated to the status of religion. Through their thirst for unlimited power, they are all victims of demonic possession, whereby a particular "natural part of the psyche [comes to] assume demonic form [because] it usurps the place of the whole." This disproportion, which takes the form of "manic excess" (Ulanov 39), deprives the patient's ego of the strength needed to create inner balance and to deal with the external world of reality.

At this point, however, Orwell makes us ask, what is reality? According to O'Brien, "reality is inside the skull" (228), and since the Party has absolute control over the mind, it assumes the prerogative of deity. In *Goldstein's Book* we see indeed that the Party has the power to annihilate the world with the help of the atom bomb. It is also capable of creating the 'new Man': in the process of his torture pilgrimage in the Ministry of Love, Winston is re-made in the image of his Maker. The Party is also able to reproduce its own duality in the children of Oceania, who are brought up to be blindly obedient to Party discipline, while "all their ferocity [is] turned outwards, against enemies of the State" (25). Going even further, Winston himself is capable of becoming a Frankenstein, and creating his own homunculus. In a grotesquely humorous episode in the Ministry of Love, where his task is to produce propaganda, he 'creates' the character of Colonel Ogilvy, the hero of Oceania (44–45). Ogilvy, a figment of Winston's imagination, assumes 'real' existence by having his name entered into official records, in sharp contrast to the vanishing of real identities and existences from the same records. Once a human being is "vaporized" by the Party, he disappears without a trace. Once a fictitious 'hero' is created by the forces of propaganda, he assumes the grotesque existence of Frankenstein's monster. No doubt, in Orwell's description of Oceania, we are constantly reminded of the work of "swift evil intelligences" (v. 2, 109) who seem to display what the theologian describes as the three salient attributes of the demonic: (1) the gratuitous and excessive eruptions of destructiveness and cruelty, (2) the rulers' premeditated design to reduce the masses to the subhuman, and (3) the potentially trans-human effects of the totalitarian state's aspiration to transform human nature and destroy our civilization. Yet, although these sinister examples of the Party's power may evoke in us a sense of the demonic, *Goldstein's Book* makes it quite clear that the source of demonic power resides in the human mind and not in the supernatural. Even if the Party's power may have superhuman effects, its source is shown to be rooted in the aberrations of a particular way of thinking, a particular mentality that is given free reign in Oceania.

Reading "the Book," we are reminded repeatedly to make a clear distinction between human source and demonic, potentially superhuman effect. Thus, the source of the Party's "superhuman powerfulness" is the conspiracy of the leaders of the three superstates against their own people in order to keep them in eternal slavery. The magnitude of the conspiracy is worldwide, indeed "trans-human," yet the agency is simply a group of ruthless executives with more than average intelligence, capable of understanding and manipulating the irrational fears of the average human being. By extension of this thought, should the masses be enlightened as to the real cause of their fear and irrationality, the "superhuman" power of the Inner Party would instantly disappear.

Searching even further to determine the ultimate source of he Inner Party's "superhuman powerfulness," we find that it is the atom bomb that ensures that no change in the social structure is possible from without, and, as a consequence, no change can come from within either. Yet, even if the effect of the bomb is superhuman, the source of this power still resides in the human mind, which had decoded the secrets of Nature; it is a human achievement and its effects should also be within the realm of human responsibility.

Orwell is definitely not alone in his time representing the totalitarian system through the spiralling of cruelty, the inability of the group and the dictator to ever stop the process of terror, the snowball effect, the chain reaction of destruction. That the modern dictator behaves like a conqueror in his own country (Arendt 417), ready to burn up his own land, ultimately himself, has been pointed out by a number of analyses of totalitarian systems *since* the publication of *Nineteen Eighty-Four* (Arendt, Lifton, Grieffenhager). It has also been recognized by Orwell himself in his capacity as political commentator years before his last illness (v. 2, 302). The plot based on O'Brien's revelation of the secret formula of "total" domination as a demonic spiral of terror is not an error in literary judgement. Nor does O'Brien's character, based on the duality between discipline and ferocity, represent Orwell's lack of skills in creating realistic characters. Both the plot and the motivation of the Masterplotter are essential to Orwell's acute psycho-historical analysis of the phenomenon of totalitarianism. As corroborated by several other psycho-historical analyses, the demonic element in Oceania belongs to the disease described, and has little to do with the diagnostician's tuberculosis, his pathological despair, or the hysteria of a personal obsession.

Notes

[1] In his 1988 *Orwell and the Politics of Despair*, Alok Rai interprets Newspeak as a sign of Orwell's "collapse of hope, that perverse deflation which, it is my argument, lies at the root of Orwell's terminal despair" (123).

[2] Of course, the critic who blames Orwell for his hysterical vision of "terminal despair" is often the same one who questions the phenomenon of totalitarianism as such. Alok Rai, for example, considers totalitarianism a purely "emotive metaphor" (18), while in his 1989 "Orwell's Political Myth and Ours," John Nelson argues that Arendt's and Orwell's "myths of totalitarianism and democracy require repair" (39).

In their *Introduction to Government: A Conceptual Approach*, Mark Dickerson and Thomas Flanegan point out that the term "totalitarianism" has become "a contentious one, enmeshed in Cold War polemics," yet "it expresses important truths about the regimes to which it is applied." Therefore, "whatever the future path of political change may be, it is important to record the historical reality of totalitarianism" (202–203).

In his 1972 study on *Totalitarianism*, Leonard Schapiro sums up the controversy in a way that fully vindicates Orwell's use of the term "totalitarian":

> Totalitarianism is a new form of dictatorship which grew up in the conditions of mass democracy after the First World War. It was characterized by the predominance of the Leader of the victorious movement, who, with the aid of his subordinate elite and a manipulated ideology, aimed at total control over state, society and the individual. Leader and elite, by claiming the right to interpret the official ideology . . . in effect embodied both church and state: they subverted the law to their own ends and claimed to control private morality. . . . In National Socialist

Germany and in Stalin's Russia these aims were achieved as nearly, perhaps, as it is ever possible to achieve them (118–119).

[3] See Alan Dutsher's "Orwell and the Crisis of Responsibility," *Contemporary Issues*, 8 (1956), 308–316; George Elliott's "A Failed Prophet," *Hudson Review* 10 (1957), 149–154; Gilbert Bonifas's *George Orwell: L'Engagement* (Paris: Didier editions, 1984); John Wain's "The Last of George Orwell," *20th Century* 155 (Jan. 1954), 71.

[4] In her *Origins of Totalitarianism* Hannah Arendt establishes that in the fully totalitarian state, "[the] innocent and the guilty are equally undesirable":

> Only in the initial stages, when a struggle for power is still going on, are [the totalitarian state's] victims those who can be suspected of opposition. It then embarks upon its totalitarian career with the persecution of the objective enemy, which may be the Jews or the Poles (as in the case of Nazis) or so-called 'counter-revolutionaries' — an accusation which in 'Soviet Russia . . . is established . . . before any question as to the behaviour [of the accused] has arisen at all — who may be people who at any time owned a shop or a house or 'had parents or grandparents who owned such things,' or who had belonged to one of the Red Army occupational forces, or were Russians of Polish origin. Only in its last and fully totalitarian stage are the . . . victims chosen completely at random, even without being accused, declared unfit to live. This new category of 'undesirables' may consist, as in the case of the Nazis, of the mentally ill, persons with lung and heart disease, or in the Soviet Union, of people who happen to have been taken up in that percentage varying from one province to another, which is ordered to be deported. This consistent arbitrariness negates human freedom more efficiently than any tyranny ever could" (432–433).

Chapter 11

The Modern Morality Play of Everyman against the Demonic Forces of Totalitarianism: Thomas Mann, Camus, Sartre, and Orwell on the Theme of Betrayal

As the author of one of the most famous dystopias of our century, Orwell is considered primarily a political writer.[1] Yet, as discussed in Chapter 4, *Nineteen Eighty-Four* is a composite of genres, successfully combining political allegory and psychological realism. In Winston's ordeal the decisive crisis of Orwell's time, the battle between totalitarianism and our civilization, is acted out in the framework of psychomachia, a war conducted between the forces of good and evil in the arena of the individual psyche. Consequently, to refute the charges of pathological despair, fragmented vision, and uneven literary achievement in Orwell's most celebrated work — charges responsible for the strange conundrum in Orwell criticism — we should try to formulate an unbiased and well-modulated definition of Orwell's political and spiritual position by comparing *Nineteen Eighty-Four* to other representative contemporary works of fiction that deal with this crisis in the mode of psychological realism.

The Theme of Betrayal

This chapter proposes a comparison of the literary expression in *Nineteen Eighty-Four* of one of Orwell's central themes, betrayal, with the expression of the same theme in Thomas Mann's "Mario and the Magician," Sartre's "The Wall," and Camus's *The Plague*. What becomes clear at the very first glance of these four works is that in the climactic scene each deals with a "boundary situation," a scene where the individual is faced with a battle of wills between victim and victimizer. Pressed to commit an act of betrayal, the victim here faces a test or trial where he fights not for his life, but for a chance to remain human.

The recurring themes of trial, betrayal, and self-betrayal are salient expressions of a crisis[2] delineated not only by Orwell but also by his three contemporaries in their confrontation with the demonic forces of the totalitarian system and the contagion of the totalitarian mentality. In this confrontation Mann, Sartre, Camus, no less than Orwell, convey to us the secular humanist's shock of being compelled to acknowledge the undeniable evidence of absolute, radical evil, when, as post-Enlightenment 'scientific' thinkers they are no longer able to call upon faith in the absolute good or the sacred. Out of their shock comes their effort to find a psychological vocabulary to diagnose an undeniably demonic phenomenon, the twentieth-century totalitarian state's attempt at the "total" domination, ultimately the transformation, of the individual psyche. Since the "demonic" is originally a theological concept, the phenomenon presents both a challenge for, and resistance to, its 'humanization' in the hands of the four writers in question. As a result, these four 'modern' works of psychological realism also carry surprisingly forceful reminders of the genre of allegory, particularly of the psychomachia of the mediaeval morality play where Good Angel and Bad Angel fight over the soul of Everyman.

Written in 1930, Thomas Mann's "Mario and the Magician" deals with what begins as the mundane experience of a middleclass German family's entertainment in an Italian sea resort. As the narrator describes the performance of the hypnotist, Cipolla, in front of a small-town audience, which not only tolerates but also 'pays for' the performance, we realize that through the metaphor of the theatre, in this case the freak show, Thomas Mann presents us with a parable about the rise of Fascism.

By the end of the story the magician's hypnotic power becomes clearly identified with the fascist dictator's charismatic powers over an entire nation mesmerized by 'magic.' Spellbound by the hypnotist's eyes and by the cracking of his whip, one by one all his subjects are broken. Deprived of their will and soul, each comes to join the "row of puppets" engaged in a grotesque, mechanical dance, all of them lined up on stage by the magician to demonstrate his uncanny power to the others. In fact, the characters' tests add up to "one long series of attacks upon the will power, the loss of compulsion of volition" (496).

The dance of the magician's victims evokes yet another powerful analogy: it is like a mediaeval *danse macabre*, thus creating an association between the dictator's irrational powers and the spell of witchcraft or demonic obsession. The association between the contemporary scene and hell is made even stronger by Mann's reference to the magician using one of the traditional names of Satan — the "betrayer" (503).

The novella culminates in the unexpected reaction of the last victim, young Mario, who is forced to give in, like the others, to the magician. Although he puts up resistance with the full force of all his being, once he falls into a trance, he is compelled to betray the girl he is secretly in love with; he is forced to give away her name in public. As if that were not enough, Mario is compelled to kiss the magician, to mistake the lips of the grotesque, perverted old man for the beautiful young lips of his beloved. Coming out of his spell, however, Mario takes revenge for his humiliation and shoots the magician.

Is Mario guilty? Is the act of murder his redemption? Would he have been damned otherwise? The narrator concludes that in spite of the consequences that Mario will have to suffer for life, the effect of his act of murder is liberation.

Sartre's "The Wall" continues the theme of the battle between victim and victimizer, a battle that also culminates in a test. Will the victim betray another human being? Set against the background of the Spanish Civil War, the story presents the battle of wills between Pablo, an anarchist, and his fascist interrogators. While he watches his comrades being led away to execution, Pablo is told he can be reprieved on condition that he denounces Ramon Gris, his leader. Having made up his mind to die a clean and honourable death, Pablo looks at his captors with contempt. And this is where he gets trapped: "They came for me and brought me back to the two officers. A rat ran out from under my feet and that amused me. I turned to one of the falangistas and said, 'Did you see the rat?'" Then, soon after this incident, still cocky with self-confidence, he turns to his interrogator, "You ought to shave off your moustache, I did" (258).

Convinced that Ramon is hiding with his cousin in town, Pablo sends the fascist officers on a wild-goose chase, telling them to look for Ramon in the cemetery. But the joke reaches an unexpected conclusion. Having quarrelled with his cousin, Ramon indeed took shelter in the cemetery; the falangistas find him exactly where Pablo had suggested. Pablo's whole world collapses; he had won his life but lost himself: "Everything began to spin and I found myself sitting on the floor. I laughed so hard that I cried" (259).

Although it has been customary to regard "The Wall" as Sartre's illustration of the futility of man's struggle in an absurd universe, I would suggest that "The Wall," just like "Mario and the Magician," makes us ask questions about the victim's complicity. Is Pablo guilty? By entering the battle of wills, by taunting his interrogators and sending them on a wild-goose chase, did he not, in effect, succumb to the conditions of his captor's game, the game of domination?

And although Pablo himself is convinced that his playfulness with the interrogator is motivated by defiance, even heroism, is he not also playing a game with himself? Didn't he, subconsciously, want to stay alive even at the price of denouncing his leader? This question is made especially poignant, since the entire idea of the 'joke' occurs to Pablo simultaneously with the sudden, unexpected appearance of the rat between his legs — a symbol, in effect a symptom, of his readiness to commit the act of betrayal.

The rat as a symbol of betrayal and self-betrayal follows us through Winston's and Pablo's trials. It is also there at the trials of the three central characters in Camus's *The Plague*. Here the battle between victim and victimizer takes the form of an individual pitted against a non-human, impersonal force of destruction. The struggle against domination of the three central characters, who are the major fighters against the plague — Rieux, Paneloux, and Tarroux — is their struggle against the fatigue of their own bodies and the temporary flagging or final despair of their own spirits. Betrayal, in their case, would consist of running away, of quitting the fight against the plague — that is, of giving in to the disease. The plague presents the spreading of the fascist mentality as a contagion. This metaphor could also be extended to all forms of the totalitarian mentality, as evidenced by Camus's reference to "the crimes of Stalinism" (qtd. in Lottman 461), and his description of Stalin's Empire as a mentally diseased "universe of trial — terror and trial" ("Prophecy" 3). Carrying the plague microbes the human organism is unable to resist, the rats are a means of laying open, of 'betraying,' the human being to the disease.

Although the victimizer is presented here through the metaphor of an impersonal force, the question of the victims' personal responsibility is also raised by Camus, as the plague becomes a test of their potential for resistance. The novel explores the kinds of resistance possible through the different tests set up for the major characters — Rieux the physician, Paneloux the priest, and Tarroux, the judge's son, who refuses to judge or condemn anyone. It is Tarroux who defines resistance as entering a game, or a match. Even if this game may end in death, the very act of exerting resistance to the disease is equivalent to "winning the match" (237). At the end of the novel the contagion abates as mysteriously as it appeared, but the threat of another outbreak is always with us; it underlies our existence, our condition of being human. The only thing we can do under the circumstances is to recognize the danger, not relax vigilance, not allow ourselves to be 'betrayed' by our condition: "One must do what one can to cease being plague-stricken, and that's the only way we can hope for some peace, or failing that, a *decent death*" (207).

Tarroux's "decent death" reiterates the concept of Pablo's honourable death, a situation where a human being can salvage the essence of human nature only in death. Camus extends this idea in his analysis of Stalin's terror as another form of the plague, concluding that in the universe of terror, where human beings are reduced to will-less objects, the victim's freedom may mean he must die hating the victimizer: "If he dies in refusing to be enslaved, he re-affirms the existence of another kind of human nature" ("Prophecy" 234). Orwell makes the same point. Close to the end of his ordeal in the Ministry of Love, Winston realizes that "to die hating them, that was freedom" (226).

Of course, Winston is not granted his wish. In the course of his 'conversion' he has to learn how to 'convert' love and loyalty to Julia into "love" for Big Brother. In the scene where young Mario is hypnotized into kissing the lips of the magician, as if he were the girl he is in love with, Thomas Mann alludes to the same sinister process inherent in the individual's emotional-sexual transferral of love to the dictator.

Mario's betrayal of the girl he loves has no practical consequences to the girl, only to Mario himself. Pablo's denunciation of his comrade helps the falangistas capture Ramon, but they seem to be just as interested in breaking the will of Pablo, the traitor. Finally, the fact that Winston betrays Julia has absolutely no practical effect on her: she is already captured and broken. Why is it necessary, then, that Mario, Pablo, and Winston be turned into traitors? Why does the victimizer feel that this is his only way of winning the game against the victim, and what is the nature of his game? The name of the game is domination. Once the victim has committed the final act of betrayal, he is no longer himself. Betraying Julia, Winston betrays himself — that is, the essence of what makes him human. Once this is accomplished, he turns into a will-less object, like Mann's "puppets," ready for further denunciations, unable to feel human affection, unable to resist the victimizer. This, once more, agrees with Camus's analysis of Stalin's "Empire," where the chain reaction of denunciations breaks the bond between human beings and reduces them to objects: "In the kingdom of humanity, men are bound by ties of affection; in the Empire of Objects, men are united by mutual accusation ("Prophecy" 235). Once the final tie of affection is broken, the victim will never again resist domination — in fact, he will want to please, to imitate, to become *like* the victimizer.

The battle of wills culminates in the victim's betrayal of another human being, which, as we have seen, is really the act of self-betrayal, the betrayal of what Orwell called the "inner heart," the "incorruptible inner self." Yet, originally, it had been the victimizer-aggressor who had been acting out the role of the betrayer-deceiver. Thomas Mann quite explicitly refers to the Magician as "the betrayer," who, in turn, makes Mario betray the name of his beloved. In Sartre's "The Wall" the fascist officers deceive Pablo. They promise to spare his life if he betrays Ramon, but all along they have no intention of keeping their bargain. They may kill Pablo any day, but first they want him to commit the act of denunciation, to become treacherous like themselves.

But once more, it is in *Nineteen Eighty-Four* that the mirror-like relationship between victim and victimizer is most well worked out. In Chapter 4 we noted that Winston's dread of the rats is connected with something he dreads in his innermost self — the ruthlessness and the uncanny ability of the starved rats to attack where the human being is most vulnerable. But when searching out the individual victim's most characteristic weakness in Room 101, doesn't Big Brother display precisely this ability? We should recognize that the child Winston who snatched away the last piece of chocolate from his starving mother and sister was indeed like the starved rats, but both he and the rats were victimized by the Party's brutality. They were starved deliberately, so that they could be turned into instruments in the hands of the Party. Ultimately, the real face behind the mask-like cage of the rats is the face of Big Brother himself. It is Big Brother who turns his subjects into ferocious, treacherous beings like himself. Winston's final 'atonement' with Big Brother can take place only after he too has committed an act of betrayal.

This mirror-like relationship between victim and victimizer may provide a clue to the focal issue in these four stories. It is the exploration of our vulnerability, the way we may become 'betrayed' to accept the totalitarian mentality, the mentality of the victimizer. At the allegorical level, Orwell's Big Brother, Sartre's fascist interrogator, and Mann's Magician, the Betrayer, are not only characters on the outside. The potential to be like the victimizer dwells within the victim's psyche. When Pablo takes a quick glance at the rat and then looks at the officer, telling him he should shave off his moustache just as Pablo had done, he suddenly sees in the officer a mirror image of his former self. His quick insight into their relatedness is connected with the appearance of the rat, symbol of denunciations and betrayals. This mysterious sense of the connectedness between victim and victimizer is also hinted at in *The Plague*: We carry no immunity against the bacilli spread by the rats. Our vulnerability to the victimizer is, and will remain, part of our nature.

In fact, each of these 'realistic' works of modern fiction explores an urgent spiritual-moral dilemma by dramatizing, in fundamentally allegorical terms, the crisis of our civilization. This crisis goes beyond the will and motives of any mad dictator who has managed to deceive and assume power over the people. The real dilemma is the diseased area in the soul of Everyman, the corroded resistance in the modern psyche that was vulnerable to the contagion of the totalitarian mentality, that allowed, even encouraged, the perverted dictatorial will to assume control over millions of ostensibly 'normal,' 'rational,' 'decent' human beings.

All four writers observe the uncanny ability of the dictator to find the weakest spot, the area of least resistance for launching his attack. Thomas Mann's magician "had the wit to make his attack at the weakest spot" (488), to "search out [the subject's] ethereal lack of resistance to his power" (498). Looking at Mario, a melancholy twenty-year-old, the magician assumes that the young man must be lovesick. He probes into this sickness, until he can gather evidence and formulate his attack against Mario's will. In Sartre's "The Wall" the fascist Belgian doctor observes the condemned men's reaction to their knowledge of impending death: he wants to find out more about the absolute limits, the "walls" of the personality. Learning about the weakness in human nature will help the fascists in their cruel work at other interrogations. Pablo recognizes the doctor's function correctly when he observes: "He came to watch our bodies, bodies dying in agony while yet alive," and when he cries out in anger: "You aren't here on an errand of mercy. . . . I saw you with the fascists" (250).

That the disease strikes at the most vulnerable spot is also central to Camus's interpretation of the crisis. Initially in Oran the disease is allowed to spread because people are not ready to face it in time; they are ashamed to admit the disease even when the dead rats are already all over the city.[3] Here also, the disease strikes at the secular humanist's weakest spot, at his disbelief in the demonic forces of the irrational, at his lack of spiritual imagination: "In this respect our townsfolk were like everybody else, wrapped in themselves; in other words they were humanists; they disbelieved in pestilences. . . . But it doesn't always pass away and . . . it is men who pass away, and the humanists first of all, because they haven't taken any precautions" (34). Camus returns to this point of the victim's vulnerability when discussing the nature of Stalin's terror, observing how well the dictator "calculates the weak points and the degree of elasticity of [every] soul" ("Prophecy" 236).

But the most memorable treatment of Everyman's vulnerability to the totalitarian will to power is Orwell's famous conceit of Room 101. Room 101 is as important to the Party psychologically as is the atom bomb politically. Here is the starting point for the "chain reaction" of trials and denunciations; here is the place where everyone can be brought to the limits, the "walls," of his or her personality.

The question is, what are the consequences of breaking down these walls, of eliminating the distinction between victim and victimizer, battering the individual psyche until it regresses to the collective self that does, in effect, reflect the dictator's own primitive psyche? To return to the terminology of Jungian psychology, the gigantic catastrophes in the political world should be recognized as "modern man . . . [being] battered by the elemental forces of his own psyche" (*Civilization* 235). The totalitarian dictator can break down the "walls" of the individual psyche because in a wider sense he is called forth by our own sense of weakness, to compensate for our sense of powerlessness by the "overwhelming power drive of the Shadow" (*Civilization* 221). In this sense the dictator's appearance is not the cause, but the symptom of, the tendency for psychic disintegration. That the victimizer represents the foil, the mirror image of the victim in each story is corroborated by Jung's concept of the Shadow. Accordingly, O'Brien, whose mind "contains" Winston's, represents a part of Winston's personality that comes to overpower his consciousness. By the end of his ordeal Winston has been driven effectively insane: he has no self left once he 'falls in love with' and identifies unconditionally with O'Brien, alias Big Brother, alias the Prince of Darkness.

When the Enlightenment philosophers introduced the idea that evil is not a permanent flaw, but only a temporary disease or weakness, they implied that human beings are perfectible, their flaws are curable by the healing power of light, education, reason. In the perspective of the totalitarian state's control over the human psyche provided by these four works of fiction, all such 'enlightened' assumptions are put on trial. The trial concerns the survival of the Everyman of our civilization who must resist the Bad Angel at a time when he can no longer call for help from the other direction. He has no one to rely on but the self, the core of personality in "the inner heart," the "incorruptible inner self" that is the driving force of the "spirit of Man," of the human species. It is the urgency of this crisis that introduces, in each of the four works in question, an element of allegory, an effect surprisingly reminiscent of Everyman's dilemma between good and evil in the mediaeval morality play.

This effect is made even stronger by the finality of the characters' tests and trials. The tests we are considering can never be repeated: their consequences are irrevocable. When Pablo and Winston betray another human being, they unmistakably damn themselves. Even if we prefer to describe Pablo's and Winston's defeat in the secular-medical terms of psychic disintegration or insanity, self-betrayal has the same finality here as the mediaeval concept of damnation: the victim is confined to hell without further hope of escape.

Although the locales for the four stories happen to be Italy, Spain, Algeria, and London, the real locale is the hellscape of the modern psyche under the spell of totalitarianism. Mann's *danse macabre* and his identification of the magician as the "betrayer" bear out this association forcefully. Sartre's white cell with the naked electric bulb, the condemned men watched by the alien, inhuman eyes of the Belgian doctor, the Other, describe hell in terms of Sartre's vocabulary. Sartre's statement in *No Exit* that "hell is other people" really means that hell is being watched by the Other. This is also an important concept in Orwell's description of Winston's dread of being continuously watched by the eyes of Big Brother.

As for Camus's Oran, we observe that it is in a condition of 'living hell' even before the appearance of the rats. Although it is described as a seaport, we see it withering away. Cut off from its connection with the sea, it is blocked from the vital sources of spiritual life; it is a wasteland, a hellscape. Finally, Orwell's tortuous spiral in the Ministry of Love, with Room 101 placed "many meters underground, as deep down as it was possible to go" (237), is a Dantesque vision of the modern totalitarian state machine reverting to the Inferno, as its mediaeval original.

Unmistakably, each of the four works is a powerful product of the moral imagination. Just as unmistakably, Mann, Sartre, Camus, and Orwell share the humanist's deep desire to provide a secular, psychological interpretation of the trials, denunciations, and betrayals characteristic of the totalitarian mentality. Yet the fact remains that each work leaves us with a haunting image of a wasteland, a contemporary version of hell. Confronted with our crisis, Mario, Pablo, and Winston, as well as Camus's plague fighters, remind us of the potentially dire consequences of the twentieth-century morality play.

Of course, there are also significant differences between the twentieth-century morality play and its mediaeval original. Although the role of the Great Enemy, the Great Betrayer, appears to be as secure as ever, there is no trace of its opposite, the Good Angel. Everyman is woefully left alone, his strength waning, up against a superlative force he cannot match.

In "Mario and the Magician," Thomas Mann vividly dramatizes this dilemma in the struggle against the Magician by his bravest victim, the Roman gentleman. In trying to salvage his dignity in his confrontation with the Magician, the Roman gentleman is trying to "save the honour of the human race" (499). He is determined not to give in, with the full force of his being. But *not to will* is not effective in itself. To withstand the hypnotic power of the Magician, the Roman gentleman should summon up an equally powerful positive will. Unable to do this, he must at last succumb like all the other victims. Although he is one of the few (next to the narrator) who recognizes that Cipolla, the Great Betrayer, is radical evil, he lacks a firm definition of the absolute good with which to oppose him. The Enlightenment philosophers who set up the framework for our contemporary morality play seem to have forgotten to include the Good Angel in the cast. Therefore, when describing the trial of modern Everyman by the demonic forces of totalitarianism, these four writers are also reporting the trial of the contemporary secular humanist. Each of the four stories bears witness to the force of radical evil which resists its positive, fully optimistic Enlightenment interpretation.

Just like Orwell, Thomas Mann, Camus, and Sartre depict the effect of dramatic struggle between victim and victimizer; Everyman's heroic will to resist is undeniable. Yet on the evidence of these representatives of mid-century fiction dealing with the catastrophic "battering" of the modern psyche by the forces of totalitarianism, one begins to wonder about the curious imbalance introduced into the post-Enlightenment spiritual landscape of twentieth-century secular humanism. God may be dead and Heaven wiped off the map, yet the Prince of Darkness, the Great Betrayer, seems to be alive and well; under the name of the "God of Terror" or the "God of Power" he could, any day, move his dominion into the very heart of the 'modern' twentieth-century psyche.

The Problem of Radical Evil:
The Modern Psychodrama

In the company of Mann, Sartre, and Camus, Orwell takes us to the very heart of the twentieth-century secular humanist's dilemma: The modern ego is not prepared to effectively resist the radical evil that emerged from the social-psychological reality in the form of the totalitarian superstate. In a way, this dilemma is inevitable: from the Enlightenment we may have received too facile an answer about human nature. According to Arendt, even in our religious framework we would have been unable to deal with the reality of the totalitarian state in its most characteristic functions of the torture chambers and concentration camps, experimental laboratories designed specifically for the domination and transformation of human nature: "It is in-herent in our entire philosophy that we can not conceive of a 'radical evil.' . . . Therefore, we actually have nothing to fall back on in order to understand a phenomenon that nevertheless confronts us with its overpowering reality and breaks down all standards we know" (459).

Obviously, the first task of the twentieth-century humanists of Orwell's time is to scrutinize the nature of this phenomenon, to give it a name, to try to understand it in order to learn to combat it. Orwell's *Nineteen Eighty-Four* emphatically and re-peatedly reminds us that in the totalitarian world-state we are confronted with a hellscape, but, as *Goldstein's Book* demon-strates, this hellscape of the Oceania of 1984 has been created by human beings through the force of false, erratic thinking in the 'present' world of the 1940s.

In the framework of psychological realism, the literary works we have just examined by Orwell, Thomas Mann, Camus, and Sartre all concentrate on this man-made hellscape by focusing on the crisis of the human psyche. Indisputably, each work sets out to remain within the fundamentally secular boundaries of the literary convention of 'realism.' Nevertheless, it seems to be in the nature of the subject matter that at times it bursts asunder the humanist's secular vocabulary, and introduces am-biguity between the human and the more-than-human. The same kind of ambiguity is apparent when we attempt to de-termine the genre of these works of fiction. Each of them dis-plays the characteristic verisimilitude of psychological realism, but each invites us, at the same time, to discern the politi-cal, even metaphysical framework of allegory. They all suggest that the "boundary situation" of the individual human drama is acted out against a larger framework of significance, where every character and every individual gesture tends to achieve an added, 'higher' meaning. As a result, although undeniably representatives of psychological realism, these particular works of Mann, Camus, and Sartre may also be approached, at least to the same extent as *Nineteen Eighty-Four*, as embodiments of the allegorical principles of psychodrama, a morality play that acts out a modern Everyman's confrontation with the cosmic forces of radical evil. It is only in reference to such a wider framework that the twentieth-century humanist is capable of contemplating the individual's resistance to the totalitarian experiment, where the survival of "human nature as such is at stake" (Arendt 459).

Notes

[1] According to Bernard Crick, "*Nineteen Eighty-Four* may show sociological rather than psychological imagination, but imagination of a high order none the less" (*Life* 397). It is my intention in this study to emphasize that in the last novel the political-sociological and psychological aspects of Orwell's imagination are integrated to a high degree.

[2] The recurring theme of trials and betrayals is indeed reminiscent here of the manifestation of another spiritual crisis, the one Wordsworth describes in *The Prelude*:

> Such ghastly visions had I of despair
> And tyranny and implements of death;
> And innocent victims sinking under fear,
> . . . .
> Each in his separate cell, or penned in crowds
> For sacrifice . . . .
> . . . . Then suddenly the scene
> Changed, and the unbroken dream entangled me
> In long orations, which I strove to plead
> Before unjust tribunals,— with a voice
> Labouring, a brain confounded, and a sense,
> Death-like, of treacherous desertion, felt
> In the last place of refuge — my own soul. (X, 402–415)

What the nineteenth-century humanist describes here is the vision of the Reign of Terror as it shatters the poet's political hope in the French Revolution to fulfill the ideals of Fraternity, Equality, and Liberty. But disillusionment with the political ideal is gradually turning into disillusionment with the entire Cosmos abandoned by God, moral principle, and meaning. Ultimately, the loss of faith reaches the inner heart, until the poet feels "a treacherous desertion . . . in the last place of refuge — my own soul." Significantly, the feeling of being betrayed is changing into the feeling of having become a traitor. Wordsworth presents the Reign of Terror as a long series of interlocking betrayals that culminate in the humanist's sense of self-betrayal — a sense of spiritual death.

This is the crisis Wordsworth struggles with in the wasteland of *The Borderers*, the only tragedy he ever wrote, shortly after the Revolution. After his tragic fall — betrayal followed by self-betrayal — Wordsworth's hero can no longer believe in the perfectibility of the human being, the foundation of the Enlightenment "religion of humanity." Feeling betrayed by his best friend, he feels he can no longer deny the existence of radical evil: "The deeper malady is better hid:/The world is poisoned at the heart" (II, 1035–1036). (For further discussion of the Romantic crisis, see my *Lost Angels of a Ruined Paradise: Themes of Cosmic Strife in Romantic Tragedy*.)

In the hellscape presented by the four twentieth-century works of fiction by Orwell, Mann, Sartre, and Camus, we are also aware of the dramatization of a political crisis that assumes cosmic, spiritual dimensions.

[3] In his 1903 novella, *Death in Venice*, Thomas Mann also refers to pestilence as "the city's secret," its "silence and denial" of decay. Like Camus in *The Plague*, Mann here presents the deadly contagion as a metaphor for the protagonist's, indeed an entire society's, mental and spiritual disease.

Chapter 12

What Turns Utopia into Dystopia? The Terror of Science and the Science of Terror — Huxley and Orwell

Like Mann, Sartre, and Camus, Orwell presents us with a haunting, psychologically credible dramatization of the crisis of the individual psyche battered by the forces of totalitarianism. The composite genre of *Nineteen Eighty-Four* also allows Orwell to pose some probing questions that directly connect the personal drama of Winston's psychic disintegration with the political system of Oceania and, significantly, with the system that preceded and led to Oceania — questions germane to dystopian satire. Consequently, to return to the issue of Orwell's alleged despair — an issue central to the Orwell conundrum — we should now also examine Orwell's diagnosis of the demonic element endemic to totalitarianism, within the framework of the Utopian-dystopian tradition. To get a fair picture of what is unique to Orwell's position, let us once more look at *Nineteen Eighty-Four* in comparison with another representative work in this genre, Huxley's *Brave New World*.

Evil in both dystopias appears as the attempt of the superstate to transform human nature until the individuality of men and women is fully sacrificed to the state machine. Even if the twentieth-century humanist faces a significant dilemma in articulating the magnitude of evil introduced by the phenomenon of the totalitarian state, in the words of Hannah Arendt, " there is . . . one thing that is discernible: We may say that radical evil has emerged in connection with a system in which all men have become equally superfluous" (27). In exploring the alarming potential of the modern State to make human beings superfluous, both Huxley's and Orwell's satires point out the absurdity of the State's claim to total domination, that is, its claim to be leading humanity towards a utopian goal that is historically determined.

Historical Determinism and Utopia

> A story is told that at a writers' conference in Moscow in the early 30s André Malraux caused consternation by rising to ask: "What happens in a classless society when a streetcar runs over a beautiful girl?" Gorky was hauled out of his sickbed to deliver the answer, arrived at after long debate: in a planned and classless [and hence perfect] society, a streetcar would not run over a beautiful girl (Robert Elliott *Shape*, 105).

Wouldn't most of us say that at the root of the charming naiveté of Gorky's answer lies the vision of a state of uninterrupted happiness, the classical promise of Utopia? But is there such a promise offered or even implied in the genre of Utopian literature?

Not quite. In fact, I would venture to say that some of the best-known classics in the Utopian genre are anti-utopian, that simultaneously with the vision of Utopia appears the warning *against* Utopia as a perfect state of uninterrupted happiness. Thomas More himself offers two ironic provisos. First, we are told that "pride would not set foot in Paradise"; hence humanity could not enter Utopia until it got rid of pride, which More does not expect it to do for "quite a number of years" (66). Given the ironic context, this means, of course, "never." The second proviso is inherent in the short poem that the book, coming alive for this purpose, recites about its own accomplishments: "Plato's *Republic* now I claim/To match or beat at its own game/For that was just a myth in prose,/But what he wrote of, I became,/Of men, wealth, laws a solid frame,/A place where every wise man goes./Goplacia is now my name" (28).

Note that Utopia is not a place where the wise man resides or will be residing: it is a direction, a goal for the process of self-perfection. That Utopia should not be seen as a state of being but a process of becoming is repeated many times. Swift's Houyhnhnmland may look like Utopia to poor gullible Gulliver, but when we hear that in their own language Houyhnhnm means the "perfection of nature," Swift's parody becomes quickly apparent. To declare yourself in the state of perfection reveals the sin of pride and immediately denies your statement. As for Voltaire's Candide, despite his lifelong quest for a place that would finally qualify for "the best of all possible worlds," and despite his miraculous good luck to find Eldorado hidden, as it should be, behind inaccessible mountains, no sooner is he permitted to enter than he takes his leave. Corrupted by civilization (as we all are), no longer can he find satisfaction in the primitive Rousseauean Paradise reserved by, and for, the innocent. Candide would rather show off his gold among people who have less than he has. Just as important, he would rather leave behind the state of uninterrupted happiness for the intense emotion implied by a Romantic pursuit of love (well may *we* know that such a course is "mad in pursuit and in possession so").

This "good place," this ideal, this heaven on earth is a valuable foil to show up the sordid way things really are in the world around us, but it is also, invariably, too much of a good thing. Like heaven, its original archetype, it is a place we all feel we should strive for, but somehow, on closer examination, find that we are in no particular hurry to get there just yet — possibly because once we enter, we are not really expected to leave again.

The anecdote about Malraux's probing question and Gorky's charming answer may, by now, assume sinister connotations. It represents a significant new stage in Utopian thought: it shows what happens when the timeless Utopian promise is taken over by a nineteenth-century ideology, and this ideology, by a twentieth-century totalitarian dictatorship. It is only now that More's renaissance promise of bringing 'heaven to earth' loses its built-in ironic proviso. Suddenly we are expected to know with absolute certainty that heaven-on-earth awaits at the stop of the next historical junction, and we are expected to envision the approach of happiness everlasting with the undisputable concreteness of a streetcar running on its tracks with unswerving precision.

Ironically, it is by insisting on a "scientific" methodology that will save the world from the tyranny of religion that Marx's dialectical materialism assumes eschatological dimension. In declaring his Socialism "scientific," Marx dismisses his ties with Utopian tradition, and presents us with an ideology that offers a "scientific," that is, irrefutable, explication of the past, the present, and the future. In that future of a classless and hence perfect society, we are told by Gorky, there can be no more accidents, because even the system of transportation will have achieved its stasis of perfection. Well may we ask, once humanity has achieved such continuous state of transport, will it still require the services of public transportation?

Be that as it may, after we have been requested to contemplate heaven on earth in dead earnest, it is probably quite natural that the irony inherent in the Utopian genre will have to surface in works that are anti-Utopian. Both *Brave New World* and *Nineteen Eighty-Four* are dystopian satires that manifest the grim, often tragic irony of disillusionment with two aspects of twentieth-century ideology that emerged from the twofold Utopian expectations of the late nineteenth-century: faith in science and faith in socialism.

A Dream Fulfilled — A Dream Betrayed

In the ideology followed by the World State of *Brave New World*, the twofold dream is allowed to run its full course and turns into a nightmare by being carried to its absurd conclusion: Huxley points out that it was a dream concentrating only on material progress, was narrowly utilitarian, and hence was lacking in spiritual dimension. In the London of 631 AF we meet Marx, Lenin, and Trotsky, all the great representatives of the Socialist Revolution; we also meet Helmholtz the physicist, Watson the psychologist, and Darwin and Freud, the geniuses of modern science. But let us take a closer look at those who carry the name of genius in the London of the future: the whining Bernard Marx, the totally mindless Lenina, the insignificant Polly Trotsky, not to mention the unsavoury journalist Darwin Bonaparte and emotional engineer Helmholtz Watson, whose creativity is thwarted by the system. They are all mediocrities: no genius can be produced once the dream of the earlier geniuses had become realized.

By contrast, *Nineteen Eighty-Four* shows us that the twofold dream of Socialism and science was deliberately distorted by those who assumed power in its name. O'Brien has nothing but contempt for those "cowards and hypocrites" who "pretended, perhaps . . . even believed, that they had seized power unwillingly and for a limited time, and that just round the corner there lay a paradise where human beings would be free and equal." O'Brien knows "no one seizes power with the intention of relinquishing it. . . . One does not establish a dictatorship in order to safeguard a revolution: one makes the revolution in order to establish the dictatorship" (211).

At first glance Huxley's and Orwell's dystopias seem to have very little in common. One presents the nightmare implied in the fulfilment of the dream — the other, the nightmare implied in the distortion, the betrayal of the same. And yet these two societies are two sides of the same coin: both are state machines running with scientific precision and both thrive on the Big Lie. That lie is that the totalitarian government serves the happiness of the people; in effect, happiness becomes a euphemism for the people's enslavement by an ideology, a secular religion that makes them worship the state and love their servitude.

Gorky's answer that in a perfect state the machine will no longer make any mistake represents the iron logic of totalitarian ideology, which finds its appropriate symbol in the consistent motion of the machine. Ironically, once the Law of History is fulfilled, the very notion of historical becoming is eliminated; the only movement imaginable is the *perpetuum mobile* of the State machine. Prerequisite to its movement is the existence of human beings whose only purpose is to conform, so that the machine may run its course undeterred. The State, the Superego, has achieved absolute control over the population, all of them forced to regress and stay at the level of Id, a condition of eternal childhood obedience. Anyone who dares to question his State-determined function must be eliminated. When the Controller sends the intellectual rebel to the islands, when Big Brother sends the heretics through the torture chamber, we see the totalitarian State ejecting the most important part of the mature personality — the Ego, the driving force of the critical intellect and the instrument of reality-testing.

In the words of Hannah Arendt, behind the totalitarian State's desire for total domination lies the desire of the totalitarian mind for a consistency, which became independent of reality, a consistency of historical determinism that, as revealed in Gorky's answer, cannot afford the spontaneity of mutations or variables:

> No ideology which aims at the explanation of all historical events of the past and the mapping out the course of all events of the future can bear the unpredictability which springs from the fact that men are creative, that they can bring forward something so new that nobody ever foresaw it. What totalitarian ideologies therefore aim at is not the transformation of the outside world [of the revolutionizing transmutation of society], but the transformation of human nature itself (Arendt 458).

Both *Brave New World* and *Nineteen Eighty-Four* present us with the paradigm of the totalitarian State as an enormous laboratory for the transformation of human nature, the creation of a species no longer human. In *Brave New World* the State machine is represented by the Hatchery in which human beings are decanted at various stages of arrested development. In *Nineteen Eighty-Four* the State machine is revealed, appropriately, in the torture chamber where Winston receives an answer from O'Brien to his gnawing question: "I understand how: I don't understand why." Since God is Power and the Inner Party is the priesthood of a cruel divinity, it depends on an unending process of victimization to appease the God of Power, to assure its own immortality, to feel its own vitality: "The object of power is power. The object of persecution is persecution. The object of torture is torture."

Not long after this revelation, Winston is taken to Room 101, where he is made to understand existentially what is the mainspring of this State machine: In Room 101 everyone is to betray, to sacrifice, his nearest and dearest — ultimately himself. When Winston emerges from the womb of the Ministry of Love, he is indeed new-born: his pink skull, thickened, coarse features, his clinging to his gin bottle, provides us with a physical description appropriate to the grotesque rebirth of his psyche. Once his old self is broken, he assumes the collective psyche of the rest of the faceless, soul-less denizens of Oceania; he is dehumanized as effectively as the bokanovskified twins in Huxley's dystopia.

Huxley's laboratory for the totalitarian transformation of human beings is the Hatchery, Orwell's the laboratory of the torture chamber. In his central symbol Huxley explores the terror of science; Orwell, the science of terror. Nevertheless, both novels suggest that the mechanism of the totalitarian superstate consists of a diabolic new birth, a new species engendered by the marriage between science and terror.

As we learn from Orwell's essays, he feared the unprecedented power of modern dictatorships to alter human nature, as easily able "to produce a breed of men who do not wish for liberty as to produce a breed of hornless cows" (v. 1, 419). At the end of *Nineteen Eighty-Four* we see this fear realized: the newborn Winston, having achieved the "happiness" of the collective psychosis, no longer wants to break free from Oceania even in his dreams. As for Huxley, he presents us with the dilemma of

John Savage and Lenina: though they are deeply in love with each other, still the obstacle in their way is insurmountable — John belongs to the human species; Lenina, predestined to be "happy" by loving her servitude, belongs to another.

The laboratories of the State machine, which spew forth creatures deprived of all those things that make us human, evoke the horror we traditionally would associate with hell. Of course, in the twentieth-century context, hell takes the form of an enormous insane asylum, and damnation becomes a psychotic breakdown, which, for the purposes of both works of fiction, is incurable. John the Savage goes insane and commits suicide; Winston Smith is made to suffer a breakdown and remain in a psychotic state until his impending execution. Both the terror of science and the science of terror induce insanity — the personality has collapsed; ego has been forcefully eliminated.

How does the State achieve this? The strategy of the Inner Party is based on its awareness of the Freudian insight that "outbreaks of anxiety and a general preparedness for anxiety were produced whenever sexual excitation was inhibited, arrested or deflected in its progress towards satisfaction" (Freud, v. 20, 110). The Party's control of the personality is based on its denial of the sexual instinct. The energy withdrawn from Eros is converted into the death instinct, Thanatos, channelled, like a blowtorch, into sadistic hatred of the enemy and adulation of Big Brother. Hysteria based on unresolved anxiety is converted into a sadism with an unfixed, ever-changing target: "Hate can be turned in any direction at a moment's notice, like a plumber's blow-flame (v. 2, 41) Orwell had observed, and in the Two Minutes Hate he repeats this observation: "the rage that one felt was an abstract, undirected emotion which could be switched from one object to another like the flame of a blowlamp" (17).

The most memorable example of this psycho-political aberration is the demonstration during Hateweek that begins as a demonstration against Eastasia. All of a sudden the loudspeaker announces that Eastasia is an ally — the enemy is and always had been Eurasia. The crowd does not halt for a moment: "The Hate continued exactly as before, except that the *target* had been changed" (161). Deprived of food, love, sexual satisfaction, the 'starved rats' of Oceania live all their lives in a "preparedness for anxiety," an anxiety the ego is never allowed to master.

In contrast to Big Brother, the Controller in *Brave New World* makes the ego regress by eliminating anxiety altogether. Here psychic manipulation is based on the State's indulgence of the pleasure principle. Sexual love is depersonalized through the state ritual of "orgy-porgy" and the enactment of the slogan, "everyone belongs to everyone else." As Freud had pointed out, "two people coming together for the purpose of sexual satisfaction, in so far as they seek for solitude, are making a demonstration against the herd instinct, the group feeling." (Freud, v. 18, 140) The conflict between personal love and the herd instinct appeared quite late in man's history and marks an advanced state of ego development:

> It is only when the affectionate, that is personal factor of a love relation gives place entirely to the sensual one, that it is possible for two people to have sexual intercourse in . . . a group, as occurs at an orgy . . . at that point a regression has taken place [to an] early stage in sexual relations, at which being in love as yet played no part (Freud, v. 18, 140).

That the depersonalization of sexual love is tantamount to the regression of ego is further explained by Herbert Marcuse, who describes how our quasi-permissive modern State has actually increased its control over the personality. Freud points out that the inherent conflict between Eros and society is one of the central concerns of the striving, maturing ego. But once the State encourages the spontaneous release of sexual energy, this energy itself "changes its social function." As soon as "sexuality is sanctioned and even encouraged by society," says Marcuse, "it loses . . . its essentially erotic quality, that of freedom from social control. . . . Now with the integration of this sphere into the realm of business and entertainment, the repression itself is repressed: society has enlarged, not individual freedom, but its control over the individual" (57).

Big Brother rules by creating anxiety, the Controller by eliminating anxiety, yet the central goal is very much the same: to make ego regress by making human relationships and personal loyalties impossible, in accordance with the Freudian insight that the family is "not only the very model of political affiliation but also exerting a limit upon it: a competing loyalty and repository of erotic capital" (Rieff 272).

Consequently, in *Brave New World* the family is dissolved by biological fiat (except for the test tube you simply can't have mother or father), in *Nineteen Eighty-Four* by political fiat (children and parents, husband and wife are encouraged to denounce each other to the State). By destroying the sexual bond and the family bond at the same time, both superstates have virtually 'nationalized' the "erotic capital" of their populations. Through being forced to give up the sexual and the family bond, the citizens both of Oceania and of London 631 AF regress to the state of infantile helplessness, worshipping the State, the exalted Father, exclusively.

Both superstates have introduced an ideology equivalent to a religious orthodoxy, and as Orwell has pointed out, any orthodoxy is intent on reducing human consciousness. The Utopian promise of "happiness" is present in the background of both systems: Big Brother pretends to the masses that he is intent on bringing about an "earthly paradise" — this is, of course, the promise that allowed him to come to power. In fact, he has never had anything but contempt for the "stupid hedonistic utopias of the past" (229). The Controller also uses the hedonistic promise of "happiness" as a trap. In *Brave New World* the people are offered the pleasure of sexual indulgence and of soma to distract them from the fact that all their responses are completely predetermined. "Happiness," the Controller explains, consists of "liking what you've got to do. All conditioning aims at that: making people love their inescapable destiny" (24). Soma, the most obvious instrument of instant happiness "has become an instrument of statecraft. The tyrants were benevolent but they were still tyrants. Their subjects were not bludgeoned into obedience. They were chemically induced to love their servitude" (Huxley, "Revisited").

The function of soma in *Brave New World* parallels that of Doublethink in *Nineteen Eighty-Four*. Like soma, Doublethink is expected to smooth over the contradictions, the temporary 'bumps' in the self-consistent fiction created by the ideology. Most specifically, soma and Doublethink are designed to blind the citizens of dystopia to the occasionally surfacing reminders of a spontaneous, genuine world outside their particular mental system. Doublethink makes the citizens of Oceania use "protective stupidity" and practise "reality control" any moment they feel that the compulsory "happiness" of the superstate is threatened by reminders of reality. Like soma, Doublethink represents the blunting of consciousness, a practice that corrupts ego in its most important function, reality testing.

The vacuum that the totalitarian state creates around itself to deny reality is emphasized by both Huxley and Orwell. The Controller admits that the average citizen "goes through life inside a bottle" (175): ego remains in a pre-natal state; even alpha pluses are to behave with "infantile decorum" (83), as if they had no consciousness whatsoever.

Big Brother also depends on creating a vacuum around Oceania by sealing it off from the outside world. But the most important factor in creating an enclosed, impenetrable world of fiction is the elimination of the past, creating a historical vacuum. The Controller declares that history is "bunk" and makes sure no one except himself is allowed to read the classics. As for Oceania, Big Brother relies on the fiction that the Inner Party brought the people happiness unprecedented in the past; hence, it is vitally interested in eliminating history, which would allow people an opportunity for comparison. The memory hole that destroys the records of history is also indispensable to another insane practice — the "vaporization" of human beings at the will of the Party: not only are they murdered, they disappear without a trace as if they "never have existed" (204).

The fact that once a human being's identity is destroyed, he also becomes disposable is also made clear by Huxley. The murder of an individual is of no consequence whatsoever: "after all, what is an individual? [asked Foster] With a sweeping gesture he indicated the rows of microscopes, the test tubes, the incubators . . . we can make a new one with the greatest ease — as many as we like" (120). Both dystopias present the principle of the totalitarian superstate as an unprecedented absurdity, where the government regards the governed as entirely superfluous except for their function to keep the State machinery going. (One is reminded of Bertolt Brecht's famous quip after the 1953 June uprising in East Germany, when the people were reprimanded by the Government. Remarked Brecht with grim humour: "The people have lost the confidence of the Government," which amounts to saying, "If the people won't behave themselves, the government will dismiss them.")

There is no doubt that both Huxley's and Orwell's dystopian satires reveal totalitarianism as radically evil — it is a world of the absurd, the criminally, diabolically insane. In the tradition of great satire we are used to the idea that when the satirist describes a topsy-turvy world that is insane and immoral, by the 'reversal of his reversal' we could expect to discover the norm, the implied ideal for the self and for society. But does such a reversal of dystopian satire lead us back to the ideal of Utopia?

To begin with the psychological aspect of this question, we should realize that both Huxley and Orwell share with Freud a view of the human personality as a dynamic process. What is more, "Freud's dictum that 'we are all somewhat hysterical,' that the difference between so-called normality and neurosis is only a matter of degree, is one of the key statements in his writing" (Rieff, 389). If we accept that psychosis and neurosis are distinct alternatives lurking in our background all the time,[1] doesn't this mean that our modern concept of "psychological man" is based on a fundamentally tragic and not on a Utopian humanism?

As for the political aspect of the Utopian ideal, on the evidence of Stalin's and Hitler's experiments in totalitarian dictatorships, doesn't it seem that the moment Utopia comes to power, its goals themselves undergo a tragic transformation? How would Orwell and Huxley have answered these questions? No doubt, these were questions vital for both.

Huxley wrote *Brave New World* in 1930, re-examined its premises in a 1946 Preface, then in a 1957 essay, then in a whole collection of essays, *Brave New World Revisited*, in 1958. Finally, just before his death, he seemed to have found the answer in *Island*. The island of Pala is everything the modern Utopians must have been searching for. But it is a good place because it refuses greed and aggression, and it is precisely for this reason that it is overrun by its greedy and aggressive neighbour. Huxley's life-long search for the "good place" in the modern world remains tragically unresolved.

In fact, Orwell comes up with far less pessimistic answers. It is true that he wants to dissociate Socialism from Utopian expectations because these are bound to end in disillusionment and despair. He is also careful to show that the hedonistic, materialistic streak in the nineteenth-century dream is bound to lead towards dehumanization. His essay on "Pleasure Spots" comes remarkably close to the conclusions of Huxley's 1946 Preface to *Brave New World*, revealing that the humanism underlying the two dystopian satires is of the same fabric.

> Much of what goes by the name of pleasure [says Orwell] is simply an effort to destroy consciousness. If one started by asking, what is man? what are his needs? how can he express himself? one

would discover that merely having the power to avoid work and live one's life from birth to death in electric light at the tune of tinned music, is not a reason for doing so. Man needs warmth, society, leisure, comfort and security: he also needs solitude, creative work and a sense of wonder. . . . If he recognizes this, he could use the products of science and industrialism eclectically, applying always the same test: Does this make me more human or less human? (v. 4, 105).

Having read Huxley's and Orwell's dystopian satires, we should conclude that the best society is the one that allows us to ask these questions, that holds maximum assurance of freedom, the unhampered striving of a dynamic, healthy ego. Our greatest fear is no longer chaos or disorder, as it was for Plato, who in *The Republic* presented us with a system that was guaranteed never to change; our greatest fear is the over-organization, the regimentation of massmen into the faceless, horrifying crowds of Oceania, forever on the march, forever hating, persecuting — or into the equally faceless crowd of bokanovskified twins standing in line, forever, awaiting their soma distribution. Our greatest fear, as Huxley and Orwell have articulated it for us, is the reverting of the human species into docile denizens of an enormous concentration camp, the structure that follows most characteristically from the machine-like consistency of the totalitarian mindset, which cannot admit of the spontaneity inherent in the creativity and freedom of a dynamic personality.

Let us now return once more to Malraux's question and Gorky's answer about the streetcar and the beautiful girl in a classless, planned, and hence indisputably perfect society. Imagine for a moment what would have happened if at this point a Soviet writer would have raised his voice to challenge Gorky's answer, which combined the fanaticism of religious revelation with the finality of a verdict delivered by the Holy Inquisition. The exchange between Malraux and Gorky should be a warning against the machine-like consistency of ideological thinking, which turned, in the hands of totalitarian dictatorships, into a frightening weapon against the individual's most fundamental right, freedom of inquiry.

To show up the sinister consequences of the totalitarian mentality was the most direct aim of Orwell's satire in *Nineteen Eighty-Four*. This, however, does not mean that Orwell gave up belief in the original dream of Socialism.

> The 'earthly paradise' [says Orwell] has never been realized, but as an idea it never seems to perish ... underneath it lies the belief that human nature is fairly decent and capable of indefinite development. This belief has been the main driving force of the Socialist movement, including the underground sects that prepared the way for the Russian revolution. (*Manchester Evening News*, 31 Jan. 1946, qtd. in Crick, "Introduction" 116).

But to avoid the pitfalls of Oceania, it is essential to reintroduce the ironic proviso of a modest, sober humanism built into the classical works of the Utopian tradition: Only when we give up looking for the "earthly paradise" as a stasis[2] reached at the end of the historical process — that is, only when we accept that we must go on cultivating our earthly gardens — can we hope to find happiness in the process of struggling for a society with the most modern and most traditional of humanist ideals: the integrity of the individual based on the freedom of a striving, dynamic personality. In spite of the undeniable power of the demonic forces around him — forces attested to by many of his contemporaries — Orwell's commitment to struggle for this ideal never wavers. In this ideal his faith in the "spirit of Man" finds its life-long spiritual centre.

Notes

[1] In *Freud — the Mind of the Moralist*, Philip Rieff points out that psychic health depends on a precarious balance, and neurosis and psychosis are distinct alternatives in our background all the time: "Neurosis does not deny the existence of reality, it merely tries to ignore it; psychosis denies and tries to substitute something else for it. A reaction which combines features of both of these is one we call normal or 'healthy': it denies reality as little as neurosis, but then, like psychosis, is concerned with effecting a change in it" (388).

[2] According to J.L. Talmon, the "yearning for salvation and the love of freedom" cannot be satisfied at the same time; we have to accept the "incompatibility of the idea of an all-embracing creed with liberty" (254). Therefore,

> like a psychoanalyst who cures by making the patient aware of the subconscious, the social analyst may be able to attack the human urge which calls totalitarian democracy into existence, namely the longing for a final resolution of all contradictions and conflicts into a state of total harmony. It is a harsh, but none the less necessary task to drive home the truth that human society and human life can never reach a state of repose. That imagined repose is another name for the security offered by a

prison, and the longing for it may in a sense be an expression
. . . of the inability to face the fact that life is a perpetual and
never resolved crisis. All that can be done is to proceed by the
method of trial and error (254–255).

Part IV

Orwell's Tragic Humanism

As we have seen in the last three chapters, when Orwell's diagnosis of the evils of totalitarianism is compared with that of his contemporaries, it becomes evident that *Nineteen Eighty-Four* was not inspired by its author's personal pathology of hysteria, paranoia, or demonic obsession. In fact, Orwell's diagnosis is remarkably close to some of the most 'sane' of his contemporaries — historians, psychologists, and writers of the stature of Thomas Mann, Camus, Sartre, and Huxley.

Nor is it true, as has often been suggested, that in his last novel Orwell's diagnosis of totalitarianism emerges as a sudden fit of pessimism due to his failing health at the end of his life. An examination of the various dimensions of Orwell's vision of reality in the course of his career should provide ample evidence that the novel incorporates Orwell's most mature and well-considered response to the dilemma puzzling so many of his contemporaries: Can the secular humanist admit the undeniable existence of radical evil without abandoning faith in human perfectibility?

But to see more closely the options of the humanist in Orwell's time, Chapter 13 will take a look at the social, psychological, and philosophical dimensions of Orwell's vision by examining his thoughtful response to Marx, Freud, and the Existentialists, the three major tributaries of the mainstream of twentieth-century realism. Noting Orwell's various reservations about the 'realism' of these three thought systems, Chapter 14 invites us to take a further look at Orwell's ties with the moral idealism inherent in the 'religion of humanity,' a 'religion' we usually associate with the Romantics and, going even further back, with the Enlightenment. Chapter 14 concludes with the suggestion that we look for Orwell's synthesis of twentieth-century realism and nineteenth-century idealism in his telling analysis of Shakespearean tragedy, where he defines what he sees as essential to the tragic dimension of the human predicament — a noble struggle for the affirmation of life, even when confronted by overpowering forces.

Far from presenting us with the fragmented or distorted vision of a sudden attack of despair, as has so often been suggested, *Nineteen Eighty-Four* is inspired by a multidimensional and well-integrated vision of reality. It incorporates the political, psychological, and spiritual dimensions of Orwell's tragic humanism, culminating in a mature, hard-won affirmation of the "spirit of Man."

Chapter 13

The "Spirit of Man":
Orwell's Response to the 'Realism' of
Marx, Freud, and the Existentialists

The Spirit of Man

In the dark, haunted intellectual landscape of the 1930s and 1940s, we have found Orwell, next to Thomas Mann, Sartre, Camus and Huxley, engaged in a desperate struggle against despair itself. Each of these writers, in his own way, is deeply committed to humanism, a secular and fundamentally positive view of the human predicament inherited from the Enlightenment, based on the denial of radical evil, and hence on the perfectibility of the human being. But when compelled to confront the unprecedented scale of the cruelty and destruction of two world wars, the concentration camps of the totalitarian systems, the threat of a nuclear holocaust — the escalation of the irrational forces capable of assuming demonic dimensions — it becomes a veritable act of faith to assert confidence in the survival of the human spirit. Therefore, when O'Brien declares the eternal, self-perpetuating reign of the God of Power and Winston, already broken in mind and body, makes his last appeal to the "spirit of Man," the scene has particular poignancy.

> "No. I believe it. I *know* that you will fail. There is something in the universe — I don't know, some spirit, some principle — that you will never overcome."
> "Do you believe in God, Winston?"
> "No."
> "Then what is it, this principle that will defeat us?"
> "I don't know. The spirit of Man." (217)

For a long time, even in the Ministry of Love, Winston clings to faith in "some spirit, some principle" still capable of defeating the Party. Since Winston never succeeds in defining this very important term, what should we understand by the "spirit of Man"?

We have seen that in Orwell's view it is due to the loss of religious belief and a concomitant loss of moral values that in the twentieth-century human beings have become susceptible to the totalitarian mentality, which is based on the worship of power. Therefore, Orwell believes, "the real problem of our time is to restore the sense of absolute right and wrong when the belief it used to rest on — that is the belief in personal immortality — has been destroyed. This demands *faith*, which is a different thing from credulity" (v. 3, 123).

What does "faith" mean in this passage, where religious belief is associated with the ignorance or self-delusion of "credulity"? In context, "faith" can refer here only to faith in mankind, in the human ability to struggle, to salvage civilization by establishing a code of universal moral values *without* recourse to religious belief in personal immortality. Still, Orwell's humanistic "faith" also implies a passionate concern about the future, even if this future is secular, that is, emphatically "independent from heaven and hell" (v. 3, 177). That under certain circumstances the individual should become capable of self-sacrifice for the entire species seems to be an essential strand in Orwell's 'religion of humanity'; he observes that "people sacrifice themselves for the sake of fragmentary communities. . . . A very slight increase of consciousness, and their sense of loyalty could be transferred to humanity itself, which is not an abstraction" (v. 2, 32). In Winston's long, often heroic resistance to O'Brien in the Ministry of Love, it becomes clear that loyalty to humanity is indeed not an abstraction.

It also becomes clear that in trying to refute O'Brien's prediction, Winston does not claim that it is a return to belief in God that will defeat the totalitarian God of Power. In fact, Winston's predicament demonstrates that nostalgia for the security and serenity of traditional religion could become highly deceptive. Driven by an irresistible urge to return to the past, Winston makes repeated visits to the antique shop and experiences an obsessive desire to purchase the old diary, the glass paperweight, and the etching of the old church — all mementos of a beauty that is no longer allowed to exist in Oceania. It is also in line with Winston's craving for this beauty that he is so deeply moved when he hears from Mr. Charrington the first fragment of the rhyme about the pealing of the church bells in old London. Yet, if we pay closer attention to the dramatic situation implied by this seemingly innocent nursery rhyme,

Winston's deep attraction to old churches and pealing church bells becomes more than simply another expression of his nostalgia for beauty. There is something ominous in the drama suggested by the nursery rhyme, and unbeknownst to himself Winston becomes a participant in this drama as he keeps searching for the missing lines.

The drama is connected with some kind of transaction, and it may be worth noting here that Winston pays for the possession of the diary and the crystal paperweight, but fails to pay for the picture of the church, and, of course, it would never occur to him that there might be a price to pay paid for the first few lines of the nursery rhyme. While he is ready to risk his life in payment for self-expression (the diary), and for creating a private world of beauty and love (the crystal paperweight), at this point he is unaware of the cost implied by his nostalgia for religious belonging.

The first line he hears from Mr. Charrington arouses Winston's interest: "Oranges and lemons, say the bells of St. Clements" (90). There is something offered by the pealing of the church bells, something that appears serene, beautiful, highly desirable. Yet, as the story progresses and Winston stumbles upon the subsequent lines, it becomes clear that implied in the offer of serenity and beauty there is a payment to be made: "When shall you pay me? say the bells of Old Bailey." This simple question becomes ominous in the light of the 'purchaser's' answer, admitting his unwillingness or inability to pay, "When I get rich — say the bells of Shoreditch." Since in the sinister-ironic context of the drama this answer means "never," in the parallel situation of the novel Winston, our spiritually impoverished Everyman, is unwilling or unable to pay. Consequently, the payment will be extracted by force, and it will be a price beyond all expectations: "Then here comes a candle to light you to bed; here comes a chopper to chop off your head." The church bells act out a cruel, painful ritual of temptation, seduction, and entrapment — a ritual highly suggestive in the light of Winston's predicament in the novel.

The picture of the old church plays a role similar to that of the church bells. Winston is fascinated by the beauty of the original building which, ironically, is now a dilapidated "museum used for propaganda displays of various kinds" at Victory Square (90). But what is Orwell's target in this ironical juxtaposition of the old church and the museum used for propaganda displays?

Does he suggest that the function of the museum of propaganda is diametrically opposed to that of the beautiful old church, or do these two functions bear a significant resemblance? I suggest that the role played by the old picture in Winston's arrest at the end of Part 2 favours the second hypothesis.

Winston's fascination with the beautiful picture of the church contributes to his passionate desire to return to Mr. Charrington's shop and rent the room above it. That room, with the crystal paperweight at its centre, becomes the symbol of the lovers' freedom away from the telescreen, the all-seeing eyes of Big Brother. However, at the time of their arrest, Winston and Julia find out that even in their room they had not been free. The telescreen had been there all along; it had been camouflaged by the seductively beautiful picture of the old church. It is at the dramatic moment of this recognition that Mr. Charrington reminds the lovers of their entrapment by repeating the jeering, sinister last lines of the nursery rhyme. The process that started with Winston's enchantment by the church bells has been brought to light ("then here comes a candle to light you to bed"), and the time has arrived for paying the price ("here comes a chopper to chop off your head").

In Part 3 Winston's powerful resistance to O'Brien is not motivated by a wish to return to religious belief in the soul's immortality. Nevertheless, Winston's faith in "some spirit, some principle" is closely connected with a concept of futurity. Although he is hard put to explain what he means by the "spirit of Man," his actions show that he is able to retain this faith as long as he is able to stay loyal to his bond with Julia and behave as if "the object was not to stay alive but to stay human" (148), as long as he "can *feel* that staying human is worthwhile" (147). He does not lose this faith so long as he can maintain freedom from the insane power worship of the Party because "to die hating them that was freedom" (226), and it is "by staying sane that you carried on the human heritage" (28).

We know, of course, that ultimately Winston fails to carry on this heritage. In Room 101 he too is reduced to the subhuman. But does Winston's predicament in the framework of the satire reflect Orwell's own loss of faith in the "spirit of Man"? It is crucial to remember that the question the satirist elicits from us here is not whether it is true that we shall inevitably have to give up faith in the human spirit in the future. Instead, within the hypothetical framework of the satire, our question should be: "Is it true that accepting the totalitarian mentality is antithetical to the human spirit, that as soon as we have consented to totalitarianism coming to power, we have irrevocably renounced our faith in the "spirit of Man"?

Orwell's Response to
Marx, Freud, and the Existentialists

Through Winston's attestation of faith in the "spirit of Man," Orwell reveals the various dimensions of his own "faith" in the ideals of a 'religion of humanity' — ideals, I submit that were the motivating force of his humanism and that were at the core of his self-appointed task as a satirist. Yet, to see more clearly what "faith" means in the vocabulary of the secular humanist, we should take a closer look at Orwell's definition of the political, psychological and philosophical dimensions of the human predicament in his characteristic response to the 'realism' of Marx, Freud, and the Existentialists, respectively.

Although at no point could Orwell be called a Marxist, a Freudian, or an Existentialist, significant strands of these three thought systems, so influential in his time, have been woven into the fabric of his vision of the world. In fact, if we want to delineate the humanist "faith" that is identifiably "Orwellian," we should probably begin by examining his individual response to these three major tributaries of the secular-humanist mainstream of twentieth-century thought.

Response to Marx

Although Orwell emphasizes that he became a Socialist because of his sympathy with the downtrodden and not due to a commitment to Marxist theory (v. 3, 456), his vocabulary reveals that he is sufficiently conversant with the central assumptions of Marxism to form his individual responses to them.[1] With the Marxists, he accepts the historical significance of class struggle, and explains that in *Animal Farm* he presents the oppressed animals' point of view from a Marxist perspective (v. 3, 459). He also contemplates "the economic theory of history" seriously but not without trepidation. It is a "dreary" theory but "quite true enough," he admits in "The Lure of Profundity" (*New English Weekly* 30 Dec. 1937, 235–236, qtd. in Bonifas 165). Orwell's vocabulary in his essays reveals the Socialist's unequivocal condemnation of economic inequality as a clear indication of the exploitation of the dispossessed; he states that "a man with 150,000 a year . . . is robbing . . . the man with fifteen shillings a week" (v. 1, 388), and demands that the Labour government should "nationalize land, coal mines, railways, public utilities and banks" (v. 3, 448).

At the same time, throughout his essays, one can also detect Orwell's resistance to aspects of the materialism fundamental to the Marxist theory of history. No doubt Orwell's commitment to Socialism, which largely grew out of his sympathy for the unemployed during the Depression years, is based on his willingness to address economic questions as issues of first importance.[2] But their priority is only chronological. The spiritual dimension of human nature is just as important to Orwell, even if "privation and brute labour have to be abolished before the real problems of humanity can be tackled. . . . How right the working classes are in their 'materialism'! How right they are to realize that the belly comes before the soul, not in the scale of values but in point of time!" (v. 2, 304–305). The single quotation marks around the word express Orwell's doubt as to whether the working class should be termed materialist at all.

In fact, what Orwell questions is the materialism not only of the proletariat, but of Marx himself.[3] It is an essential feature of Marx's historical materialism that "he divides social life into an economic or material base . . . and an ideological *superstructure* which reflects that base." This division is essential to the concept of economic determinism, to Marx's claim that it is "the material productive life of men . . . which determines social consciousness," including ideas and ideologies (Kamenka 569). Hence Marx's famous statement that "the ruling or dominant ideology of any social period is the ideology of the ruling class" (Kamenka 571). Orwell gives a characteristically nonmaterialist interpretation to this key concept; he asserts that

> the most important part of Marx's theory is contained in the saying: "Where your treasure is, there will your heart be also". But before Marx developed it, what force had that saying had? Who had paid any attention to it? Who had inferred from it . . . that laws, religious and moral codes are all a superstructure built over existing property relations? It was Christ, according to the Gospel, who uttered the text, but it was Marx who brought it to life (v. 3, 121).

Characteristically, Orwell interprets Marx's division between the economic base and the superstructure of ideas — an essential feature of Marx's materialism — to prove Marx's *spiritual* affinity with the ideals of Christian humanism. Along the same lines Orwell analyzes "Marx's famous saying that 'religion is the opium of the people.'" Orwell argues that

> Marx did not say . . . that religion is merely a dope handed out from above; he said that it is something that people create for themselves to supply a need he recognized to be a real one. "Religion is the sigh of the soul in a soulless world. Religion is the opium of the people". What is he saying except that man does *not* live by bread alone, that hatred is *not* enough, that a world worth living cannot be founded on 'realism' and machine guns? (v. 2, 33).

Whether Orwell's interpretation of Marx is objectively correct, it is important for us to see that Orwell the satirist, Orwell the pamphleteer, attacks his Adversary, the Leftist intellectual, for forgetting the moral-spiritual dimension of the Socialist Movement,[4] which should therefore "be reminded of the original, half-forgotten objective of human brotherhood" (v. 4, 485).[5]

In harmony with his life-long search for universal moral and spiritual values, we noted in Chapter 3, in Spain Orwell turned to Socialism as not only a political commitment but also a spiritual faith, the core of his humanism. The emotional intensity of this faith finds expression in a poem he addresses to a working-class Italian soldier ready to sacrifice his life for his brothers in Spain, for a better future for humanity as a whole. Orwell here introduces the image of the "crystal spirit," as if to pledge faith to the survival of the human spirit through the purity and indestructible vitality of the working class: "But the thing that I saw in your face/ No power can disherit/ No bomb that ever burst/ Shatters the crystal spirit" (v. 2, 306).

When in *Nineteen Eighty-Four* Winston wants to articulate his faith to O'Brien, he too associates the "spirit of Man" with the proles' vitality, pitted against the "dead" intellectuals who are paralysed by the Party's moribund "world view . . . [that is] imposed by the dead upon the living" (180). By contrast to the Party members, the "proles [are] immortal." Still able to sing, cry, and enjoy the process of life, they have "the vitality which the Party did not share and could not kill" (188).

Although, seeing the proles in their debased, brutalized condition in Oceania, Winston requires a real "act of faith" (77) to think highly of them, undoubtedly they are the source of the vitality he is looking for when he makes his last appeal to the "spirit of Man" in order to refute O'Brien's prediction:

> "You could not create such a world as you have just described. It is. . . . It is impossible."
> "Why?". . .
> "It would have no vitality. It would disintegrate. It would commit suicide." (231)

The vital promise of our inextinguishable humanity depends upon the proles. They will, in spite of so many defeats and betrayals, keep growing towards the sun like a plant (v. 2, 299), continue to be fertile like the washerwoman, mother to fifteen children (187). In their "vitality" which is "immortal," the proles of Oceania still remind us here of Orwell's 1937 celebration of the "crystal spirit" that "no bomb can ever shatter." Their strength and vitality are still undeniable. In his Preface to *Animal Farm*, Orwell tells us that the metaphor for the workers' oppression came to him when seeing a cart-horse being whipped by a little boy (v. 3, 458), and in *Nineteen Eighty-Four* we hear the proles "needed only to rise up and shake themselves like a horse shaking off flies" (64). But Winston recognizes a paradox: "until they become conscious they will never rebel, and until after they have rebelled they cannot become conscious" (65). The horse is unaware of his strength being superior to his master's; he lacks the capacity of consciousness, the Word. Will the proles of Oceania ever attain that capacity?

In *Nineteen Eighty-Four* the satirist demonstrates that Oceania suffers from the escalation of a phenomenon already rampant in our world: the corruption of consciousness, the corruption of the Word. No revolutionary action can redeem the world of Oceania without first addressing the 'Big Lie' responsible for this corruption. Therefore, even if Winston's "spirit of Man" still carries a clear allusion to Orwell's originally exalted image of the working class's "crystal spirit," significantly in *Nineteen Eighty-Four* the responsibility for upholding the future of our species rests upon a writer. "The last man of Europe" is not a prole; he is one of the last literati. He may look to the proles for vitality and hope, but he is unlike them in still having command of the Word, consciousness, memory, and at least some concept of our cultural heritage. His heroic struggle for authenticity is therefore directed at finding the Truth, and combating the corruption of the Word. Consequently, to find the proper perspective on the "spirit of Man" in *Nineteen Eighty-Four*, we should turn from the "crystal spirit" of the proletariat to the "crystal paperweight" that becomes the symbol of the "last man's" private world, his "incorruptible inner self" (v. 4, 402), the uniqueness and integrity of each individual psyche.

It is noteworthy that the "crystal paperweight" still carries a reminder of the role of the working class, since Winston finds this mysterious object, together with the other cherished mementos of the past, in the prole quarters. Nevertheless, in *Nineteen Eighty-Four* the central drama of resistance does not focus on the collective will of a class; it focuses on the individual psyche as the last stronghold of our civilization, the spirit of our species. Orwell's concept of the human psyche incorporates (although it is not defined by), his characteristic response to aspects of Freudian thought.

Response to Freud

According to Rees, Orwell was indifferent to Freud's ideas (13), and in Paul Roazan's opinion, "George Orwell and Sigmund Freud seem mutually uncongenial figures in intellectual history" (675). Yet, as noted in Chapters 4, 8, and 12, Orwell's view of human nature was profoundly influenced by that new, fundamentally Freudian,[6] model of "psychological man" that emerged on the literary scene in the first decades of the twentieth-century, even if he was not in agreement with some of the well-known implications of Freudian ideology. As noted in Chapter 4, Orwell was not impressed by Freud's concept of the Oedipus complex, and did not accept that human behaviour was determined by the forces of the subconscious. We have seen in the discussion of Winston's dream sequence that Winston is driven by a fundamentally moral attitude: he feels compelled to recall the degree of his responsibility in his mother's disappearance. After his breakthrough dream that helps him understand the past, Winston makes a moral commitment for the future by determining not to betray Julia. Since sanity and moral commitment mean virtually the same thing in Orwell's vocabulary, he admits discomfort when faced with the neutral attitude psychology tends to take to moral questions.[7]

Are critics nevertheless right in stating that Orwell finds Freud's concepts uncongenial? Is there a way to read the novel, as some critics have, as a parody of Freudian psychoanalysis? Careful reading would suggest that the answer is no to both questions. As we have seen in Chapters 4 and 12, as long as Winston acts as his own psychoanalyst, his character shows growth and increasing self-awareness. The parody of the psychoanalytical process takes place in Part 3, in the Ministry of Love, and the process leads to Winston's destruction, not because psychoanalysis is useless or harmful, but because it is used by O'Brien in a diabolic reversal of its original function, not to heal but to destroy the individual psyche.[8]

Orwell's sophisticated use of such Freudian concepts as the dynamic relationship between id, ego, and superego as an energy system is endemic to his psycho-historical analysis of the totalitarian system. That he identified the Inner Party with the superego is confirmed by Alex Comfort: "We talked about his book which I took to be a political statement against dictatorship. His reply was astonishing — that it was, but the model in his mind was also that of a neurotic internal 'thought police' with Big Brother as the superego" (17).

In fact, the Inner Party fulfils the role of a punitive, sadistic superego, which deflects the energies needed for a maturing ego by tampering with the sexual instinct. As noted before, it is one of the central tenets of Freudian psychoanalysis that the "outbreaks of anxiety and a general preparedness for anxiety were produced . . . whenever sexual excitation was inhibited, arrested or deflected in its progress toward satisfaction" (v. 20, 110). Consequent to what Freud would call their "undischarged sexual excitation or enforced abstinence" (v. 20, 110), the Party members of Oceania live in a state of hysteria that can be channelled into sadistic hatred of the 'enemy' or mystical adulation of the leader. In his study on the fascist personality, Wilhelm Reich elaborates on Freud's insight, when arguing the close connection between mysticism and sadism, and pointing out that both "religion and tyrannical political systems . . . provide excitement that is both antisexual and a substitution for sexuality" (168).

Orwell's picture of Oceania is clearly in accord with Freud's views on the role of sexual denial, an interpretation also confirmed by historical accounts of totalitarianism. Thus, "it was Hitler himself who pointed out that the effect of his speeches was the seduction and sexual ravishing of the crowds, and a former confidant of the Fuehrer who noticed that Hitler made the strongest impression on people who were highly suggestible or somewhat effeminate" (Tolstoy 335).

In the light of the historical evidence for the strong connection between enforced sexual puritanism and a hysterical excitement generated by, and for, the worship of the leader, it is rather unexpected that Professor Crick should suggest that Orwell's description of the sexual practices in Oceania is largely irrelevant to the satire of totalitarianism ("Introduction" 120). A closer look at the State's strict control of sexuality in the U.S.S.R. under Stalin should make it clear that Orwell's Freudian analysis is here clearly on target.

It is true that the moral code of the early Bolshevik revolutionary did allow for free love, but the sexual instinct was clearly subordinated to the Bolshevik's primary function: to advocate the cause of the Revolution. In the course of the "Stalinist revolution" in the 1930s, the Party's relaxed position on sexuality changed into a strictly repressive, controlling attitude. Birth control methods were discouraged, abortion was severely punished, divorce was virtually impossible to obtain. Also, the family as a whole became legally punishable for acts of sabotage or dissent proven against any of its members. As a result, "the State was admitted as a new member of the family." These new family laws were essential to the machinery of Stalinist terror, which relied on the denunciation of parent by child and spouse by spouse (and instituted the death penalty against children of twelve). The subordination of sexual and family love to the State

> was a constant theme in literature, the cinema, and every form of art. The family is an important form of the collective, so the argument ran, but the state is an incomparably more important one. That is why, in the 1936 movie, *Party Card*, the wife denounces the husband to security organs. . . . This call for the betrayal of one's kin was directed to all family members without distinction (Geller 286).

Orwell was familiar with these developments, which were well documented in books he reviewed on the U.S.S.R., such as Koestler's *The Yogi and the Commissar*. Therefore, young Miss Parsons' betrayal of her father, and Winston's fear that his wife Katharine might betray him, are not figments of an erratic imagination: they are allusions to a policy central to totalitarian dictatorships. Of course, Orwell uses the satirist's licence for overstatement when he makes O'Brien boast that the Party is intent on eliminating the orgasm in the near future. But when the novel makes clear that Winston cannot even dream of obtaining a divorce (61), that Julia has to deny her sexuality in the youth movement, that Katharine refers to making love as "doing our duty to the Party" (62), Orwell's allusions to the grim, restrictive attitudes toward sexuality under Stalin's regime are unmistakable.

Of course no one, in actual fact, would have prevented people, even in Stalin's regime, from getting married because they were attracted to each other, but there was a severe contradiction between private loyalties, sexual attraction, family love, and the loyalty both sexes owed to the Party. Women whose husbands were arrested during the mass arrests of Stalin's purges were expected to sue for divorce so that they and their children could not be further associated with the husband's "dissent." These women were expected to demonstrate loyalty to the State over personal loyalty to their spouses. (In *The Gulag Archipelago* Solzhenitsyn describes his encounter in the camps with a "wave of wives arrested for failure to renounce their husbands" [77].)

To respond to Professor Crick's point, then, Orwell's analysis of the sexual puritanism in totalitarian regimes coincides with historical evidence; it also shows his agreement with Freud's analysis of the connection between sexual denial and hysteria.

In fact, Orwell describes O'Brien as a "mixture of psychologist and inquisitor" (169), who uses the sophisticated insights of modern psychology not for the healing of the psyche but for its destruction. Winston's ordeal in Room 101 reveals the Party's uncanny awareness of Freud's theory on repetition. Freud observes that a little boy, suffering from a relatively minor trauma, tends to "reproduce every distressing impression" (v. 20, 167) of the trauma in his play. The adult, driven by the anxiety related to a major trauma, tends to return to its scene to 'repeat' it, that is, to act it out deliberately, so that "the ego, which [originally] experienced the trauma passively, now repeats it actively in a weakened version, in the hope of being able itself to direct its course" (v. 20, 166). Forcing Winston to confront the hungry rats, O'Brien is fully aware of Winston's phobia originating in his childhood crisis. Winston does not *choose* to relive this trauma. Nor does the repetition present the trauma in a "weakened version." O'Brien's purpose is not to allow the ego to direct its own course and thereby liberate itself from guilt and anxiety. On the contrary, his purpose is to crush the ego and thereby produce in the 'patient' a sense of infantile helplessness.[9]

This diabolical reversal of modern psychology's healing function is at the very centre of the concept of Room 101, the Party's greatest psychological invention, which is based on the recognition that there are different walls, different limits, to each personality. This concept is articulated quite clearly by Freud: "Each individual has in all probability a *limit* beyond which his mental apparatus fails in its function [of] *mastering* the quantities of excitation which require to be disposed of" (v. 20, 148). O'Brien's description of Room 101 carries a strong Freudian echo: "for everyone there is something unendurable — something that cannot be contemplated. . . . [The rats] are a form of pressure you cannot withstand, even if you wished to" (245).

Another important Freudian echo that works in combination with the metaphor of Room 101 is the shattering of the crystal paperweight. In his "Dissection of the Personality," Freud offers the metaphor of a crystal for the disintegration of the psyche: "If we throw a crystal to the floor, it breaks; but not into haphazard pieces. It comes apart along the lines of cleavage into fragments whose boundaries, though they were invisible, were predetermined by the crystal's structure. Mental patients are split and broken structures of the same kind" (v. 22, 59). Orwell's brilliant analogy between the shattering of the crystal and the shattering of the individual psyche in Room 101 seems here to be inspired by the concepts, even the images, of Freud. Because Room 101 is a place where each individual psyche can be destroyed, disintegrated, as it were 'unravelled' in a way that is specific to its particular structure, the shattering of the crystal paperweight by the Thought Police at the moment of Winston's arrest is a most telling foreshadowing of the "last man's" greatest fear, his irrecoverable loss of the "spirit of Man" not through the loss of physical existence, but through the disintegration of his individual psyche.

Response to Existentialist Thought

Since it represents the lovers' private world, their private values, the crystal paperweight also invites an existential analysis of Winston's search for authenticity in defiance of the public values of the Party. In fact, recently several of Orwell's novels have been interpreted from an Existential point of view.[10] This, of course, does not imply that Orwell had subscribed to the tenets of Existential thought, nor even that he had first-hand knowledge of Existentialist writers such as Kierkegaard, Nietzsche, or Jaspers. Nor did he have an intellectual exchange with such contemporaries as Camus and Sartre. As a matter of information, we know that when Orwell was in Paris in 1945, he had an appointment with Camus, but on account of illness, Camus was unable to come (v. 4, 457).[11]

As for Sartre, Orwell reviewed his book on anti-Semitism rather unfavourably and wrote to a friend that Sartre was a "bag of wind, though probably when it comes to existentialism, which I don't profess to understand, it may not be so" (v. 4, 510). It seems clear that Orwell dislikes not only Sartre's book, but also the voice and the persona. Nevertheless, just like the ideas of Marx and Freud, the ideas of Existentialism were in the air, and Orwell's claim that he does "not profess to understand" them sounds more like a dismissal of what he does not like than an innocent plea of ignorance. According to Rees, Orwell was "unimpressed by the Existentialist philosophies in vogue towards the end of his life and here, I think, there was a temperamental barrier; though it might nevertheless be claimed that he was in real life a better Existentialist, more authentic and more 'engaged' than many philosophers whose Existentialism exists mainly between the covers of a book" (13).

Rees is undoubtedly right in drawing attention to the fact that Orwell's life shows evidence of attitudes embraced by Existentialism. But the purpose here is to determine Orwell's familiarity with, and his characteristic response to, Existentialist ideas in his writing. Like Nietzsche and Kierkegaard, who warned against accepting meaningless abstractions, Orwell is sceptical of abstractions, theories, and theoreticians, a position also in harmony with the empirical tradition.[12] Ironically, he claims he "never had the slightest fear of a dictatorship of the proletariat," but admits "to having a perfect horror of a dictatorship of theorists" (v. 1, 583).

We should also remember that Winston shows true existential courage when he risks torture and death in his effort to form his own thoughts and values, by breaking out of the intellectual strait-jacket of abstractions, clichés, and empty Party slogans.

It is also part of his search for authenticity that he insists on re-assembling the fragments of the nursery rhyme and on buying the diary and the crystal paperweight, mementos of a past the Party "controls" through a network of lies.

As for Orwell himself, his 'existential' mistrust of the dishonesty inherent in accepting ready-made opinions is clearly manifest, not only in his angry attacks on "smelly little orthodoxies" (v. 1, 504), but also in the probing, speculative tone in his essays, in the emphasis on first-hand experience in his 'documentaries,' in the autobiographical strain in his fiction. Nevertheless, Orwell's treatment of the first-hand, autobiographical experience in the following instance reveals not only his affinity with, but also his resistance to, the 'pure' Existentialist position.

At the time of writing *Homage to Catalonia*, Orwell admits that including an entire chapter of documentation to defend "the Trotskyists who were accused [by the Stalinists] of plotting with France" might "ruin the book" within a few years. But, he explains, "I could not have done otherwise. I happened to know what few people in England have been allowed to know, that *innocent people were falsely accused*. If I had not been *angry* about that I should never have written the book" (v. 1, 29, my italics).

The first-hand experience of knowing about "innocent people falsely accused" goes back to Orwell's personal experience of "the horrible atmosphere of suspicion and hatred, the lies and rumours circulating everywhere, the posters screaming from the hoardings that *I and everyone like me* was a fascist spy" (*HC* 238–239, my italics). Fighting against Franco in the "POUM, militia — i.e. the Spanish Trotskyists," Orwell explains, "at Huesca a Fascist sniper shot me through the throat. . . . [Then] in the middle of 1937, when the Communists gained control . . . and began to hunt down the Trotskyites, . . . both [my wife and I] found ourselves among the victims. We were lucky to get out of Spain alive" (v. 3, 456).

Orwell knows 'existentially' what it is like to be falsely accused, threatened by death, betrayed by the very people who had been generally regarded as the staunchest champions of one's own cause. The satirist's "generous anger" (v. 1, 504), however, takes Orwell a long way beyond the personal experience: "My wife and I both saw innocent people being thrown into prison because they were suspected of unorthodoxy. Yet on our return to England we found numerous sensible and well-informed observers believing the most fantastic accounts of conspiracy, treachery and sabotage which the press reported from the Moscow trials" (v. 3, 457).

Clearly, the continued anger against injustice and betrayal that triggered not only *Homage to Catalonia* but also *Animal Farm* and *Nineteen Eighty-Four* has an existential nucleus in the personal experience of betrayal. This experience, however, becomes the source of compassion for everyone else in the same predicament, until the satirist's "generous anger" at the victimization of the innocent swells into "savage indignation" against the "protective stupidity" of all who obstruct justice by refusing to face the truth, a tendency Orwell finds particularly dangerous in the case of powerful Stalinist propaganda.

Orwell's existential emphasis on the authenticity of the writer's lived experience notwithstanding, it seems to me most Existentialists among Orwell's contemporaries would be lacking in Orwell's "generous anger" which was admittedly so vital for him in turning on the dynamo of his satirical vision. In fact, Orwell's intellectual passion as a satirist derives from the capacity for approval and disapproval inherent in a fundamentally moral imagination. I suggest this quality describes Orwell's stance more faithfully than the more typically dispassionate Existentialist attitude which, denying the universality of any value system, tends towards moral relativism.

Orwell's concept of the connection between subjective and objective truth is also worth examining in this connection. From an early age, Orwell tells us, he developed the inner voice of the witness, the first-hand observer and recorder of facts and events (v. 1, 24), and considered it the writer's duty to render his first-hand experience of any situation with sincerity, for better or worse. Hence his emphasis in *Homage to Catalonia* that the book contains *his* truth and not necessarily the whole truth: "Beware of my partisanship, my mistakes of fact and distortion inevitably caused by my having seen only *one corner* of events" (*HC* 230–231, my italics).

That one's truth must be founded on one's lived, subjective experience is an Existentialist pronouncement reiterated in "Inside the Whale" and "Writers and Leviathan," among other writings. Yet, unlike the 'pure' Existentialist, Orwell does not imply that since all truth is limited by the parameters of our subjective experience, all truth is relative and the search for universal truth is futile. On the contrary, Orwell's writing implies that the more difficult the attainment of truth, the greater the need for its unhindered pursuit: hence his genuine anguish when he saw that the totalitarian state falsified historical facts and forced writers to practise emotional and intellectual self-censorship, thereby denying the very existence of truth.

As noted in Chapters 5 and 7, Winston's struggle for authenticity, for finding the "inner core" of his private self, also engages him in the pursuit of historical truth. If, as Rees suggests, Orwell can be described as a "conscience-stricken man," Winston should be described as truth-stricken. Confiding his knowledge to Julia that the trial of Aaronson, Rutherford, and Jones, many years earlier, had been rigged and their confessions untrue, Winston still feels so outraged by the discovery that Julia is genuinely puzzled: "Were they friends of yours?" she asks innocently. (Or, perhaps, she is the 'pure' Existentialist in the novel?)

One would expect Orwell's ties with an Existentialist definition of the subjective nature of truth to be most obvious when it comes to his critique of the orthodox Marxist Adversary's uncritical obedience to ideology, including its eschatological framework. Orwell defines the totalitarian state as a theocracy, with a semi-divine fuehrer who claims infallibility on the basis that he is leading his people along the path towards historical fulfilment. Orwell's career as a political writer can be seen as an Existentialist protest against the scientific determinism claimed by the Marxist theoreticians, in that he regards the 'scientific' claim as a sham used by the power-hungry for their own purposes, and he also argues that prophetic predictions of our future deny our freedom of choice. In his critique of Burnham's *Managerial Revolution*, Orwell points out that once we hear the prediction of peril, we can exercise our freedom to change our course and disaster can be averted: the future is not predetermined (v. 4, 207). Orwell argues even more strongly against the historical determinism inherent in Marxist theory, and the fraudulent way Stalinists use the "dialectic" to vindicate their regime of the present today, in the name of the inevitable "final synthesis," the Communism of the future. Orwell's castigation of his Adversary, in "Catastrophic Gradualism," for condoning Stalin's enslavement of the present generation in the name of liberating mankind in the future (v. 4, 33), and his insistence that Stalin's brutal oppression of human rights today cannot be vindicated in the name of building an ostensibly humane society for tomorrow, place him in a philosophical position that combines Existentialism and humanism. However, when a choice between Existentialism and humanism is presented, for Orwell the latter always takes precedence. Of course, if "by humanism one understands a doctrine according to which individual persons are the source of value and intelligibility, existentialism itself is humanistic" (Olson, *Existentialism* 47). Nevertheless, Existentialists oppose a fundamental doctrine of humanism, "according to which the individual can and should identify with the species of mankind, putting the interest of mankind at large above his own or those of any other single individual" (Olson, *Existentialism* 47). Hence "the basis of the Existentialist attack upon humanism is quite clearly related to the anguish of the here and now. If man is tied to a limited region of space and time, then he cannot identify with mankind at large . . . the future of mankind is unknown, and the individual cannot identify with the unknown" (Olson, *Existentialism* 49).

Clearly, Winston's wordless lament over the shattering crystal expresses existential anguish about the frailty of man's and woman's hope for futurity: "The fragment of coral, a tiny crinkle of pink like a sugar rosebud from a cake rolled across the mat. How small, thought Winston, how small it always was" (190).

He also expresses anguish about an unknowable future when it comes to the question of communicating with an audience through his diary: "How could one communicate with the future? It was of its nature impossible" (12). Nevertheless, Winston asserts not only the psychological need but also the moral imperative to communicate with the future: "He was a lonely ghost uttering a truth that nobody would ever hear. But so long as he uttered it, in some obscure way the continuity was not broken. It was not by making yourself heard but by staying sane that you carried on the human heritage" (28).

Central to Winston's quest for authenticity is his attempt to assure the continuity of the human heritage by producing in his diary an unchangeable record of the past that will serve as a link with the future.[13] He is the "last guardian of the human spirit" in Oceania because he is the "last man" (233) who carries such a commitment to the past and the future. It is precisely because of the humanist's commitment to the continuity of the human species that Orwell is so critical of ideological

predictions of the future that deny us one of the most important attributes of being human — our freedom of choice. In
his 1950 "The Failing of the Prophecy," Camus echoes Orwell's
objections to historical determinism. Unlike Camus and Orwell, however, Sartre insists that in spite of the aberrations of
Stalin's regime, the inevitable long-term results of the Marxist
dialectic still justify the Western intellectual's commitment to
the Communist Party. Sartre here changes the parameters of
his philosophy significantly; he identifies with an existentially
unknowable future and challenges the individual's freedom of
choice, a concept central to Existentialism.

Is Existentialism, then, a significant aspect of Orwell's humanism? The particular brand of humanism that may be described as 'Orwellian' resists any 'package,' any ready-made theory or body of thought. His parallels with the Existentialists
and their precursors are undeniable, but so are his personal differences. Like Nietzsche, Orwell is concerned with the 'vacuum,'
the spiritual void created by the loss of religious belief, and he
warns us not to accept hypocrisy, abstractions, and the false values of an old and outgrown morality. Yet he has no sympathy
for Nietzsche's "blond beast," the Superman of a new morality
advocated by the philosopher. Orwell's courage as a humanist
lies precisely in his insistence on facing the vacuum with dignity,
relying on the "decency" of human beings who "know that they
are mortal and are nevertheless willing to act as brothers" (v. 2,
32). Like Jaspers, Orwell is interested in boundary situations
and explores the dilemma of human relationships. For Orwell
personal love, like genuine communication, is "hard work" (v. 4,
528), yet a fundamental criterion of our humanity. Like Sartre,
Orwell is preoccupied with the human being's capacity for freedom, but he also draws attention to the crucial question of our
social responsibility to maintain our *right* to freedom, because
in certain societies men and women can become stripped of
freedom and hence of their essential nature as human beings.[14]
But I believe that among all the Existentialist thinkers of his
time, it is Camus with whom Orwell shows the greatest affinity;
both pose the question "What is Man?" and assert that it is
less difficult to become a saint than to remain human.

Winston's commitment to uphold our cultural heritage in order to remain human is a reflection of Orwell's vital interest in
the great thinkers of the past and of his own time. Respect
for this "heritage," however, does not mean slavish adulation;

probably Orwell's closest tie with Existentialism is to be found in that lively, spontaneous, 'existential' process in which he explores and tests the validity of the various thought systems of his era against his own lived experience and temperament.

A case in point is Orwell's temperamental disagreement with the 'realist's' approach to moral questions, although elements of Marxist, Freudian, and Existentialist thought have entered his vision significantly. As noted in Chapter 7, in the "blackwhite" aspect of Doublethink Orwell parodies Marx's concept of the dialectic that allows the same act to be assessed as negative or positive, depending on its position in a particular historical phase of the dialectical process. Orwell also expresses dismay at the tendency in modern psychology to substitute psychological terms for moral ones, and he forcefully asserts the universality of moral values, over the Existentialists' denial of them.

Some of Orwell's most typical responses to the thought of Marx, Freud, and the Existentialists reveal salient characteristics of his own intellectual temper. Thus, Orwell shows a tendency to give a spiritual-moral reading to Marx's concept of Socialism, although Marx is known for a materialist approach to history. In his response to Freudian thought, Orwell shows a similar tendency to 'moralize' the subconscious, to attribute moral intent to our "dreamthoughts" which guide us not only to sanity and self-knowledge but also to moral conduct. Characteristically, in spite of many strongly existential elements in his writing — particularly in the autobiographical strain in his fiction and in his characters' search for authenticity against the public values imposed on them by their society — Orwell also tends to 'negate the negation' inherent in the Existentialists' concepts of alienation and their denial of unifying moral values. This is to say, Orwell's definition of the "spirit of Man" contains many of the insights of the 'realism' of the twentieth century, but it is by no means contained by any one of these thought systems. Therefore, to get a fuller view of the "faith" essential in a great twentieth-century satirist's struggle against despair, we must go back to the roots of this humanistic "faith" in the moral idealism of the nineteenth century.

Notes

[1] In "The Lure of Profundity," Orwell admits that "Marx is a difficult author to read" (*New English Weekly* 30 Dec. 1937, 325, qtd. in Bonifas 165).   Yet, according to his friend Rees, in the

circle of the *Adelphi* Orwell impressed Marxist theoreticians with his sophisticated command of Marxist terminology (147). Gilbert Bonifas also points out that Orwell was engaged in dialogue with Murry, Rees, and Common, contributors to the *Adelphi*, who all possessed an excellent knowledge of Marxism, and while working on *The Road to Wigan Pier* he "assisted in the [Socialist] Summer School organized by Murry and the *Adelphi* in Langham, close to Colchester" (159). Even more important than biographical evidence, Orwell's essays and his early novels, particularly *Keep the Aspidistra Flying*, show that he was well acquainted with the various tenets of Marxism even before the writing of *Road to Wigan Pier*.

[2] Never fully satisfied with an exclusively Marxist interpretation of political events, by the 1940s Orwell feels "it is not easy to find a direct economic explanation of the behaviour of the people who now rule the world. The desire for power seems to be much more dominant than the desire for wealth" (v. 4, 289). In fact, nationalism, racism, and totalitarianism have psychological roots that require consideration prior to the economic 'realities,' and "so long as the world tendency is towards nationalism and totalitarianism, scientific progress simply helps it along" (v. 3, 175).

[3] According to Orwell's 'spiritual' interpretation of Marx, "any *thinking Socialist* will concede to the Catholics that when economic injustice had been righted, the fundamental problems of man's place in the universe will remain. . . . It's all summed up by Marx's saying that after Socialism has arrived, human history can begin" (v. 3, 83).

[4] Orwell declares what the Soviet experience should have made clear to any objective observer: "Socialism used to be defined as 'common ownership of the means of production', but it is now seen that if common ownership means to have centralized control, it merely paves the way for a new form of oligarchy. Centralized control is a necessary precondition of Socialism, but it no more produces Socialism than my typewriter would of itself produce this article I am writing" (v. 4, 36).

[5] Orwell's faith in man's "international brotherhood" notwithstanding, Orwell makes fun of "Marxist phraseology [which] is peculiar in that it consists largely of translations. Its characteristic vocabulary comes ultimately from German or Russian phrases which have been adopted in one country after another with no effort to find suitable equivalents" (v. 3, 133). In the British political landscape — so obviously different from that of Germany or Russia — it is simply ludicrous to repeat Marxist-Stalinist clichés unthinkingly: "Just talk about hydra-headed jack boots riding roughshod over blood-stained hyenas, and you are all right. For confirmation of which, see almost any pamphlet issued by the Communist Party" (v. 3, 134).

[6] Orwell the essayist makes frequent reference to the Freudian concepts of psychoanalysis, neurosis, guilt complex, repression, and projection; witness, for example, his review of Koestler's *Arrival and Departure* (v. 3, 279–280). Orwell's awareness of Freud's dream analysis plays a significant role in Winston's dream sequence in *Nineteen Eighty-Four,* and analyzing his own dreams Orwell is fully aware of the Freudian connotations: "The night before the Russo-German pact was announced I dreamed that the War had started. It was one of those dreams which, whatever *Freudian inner meaning* they may have, do sometimes reveal to you the real state of your feelings" (v. 1, 590, my italics). Orwell also refers to Freudian slips, or "Freudian errors" (v. 4, 190), when discussing the bad English of politically orthodox writers.

Going beyond the subconscious motives of his political opponent, he is also sensitive to the Freudian motives of his fictional characters, and even to the subconscious 'subtext' of his own politics. Thus, he claims, in spite of his speeches and pamphlets *against* the war before the Russo-German pact was announced, his dream "taught [him] two things, first, that [he] should be simply relieved when the long-dreaded war started, secondly, that [he] was patriotic at heart" (v. 1, 590). In fact, Orwell was profoundly interested in Freud's seminal thought on the subconscious, as evidenced by his own speculations on our "dreamthoughts" (v. 2, 18) in a passage that has, incidentally, been chosen as a motto for an educational film under the title *Freud: The Hidden Nature of Man,* released by the Learning Corporation of America in 1970.

[7] I would suggest that Orwell's negative attitude to certain aspects of Freudian thought stems from the neutral attitude psychology takes to moral questions. Orwell found the characters of D.H. Lawrence, for example, to move in such an exclusively psychological dimension that "there did not seem to be any classification of characters into 'good' or 'bad'. Lawrence seemed to sympathize with all of them about equally, and this was so unusual as to give me the feeling of having lost my bearings" (v. 3, 259). In contrast to this lack of moral differentiation in the "serious novel," in "lowbrow fiction one still expects to find a sharp distinction between right and wrong, and between legality and illegality. The common people, on the whole, are still living in the world of absolute good and evil from which the intellectuals have long escaped" (v. 3, 259). Finally, due to the "mingled boredom and brutality of war," the intellectuals are followed by the others, until "emancipation is complete. Freud and Machiavelli have reached the suburbs" (v. 3, 260). Apprehensive of what he sees as moral neutrality and the overemphasis on sexuality in Freudian thought, in his study on Dali Orwell even suggests that "a psychiatrist usually has a leaning towards some sexual aberration himself" (v. 3, 193).

[8] Here Orwell seems to be in agreement with Freud's interpretation of "group feeling" which, in too many instances, hinges on scapegoating, on the projection of evil on the outsider. Ironically, Freud points out, "when once the Apostle Paul posited universal love between men as the foundation of his Christian community, extreme intolerance on the part of Christendom towards those who remained outside it became the inevitable consequence" (v. 21, 114). Freud also draws a comparison between the scapegoating in the early Christian communities and in the newly formed Soviet Union: "One only wonders what the Soviets will do after they have wiped out the bourgeoisie" (v. 21, 115). Years later, Orwell also ponders the indispensable role of the scapegoat in a secular religion: "It occurred to me yesterday," he notes in his diary after the assassination of Trotsky, "how will the Russian state get on without Trotsky? Probably they will be forced to invent a substitute" (v. 4, 418).

Orwell seems to be in agreement with Freud as well that the "group feeling" associated with the rituals of religion or the "secular religion" of totalitarianism represent a regression for the mature ego. According to Freud, "the origin of religious attitudes can be traced back in clear outline as far as the feeling of infantile helplessness" (v. 20, 72). Also, what Orwell describes as a childhood ambivalence to the God he is expected to love and fear at the same time, (v. 4, 412) is in Freud's eyes the prototype of the "double significance of taboo" in primitive religion, and in "An Autobiographical Study" he argues that "the primal father, at once feared and hated, revered and envied, became the prototype of God himself" (v. 20, 68).

[9] By starving and corrupting the id, the Party manages to 'starve' the ego, depriving it of its energies, until it gives up or breaks down in its ultimate function, the testing of reality. "Reality control" is one of the synonyms for Doublethink, the ability of the Party to exert "total" control over reality by assuming "total" control over the mind (214). Another synonym for "reality control" is "controlled insanity" (185), a state of mind that relies on the most rigorous practice of psychological defence mechanisms to be able to cope with, or screen out, reality. While a defence mechanism is a self-protective function of the ego, designed to diminish anxiety temporarily, if these mechanisms become too numerous or too powerful, they may lead to a total blocking out of reality. Thus Parsons represses his fear and hatred of Big Brother to the point that he *overcompensates*; he keeps repeating the Party slogans to convince everyone, above all himself, of his unlimited love for Big Brother. At the peak of his anxiety in the Ministry of Love, he *identifies with the aggressor*," (201) by expressing a genuine wish to be severely punished for his 'transgression' (201). But of all defence mechanisms, it is *projection* that characterizes the behaviour of the 'starved rats' of Oceania most conspicuously. All of

them potential victims, they repress their own fear and hatred of the Party, feelings that cause them great anxiety. Deeply anxious about their own sinful desire to dissent, they project this on one another, denouncing everyone else for harbouring the desire.

The prominence of these defence mechanisms, often leading to insanity, has been observed during witch-hunts in the past — witness *The Crucible*, where Arthur Miller explores the dynamism of the Salem witch trials as a metaphor for the anti-Communist 'witch trials' of the McCarthy era. They have been observed on an even vaster scale during Hitler's persecution of scapegoats in Germany, and during the waves of purges and mass deportations during Stalin's regime in the U.S.S.R. and Eastern Europe. Orwell's profound understanding of these phenomena in their psycho-political context is essential to his satire of a ruling class that depends on the practice of Doublethink, on the "controlled insanity" of the people, for its existence.

[10] According to Michael Carter, Winston "exemplifies classic existential action" (217). Carter finds the themes of Orwell's fiction "reducible to the prevailing orthodoxy's power to demand of the private authentic individual that he generate a public unauthentic self; and it is the conflict which arises from this demand which forms the thematic centre of every Orwell novel. It is also the great theme of existential thought" (28).

[11] Herbert Lottman, in *Albert Camus: A Biography*, points out that Orwell and Camus exchanged letters in connection with the "creation of a Committee of Support for Spanish Republican Émigrés" (461) and Camus's "journal notes show he was also reading George Orwell" (413), but he does not specify which work of Orwell (413). Nor is there evidence that Orwell read *The Stranger* or *The Plague*.

[12] Alan Sandison draws attention to the importance of empiricism in Orwell's thought, pointing out that Orwell regarded "the senses . . . inalienable, and in the reception of their independent and particular report of the natural world [there] is proof of our individuality" (10).

[13] Here Winston's commitment is a direct reflection of Orwell's. According to Richard Rees' 1951 "George Orwell" in *Scots Chronicle*, Orwell believed that "to care passionately about the fate of mankind after your death was an ethical imperative" (11, qtd. in Rodden 401).

[14] In discussing the dilemma of freedom, Sartre comes up with the famous paradox that "we were never more free than during the German occupation," arguing that human beings become free in the process of asserting their freedom in situations of high risk and danger. In fact, Sartre argues, it is in the torture chamber that the individual faces the ultimate test of freedom: "All those among us who knew any detail concerning the resistance asked themselves anxiously, 'If they torture me, shall I be able to keep silent?' Thus the basic question

of liberty itself was posed, and we were brought to the verge of the deepest knowledge that man can have of himself . . . *the limit of his own liberty, his capacity for resisting torture and death*" (qtd. in Olson 109, my italics).

By contrast, Winston takes it for granted that under torture one is no longer free; Orwell has little interest in the question of how long one's body or nerves can withstand torture. On this score Winston has no curiosity, aware of "the treachery of the human body which always freezes into inertia at exactly the moment when a special effort is needed" (91). Having no faith in physical heroism, Winston knows right from the beginning that one can no longer be free in the torture chamber. He also knows, instinctively, that the totalitarian state reveals its essence in the torture chamber: "the grovelling on the floor and screaming for mercy, the crack of broken bones, the smashed teeth, the bloody clots of hair. Why did you have to endure it, since the end was always the same. . . . Why then did that horror, which altered nothing, have to lie embedded in future time?" (90–91).

For Sartre the greatest "secret" about the human being is the "limit of his liberty." For Orwell the mysterious "horror" embedded in the future is the individual's inevitable defeat in the totalitarian state. Instead of asking, "what is the extent of our freedom in the torture chamber?" Orwell emphasizes that once there, there is no freedom, and we should exert all our energies to prevent the approach of a society whose very essence is revealed in the torture chamber. Unlike such Existentialist thinkers as Sartre, Frankel (1963) and Bettelheim (1960), who emphasize that human beings maintain their freedom of choice even under torture, because even then they have a say in how fast or how painfully they are willing to die, Orwell's satire is inspired by his "savage indignation" about the indisputable loss of freedom in a totalitarian system, by his conviction that we should prevent the spreading of the totalitarian mentality. Orwell's position on the dilemma of freedom seems to me ultimately less pessimistic than that of Sartre, Frankel, or Bettelheim.

Chapter 14

Orwell's Concept of the Tragic: The Synthesis of Nineteenth-Century Moral Idealism and Twentieth-Century Realism

The conclusion of Orwell's life-long search for a secular, accessible, and universally acceptable moral code coincides with his coming of age as a great writer; hence it is no accident that his two last and most mature novels are satires, indicative of that relatively old-fashioned phenomenon, the moral imagination. Satire as a genre relies on a "militant irony" to score its points against our topsy-turvy, insane, and immoral world of reality in order to accomplish a reversal to the unstated yet firmly held 'norm' of sanity and morality. To expect such a restitution, the satirist has to rely on his various readers' uniform sense of rightness and justice — that is, on moral values he must assume to be universal.

The capacity of the moral imagination for genuine affirmation that is endemic to the mood and moral temper of great satire is, regrettably, often overlooked by those critics who claim that *Nineteen Eighty-Four* conveys a message of pessimism and despair of life. In fact, where Orwell's fiction reveals his most significant difference from his Existentialist contemporaries is in his affirmation of the world of the senses, of his enjoyment of the beauty of the surface of the earth. Sartre's world in his *Words*, *Nausée*, and even his plays, is rarely enticing to the sensual imagination. Camus's *The Chute* and *The Plague* are dominated by grayness and drabness; even when there is sensual exuberance, as in *The Stranger*, this is also a source of the character's deep psychical turbulence. On the whole, the twentieth-century Existentialist tends to perceive the world characteristically in terms of Man's alienation from Nature. Underlying this perception is the philosophical belief that "consciousness is inevitably unhappy consciousness" (Olson 25), that the very process of becoming conscious is equivalent to becoming aware of suffering and the alienation between Man and the Universe.[1]

Unlike these Existentialist writers, Orwell shows reverence for the tangible beauty of Nature, the world of the senses, and the acuteness of sense perceptions. We have seen in Chapter 3 that even in the rather subdued atmosphere of his early novels, the central characters occasionally experience a rush of joy, at least one perfect moment, which is derived from feeling at one with the flow of life in Nature. And, of course, it would be useless to attempt to 'decode' the satire in *Nineteen Eighty-Four* if we did not realize that the love scenes in the Golden Country and in the room over the antique shop create a foil; they establish the natural, human context, allowing us to gauge how unnatural and dehumanized the world of Oceania has become. The moments of alienation, the ugliness of the city, the unpleasantness of sense impressions in Victory Mansions are not a reflection of the human being's inevitable alienation from the Universe; they reflect the alienation created deliberately by a monstrous, *unnatural, inhuman* political system.

As for the characters' epiphanies of happiness and joy, they may be called "Existentialist" moments because they are deeply felt and lead to a higher degree of self-awareness. But are all such moments necessarily Existentialist in the twentieth-century definition of the term?

In effect, I suggest that the epiphanies of Orwell's characters often convey more than an echo of those characteristically Romantic epiphanies familiar from the works of Wordsworth, Keats, and Shelley, which celebrate the fusion, the union between Man and Nature. For example, Orwell's description of Dorothy Hare's pantheistic experience in Nature (*CD* 287) contains echoes of Wordsworth: the landscape becomes fused with the internal landscape of the human mind in meditation, and we are made to feel that in this oneness Man and Nature come fully alive. In those exceptional moments when George Bowling (*CUFA* 528) or Gordon Comstock (*KAF* 737) experience the joy of being alive, Orwell is capable, like Wordsworth, of conveying the humanist's epiphany, a sense of deep affirmation of the process of life: "Not in Utopia,–subterranean field,–/ Or some secret islands, heaven knows where!/ But in the very world, which is the world/ Of all of us–the place where in the end,/ We find our happiness, or not at all!" (*Prelude*, 11, 140–144).

The point here is that Orwell is probably closer to the nineteenth-century Romantic precursors of Existentialism than to the Existentialism of his contemporaries. When, for example, he describes the lovers' meeting in the Golden Country, Winston and Julia's sexual union also becomes the celebration of the union between the human being and Nature in a moment that transcends alienation.

Nor should one overlook some other surprisingly 'Existentialist' manifestations in the Romantic period, such as Byron's description of attending an execution in Italy. Watching the event with opera glasses and recording his own reactions with impassioned objectivity, Byron admits that he was sickened by the sight, yet "determined to see, as one should see everything once with attention" (*Self-Portrait* 408). No doubt there is existential reverence here for the first-hand experience of the witness, the recorder, foreshadowing a similar reverence in Orwell's voice in "A Hanging," in "Shooting an Elephant," and in key scenes in *Homage to Catalonia*. At the same time, just as in the case of Byron, Orwell's intensely 'Romantic' compassion with the victim emerges over and against the meticulous objectivity of a seemingly tough-minded neutral observer. Although the narrative is interspersed with reflections on the narrator's own objectivity, no perceptive reader would miss the writer's passionate — and compassionate — moral commitment.

There is another aspect of Romantic idealism demonstrated by the resemblance between the two Eton boys, the "mad Shelley" and the rebel Eric Blair, more than a hundred years later, both of them "lonely heretics" whose search for authenticity begins with their refusal to conform to the behaviour expected from their class and age group. Professor Crick draws attention to the marginal notes Orwell wrote at Eton on the last page of Shelley's *Prometheus Unbound*. "Courage even in defeat," wrote the schoolboy Eric Blair ("Introduction" 136). In his later years George Orwell returns to this 'Romantic' thought in his essay on Shakespeare. In spite of Orwell's reputation for the tough-mindedness of an almost documentary realism, his analysis of tragic drama and the tragic dimension in the life of the creative artist ("all novels are failures") can come, on occasion, remarkably close to a Romantic, Shelleyan interpretation of the poet-hero's Promethean quest to liberate mankind by struggling against the tyrannical mental habits of political orthodoxy. Especially in *Nineteen Eighty-Four*, expressed through Winston's heroic attempts to uphold the human heritage for the future, Orwell's concept of authenticity, to me, frequently seems closer to a fundamentally Romantic, nineteenth-century definition of the 'religion of humanity' than to the concept of his Existentialist contemporaries.

Even Orwell's debt to Freud does not remain untouched by the epistemological idealism of the Romantics. No doubt Winston's dreams are significant signposts in his journey for self-discovery, and we cannot overlook here Orwell's sophisticated insights into Freudian dream analysis. Still, it is worth noting that Orwell makes Winston stumble upon the Golden Country with "a curious, slow shock of recognition" (110) *after* or *because* he had a dream about it beforehand (31). And it is Winston's "dreamthought" about the girl with dark hair in the Golden Country that prepares him to meet and make love to the real Julia in the real landscape. In this instance Orwell attributes the kind of power to our "dreamthoughts" that Keats would attribute to the visionary power of the Creative imagination: "What the Imagination seizes as Beauty must be truth — whether it existed before or not. . . . The Imagination may be compared to Adam's dream — he awoke and found it truth" (Keats, *Letters* #43).

In its spiritual-heroic aspects, its concern with posterity, its commitment to the universal moral virtues of human decency, its affirmative stance on Man's position in Nature, and its emphasis on the creative power of our dreams and Imagination, Orwell's humanism reveals ties with the Romantics' 'religion of humanity.'

Some of the central tenets of this 'religion' the Romantics had inherited from the Enlightenment. It is no accident that The Appendix of Newspeak ends with a passage from the Declaration of Independence (267), a reminder of the Enlightenment philosophers' definition of fraternity, equality, and liberty as the highest ideals of democracy, to be claimed as the birthright of all humanity. It is pertinent to this point that Orwell's original commitment to Socialism in Spain was a commitment to democratic ideals in their highest form, including the freedom of the critical spirit.[2] In his essays Orwell is consistent in emphasizing that even if criticism of the U.S.S.R. might be considered unpopular in the 1940s, it is due to "individuals willing to face unpopularity that the Socialist movement exists at all" (v. 3, 443). In *Nineteen Eighty-Four*, the satirist's last message to his reader is the humanist's warning: to condone the intellectual constraints of the totalitarian mentality in the name of the long-term ideals of Socialism is equivalent to allowing these very ideals to perish without a trace.

Through its affinity with the eighteenth- and nineteenth-century idealism of the 'religion of humanity,' Orwell's writing reveals its significant differences from the basic position of twentieth-century realism, particularly from the philosophy of Existentialism: Orwell does not accept the human condition as being, by definition, absurd, mean, and unappetizing. Instead of seeing nausea as an appropriate metaphor for the human predicament, Orwell's work makes a claim for the beauty of existence. When he describes ugliness, poverty, and brutality — and he is deservedly famous for describing these most convincingly — his voice does not convey acceptance of man's alienation in the universe, but outrage against the emptiness of a machine civilization, or against the deceptive and wasteful world of totalitarian systems which are *responsible* for alienating Man from Nature.

The word "responsibility" is important here to remember. Orwell the satirist is Orwell the humanist: he makes us individually and collectively responsible for our predicament because he is unwilling to accept any form of determinism as a given. Just as he is suspicious of the tendency to moral neutrality in Marxist, Freudian, and Existentialist thought, he would reject their particular tendencies towards determinism: the historical determinism of Marx and his followers, the psychological determinism inherent in the thought of Freud, and the Existentialists' definition of alienation as a precondition of the human predicament.

Far from accepting alienation as natural, Winston embarks on his pursuit of the truth because he wants to find out whether life had always been as ugly and joyless as it is in Oceania. His whole body and his central nervous system carry a "sort of protest" (66), a rebellion against such a world; instinctively, he knows Ingsoc must be unnatural because by deliberately alienating human beings from their physical environment and from one another, it denies something that is their natural birthright. It seems to me that what Rees sees as Orwell's temperamental difference from the Existentialist writers of his time and as his indifference to Freud lies in Orwell's rare capacity for passionate approval and genuine affirmation of the "process of life"; he is also capable of bitter condemnation of those who would prevent human beings from exercising their freedom, their right to pursue the truth. Underlying this uniquely Orwellian attitude is the unstated but firmly held moral standard of the great satirist whose "generous anger" against Man's degradation is the consequence of his originally high expectations for the "spirit of Man."

The characteristically nineteenth-century roots of Orwell's moral idealism notwithstanding, the twentieth-century overtones of Existentialist, Marxist, and Freudian thought provide Orwell's humanism with the sombre colouring of modern realism; and this sombreness may offer a healthy corrective to some of the overly optimistic tunes of those humanists who would insist on the "joyous service of mankind," and on an "unrelenting faith" (Lamont 121) in the future and in the progress of humanity. Unlike the facile optimism sometimes associated with humanistic thought, Orwell's work does not suggest that the service of humanity is necessarily joyous, that the humanist's faith is unrelenting, that the spiritual-moral progress of mankind is guaranteed (v. 3, 83), and that evil is only a matter of a temporary obstacle that, upon closer examination, will reveal itself as mere ignorance and therefore not 'really' evil. In *Nineteen Eighty-Four* Orwell presents us with an unforgettable image of a demonic world that worships the God of Power, and he compels us to realize that such a world is not only a figment of the imagination. The radical evil of Oceania is not a philosophical hypothesis; it is a historical phenomenon that has assumed vast proportions in the past and has the potential for assuming even vaster proportions in the future.

The "blackwhite" characteristics of the totalitarian habit of mind are an ever-present temptation for irrationality in all of us. Pointing out these dangers, Orwell indirectly also presents us with his own habit of mind: His rationalism is characterized by the give and take of exchange, seeking consciously for a "middleterm" between contraries that will allow the thinker to avoid the dynamism of the "blackwhite" mentality. (In Orwell's presentation of Doublethink, this dynamism begins with the reduction of the whole world into black and white; then it assumes that we must choose either black or white; and finally, after a process of mirroring white in black and black in white, it produces their coalescence in the "coincidence of opposites.")

One of the most delightful qualities in the majority of Orwell's essays is the earnest yet urbane tone, the writer committed not to the particular politics of a particular party, but to the process of critical thought itself; hence the spontaneous, surprising turns and insights in his argument, whose rationality is always far from rigid or predictable.

In discussing a great satirist's cautious respect for Reason, we may note here that, according to Patrick Reilly, Orwell's portrayal of Swift contains a self-portrait as well. Orwell's essay on Swift indeed reveals admiration for a great predecessor in satire, and he would probably agree with the Swiftian verdict that man is only "an animal *capable* of reason" and not a "rational animal." Yet, Orwell's compassion and, probably most important, his genuine reverence for the "process of life" make his voice of Reason quite distinctly different from that of Swift, whom he condemns for advocating "a simple refusal of life" (v. 4, 256), which is a refusal to believe that "man is a *noble animal* and life is worth living" (v. 4, 259, my italics).

On the whole, Orwell's vision is a humanism based on genuine faith in the nobility of the "spirit of Man," but a faith not easily acquired. It is a tragic humanism, and to identify the unique resonance of the "Orwellian" synthesis of idealism and realism, we must finally turn to the important connection Orwell creates between a genuine affirmation of the "process of life" and the acceptance of the tragic dimension of existence. His views on this inextricable connection are best expressed through his analysis of Shakespeare.

The Synthesis:
Orwell's Definition of the Tragic

Orwell's definition of the tragic spirit offers a suggestive reconciliation between a genuinely spiritual, even Romantic version of moral idealism and a sober, tough-minded version of twentieth-century realism.

To begin with, we should remember that Orwell's definition of tragedy is secular; he shares the conviction with Marx, Freud, and most of the Existentialists that modern man's loss of religious belief is irrevocable — in the twentieth century we cannot return to faith in personal immortality. In fact, Orwell quite consistently reminds us that the humanist's position is irreconcilable with that of the religious thinker. Scrutinizing the views of such "otherworldly" thinkers as Graham Greene, Tolstoy, and Gandhi, Orwell insists that there can be only "a *seeming* truce between the humanist and the religious believer" (v. 4, 344).

In his discussion of Tolstoy's "otherworldly" criticism of Shakespeare in "Lear, Tolstoy and the Fool" (v. 4, 331–348), Orwell's own definition of the humanist's position emerges with great clarity. Although he respects Tolstoy for his literary achievement, in this essay Orwell discusses Tolstoy's position as if he had never written anything other than his criticism of Shakespeare, a piece of writing that actually came relatively late in Tolstoy's life, following his conversion. Tolstoy happens to express here a great deal of antagonism towards Shakespeare, particularly towards *King Lear*. Orwell attributes this hostility to Tolstoy's "otherworldliness" in the face of Shakespeare's humanism. It is important to note that for Orwell the tragic spirit has its roots in a humanistic affirmation of the process of life. In effect, Orwell argues that Tolstoy's unfair judgement of Shakespearean tragedy is attributable to Tolstoy's failed humanism, because Tolstoy "tried very hard to make himself into a saint, and the standards he applied to literature were otherworldy ones" (v. 4, 344).

Whether Orwell is objectively correct in his assessment, we should note that here he accuses Tolstoy of the same thing he is to accuse Gandhi of later (v. 4, 528): the "saint" or the "yogi" would "save his soul at the expense of ignoring the community" (v. 4, 36). In concentrating on the transcendental, the superhuman, "the saint, at any rate Tolstoy's kind of saint, is not trying to work an improvement in earthly life: he is trying to bring it to an end and put something different in its place" (v. 4, 344). Therefore, Orwell feels, "the difference between a saint and an ordinary human being is a difference in kind and not in degree" (v. 4, 344). Implied in Tolstoy's criticism of Shakespeare is the "saint's" conviction that

> if we could stop breeding, fighting, struggling and enjoying, if we could get rid not only of our sins but of everything else that binds us to the surface of the earth — including love, in the ordinary sense of caring more for one human being than another — then the whole painful process would be over and the Kingdom of Heaven would arrive" (v. 4, 344).

By contrast, the humanist (who represents for Orwell the "normal human being") "does not want the Kingdom of Heaven; he wants life on earth to continue." His affirmation of life on earth also means acceptance of struggle. Life is worth living; it is worth struggling for: "The humanist attitude is that struggle must continue and that death is the price of life: 'Men must endure/ Their going hence, even as their coming hither: Ripeness is all' — which is an un-Christian sentiment" (v. 4, 344).

In fact, this "un-Christian sentiment" is uttered by Edgar, probably one of the least "un-Christian" among the characters in *King Lear*, but Orwell's interpretation of Edgar's lines draws attention to his own position as a secular humanist. It is Orwell who would argue that "ripeness is all," that there is no transcendence of the human condition, which is rooted in Nature. Nevertheless, as we have just seen, in those rare moments when his characters feel at one with the world of Nature or join in love with another human being, Orwell's own writing conveys a deep sense of affirmation, not unlike moments of epiphany in Romantic poetry. Hence the moving emotional power of the love scene between Winston and Julia in the Golden Country, while they listen to the thrush singing. Winston insists that the thrush sings to *them*, that it is singing in ecstasy. Sober and unromantic, Julia argues a point with Winston she could also argue with the authors of "To a Skylark" or "Ode to a Nightingale." She insists that the thrush sings to itself, or that it simply sings (188). She too, however, finds it worthwhile to go on with their meetings at the risk of her life, and when it comes to the bond of their commitment to each other, she takes the final, greatest risk: she joins the Underground for and with Winston. Nor should we forget that it is sober and 'unromantic' Julia who upholds the supremacy of the lovers' private world when she responds to O'Brien, very quickly, that whatever else the Brotherhood might demand from them, they are not ready to separate from each other. Typically of Orwell, it is the fulfilment of their sexual desire, their affirmation of the "process of life" in Nature, that gives the lovers strength to pursue their "noble," tragic-heroic commitment.

To show that the "noble," sacrificial dimension of tragedy is inseparable from a vital affirmation of existence, Orwell emphasizes that Shakespeare "loved the surface of the earth and the process of life — which, it should be repeated, is *not* the same thing as wanting to have a good time and stay alive as long as possible" (v. 4, 345). It is significant that in "Why do I Write?" Orwell describes his own affirmation of existence very much in the same terms: "I shall continue to feel strongly about prose style, to love the surface of the earth, and to take pleasure in solid objects and scraps of useless information" (v. 1, 28).

Unlike Swift, who refuses to see man as "a noble animal" (v. 4, 259), Shakespeare grants human beings the nobility of their struggle and implies that life is worth living in spite of irrecoverable losses. This is the vision that strikes Orwell as truly 'tragic' — that is, conducive to the writing of great tragedy. In this interpretation, tragedy implies faith in the nobility, the dignity of the human spirit; this is the only form of transcendence Orwell acknowledges:

> It is doubtful whether the sense of tragedy is compatible with belief in God: at any rate it is not compatible with disbelief in human *dignity* and with the kind of 'moral demand' which feels cheated when virtue fails to triumph. A tragic situation exists precisely when virtue does *not* triumph, but when it is still felt that *man is nobler than the forces that destroy him* (v. 4, 338, my italics).

His essay on Shakespeare makes clear that Orwell's self-definition as a satirist who warns his contemporaries about the necessity of struggle follows quite directly from his interpretation of humanism. The tragic element in his vision is also part of his humanism. Even "when virtue does not triumph," man has to go on with the struggle. To continue the struggle — that is, to keep on enjoying the process of existence while "trying to work an improvement in earthly life" (v. 4, 344) — is the only way to demonstrate that "man is nobler than the forces that destroy him."

In *Nineteen Eighty-Four* the recurring image of the mother, "blue with fright herself," but trying to cover up her child "as much as possible as if she thought her arms could keep the bullets off him" (13), is a most moving illustration of what Orwell considers "noble" in the human spirit.

Winston's excitement over the refugee mother's tragic-heroic gesture he had seen on the screen makes him start writing in his diary. This leads him, through the 'underground' of his subconscious, to a memory of his own mother, who offered the same gesture to her children in the face of overpowering forces. Winston's recognition of what tragedy had meant in the past forms a significant step in his understanding of his first dream, and also starts him on his own tragic-heroic quest for love, commitment, and individuality against the State's overpowering forces:

The thing that now suddenly struck Winston was that his mother's death, nearly thirty years ago, had been tragic and sorrowful in a way that was no longer possible. Tragedy, he perceived, belonged to the ancient time, to a time when there was still privacy, love, and friendship, and when the members of a family stood by one another without needing to know the reason (31).

The simple dignity of the mother's self-sacrifice based on her "deep and complex sorrows" and private loyalties reminds Winston of a world that, unlike his own, had been noble, tragic, that is, human.

But Winston's dream of the light-flooded Golden Country that immediately follows the dark landscape of tragedy should also be examined in conjunction with the mother's tragic gesture. The image that creates the connection between the two dreams is the "magnificent gesture" of the girl with the dark hair, a gesture asserting political and sexual freedom, the breaking away from the world of Oceania. This second dream must evoke in Winston vague memories of the golden-green landscape associated with Shakespeare's romantic comedy, the background of pastoral, because we hear that he "woke up with the word 'Shakespeare' on his lips" (31). Nevertheless, since the two dreams are interconnected, in fact Winston must feel that "the word Shakespeare" is somehow connected with the *combined effect* of the two gestures — that is, with both the dark landscape of tragedy in the first dream, and the light-flooded landscape of romance in the second one. In Orwell's reading Shakespeare's vision demonstrates the dignity of tragic heroism precisely because it also affirms the "process of life."

In the mother's protective, loving gesture of sacrifice Orwell leaves us with one of his most memorable images of the "crystal spirit," the nobility of the "spirit of Man" (and woman):

> If you loved someone, you loved him, and when you had nothing else to give, you still gave him love. When the last of the chocolate was gone, his mother clasped the child in her arms. It was no use, it changed nothing, it did not produce more chocolate, it did not avert the child's death or her own, but it seemed natural to her to do it (146).

At this point Winston also recalls "the refugee woman in the boat [who] had also covered the little boy with her arm, which was no more use against the bullets than a sheet of paper" (146). The timeless, tragic gesture of protecting the child against bombs and bullets should remind us, once more, that due to its potential for reaching a purity that is incorruptible by external forces, "No bomb that ever burst/ Shatters the crystal spirit" (v. 2, 306).

The fact that one of the most moving vignettes of the human being's tragic dignity, the very essence of the "spirit of Man," is represented by Winston's mother should, I believe, also be something to ponder when responding to the Feminist critics' twofold objection to Orwell's humanism. According to Daphne Patai's reading of *Nineteen Eighty-Four*, Orwell's point of view was sexist, if not downright misogynist, and due to his unsound gender ideology he ended up in despair about the future of humanity. I suggest that the mother's recurring image in the novel conveys Orwell's tragic affirmation of the human beings' nobility, which transcends "the forces that destroy" them: his choice of the mother as the symbol of the tragic-heroic spirit of mankind should clear Orwell's humanism from the Feminist critics' twofold charges of misogyny and despair.

In the context of *Nineteen Eighty-Four*, Orwell's faith in the "spirit of Man" is revealed in the perspective of a tragic humanism; it is an affirmation of the vitality, the stamina, and the decency of the downtrodden, of the "crystal spirit" of heroic struggle for equality and freedom — a struggle in defence of the individual's private loyalties, the love and trust among human beings, and the heritage of the greatest documents of human consciousness. Winston's last appeal to the "spirit of Man" is also a reminder, however, that the crystal may indeed shatter, and that the forces of both physical and spiritual destruction could become overwhelming.

Still, one may point out, Orwell would insist to the very end that no force external to man could "shatter the crystal spirit." In the novel the shattering of the crystal paperweight is instigated by the Thought Police, and at the most universal level of the satire, the Thought Police in Oceania represents the final development of *our generation's* present practice of self-censorship and self-delusion. It is in the spirit of a hard-won, tragic humanism that the satirist reminds us that as human beings we carry the threat of the destruction of our civilization, but also the power to avert it, within ourselves.

Notes

[1] In his *Introduction to Existentialism*, Robert Olson points out that the Existentialists "declare that consciousness is inevitably un-happy consciousness. Sartre, for instance, cites as 'self-evident truth' that the 'human reality . . . is by nature an unhappy consciousness with no possibility of surpassing its unhappy state.' . . . 'Suffering,' avers Unamuno, 'tells us that we exist'" (25).

[2] Orwell's critique of his Adversary follows the major premises of democratic Socialism. As summarized in Norman Thomas's 1963 *Socialism Re-examined*, the "Communist Theology" should be seen as fundamentally alien to the original spirit of Marxism: "Commu-nism falsely claims to share in the Socialist tradition. In fact, it has distorted that tradition beyond recognition. It has built up a rigid theology which is incompatible with the critical spirit of Marxism" (217).

Part V

Coming Through the Other Side:
The Metamorphosis of Tragic Irony into
the Militant Wit of Satire:
An Ultimate Faith in the "Spirit of Man"

As revealed by the examination of Orwell's response to the major currents of thought in his time, the vision that informs *Nineteen Eighty-Four* is the world view of a tragic humanism: Orwell asserts hope in human perfectibility and in the future of our civilization precisely by calling attention to the presence of those dark and potentially "overpowering forces" we have to struggle against. The novel does not convey the message of the hysterical outcry, or the fragmented vision of a sudden attack of despair or personal obsession, but the mature, well-integrated synthesis of Orwell's thought in all its political, psychological, and spiritual dimensions.

Part V will conclude this study with a discussion of the unique literary merits of *Nineteen Eighty-Four*, a work that embodies the subtle yet powerful interplay between the various components in Orwell's tragic humanism. In fact, the clarity, coherence, and uniqueness of the novel as a literary work are inseparable from the mature and well-integrated vision of reality that informs it. But how does the oxymoron of tragic humanism find its literary expression in *Nineteen Eighty-Four*? What is the relationship between the tragic element demonstrated by Winston's inevitable defeat, and the satirical argument that is by definition didactic, inspired by the ultimately optimistic assumption that, once human folly can be cured, disasters can be averted?

To answer these questions, Chapter 15 will concentrate on the relationship between tragic irony and satire in the structural interaction between the narrative text and the 'documentary' Appendix, the *Dictionary of Newspeak*. By focusing on their thematic interaction, Chapter 16 will offer a solution to the Orwell conundrum and conclude the discussion of the novel.

Chapter 15

The Structural Function of Newspeak —
The Catharsis of Satire

Tragic Irony and
the Militant Irony of Satire

Although Orwell referred to the novel as both satire and parody,[1] many of his critics had difficulty reconciling the stark hellscape of Oceania and the irony or humour popularly associated with satire. Indeed, in most works that are considered satirical, moral instruction is conveyed through "laughter, ridicule and mockery . . . [since] by and large the satiric spirit seems to fuse most readily with the comic genres" (Robert Elliott, "Satire" 780). Nevertheless, it is not unprecedented that great works of satire should have a serious, even tragic dimension, represented by a sense of the "grotesque or absurd," which is quite distinct from the more popular, comic, or light-hearted examples of "wit and humour." In these works of dark satire the satirist's attack on his target may assume the attributes of "serious wit" — for example, Donne's typically "metaphysical" wit, which C.S. Lewis has aptly described "as if Donne performed in deepest depression those gymnastics which are usually a sign of intellectual high spirits" (Donne 97). In some works of Swift, Voltaire, Blake, and particularly Kafka, serious wit may turn "tragic and deeply prophetic," and thus "may rise above the bonds of the comic." In such instances we are invited to contemplate the tragic potential of man's deviation from reason. This, of course, also implies the existence of a norm — sanity — which the satirist feels human beings must preserve in order to be called human.

But whether we laugh or cry out in shock or horror, our most unmistakable sense of the satirical comes from a sense of irony — the sense of reversal. To borrow Northrop Frye's term, satire is characterized by a particular type of irony that is "militant" (*Anatomy* 223) — that is, used to 'militate' against a world that has been stood on its head — a forceful reminder that it should return to its 'right-side-up' norm of sanity and morality, to the way things should be. Depending on the satirist's personality, and to some extent, on the intellectual climate, the degree of militancy may vary. Thus, *Nineteen Eighty-Four* is obviously closer to Juvenal, whose "*saeva indignation* and flights into tragical seriousness . . . contrasts with the urbane mockery characteristic of Horace" (Robert Elliott, "Satire"). But the moral conviction that turns the barbs of "militant irony" in the direction of its target is still unerring, whether we find it in the form of an urbane, rationalist, "Horatian" irony (characteristic of the voice in many of Orwell's essays), or in the corrosive irony descriptive of the "savage indignation" of satirists such as Swift, Voltaire, or Kafka. Finally, there is a quality of irony Orwell himself defined in his analysis of Dickens as a "generous anger" (v. 1, 504), which is probably as typical of Orwell in *Animal Farm* as is the prophetic power of "savage indignation" informing *Nineteen Eighty-Four*.

That the irony is "militant" also implies that in satire "the moral norms are relatively clear, and it assumes a standard against which the grotesque and the absurd are measured" (Frye, *Anatomy* 223). We should probably also add here that great satire, like great tragedy, often appears at periods of transition, when ideals that have been taken for granted by long-standing tradition are being challenged. It is important, however, that the memory of these ideals still be relatively clear, since "at least an implicit moral standard [is] essential to a militant attitude to experience" (Frye, *Anatomy* 224). There is no question that *Nineteen Eighty-Four* demonstrates such a "militant irony." This also reveals Orwell's assumption that he can appeal to his reader's implicit moral standard. The satirist would not stand on his head and perform mental gymnastics to show how equality, freedom, and individuality are debased in Oceania, had he not assumed that equality, freedom, and individuality still mattered to his readers.

In Chapter 6 we observed some examples of Orwell's most characteristic devices, such as the reversals of cause-effect relationships and the apposition that creates unexpected analogies or equations. Right from the first page of the novel we are expected to recognize that Oceania is an irrational world, where riddles and contradictions are accepted at face value and the normal emotions of basic human relationships are diametrically reversed. Thus the Party quite openly advocates Hate and not Love as a most desirable emotional state; children are taught to spy on and denounce their parents, going against the most obviously natural feelings of the family bond and loyalty; it is a world in which Winston is made, at the end, not only to accept but also to celebrate the prospect of his own torture and execution (256).

Another significant device is allusion, which often works in combination with the changing of cause-effect or ends-and-means relationships. Through these various devices, Oceania is defined as a world where there is no reliable connection between the sign and the signified, where the unnatural is considered natural, where punishment and reward are entirely gratuitous — in short, a world not merely of the absurd but of deliberately induced, controlled insanity. Here the reversal into the realm of the irrational evokes horror, shock, and not laughter. Although we may smile, at least initially, when recognizing that the grotesque, absurd world of London in 1984 is simply a logical extension of the 'normal,' familiar London the reader has always known, this recognition does not lead to a smile of comic relief. But does satire provide such relief? Does satire as a genre offer an emotional catharsis? Does *Nineteen Eighty-Four*, the grimmest of all satires, offer any kind of catharsis?

By recognizing the satirist's numerous allusions, we acknowledge the connection between our 'present' and the future; we also see that simply allowing this present trend to be carried to its logical conclusion, we have entered the world of the clinically insane. For example, the quick changing of partners among Eastasia, Eurasia, and Oceania takes place *so that* one may betray one's erstwhile partner by forming a new alliance, *so that* one may create confusion among the masses. This is an obvious allusion to the quick shifts of *realpolitik* practised by the three power blocks before, during, and after World War II. Beyond recognizing such historical allusion, we can also see that Orwell stretches the familiar historical situation much further. In the historical theatre the quick shifts in alliances and betrayals were a means to an end; they were intended to serve the purposes of the given world power and help win the war. In *Nineteen Eighty-Four* the means have become an end. War is simply an "imposture" (173). The mechanism of shifting alliances and betrayals is an artifice fabricated and kept in motion deliberately to confuse, distract, and make the population collaborate in its own enslavement. What may have started as a trend, as a means to be justified, has become an end in itself. The process of lies, betrayals, and violence set in motion in the 1940s has become legitimate and desirable. It has turned into an unstoppable machine that runs the totalitarian world system.

As we discover the connection between each of Big Brother's tactics and those of his historical models, Hitler and Stalin, we realize the true wit of Orwell's demonstration of how even the most outrageously irrational tactics in 1984 carry their origins in historical precedents, in the facts of the 1940s. This recognition is not connected with the wit normally associated with the catharsis of laughter. Instead, it evokes the "wit" of the grotesque, the shocking. The satirist's point is to show that our acceptance of the totalitarian mentality even for a moment would be tantamount to our entrapment in the unstoppable escalation of the irrational, associated with obsessive mental disease or schizophrenia.

The effect of Orwell's irony is frequently closer to tragedy than comedy. In order to identify its overall effect, I suggest turning to Northrop Frye's *Anatomy of Criticism*, which defines the various stages of tragedy "as they move from the tragic to the ironic" (219). In delineating the range of heroic and ironic dimensions in tragedy, Professor Frye describes the heroic stage as the one in which the central character assumes a mythical stature: he is at a level of freedom higher than his audience. By contrast, at the "low mimetic" and the "ironic" stages, the hero is at a level of freedom that, respectively, equals or is below that of the audience.

Where does Winston belong? Is his position characterized by the "mimetic" mode of psychological realism and verisimilitude, in which he would assume a degree of freedom identical to that of his audience? Or is his existence delineated by the "ironic" mode in which his freedom would be at a level lower than that of the audience? My suggestion is that his case is defined by the third position. I also would like to propose that it follows from the structure of dystopian satire that the audience is granted a higher level of freedom only when, and as a direct consequence of, recognizing the protagonist's lower level of freedom.

But before exploring these suggestions further, it is important to remember Professor Frye's observation that "as the ironic element increases, the heroic decreases," and, in effect, the ironic perspective is equivalent to "putting the character in a state of lower freedom than the audience" (*Anatomy* 221). If we look for a classical illustration, we find that in *Oedipus Rex* the hero labours in bondage to Fate, and is hence in a state of freedom that is remarkably lower than that of the average man, the chorus, or the audience. According to Frye, *Oedipus Rex* already moves on to the last stage of tragic irony, "a world of shock and horror in which the central images of *sparagmos*, that is, cannibalism, are images of cruelty and outrage" (*Anatomy* 229). But aren't these images of tragic irony also familiar to us from great satire? In *Candide*, Voltaire offers a 'Swiftian' understatement of the inhumanity of human beings by presenting us with the life story of the Old Woman, who is a matter-of-fact survivor of an act of cannibalism, made no less horrifying by the fact that it was practised in installments. In his "Modest Proposal" Swift makes his quasi-sensible persona attempt to persuade us that the new-born babies of the Irish poor should be sold for human consumption, implying, of course, that the poor would be better off having their children eaten, compared to the way they live. In Kafka's *Penal Colony* the victims are subjugated to the most merciless torture imaginable, and, of course, in *Nineteen Eighty-Four*, in the course of Winston's "torture pilgrimage" in the Ministry of Love, we witness the self-revelation of a cannibalistic, cruel Godhead whose life-force comes from devouring its victims. Behind the benevolent mask of Big Brother is the real two-faced divinity of Oceania, the God of Power symbolized by the rationality of O'Brien's iron logic and the ruthless 'cannibalism' of the rats starved until they are ready to devour one another. As Northrop Frye points out, the sixth or last stage of tragic irony is identical to an "undisplaced demonic vision," and he chooses *Nineteen Eighty-Four* as the most powerful modern exponent of this irony:

> The sixth phase presents human life in terms of largely unrelieved bondage. Its settings feature prisons, madhouses, lynching mobs, and places of execution, and it differs from a pure inferno mainly in the fact that in human experience suffering has an end in death. In our day the chief form of this phase is the nightmare of social tyranny, of which *1984* is perhaps the most familiar. . . . In *1984* the parody of religion in the final scenes is more elaborate: there is a parody of the atonement, for instance, when the hero is tortured into urging that the torments be inflicted on the heroine instead (*Anatomy* 227).

Frye's analysis draws attention to a particular dynamism according to which, after reaching the "dead centre" of the darkest tragic vision, a sense of reversal occurs.

> This brings us around again to a point of demonic epiphany, the dark tower and prison of endless pain . . . , the *tour aboli*, the goal of the quest that isn't there. But on the other side of this blasted world of repulsiveness and idiocy, a world without pity and without hope, satire begins again. At the bottom of Dante's hell, which is also the centre of the spherical earth, Dante sees Satan standing upright in the circle of ice, and as he cautiously follows . . . , he passes the centre and finds himself no longer going down but going up, climbing out on the other side of the world to see the stars again. . . . Tragedy can take us no further; but if we persevere with the *mythos* of irony and satire, we shall pass a *dead centre*, and finally see the gentlemanly Prince of Darkness bottomside up" (*Anatomy* 227).

I suggest that we see this dynamism as the reversal of "tragic irony" into "militant wit," the irony most appropriate to satire.

Of course, Professor Frye's provocative suggestion about the reversal between the modes of tragic and satirical vision was meant to establish a relationship between various modes, various genres. Can such a reversal occur within one work? Do we experience such a reversal in *Nineteen Eighty-Four* between the darkest revelations of 'black tragedy' and what is ultimately the hopeful assertion of the satirist's "militant" irony, traditionally aimed at warning, in order to avert catastrophe? How can there be such a reversal *after* we have seen the last stage of Winston's struggle and defeat in his "*tour aboli*," the "goal of the quest that isn't there"? Are we, in *Nineteen Eighty-Four*, taken down to the darkest stage of tragic irony only to break through to the other dimension of a new enlightenment brought on by the liberating "militant" wit of the satire?

From the Narrative into the Appendix of Newspeak: The Structural Reversal from Tragic Irony to Satire

There is indeed such a sense of reversal in *Nineteen Eighty-Four*, and it can be illustrated both in the context of the novel's composite genre and in one of its most significant themes, that of the corruption of language. The evidence is presented in the last few pages of the book, the Appendix containing the Principles of Newspeak, which I suggest should be considered an organic part of the novel. Orwell himself felt strongly that the Appendix had an essential function; as in the case of *Goldstein's Book*, he resisted both publisher and critic who advised him to exclude this second document of expository prose from the novel. In fact, following the harrowing last scene in the narrative, the Appendix has a function similar to *Goldstein's Book*: It helps create a sense of emotional distance between the central character and the reader. It allows us to take a purely cerebral overview of the satire's target, the totalitarian mentality.

While *Goldstein's Book* made us return to Oceania's past — that is, our present, the Appendix of *Newspeak* takes us to yet another timeplane. It emphasizes that there was to be a stage *after* the events we have been witnessing in 1984, a stage that was to arrive in 2050 as a consequence of the "blackwhite" mentality of 1984, which was, in fact, a logical consequence of the same mentality already rampant in 1948. The fact that we are not quite certain whether this final stage, predicted by the Party to occur about the year 2050, had indeed materialized, adds to the ambivalence created by the conditional mood of the hypothesis. Through the Appendix, we are invited, quite emphatically, to speculate about a world in terms of "what if?" instead of the world "the way it is." The words of the introduction establish ambiguity immediately: "It was expected that Newspeak would have finally superseded Oldspeak (or Standard English, as we should call it) by about the year 2050" (257). Has this expectation been fulfilled? Who is the narrator? Who is his audience? Once we have stepped out of Winston's story, which we had witnessed exclusively through Winston's consciousness, the identity of the narrator is left deliberately in the background. The voice is impersonal, omniscient, assuming some kind of an official, institutional consciousness, emphasized by the use of the passive voice. Thus we hear that "it was expected" that certain things would happen, but it is left undetermined whether the changes that were meant to take place have indeed occurred. Reading the Appendix, we are enticed into entering a musing, speculative frame of mind, invited to focus attention on yet another reality removed from our own, both in terms of time and in the degree of its substantiality or concreteness.

The Readers' Dissociation from
Winston's Consciousness

In the context of the composite genre of *Nineteen Eighty-Four*, the reversal from tragic irony to the militant wit of liberating satire is brought about by the interaction between the narrative and the two 'documents,' the Appendix of *Newspeak* and *Goldstein's Book*.

As the satirist indicates a cause-effect relationship between our present and our future, the protagonist of the dystopian satire assumes a particular, quasi-filial relationship to the 'ideal reader.' Winston carries the burden of the 'parents' sin' visited upon the following generation. His world has come about as a logical consequence of certain trends *we* have allowed to run rampant in ours; he is in effect taking the consequences — paying for our sins of omission. In *Nineteen Eighty-Four* this causal relationship is made quite explicit by Orwell's insertion of *Goldstein's Book* at the height of the rising action, making us aware that there is a difference between Winston's world and the readers'. We are reminded of this difference again when we are asked to read the *Dictionary of Newspeak after* watching the fulfilment of Winston's fate.

It is only at these two points that the reader is detached, suddenly, and as if by force, from the sphere of Winston's consciousness. In the rest of the novel, every thought, every single descriptive detail of the environment is filtered through his perceptions. In this way we enter a highly limited, by its very nature fragmented, subjective view of Winston's world, which exists exclusively in his perceptions, uninfluenced by the balance of other opinions and other views about 'objective' reality. This adds to the intensity of the vision described, and increases the suspense. We follow, for example, Winston's perception of O'Brien as a friend, a potentially intimate companion and fellow conspirator in the Underground, only to be shocked together with him when O'Brien reappears at the Ministry of Love and is revealed in his true colours as *agent provocateur*, mastermind, and quite possibly the real Big Brother hidden behind the icon.

Throughout the novel, Winston's consciousness is our consciousness, and it is simply impossible for us not to identify with him and accept his perceptions about the world of Oceania; his consciousness is the readers' only guide in the novel.

It is remarkable that Orwell achieves this effect without narration in the first person singular, a technique usually associated with the "stream of consciousness" characteristic of the modern psychological novel (Edel 19; 198–200).

The narrator's reference to Winston in the third person singular still allows him to describe in great depth what Winston does, sees, feels, and thinks at the same time. Should Winston tell us his whole story in the first person singular — as he does in his diary entries — we would, in effect, know somewhat less about his sensations, perceptions, feelings, and thoughts; by using the third person singular narration Orwell can give us a sense of simultaneity of internal and external action, often also hinting at the "stream of consciousness" below the level of the continuous external action.

Thus we hear that at the Two Minutes Hate Winston talks in one way and thinks in another, and at one point he loses control: "In a lucid moment Winston found that he was shouting with the others and kicking his heel violently against the rung of his chair. The horrible thing about the Two Minutes Hate was not that one was obliged to act a part, but, on the contrary, that it was impossible to avoid joining in" (17).

Winston's observations of others and of himself underline the factual description of the group's hysterical behaviour where "the rage one felt was an abstract, undirected emotion which could be switched from one object to another like the flame of a blowlamp" (17). Orwell describes the oscillation of Winston's hatred as it turns from Goldstein to Big Brother and than back again to Goldstein, apparently quite independently of his will. Then, by a "voluntary act," he switches his hatred to the dark-haired girl behind him while "vivid, beautiful hallucinations flashed through his mind." His free associations below the level of consciousness underline his fundamentally 'objective' observations throughout the entire scene in a quick staccato motion. Sometimes these associations briefly reach the level of consciousness, when, for example, he realizes that his hatred and sadistic fantasies about the girl are the consequence of his frustrated desire for her. Sometimes they barely reach the level of consciousness and disappear from view altogether, when, for example, he associates the chant of "B-B!" with the primitive tribal "stamp of naked feet and the throbbing of tom-toms" (18). It would be simply impossible to render all these events, flashbacks, memories, and hallucinations with such an effect of synchronicity in a first person singular narration.

As a result, Orwell allows us to proceed with a linear story line, while also rendering the interaction between various levels of consciousness in Winston's own thinking, emphasizing the emotional significance of certain thought patterns by letting us hear about Winston's physiological response to particular situations that trigger unpleasant memories. For example, while struggling with his first diary entry and getting closer to the source of his yet unrecognized guilt about his mother's disappearance, we hear that his "varicose ulcer had begun itching unbearably . . . above his ankle" (12), and when Julia arrives at their first meeting with a piece of real chocolate, "the first whiff of its scent had stirred up some memory which he could not pin down, but which was powerful and troubling" (108). Finally, the gin he drinks after he is released from the Ministry of Love has a smell "which dwelt with him night and day, was inextricably mixed up in his mind with the smell of those — " (248). The effect of the narrative method is a remarkably rich rendering of the complexity of the central character's subjective universe, without the risk of making the reader lose sight of the 'plot,' the external events, and the characters that appear and disappear on Winston's horizon.

We do, however, step out of the orbit of this all-encompassing central consciousness when we start reading *Goldstein's Book*. Although we are still expected to read the Book simultaneously with Winston, we are clearly aware that the information, the perception, and the explication come from another source than Winston's consciousness. This is the first time we are forced to create a distance between ourselves and the central character. Doing so, we are forcefully reminded that we exist on a different timeplane than Winston: when Winston reads about his past — the historical events of the 1940s, for example — the readers gradually discover that what is described as Winston's past is the readers' *present*.

This realization has several consequences. Winston's predicament is *potentially* the predicament awaiting us in the future. Also, the readers should realize that Winston's predicament is predetermined by the totalitarian world State, which is the clear consequence of trends we may have accepted and condoned in our own world as harmless and normal. Reading *Goldstein's Book* about the genesis of Oceania, it becomes apparent that

Winston is enslaved by *his* past: he has no choice but to lose because he suffers the consequences of our mistakes. Born into the prison that is of our making, his predicament has been determined by our deeds in the 'present,' which allowed the enormous prison-house of the totalitarian world State to come into being.

If Winston is at a lower level of freedom than the readers, it is due to the fact that the generation of the late forties allowed the world to develop into the world of the eighties. His loss of freedom is, in fact, ascribed to the readers, or at least to the readers' generation. It follows then that Winston cannot be the butt of the satire: his effort towards liberation and self-realization is nothing short of heroic, his fall entirely undeserved. As a matter of fact, Winston is *our* pharmakos, our scapegoat: he suffers due to our flaws; we see him swallowed up by the forces of hero-worship and hatred that we have allowed to come to power.

The Catharsis of Tragedy vs. The Catharsis of Satire

We are now in a position to take a closer look at the interaction between the elements of tragedy and satire. Orwell's definition of tragedy emphasizes the tragic affirmation of man's struggle against overwhelming odds, and implies that in tragedy the loss sustained by the character also affirms the value of what is being lost. It is precisely through Winston's loss of memory, common sense, his attachment to Julia, and through his loss of memory about his childhood love for his mother (264), that we affirm the essential value of memory, common sense, loyalty, and love as dimensions of *our* freedom.

Another characteristic of great tragedy in *Nineteen Eighty-Four* is the inevitability of the loss Winston suffers. But does Winston achieve a sense of tragic catharsis as the result of his inevitable end? Does he receive new light, emerging out of the darkness of tragic knowledge?

It is generally accepted that the emotional reversal implied by tragic catharsis follows from the tragic hero's completion of his predicament and his reaching of an understanding or acceptance of this predicament. In *Nineteen Eighty-Four* Winston does not achieve a sense of a higher understanding. He reaches no light at the end of the tunnel of darkness, except the light of the corridor leading to the torture chamber, and finally to the executioner's cell. The tragic knowledge that might have emerged from Winston's spiritual journey is not accessible to him; he has to reject his entire past as "false memory." In other words, the moment he reaches "Acceptance" of the system, he also has to deny the insight of a previous tragic understanding. This denial is endemic to Doublethink, as expressed in the third Party slogan, "Ignorance is Strength." As a result, Winston cannot benefit from the revelation or recognition the hero of tragedy usually experiences after the reversal of peripeteia: for Winston there can be no new tragic knowledge, no new illumination. Nor do the readers experience the kind of emotional reversal that is usually associated with tragic catharsis. Our feelings of pity and fear remain, to a large extent, unpurged as far as Winston's predicament is concerned.

Yet there is a knowledge that should emerge from the spark between the book and the reader. Winston's predicament becomes the source of our illumination. But the nature of this illumination will become clear only if we realize that we are looking at Winston's predicament from a different timeplane. He becomes our pharmakos because in drawing attention to his total lack of freedom, he makes us realize that his chains are forged by us, by *our* decisions in *his* past. This, of course, means that Winston's enslavement draws attention to the decisive significance of our freedom at the present moment. What is inevitable for Winston is still in our future, a cautionary tale only. Our chance for freedom lies in this moment of recognition. This is to say, the tragic irony emerging from his lower level of freedom becomes the guarantee of our higher level of freedom, the built-in guarantee of freedom assumed by the present in relation to the future.

It has been acknowledged that great tragedy asks some of the most universal questions about the human being's predicament in the universe and claims to offer no specific answers. Tragedy remains satisfied with being able to ask the important questions. By comparison, dystopian satire may also ask some fundamental questions about the foundation and the limits of our humanity, but does so within a societal framework. Unlike tragedy, it is not satisfied with asking the question; it also has a message, a didactic intent. Consequently, as a cerebral genre, it makes a more direct appeal to the rational thought process, and the nature of the catharsis must be appropriate to the genre. *Nineteen Eighty-Four* is the prototype of dystopian satire, which allows us to see this movement quite clearly: in reading *Goldstein's Book* at the end of Part 2, and the *Dictionary of Newspeak* after Part 3, we are recalled to the realization that what for Winston became an inescapable, predetermined fate is still only a possibility in our future. This realization should create a sense of distance and herein, I suggest, lies the possibility for the only catharsis implicit in satire.

"What happened had to happen" is the recognition reached at the end of tragedy. Only by confronting the darkness of evil and suffering can we liberate ourselves from it. Liberation comes here as a result of, *after*, the catastrophe. In satire the catharsis consists of another kind of recognition and I suggest that it is the sense of relief that comes from a revelation accomplished by the force of Reason; it consists of the recognition that we are still *before* the catastrophe, and hence in possession of the freedom to avert it. When reading *Goldstein's Book* and the *Dictionary of Newspeak*, dealing with the past and the future of Oceania, respectively, we are reminded that Winston's story which we have just been reading, has not happened yet. Unlike Winston, we still have the freedom to shape the future according to our higher understanding and according to our free choice. The God of Power is the God of cruelty and destruction, but ultimately it is not God who creates the human being, but the human being who creates God in the image of the highest self. In other words, we can still stop those alarming trends of power worship and self-deception around ourselves that could lead to an invincibly demonic world in the future.

The most memorable message of Orwell's satire is that totalitarianism dehumanizes human beings by denying them freedom and thus it swallows up, eliminates the personality. It would be unfair, therefore, to argue that Orwell denies the freedom of the will as a prerogative of our humanity. The imaginative leap of satire can take place either in terms of space or in terms of time; in *Nineteen Eighty-Four* we take a leap into the future. It is in the nature of dystopian satire that we are expected to accept the satirical framework, to suspend disbelief, while reading Winston's story. However, we are then also expected to step back from the future and contemplate the story from our time-plane. Therefore, the question raised by *Nineteen Eighty-Four* is not whether humanity will indeed deteriorate in the future to the extent Winston is seen to have deteriorated. The question has to follow a great "if," and properly phrased it should read as follows: "Is it true that if totalitarianism is allowed to become a world power, even heroic resistance like Winston's would become useless?" It is part of the satirist's strategy to suggest that Winston's predicament, the annihilation of the self, is simply inevitable after the totalitarian world state has been allowed to assume its final shape. In the meantime, however, we are also strongly reminded by *Goldstein's Book* and the *Dictionary of Newspeak* that we should not regard ourselves as Winston's contemporaries. Consequently, in the perspective of the distancing effect of these two 'documents' of expository prose, Winston's tale is revealed to be only hypothetical, receding, as it were, into the conditional mood forever.

Can we return, then, to what Northrop Frye describes as the reversal between tragic and satirical dimensions, a dynamism I proposed we examine in terms of the reversal of tragic irony into the liberating force of the satirist's militant wit? Through the novel's composite genre, our missed tragic catharsis leads us to the more restrained, more cerebral catharsis of the satire: the rational recognition that Winston's tragic story has not been acted out yet. The vision of the future is still only a vision as far as the readers' own existence is concerned. At the same time, the tragic elements and the identification required by psychological realism prepare us for a shocking, moving experience, so that we are ready for the "passionate contemplation" of the disintegration of the human psyche, the process of dehumanization as an inevitable consequence of the totalitarian mentality. There is no doubt that due to the great emotional impact created by our identification with him, it is extremely difficult to tear ourselves away from Winston and his gin-scented tears after the final scene of the novel. Nevertheless, when presented with the *Dictionary of Newspeak* in the Appendix, this is precisely what we are asked to do. Having been compelled to contemplate the abyss, at the end we receive the illumination appropriate to satire: it is our recognition of Winston's absolute bondage to the historical events of the past that brings home to us our sense of freedom. Having been compelled to look into the abyss, we are reminded that we have not made our jump yet; we may still avoid it. Having faced the emotional depths of tragic irony, we are moved towards a sense of intellectual reversal, thanks to the liberating power of the "militant wit" of satire.

Note

[1] To begin with the elements of satire, we should look at Orwell's own comments on his novel, which he intended "as a show up of the perversions to which a centralized economy is liable and which have already been *partly* realized in Communism and Fascism" (v. 4, 564). His second topical target was the "implications of dividing the world into 'Zones of influence'" (v. 4, 520). But in more general terms, he intended to write a parody of "the intellectual implications of totalitarianism" (v. 4,520), because he believed that "totalitarian ideas have taken roots in the minds of intellectuals everywhere, and I have tried to draw these ideas out to their logical consequences" (v. 4, 564).

He points out that the book is not a prophecy: "I do not believe that the kind of society I do describe necessarily *will* arrive, but I believe (allowing of course for the fact that the book is a satire) that something resembling it *could* arrive" (v. 4, 564). There is no doubt that the satire is a warning: "The scene in the book is laid in Britain in order to emphasize that the English-speaking races are not innately better than anyone else and that totalitarianism, *if not fought against*, could triumph everywhere" (v. 4, 564).

Chapter 16

The Thematic Function of Newspeak: The Reversal of Tragic Irony into the Militant Wit of Satire — Concluding Remarks

The structural reversal from tragic irony to the militant wit of the satire leads us to the only kind of catharsis satire can afford, intellectual illumination. This reversal is also vividly demonstrated in one of the major themes of the novel, the Party-instigated destruction of the English language planned to culminate in the language of Newspeak. Ending the novel with "The Principles of Newspeak," Orwell leaves us with the notion that the system created by the Party is not merely criminal: it is totally absurd. By diminishing the vocabulary in order to diminish consciousness, the Party deliberately introduces an entropy, the irreversible tendency of a system towards disorder and dissolution. Being able to reduce Oldspeak into Newspeak signals the Party's greatest triumph, its total control over individual consciousness. At the same time, and precisely for the same reason, Newspeak also signals the Party's ultimate destruction.

The Party's Triumph in Newspeak

Examining the tendencies to the suppression of free speech, censorship, the rewriting of history, and the self-censorship of the intellectual in the service of political parties, in a 1940 essay (v. 1, 576) Orwell bitterly condemns his contemporaries' adherence to political orthodoxy, which will lead to "an age in which freedom of thought will be at first a deadly sin and later on a meaningless abstraction" (v. 1, 576). Clearly, with the ever-changing dogma of Doublethink, the theatricals of rigged trials, and the public executions of the satanic freethinker, the Oceania of 1984 represents the stage where free thought has been declared a deadly sin. The Newspeak society of 2050, its range of thought diminished, represents the last stage, where free thought has disappeared altogether.

Orwell's satire here moves in two directions. First, Newspeak implies that since political language in the 1940s already served either to "defend the indefensible" or to regiment thinking in the service of various orthodoxies, the Party's announcing of its outrageous policy "not to extend but to diminish the range of thought" (258) only puts into words the practice of Orwell's contemporaries. In the mental impoverishment of 2050, the reader is asked to recognize a current, familiar trend being turned into a principle and taken to its ultimate conclusion.

Second, Orwell demonstrates how this general linguistic process affects specific words and specific concepts. In the age of Newspeak there is no word available for freedom; the concept can no longer be articulated except in the deprivatory sense of being free of something. The difference between the original word and concept and the corrupted word and corrupted concept acts as a reproach to the Adversary for submitting to the deterioration and the elimination of the ideal itself. The same kind of difference we can perceive between "freedom," as we understand it, as opposed to "being free from lice," exists between "the International Brotherhood of Man" and the denial of this very concept in the "Comintern"; between our concept of the feeling, thinking individual and the Party's "goodthinker"; between our concept of sexual love and its Party definition as "sexcrime"; between the Socialist promise of the intellectual development of the proletariat and the Party's deliberate corruption of their minds through the junk literature of "prolefeed"; between the critical, empirical mode of thinking represented by Oldthink, and the vacuous gramophone speech of "duckspeak." In the discussion of the "B vocabulary" Orwell's criticism of his own contemporaries becomes quite specific, especially of those guilty of using the terminology of political pamphlets, with their "ready made phrases" that "anaesthetize a portion of one's brain" (167):

> Even in the early decades of the twentieth century, telescoped words and phrases had been one of the characteristic features of political language; and it had been noticed that the tendency to use abbreviations of this kind was most marked in totalitarian countries and totalitarian organizations. Examples were such words as *Nazi, Gestapo, Comintern,* . . . *Agitprop* (264).

Once more, Orwell uses the satirical device of apposition when he utters the choice words of Fascism (Nazi, Gestapo) in the same breath with the choice words of Communism (Comintern, Agitprop). The apposition points to the fact that Newspeak, the linguistic model of Ingsoc, originates in the vocabulary of *both* Fascism and Communism. On this point the satire zooms in on some key concepts about the Comintern, by elaborating on its linguistic difference from the "Communist International":

> The words *Communist International*, for instance, call up a composite picture of universal human brotherhood, red flags, barricades, Karl Marx, and the Paris Commune. The word *Comintern*, on the other hand, suggests merely a tightly knit organization and a well-defined body of doctrine. It refers to something almost as easily recognized, and as limited in purpose, as a chair or a table. *Comintern* is a word that can be uttered almost without taking thought, whereas *Communist International* is a phrase over which one is obliged to linger at least momentarily (264).

The linguistic difference between the two words exemplifies the betrayal of the original ideal of Socialism — the institution originally designed to eradicate nationalism became, in reality, a branch of the Soviet foreign service.

In Oceania contractions on the pattern of the "Comintern" still remind us of their origin, but what may seem like continuity is, in fact, camouflage for the total reversal of meaning. This was a device Orwell also used in *Animal Farm,* where Squealer went on secretly changing the original wording of the seven commandments until the new version came to reverse the original meaning, yet in a way that allowed the pigs to maintain the semblance of continuity between pre-revolutionary ideals and post-revolutionary practice.

On the whole, Newspeak in 2050 embodies the last stage of a three-step process of entropy — that is, a three-step linguistic and moral decline: the betrayal of the Revolution (*Animal Farm*); the aftermath of the betrayed Revolution (*Nineteen Eighty-Four*); and the total elimination of free thinking (Newspeak, 2050). It is important to pay attention to this three-stage process, particularly in the light of Bernard Crick's point that Orwell may have intended to write three novels in sequence. Thus, we have in his Notebook references to a story in which Boxer is a human character — an indication that Orwell may have indeed intended to write a trilogy. There is a significant sense of continuity between *Animal Farm* and

Nineteen Eighty-Four, in spite of the difference in genre. It is fair to speculate that the Appendix containing the "Principles of Newspeak" may be the vestige of what could have become the third volume of the trilogy, depicting the stage that follows the totalitarian practice of 1984.

The language of Newspeak to be spoken in 2050 is the terminal stage of the linguistic decline that started in Orwell's lifetime. The Party makes it clear that its purpose is to make language mechanical, "as nearly as possible independent of consciousness," until a person becomes so skilled in talking automatically that it sounds like "a machine gun spraying forth bullets" or like "duckspeak" (265). Once more, the Party simply turns a tendency of the 1940s into a principle. Many times in his essays, Orwell points to the connection between the mindlessness and the ugliness of political language and to the connection between the use of debased language and the dehumanization of the speaker:

> When one watches some tired hack on the platform mechanically repeating the familiar phrases — bestial atrocities, iron heel, blood-stained tyranny, free peoples of the world, stand shoulder to shoulder — one often has the curious feeling that one is not watching a live human being but some kind of dummy: a feeling which becomes stronger at moments when the light catches the speaker's spectacles and turns them into blank discs which seem to have no eyes behind them. And this is not altogether fanciful. A speaker who uses that kind of phraseology has gone some distance towards turning himself into a machine (v. 4, 165).

It is the corruption of the political language of the 1940s that gave the Party the idea to further reduce consciousness to the point where the original ideals of democracy and Socialism are no longer thinkable. It is probably not without significance that if we accept the *Dictionary of Newspeak* as an organic part of *Nineteen Eighty-Four*, we must also recognize that Orwell's critique of the totalitarian mentality ends with a quotation from the Declaration of Independence (267), a document that articulates the central struggle of the "spirit of Man," the humanist's pursuit of equality, fraternity, and liberty. Orwell felt these ideals to be endemic to the cause of Socialism as the highest form of democracy. Since rhetorically the end of a text carries special emphasis, we should recognize that in *Nineteen Eighty-Four* the *Dictionary of Newspeak* carries the most emphatic part of the satirist's message: Socialism, which started out as a movement to realize the highest ideals of humanism, was betrayed until it led to the debasement of these ideals, and ultimately to their total elimination from human consciousness. In the language of Newspeak the entire spirit embodied in the Declaration of Independence is reduced and dismissed in one vague and therefore ominous word: crimethink.

By accepting the repression of criticism and the uglification and corruption of language, the satirist's Adversary can be held responsible for contributing to the ultimate destruction of consciousness. By giving up his right to criticize and his right to free thinking, he has acquiesced in the coming of a society in which thinking itself becomes a crime.

In showing how the significant documents of the human spirit are sacrificed to Newspeak, Orwell points out that our tendency to accept lies, corruption, and the falsification of history could lead to the annihilation of the best examples, the most moving documents, of the "spirit of Man." Seemingly the Party is eager to appropriate the works of Shakespeare, Milton, Swift, Byron, and Dickens by translating them from Oldspeak, but the reduction of these works to Newspeak is tantamount to their annihilation; hence, it is through the act of their translation that "our last link with the past would have been severed" (267) and that our heritage consisting of "their original writings with all else that survived of the literature of the past would be destroyed" (268).

That the annihilation of the great documents of the human spirit would lead to the destruction of civilization is proven beyond doubt by the Appendix. The "spirit of Man" lives in the Word; the Word is our only link with previous and future generations.[1] The elimination of Oldspeak, then, leads us to the deepest stage of tragic loss, the catastrophe of the cumulative loss of consciousness. Nevertheless, after reaching this "dead centre," the Appendix also offers Orwell an opportunity for the reversal of tragic irony into the militant, liberating wit of satire.

The Party's Downfall in Newspeak

The impersonal passive voice and the conditional mode introduced by the Appendix lead the readers to contemplate the events of 2050 with genuine uncertainty. Were the events expected to take place brought to their expected conclusion, or were they prevented by some circumstance unforeseen by the Party? In the course of this contemplation we will also develop serious doubt about O'Brien's announcement of the Party's eternal, unbreakable hold over the future. In effect the Party's ultimate triumph in diminishing the range of thought by reducing our language to Newspeak would be tantamount to its self-destruction. There are several 'books within the book' which should contribute to this lesson implied in Newspeak, and each contributes to the overall tenor of the satire. The first book we hear about, the *Children's History Book* Winston borrows from Mrs. Parsons, is the false Bible. It includes the official — that is, false — Genesis of the Party, designed to deceive the masses. It declares that Big Brother came to power to overthrow the capitalist exploiter and establish the equality of the workers, and that his promises of establishing equality and higher living standards have been fulfilled. As we saw in Chapter 5, *The Children's History Book* regurgitates the worst clichés of the twentieth-century Marxist theoretician, and of course it is also Orwell's allusion to the new version of the history of the Bolshevik Party, including its drastic revision of Trotsky's role in the Revolution, according to which he, the founder of the Red Army, was represented as a conspirator against the Red Army right from the beginning. This revised history was published in Russia in 1936 in millions of copies, and used as a textbook in schools (Geller). The revisions were also accepted, often unquestioningly, by members of the Leftist intelligentsia in the West.

A counterpoint to this 'official' and therefore false Bible is the "Book" of the Underground, also called *Goldstein's Book*. By contrast to the *Children's History Book*, *Goldstein's Book* gives us an adult version of the Party's Genesis. Thus we find out that Big Brother and the Inner Party prepared the Revolution, using the Socialist slogan of equality as camouflage to set up their own rule, whereby inequality was made permanent. To pursue our analogy between the "Book" and the Bible, we may look at *Goldstein's Book* as *Genesis* and the *Dictionary of Newspeak* as *The Book of Revelation* — a secular, restrained, yet highly suggestive parallel with the vision of the Apocalypse. If Big Brother echoes the biblical Antichrist, the *Dictionary of Newspeak* is the Anti-Word, the final destruction of human consciousness without hope for resurrection.

Within the same frame of reference, there is another counterpoint to *Goldstein's Book*. It is the 'Anti-Book' Winston is
working on in the Ministry of Truth, which, as we have seen, is
really the Ministry of Untruth, the Ministry of Lies. It is the
machinery designed by the Party for the continuous changing
and falsification of history until all reliable records of the past
will disappear in the "memory hole." There is no doubt that
Orwell considers the "memory hole" just as horrifying as the
"vaporization" of human beings — their disappearance without a trace. In fact, the act of vaporization is the inescapable
result of the planned corruption of language. Deceit and dishonesty lead not only to murder, but also to the planned denial
of the value of individual existence. The process demonstrates
the demonic destruction of the World through the destruction
of the Word.

The monstrosity of the Party's attempt to produce the Anti-
Book by the continuous rewriting of records is paralleled by
their attempt to produce the Anti-Novel — novel by machine.[2]
Julia is working on one of these bookwriting machines. Her job
is to contribute to the production of pornography, a product
the Party calls, quite cynically, "prolefeed." This is another attempt to design a substitute and wipe out the moral, emotional,
and psychological records of human consciousness incorporated
in the classics, the great works of fiction of the past. In fact, the
Party has taken care to remove these books from every house
in the prole quarters.

Although *Goldstein's Book* serves as a counterpoint to the
Children's History Book's intent to falsify the Word, *Goldstein's
Book* is itself a public document and there is some doubt about
its authorship and the purpose it serves in the hands of the
Inner Party. Therefore, when we are looking for the purest,
most unambiguous counterpoint to the Party's attempt to destroy the Word through the *Dictionary of Newspeak*, we should
probably look at Winston's diary. It is Winston's diary that
contains, in miniature, Orwell's own *ars poetica* as a novelist,
his commitment to witness his world for the future and become
a link to the best manifestations of the "spirit of Man": "To
the future or to the past, to a time when thought is free, when
men are different from one another and do not live alone — to
a time when truth exists and what is done cannot be undone:
From the age of uniformity, from the age of solitude, from the

age of Big Brother, from the age of doublethink — greetings!" (28).

If we realize that the diary is the counterpoint to Newspeak, it becomes clear that once Newspeak came into being, Winston would no longer be able to even think about freedom, let alone express his yearnings in the diary. He would lack the words and the concepts. Orwell made a significant point in his essays "The Prevention of Literature" (v. 4, 81) and "Literature and Totalitarianism" (v. 2, 163): In a totalitarian society expression, even thinking, will become impossible, and therefore the novel, the truly "Protestant" genre of individuality, will also have to die out (v. 4, 88–92). That the novel is also our best weapon against the totalitarian mentality remains unsaid in the essays, but it is a thought implicit in and essential to the understanding of all the 'books within the book' in *Nineteen Eighty-Four*. Since, once Newspeak is established, Winston could no longer be able to undertake his journey towards self-expression and self-understanding, Winston's diary — this humble, fragmentary, and subjective 'private' document — is in fact the last novel, the last testimony of the individual's private conscience, his uncorrupted consciousness, and hence the last representative of the "spirit of Man" in Oceania.

But in the ultimate irony of Orwell's concept of Newspeak, by destroying language and consciousness the Inner Party is also driven to destroy itself. Inherent in the dynamism of domination there is a paradox, a cruel joke Orwell had observed many years before the writing of the novel. In the context of *Nineteen Eighty-Four*, this paradox means that O'Brien's pronouncement about the Party's eternal domination should also be seen in the light of the satirist's "militant irony."

The paradox is this. If the effects of the victimizer's victory are taken to their ultimate conclusions, the victimizer will be inevitably reduced to the level of his victim. There is probably no great spiritual uplift coming from this 'joke' because the victimizer's demise at the end of the process will still not resurrect his innumerable victims along the way; nevertheless, it is a point worth observing. The parasite that devours the vitality of a living organism may reach the peak of its own parasitic power only to be faced with the final effect: by the very act of having fulfilled its energies, it has also devoured the organism it fed upon and must therefore die. When O'Brien reveals the *perpetuum mobile* of terror and lies as the mainspring of the

Party's existence, he makes clear that the God of Power depends on victims, on human sacrifice, to maintain its vitality: "The object of persecution is persecution. The object of torture is torture. The object of power is power" (227). O'Brien is convinced that the cat-and-mouse game he has played with Winston for seven long years will go on forever, always with new victims. As a "priest of power," he can feel alive only when he exercises power, and he can feel power only when engaged in the process of breaking down the personality of the rebel, the heretic, the thinker. But we have just seen that once Newspeak has come into effect, the Inner Party can have no more Winstons to match wits with. It is no accident that the Principles of Newspeak could not have been in full force in the course of Winston's story: none of Winston's rebellion against the Party would have been possible without his high level of articulation, his respect for and his command of the Word. By destroying the Word through the introduction of Newspeak, the Party makes "free thought" no longer a "deadly sin," only a "meaningless abstraction" (v. 1, 576). As a result, the destruction of language must also eliminate the entire concept of heresy on which O'Brien depends for the exercising of his power.

Moreover, if O'Brien wants to keep his vitality, he has to be of an intelligence equal or superior to that of Winston (222). His position as the "priest of power" depends on knowing the difference between the smiling icon on the poster and the true identity of the God of Power. He has to have access to the 'Big Lie' and be able to keep his knowledge from the rest of the population. When confronted with Winston's question as to whether he had read *Goldstein's Book*, O'Brien answers: "I wrote it. That is to say, I collaborated in writing it" (225). Whether or not he has written the "Book," he has to be familiar with it, be in possession of the secret truth of the Party's Genesis so that he can guard the secret of the Party's real identity from the uninitiated. The "priests's" ultimate secret is connected with the 'Big Lie' in the *Children's History Book*: only they know that Big Brother is not the people's Saviour from the enemy; Big Brother is the enemy itself. It is essential for O'Brien and all the 'ministrants' of Untruth, all the "priests" of power, that they hang on to their secret code: it is their only weapon, the only means to sustain their superiority over the masses. But once the works of all the great writers of the past have been eliminated through translation into Newspeak, language is destroyed and, with it, the Inner Party's secret code. As Syme announces to Winston during their discussion of Newspeak, by 2050 there will be no one left who can understand the very principles of Newspeak (49). Hence, the victimizer who had planned the deception in 1984 will by 2050 inevitably sink to the level of his victims and thereby, also inevitably, lose the power over others that keeps him alive.

This paradox is further reinforced if we remember that without the language of Oldspeak, the Party could no longer practise Doublethink, which is based on the twisting and corruption of words to produce the effect of self-delusion; without Doublethink the Inner Party would no longer be able to justify its function to itself. The power of the Inner Party depends on the deception and self-deception of a corrupted consciousness even more than it depends on violence. But if in the end the totalitarian mentality leads to the destruction of consciousness, the Word altogether, inevitably the Inner Party will also destroy itself in the process. The total elimination of consciousness will also have to include the instigator of the 'Big Lie' that keeps the machinery of terror in motion. And here we have reached what Northrop Frye called the "dead centre" of tragic irony and caught a glimpse of "the gentlemanly Prince of Darkness bottomside up" (227).

It is significant that Orwell uses the debasement of language as the central metaphor to show the debasement of our humanity in the totalitarian system, a system based on a corrupt and corrupting mentality we may all succumb to if we are not vigilant. Orwell's emphasis is unmistakable: even in the days of nuclear weapons, it is through the corruption of the Word that the World could suffer the final blow to the "spirit of Man." In this sense, to the very end of the novel Orwell maintains the tenets of his 'religion of humanity' by insisting that "no bomb that ever burst/ Shatters the crystal spirit." Nevertheless, Winston, the last representative of this spirit in the novel, has been shattered. The crystal representing the wholeness and uniqueness of his personality has been broken by the Thought Police. The destruction of critical thought and free expression, the destruction of the truth of the Word, is tantamount to the disintegration, the dehumanization of the psyche. By extension of this thought, it is only through the Word, through respect for objective truth, through the careful, critical investigation of our own consciousness that we can hope to remain human.

In the beginning there was the Word. In the Appendix of *Newspeak* Orwell presents us with an apocalyptic vision of the World uncreated by the destruction of the Word, bereft of the human heritage, the record of human consciousness. However, in the context of the novel, and in the context of the *Dictionary of Newspeak*, Orwell also emphasizes that what appears to be an Apocalypse is not a God-ordained catastrophe; it is simply the final stage of the same disease we see around ourselves in the present and that we must prevent from devouring the hope for the "spirit of Man." In the beginning there was the Word. In the end, our final hope is still faith in the redeeming power of the Word.[3]

The Reader and the Satirist's Message — Concluding Remarks

Orwell's decision to place the *Dictionary of Newspeak* as the last thing the reader is left to contemplate may also point to a very important question that has not been explored in the course of this study, except perhaps indirectly. The question is: What does Orwell's satire, addressed to his contemporaries, with a particular emphasis on the Leftist intellectual in the West, have to say to the readers of the 1990s, or indeed to readers at any time or place?

We have seen that the decoding of the targets of Orwell's dystopian satire hinges upon our understanding of the special relationships between the Satirist and his Adversary; the Adversary and the Ideal Reader; and finally, the Reader and the Protagonist. All of these, without doubt, are drawing attention to the cause-effect relationship between trends in 1948, the time the novel was written, and the world of the future (established quite arbitrarily as 1984). Therefore, it is worthwhile to ask, what does the novel tell us, readers of the 1990s, or indeed, readers at any time after 1948, the time of its writing? What response should we expect from the reader who responds to the novel today? It seems to me that Orwell's strategies in writing a work with the high degree of credibility expected from the psychological novel imply that for the book to have appropriate impact, the reader should take away a sense of his or her *own* crisis, the foreboding that Winston's predicament could become the reader's own. The possibility of such a predicament seems to be extremely far-fetched to young Western readers today and they may well wonder whether there is any connection between Winston's situation and their own reality.

In fact, the fate of Winston Smith, nightmarish as it may appear to such readers, is not at all the product of Orwell's fevered imagination. People have been watched, trapped, and tortured both in Stalin's Russia and in Hitler's Germany in a strikingly similar fashion. The scapegoat hunts, the purges, the rigged public trials and public executions — the evidence is there in the historical documents of the past, and due to the political changes introduced in recent years in the U.S.S.R. and Eastern Europe, more and more evidence is coming to the surface that should reassure the informed reader that the grimness of Winston's fate is not the consequence of Orwell's paranoia. For that matter, there is ample evidence of such systems of physical and psychological terror in more recent times in the records about prisoners of war in Japan, Korea, South America, and Cambodia. Records testifying to Orwell's analysis of the "blackwhite" mentality of terror and lies come from both the Rightist and the so-called Leftist dictatorships, from the theocracies such as Iran and Iraq, and from the "blackwhite" mentality associated with fundamentalist groups in the United States, for example. In our age, just as in the 1940s, the various isms, including racism, nationalism, religious fanaticism produce the same threatening symptoms of "blackwhite," "protective stupidity," or Doublethink Orwell was so accurate in diagnosing among his contemporaries.

I believe that it is important to emphasize here that, like all great satirists, when Orwell was writing, he must have seen his Adversary, or his Ideal Reader, as his contemporary who had to respond to the urgent matters of political reality in the late 1940s, the time of the writing of the book, and my argument about the novel's literary merits does not depend on the success of Orwell as a political prophet of the future: I argue that the novel is a strikingly accurate satirical 'anatomy' of totalitarianism and the reception of totalitarianism in the West in Orwell's own time. However, it so happens that at least three of Orwell's major targets have received vivid illumination in the course of the past forty years, culminating in what *The New York Times* describes as the "domino effect" of political changes between

1989 and 1990, resulting in the "collapse of Communism" in Eastern Europe and the U.S.S.R.

These events, I believe, have vindicated Orwell's position on issues relating to three of his most significant targets: They indicate that (1) the sense in which Orwell used the term "totalitarian" for Hitler's Germany and Stalin's Russia both in his essays and in *Nineteen Eight-Four* is still valid and meaningful, (2) Orwell was right in emphasizing that the unprecedented scale of "organized lying" in order to systematically repress the Truth is possibly the single most essential attribute of a totalitarian system, and (3) only by pursuing and facing up to the uncorrupted truth of History can we prevent the spreading of the totalitarian mentality in the future. Let us examine each of these points.

1. In his 1972 *Totalitarianism*, Leonard Schapiro delineates the controversy about the term "totalitarian," pointing out that "in Soviet Russia, according to the Dictionary of the Soviet Academy, it was used in 1940 and thereafter, and applied exclusively to 'Fascist' regimes. Official Soviet writers strongly deprecate the use of the term 'totalitarian' as applied by non-Soviet writers, and contend that this is an aspect of 'cold war' propaganda." Schapiro also adds, however, that "the term is frequently applied to the Soviet regime in the very extensive secretly disseminated writings by various dissent movements which have been circulating in the Soviet Union in the past years" (14).

By the end of 1990, the term "totalitarian" has become officially acceptable in the Soviet Union. In his article entitled "30 Political Parties Join in One Opposition Group," which appeared in *The Toronto Star* on October 22, 1990, Stephen Handelman gives an account of a Soviet resolution "passed by a new organization, which calls itself Democratic Russia," that insists that "the country can only be saved by uniting all democratic forces in a wide popular movement which says no to *totalitarian government* and yes to the formation of civil society" (3). The language of this resolution makes it clear that in the Soviet Union of 1990 the term "totalitarian" has become widely acceptable when referring to the Soviet system before Gorbachev, particularly to the regime of Stalin.

Of course, parallel with the acceptance of the term "totalitarian" comes the Soviet historian's acknowledgement of the facts about Stalin's terror. Thus, as Bill Keller reports to *The New York Times* from Moscow, on February 3, 1990, in the past few years "the Soviet press has left little unsaid about Stalin's shortcomings, probing into sacred myths like his conduct of World War II, likening him to Hitler, dissecting his cruelties period by period. But official historians have shied away from putting a number to it all" (*Collapse* 13). Therefore it created quite a stir when

> the estimates, by the historian Roy Medvedev, were printed in the weekly tabloid *Argumenti i Fakti*, which has a circulation of more than 20 million. . . . The estimated number of deaths is about equal to the number of Soviet soldiers and civilians believed killed in World War II. . . . In all, Mr. Medvedev calculated about 40 million victims of Stalin's repressions, including those arrested, driven from their land or blacklisted. . . . Although the bookkeeping of Stalin's terror is an inexact and controversial science, Mr. Medvedev's estimates are generally in line with Western calculations that have long been disparaged by . . . official Soviet historians (*Collapse* 13).

It is essential to recall here that Orwell's insistence that the Soviet regime is totalitarian and *therefore* it cannot be truly Socialist is at the very heart of his argument with his Adversary in the thirties and the forties. The significance of Orwell's clear-sightedness is highlighted by the fact that such prominent intellectuals among Orwell's contemporaries as Simone de Beauvoir, for example, still argued in the early fifties that "since no Soviet leader had yet dared to tell the whole truth, the whole truth did not yet exist. Hence her astonishing remark: 'No one, neither in the USSR nor elsewhere, has yet satisfactorily explained the Stalin period'" (Caute 106). A similar instance of Doublethink is revealed "when Sartre laments that 'a socialist government, supported by an army of bureaucrats, could have reduced men to slavery.' The madness lies in the inability to ask a simple question: what does a regime have to do before it becomes no longer useful to call it socialist?" (Caute 105). By contrast, Orwell was consistent in denying that the Stalin regime was Socialist, and in *Animal Farm* and *Nineteen Eighty-Four* he set out to destroy this "Soviet myth" as a pre-condition for reviving democratic Socialism in the West.

It is interesting to note that even the forty eventful years since Orwell's death have not been enough to resolve his argument with his long-time Adversary, a persona resurrected in those of his literary critics who insist, to this day, that Orwell must have been "hysterical" when describing Stalin's regime as totalitarian, an "emotive term" (Rai) that allowed Orwell's work to be exploited by the propagandists of the Cold War.

Yet, the various paradigms defining totalitarian governments designed by Western political scientists such as Friedrich, Brzezinsky, Kirkpatrick, and Talmon should be sufficient indication that the picture of totalitarianism in *Nineteen Eighty-Four* is clearly on target. All these scholars would agree with Leonard Schapiro that "totalitarianism is a useful term" when applied to Hitler's Germany and to countries "whose political regimes were modelled closely on that of the Soviet Union under Stalin" (101). Although Schapiro admits that since all these governments "are not identical in origin and structure," and therefore "the search for the definition of 'totalitarian' has proceeded unremittingly for twenty-five years or more" (101), he argues that it would be a mistake to say "that the use of the term 'totalitarian' as equally applicable to national Socialist Germany and the Soviet Union under Stalin is subsequent to, or a consequence of the 'Cold War'" (108). It is also interesting to observe that Orwell's Adversary still fails to see that Orwell's definition of Stalin's U.S.S.R. as totalitarian is not a sign of disillusionment or despair: it was precisely by dissociating Socialism from Stalin's *totalitarian* regime that Orwell managed to salvage hope in his long-term goal of democratic Socialism, (a point, incidentally, also quite easily overlooked in the Eastern Europe of the 1990s).

2. Although the definition of totalitarianism in *Nineteen Eighty-Four* coincides with the whole range of phenomena political scientists established as the "symptoms," the "syndrome," or the "contours" of totalitarian governments, in exploring the "intellectual implications of totalitarianism" (v. 4, 520) the novel gives political and psychological prominence to one particular aspect of totalitarianism — its concentrated effort to suppress truth, freedom of expression, and free thought. The developments of the last twenty years, but particularly those of 1989 and 1990, have also vindicated Orwell's major insight that

> the organized lying practised by totalitarian states is not, as sometimes is claimed, a temporary expedient of the same nature as military deception. It is something *integral* to totalitarianism, something that would still continue even if concentration camps

and secret police forces had ceased to be necessary. . . . Totalitarianism demands, in fact, the continuous alteration of the past, and in the long run probably demands a disbelief in the very existence of objective truth (v. 4, 85–86).

In his 1972 study Leonard Schapiro reinforces Orwell's focus when pointing out that

> totalitarian rule depends for its success on secrecy, isolation from the outside world, and successful deception of the outside world. The fact that the "iron curtain" has now been breached to the extent that news which the Soviet authorities wish to conceal can nevertheless reach the foreign press . . . was decisive in this case. For there can be no doubt that if the Soviet authorities could have prevented news from [human rights activist] Medvedev's detention in the asylum from reaching the outside world, . . . he would be still under forcible narcotic treatment in a ward for dangerous lunatics in the Kaluga mental hospital (117).

The intellectual passion informing *Nineteen Eighty-Four* is inextricable from the intensity of Orwell's moral conviction that the Western intellectual, particularly the writer, had a vital responsibility to the community because only he had the potential to shatter the Big Lie, to avoid the traps of Doublethink, and thereby *prevent* the spreading of the totalitarian mentality. No doubt the startlingly quick collapse of an entire power block in 1989 and 1990 was the result of a combination of complex econo-political forces, and we may have to wait for a long time before receiving a comprehensive historical explanation of their dynamism. Nevertheless, no one would question that at the spiritual-political roots of this tremendous mass movement was the determination of a small number of "dissident" intellectuals who, like Winston Smith, took it upon themselves to express dissent, to expose the truth, and to insist on being heard by the world. As *The New York Times* correspondent's analysis of this process indicates, Orwell's intense concern with the unlimited freedom of thought, expression, and communication as the most vital weapons against totalitarianism was absolutely on target:

> It turned out that a few dissidents using nonviolent means, and exploiting the freedom of the press and airwaves beyond their borders, could in this increasingly interconnected world bring down autocrat after autocrat. Foreign correspondents wrote for their own papers, but their reports were translated and beamed back

to countries where such information as they were writing was banned. The spread of portable radios and videos made such information more accessible. The official press was forced to offer more information, more truth, as it was forced to compete for credibility with the outsiders. East Germans watched West German television and learned what had been achieved in Poland. In Romania people were moved to boldness when they learned from Yugoslav stations that their countrymen had been killed by Caecescu's security forces. Once informed, they were mobilized. In most places, they marched and chanted and drew placards, and with the world press watching, such means proved sufficient *to expose previously forbidden truths* and to make revolutionary changes that had so recently seemed impossible (*Collapse* 353, my italics).

Doublethink — a network and a methodology for lying — is a warning to Orwell's contemporaries in the late 1940s that exposing the Truth is the first step in *preventing* the spreading of the totalitarian system. Undoubtedly, the fact that in the late 1980s the exposure of "previously forbidden truths" had proven to be the single most important weapon in *destroying* this system, confirms Orwell's analysis.

3.   Orwell's emphasis on the distortion of historical records as an undeniable characteristic of totalitarian regimes also gains new illumination in the light of these events. In the aftermath of the "collapse of Communism," Orwell would probably warn us that the totalitarian mentality that had been rampant in a particular system for an extended period does not disappear all of a sudden upon the defeat of that system. If it is true, as he suggest, that "totalitarianism demands . . . the continuous alteration of the past, and in the long run probably demands a disbelief in the very existence of objective truth" (v. 4, 86), it should follow that only through the unremitting pursuit of uncorrupted historical truth could we expect to overcome the totalitarian mentality. There have been a number of books and films in the past few years that dwell on this profoundly "Orwellian" insight about the power of the past to "control" the present. *Repentance*, a 1984 Georgian film directed by Tengiz Abuladze, is a powerful political allegory that satirizes the denial of the post-Stalin generation and its refusal to come to terms with its own role in the totalitarian system. The film suggests that the dead dictator — a composite figure comprising Stalin, Hitler, and Mussolini — cannot be truly buried until his

successors are ready to assess the true nature of his regime and accept their own responsibility in his rule of terror, lies, and denunciations. Until the people are ready to face the painful truth about their own past, the dictator's corpse refuses civilized burial; it keeps resurfacing as a terrible reminder of the evil and corruption of the past, which had been ignored or denied by the survivors.

In his 1989 film *Nasty Girl*, Director Michael Verhoeven explores the same dilemma through the perspective of a small-town German girl who takes it upon herself to find out what life was like in her native town, Pfilzen, during Hitler's regime. Her historical research is hampered by the functionaries at City Hall, originally faithful followers of Hitler who are still in power in the seventies. At first they deny her access to the documents, then they try to intimidate her with veiled threats, and finally they resort to violence. Needless to say, she insists on pursuing her historical research, regardless of the dire consequences to her and her young family. Both films suggest that ignoring or denying the atrocities committed in the past by one's community is equivalent to giving consent, participating in the 'Big Lie,' keeping alive the totalitarian mentality. Both the German and the Georgian film explore the Orwellian theme that we cannot achieve control over our present and future without coming to terms with, being able to "control," our past.

In fact, by now Orwell's analysis of the political-psychological mainsprings of totalitarianism has become widely accepted in most parts of the world. Since the days of Glasnost, we have seen the U.S.S.R. becoming increasingly more open to Orwell's point of view. *Nineteen Eighty-Four* had been translated into Russian, Polish, and Hungarian before; now it is being allowed to circulate. As for Western historians and political scientists, many of them have accepted and vindicated Orwell's insights emerging from his analysis of revolution, mass communication, propaganda, and increasing state control, to mention only some of the most popular areas that show Orwell's lasting influence.

Nevertheless, the 'timeliness' or topicality of Orwell's targets should not distract us from recognizing in *Nineteen Eighty-Four* the 'timeless,' universal dimensions of great literary achievement. Therefore, while it is important to acknowledge that the specific target of Orwell's satire was the "blackwhite" mentality of ideological thinking, a target that emerged from his own time and place, *Nineteen Eighty-Four* was never designed as a weapon against Russia in the Cold War, and Orwell resisted critics who welcomed the novel as such.

Neither would he have accepted, I believe, the later attempt of some of his critics to turn the novel into an anti-American satire, although in his essays and letters he had indeed voiced anti-American sentiments whenever he was confronted with what he saw as evidence of American versions of nationalism, success worship, or expansionism.

Although the satirists "savage indignation" or "generous anger" must be, by definition, directed at what he deems to be aberrations of the world of his contemporaries, ultimately his "militant irony" is directed at the propensity of the human mind to accept lies, to condone dishonesty, and to seek shelter in the "protective stupidity" of any orthodoxy. The "blackwhite" mentality of totalitarian terror is merely the superlative stage of *our* propensity to give in to this mentality. The horrors that were produced and could be produced by the totalitarian mind are potentially always with us. They are a threat to our sanity, and we must vigilantly guard against them at all times and places. In the words of Hannah Arendt,

> the crisis of our time and its central experience have brought forth an entirely new form of government which as a potentially and ever present danger is only too likely to stay with us from now on, just as other forms of government which came about at different historical moments and rested on different fundamental experiences have stayed with mankind regardless of temporary defeats — monarchies, republics, tyrannies, dictatorships and despotisms (478).

Actually, the universality and timeless appeal of the novel comes from the readers' recognition that the patterns of thought Orwell has attributed to Oceania are a clear and present danger around us and within us. By recognizing the lure of the "blackwhite" mentality, the herd instinct, the sense of emotional satisfaction provided by the "secular religion" of isms, the modern reader of *Nineteen Eighty-Four* will get a glimpse of the courage required to uphold the "spirit of Man," and to act out Orwell's motto: "Dare to be a Daniel,/ Dare to stand alone;/ Dare to have a purpose firm,/ Dare to make it known" (v. 4, 82).

At the same time, when reading the 'black mass' of Winston's joining of the Underground, the reader is also warned to be careful that the heretic's commitment to resistance against the mental tyranny of orthodoxy does not turn, inadvertently, into a fanaticism of its own kind, into a counter-orthodoxy. In times of crisis, frequently "the best lack all conviction, while the worst are full of passionate intensity."

The authorial voice in the essays and in *Nineteen Eighty-Four* bespeaks of the uniquely Orwellian balancing act between the powerful commitment of the visionary and the intellectual modesty of the rationalist. Orwell's thought itself reveals the striving for balance between the apathy of despair and the fanatical, arrogant self-assurance of the "blackwhite" mentality. The balance is not easy to achieve. Its success depends on the incessant monitoring of criticism, self-doubt, self-irony. Therefore, ultimately the most universal message of the satire is Orwell's insistence on the importance of critical thought, the freedom of thinking and expression: As long as the writer is allowed to say that 2 plus 2 makes 4, everything else must follow. His passionate commitment to intellectual liberty transcends the particular controversies of his time, to remind us that in this respect we must remain forever our brothers' keepers: "When one sees highly educated men looking on indifferently at oppression and persecution, one wonders which to despise more, their cynicism or their shortsightedness. . . . They do not see that any attack on intellectual liberty, and on the concept of objective truth, threatens in the long run every department of thought" (v. 4, 94).

That one needs to stand up for one's sense of truth and freedom even when one is a "minority of one," that "truth is not statistical," is probably the most memorable and truly timeless message of Orwell's final satire, a far cry indeed from despair or apathy. Courage to stand up for the uniqueness of the individual, for the liberation of the downtrodden; the nobility of the moral act even when it has no immediate, measurable result; to stand up for what is most essential in our human heritage, the uncorrupted consciousness, the Word: this is the essence of the struggle that is inseparable from Orwell's faith in the human spirit. Rooted in his own time, Orwell's satire also offers the timeless perspective of those very documents Newspeak was so intent on eradicating. A masterpiece of twentieth-century humanism, *Nineteen Eighty-Four* takes us through tragic irony and militant wit to faith in the "spirit of Man."

Notes

[1] When Orwell points out that in order to remain human we must hold on to our cultural heritage, he comes remarkably close to the position of another great advocate of the moral imagination, Matthew Arnold. In discussing his famous concept of "Sweetness and Light," in *Culture and Anarchy* Arnold points out that true culture "seeks to do away with classes; to make the best that has been thought and known in the world current everywhere; to make all men live in an atmosphere of sweetness and light, where they may use ideas, as it uses them itself, freely, — nourished, and not bound by them" (216–217). He would agree with Orwell that our cultural heritage is essential to the survival of our species, and that in a true democracy every human being could, and should, become "cultured." He also shares Orwell's concern that our cultural heritage should not become a canon we are "bound" by, but the source of our sense of continuity that we are "nourished" by as members of the human species.

[2] In the "Age of Doublethink" (a chapter in his 1986 *Filming Literature: The Art of Screen Adaptation*), Neil Sinyard points out that Orwell

> distrusted the industrial structure of film and the consequent mechanisation of art. "Disney films," he says darkly, "are produced by what is essentially a factory process, the work being done partly mechanically and partly by teams of artists who have to subordinate their individual style" [v. 4, 92]. . . . He makes Disney Studios sound like a labour camp. In that description, the cinema becomes an aspect of Orwell's distrust of totalitarianism, his fear of art being appropriated by the state (56).

Orwell's distrust of the cinema notwithstanding, Sinyard argues that Chaplin's "*The Great Dictator* exerted a greater influence on Orwell than he, or anyone else realized" and that the film actually "anticipates the satirical vein" of Orwell's great satires.

[3] In their "Language as Political Control: Newspeak Revisited" (*George Orwell: A Reassessment*, Vancouver, Nov. 23–24, 1984), Bernard Gorfman and Jonathan Pool argue that Orwell made a mistake by devising a language that would be easy to learn and would therefore eradicate the distinction between the ruling oligarchy and the rest of the population. Like those critics who blame Orwell for designing Oceania in a way that contradicts O'Brien's statement about the system's timelessness, both Pool and Gorfman fail to see Orwell's 'joke,' the paradox about the self-destructiveness of evil. The paradox, as many analysts have perceived, is that the system of totalitarianism carries the seed of its own destruction. Any tyranny, any

system of domination must, inevitably, end in defeat — the demise of the victimizer after his elimination of his victim.

The same paradox lends itself to analysis in terms of the "double action" characteristic of tragedy. The demonic element in the human being may assume its power through the Word, when language is allowed to become an instrument for creating lies and hatred. Thus, in his *Portage to San Cristobal*, George Steiner presents us with an apocalyptic vision of language in the mouth of the totalitarian dictator: "When He made the Word, God made possible also its contrary. . . . No, He created on the night side of language a speech of hell. Whose words mean hatred and vomit of life. Few men can learn that speech or speak it for long. . . . But there shall come a man whose mouth shall be as a furnace and whose tongue as a sword laying waste. . . . Where God said, let there be, he will unsay" (162–163).

Although the language of lies and hatred is the means of destruction, the Word by itself is also a healer. In the words of Northrop Frye, "If we know we are in hell, we are no longer wholly there: it is our consciousness that tells us we are, and consciousness is a function of language, not the other way around ("Authority" 3).

Rollo May also stresses the therapeutic effect of the Word, its power over the demonic:

> What did the ancients mean by this "Word" which has power over the daimonic? They were referring to the logos, the meaningful structure of reality, which is man's capacity for language as well as dialogue. "In the beginning was the Word" is true experientially as well as theologically. For the beginning of man as man, in contrast to apes or the pre-self-conscious infant, is the potentiality for language. We find that some of the important functions of therapy rest on fundamental aspects of the structure of language; the Word discloses the daimonic, forces it out into the open where we can confront it directly. The Word gives man a power over the daimonic (176).

Orwell's concept of Newspeak makes us aware of the power of the Word to create and uncreate the World. He draws our attention to language as the single most significant weapon in the hands of, and in our fight against, the totalitarian forces in our world.

Works Cited

1. All references to George Orwell's *Nineteen Eighty-Four* are to the novel's 1984 Penguin edition. Page references are indicated in brackets immediately after the quotation.
2. References to Orwell's other novels are to *The Penguin Complete Novels of George Orwell*, 1983.
3. All quotations from George Orwell's essays, articles, and letters refer to *The Collected Essays, Journalism and Letters of George Orwell* in 4 volumes, ed. Sonia Orwell and Ian Angus, Penguin Books, in association with Secker and Warburg, 1970. Page references are indicated in brackets immediately after the quotation, and include both volume and page number.

Arendt, Hannah. *The Origins of Totalitarianism*. New York: Harcourt, Brace and World, 1951 (originally *The Burdens of Our Times*; London: Secker and Warburg, 1951).

Armytage, A.G.H. "Orwell and Zamyatin." *Yesterday's Tomorrows: An Historical Survey of Future Societies*. London: 1963.

Arnold, Matthew. "Culture and Anarchy." *Selected Poetry and Prose*. New York: Rinehart, 1952.

Ashe, Geoffrey. "The Servile State in Fact and Fiction." *Month* 4 July 1950, 57–59.

Auden, W.H. "George Orwell." *Spectator* 16 Jan. 1971, 86–87.

Baruch, Elaine Hoffman. "The Golden Country: Sex and Love in *1984*." *1984 Revisited*. Ed. Irving Howe. New York: Harper and Row, 1983.

Beadle, Gordon. "George Orwell and the Death of God." *Colorado Quarterly* 23 (1974), 51–63.

Beauchamp, Gorman. "Of Man's Last Disobedience: Zamyatin's *We* and Orwell's *1984*." *Comparative Literature Studies* 10 (1973), 285–301.

Berger, Harold. *Science Fiction and the New Dark Ages*. Bowling Green: Bowling Green University Popular Press, 1976.

Bettelheim, Bruno. *The Informed Heart: Autonomy in a Mass Age*. New York: Free Press, 1960.

Billington, Michael. "A Director's Vision of Orwell's '1984' Draws Inspiration from 1948." *New York Times* 3 June 1984, 19 and 29.

Birrell, T.A. "Is Integrity Enough? A Study of George Orwell." *Dublin Review* 224 (Autumn 1950), 49–65.

Bonifas, Gilbert. *George Orwell: L'Engagement*. Paris: Éditions Didier, 1984.

Borkenau, Franz. "Communism as an International Movement." *World Communism*. New York: Faber, 1939.

Bracher, Karl Dietrich. "The Disputed Concept of Totalitarianism." *Totalitarianism Reconsidered*. Ed. Ernest Menze. Port Washington, New York: Free Press, 1981.

Buitenhuis, Peter, and Ira Nadel, eds. *George Orwell: A Reassessment*. London: Macmillan, 1988.

Burgess, Anthony. *The Novel Now*. New York: 1970.

Byron George Gordon. *Byron: A Self-Portrait: Letters and Diaries 1798–1821*. Ed. Peter Quennell. London: Murray, 1967.

Calder, Jenni. *Chronicles of Conscience: A Study of George Orwell and Arthur Koestler*. London: Secker and Warburg, 1968.

Camus, Albert. "The Failing of the Prophecy." *Existentialism versus Marxism: Conflicting Views on Humanism*. New York: Dell, 1966.

——— . *Notebook 1942–1951*. Trans. Justin O'Brien. New York: Knopf, 1966.

——— . *The Plague*. Trans. S. Gilbert. Harmondsworth: Penguin, 1948.

Carrère d'Éncausse, Hélène. *A History of the Soviet Union 1917–1953*. Trans. V. Ionescu. London: Longman, 1970.

Carter, Michael. *George Orwell and the Problem of Authentic Existence*. London: Croom Helm, 1985.

Caute, David. *The Fellowtravellers: A Postscript to the Enlightenment*. London: Weidenfeld and Nicolson, 1973.

Claeys, Gregory. "Industrialism and Hedonism in Orwell's Literary and Political Development." *Albion* 18.2 (Summer 1986), 219–245.

The Collapse of Communism. By Correspondents of *The New York Times*. Ed. Bernard Gwertzman and Michael Kaufman. New York: Random House, Times Books, 1990.

Comfort, Alex. "1939 and 1984: George Orwell and the Vision of Judgment." *On 1984*. Ed. Peter Stansky. New York: Freeman, 1983.

Connelly, Mark. *The Diminished Self*. Pittsburgh: Duquesne University Press, 1987.

Connolly, Cyrill. "George Orwell." *The Modern Movement: 100 Key Books from England, France and America, 1880–1950*. London: 1965.

Coombs, James. "Towards 2084." *The Orwellian Moment*. Ed. Robert Savage, James Coombs, and Dan Nimmo. Fayetteville: University of Arkansas Press, 1989.

Coppard, Audrey and Bernard Crick, eds. *Orwell Remembered*. London: B.B.C. Ariel Books, 1984.

Crick, Bernard. "Critical Introduction and Annotations to George Orwell's *Nineteen Eighty-Four*." *Nineteen Eighty-Four*. By Orwell. Oxford: Clarendon Press, 1984.

———. *George Orwell: A Life*. London: Secker and Warburg, 1980.

Deane, Herbert A. "Harold Laski." *The International Encyclopedia of the Social Sciences*, vol. 9, 30–33. New York: Macmillan and Free Press, 1968.

Deutscher, Isaac. "The Ex-Communist's Conscience." *Heretics and Renegades*. London: Hamish Hamilton, 1955. (Originally "Review of *The Gods that Failed*" in *The Reporter* [New York], April 1950.)

———. "*1984* — The Mysticism of Cruelty." *Heretics and Renegades*. London: Hamish Hamilton, 1955.

Devroey, Jean Pierre. *L'Âme de cristal: George Orwell au présent*. Bruxelles: Éditions de l'Université de Bruxelles, 1985.

Dickerson, Mark, and Thomas Flanegan. *An Introduction to Government: A Conceptual Approach*. Toronto: Nelson Canada, 1990.

Dutsher, Alan. "Orwell and the Crisis of Responsibility." *Contemporary Issues* 8 (1956), 308–316.

Eckstein, Arthur. "Orwell, Masculinity, and Feminist Criticism." *The Intercollegiate Review* 21.1 (Fall 1985), 47–54.

Edel, Leon. *The Modern Psychological Novel*. Gloucester, Mass.: Peter Smith, 1972.

Edwards, Paul, ed. *The Encyclopedia of Philosophy*. 8 vols. New York: Macmillan and Free Press, 1967.

Ehrenpreiss, Irwin. "Orwell, Huxley, Pope." *Revue des langues vivantes* 23 (1957), 215–230.

Eliade, Mircea. *Occultism, Witchcraft and Cultural Fashions*. Chicago: University of Chicago Press, 1976.

Elliott, George. "A Failed Prophet." *Hudson Review* 10 (1957), 149–154.

Elliott, Robert. "Satire." *Princeton Encyclopedia of Poetry and Poetics*. Ed. O. Preminger. Princeton: Princeton University Press, 1965.

———. *The Shape of Utopia: Studies in a Literary Genre*. Chicago: University of Chicago Press, 1970.

Faulkner, Peter. "Orwell and Christianity." *New Humanist* 89 (Dec. 1973), 270–273.

Fiedler, Leslie. Keynote address. *1984 Forum*. Seneca College, Toronto. February 27, 1984. Verbatim.

Fiderer, Gerald. "Masochism as Literary Strategy: Orwell's Psychological Novels." *Literature and Psychology* 20 (1970), 3–21.

Fink, Howard. "Orwell versus Koestler: *Nineteen Eighty-Four* as Optimistic Satire." *George Orwell*. Ed. C. Wemyss and Alexej Ugrinsky. Contributions to Study of World Literature #23. Westport: Greenwood, 1987.

Forster, E.M. "George Orwell." *Two Cheers for Democracy*. New York: Harvard, 1951, 60–63.

Frankel, Viktor. *Man's Search for Meaning*. New York: Washington Square Press, 1963.

Freud, Sigmund. *Complete Works*. Trans. James Strachey. 29 vols. London: Hogarth Press, 1955.

Freud: The Hidden Nature of Man. Dir. George Kaczender. The Learning Corporation of America, 1970.

Friedrich, Carl, and Zbigniev Brzezinsky. *Totalitarian Dictatorships and Autocracy*. New York: Praeger, 1956.

Frye, Northrop. *Anatomy of Criticism: Four Essays*. Princeton: Princeton University Press, 1957.

——. "The Authority of Learning." Lecture delivered at the Empire Club, Toronto, Jan. 19, 1984.

Fyvel, T.R. "A Writer's Life." *World Review*. June 1950, 7–20.

Geller, Mikhail, and Aleksandr Nekrich. *Utopia in Power: The History of the Soviet Union from 1917 to the Present*. New York: Summit Books, 1986.

Gerber, Richard. *Utopian Fantasy: A Study of English Utopian Fiction since the End of the Nineteenth Century*. London: 1955.

Golding, William. *Lord of the Flies*. London: Faber, 1954.

Good, Graham. "Orwell and Eliot: Politics, Poetry and Prose." *George Orwell: A Reassessment*. Ed. P. Buitenhuis and I. Nadel. London: Macmillan, 1988.

Goodey, Chris. "The Abyss of Pessimism." *GRANTA* 69 (25 April 1964), 7–9.

Gorfman, Bernard. "Pig and Proletariat: *Animal Farm* as History." Delivered at Southwest Political Science Association, Houston, Texas. April 12–15, 1978.

Gorfman, Bernard, and Jonathan Pool. "Language as Political Control: Newspeak Revisited." Delivered at *George Orwell: A Reassessment*. Vancouver, B.C. Nov. 23–24, 1984.

Gottlieb, Erika. "Orwell in the 1980's." *Utopian Studies* 3, No. 1 (1992), 108–120.

——. "Review of Daphne Patai's *The Orwell Mystique: A Study in Male Ideology*." *Dalhousie Review* (Halifax) 64.4 (1984–1985), 807–811.

Greenblatt, Stephen. *Three Modern Satirists: Waugh, Orwell and Huxley*. New Haven: Yale University Press, 1965.

Grieffenhager, Martin. "The Concept of Totalitarianism in Political Theory." *Totalitarianism Reconsidered*. Ed. Ernest Menze. Port Washington, New York: Free Press, 1981.

Gulbin, Suzanne. "Parallels and Contrasts in *Lord of the Flies* and *Animal Farm*." *English Journal* 55 (1966), 86–90.

Hamilton, Alice. "The Enslavement of Woman." *Nazis: An Assault on Civilization*. Ed. P. Van Paassen and James Waterman Wise. New York: Harrison Smith and Haas, 1934.

Handelman, Stephen. "30 Political Parties in One Opposition Group." *Toronto Star* October 22, 1990, 13.

Heller, Peter. *Dialectics and Nihilism: Essays on Lessing, Nietzsche, Mann and Kafka*. Amherst: University of Massachussetts Press, 1966.

Hilferding, Rudolf. "State Capitalism or Totalitarian State Economy." *The Modern Review* June 1947, 266–271.

Howe, Irving, ed. *1984 Revisited*. New York: Harper and Row, 1983.

Huxley, Aldous. *Brave New World*. Harmondsworth: Penguin, 1955.

——. "Brave New World Revisited: Proleptic Meditations on Mother's Day, Euphoria and Pavlov's Pooch" from "The Study of Aldous Huxley." *Esquire* July 1956.

Inge, W.R. *Christian Mysticism*. New York: Meridian, 1956.

Jung, Carl. *Civilization in Transition*. Trans. R.C. Hull. 2d ed. Bollingen Series. Princeton: Princeton University Press, 1970.

——. "The Undiscovered Self" (1957). *The Essential Jung*. Sel. and introd. Anthony Storr. Princeton: Princeton University Press, 1983.

Kamenka, Eugene. *The Portable Karl Marx*. New York: Viking, 1983.

Keats, John. *The Letters of John Keats*. Ed. Hyder Edward Rollins. Cambridge: Harvard University Press, 1958.

Kirkpatrick, Jeane. *Dictatorship and Doublestandards: Nationalism and Reason in Politics*. New York: Simon and Schuster, 1982.

Klaits, Joseph. *The Age of Witch Hunts*. Bloomington: Indiana University Press, 1981.

Koestler, Arthur. *Darkness at Noon*. Tr. Daphne Hardy. New York: Macmillan, 1941.

——. Foreword. *Stalin's Russia*. By Susan Labin. London: Gollancz, 1949.

——. "A Rebel's Progress." *Observer* 29 (January 1950), 4–5. (Reprinted as "In Memory of George Orwell" in *Bricks to Babel: Selected Writings and Comments by the Author*. London: Hutchinson, 1980.)

——. *The Yogi and the Commissar*. New York: Macmillan, 1945.

Labedz, Leopold. "Will George Orwell Survive 1984? Of Double-think, and Double-Talk, Body-Snatching and Other Silly Pranks." *Encounter* 63 (July/August 1984), 25–34.

Labin, Susan. *Stalin's Russia*. Trans. Edward Fitzgerald. Foreword Arthur Koestler. London: Gollancz, 1949.

Lamont, Corliss. *The Philosophy of Humanism*. 5th ed. New York: Ungar, 1965.

Lee, Robert. *Orwell's Fiction*. Notre Dame, Indiana: University of Notre Dame Press, 1969.

Leites, Nathan. "Psychology of Political Attitudes." *Psycho-Political Analysis: Selected Writings of Nathan Leites*. Ed. Elizabeth Wirth Marvick. New York: John Wiley, Sage Publications, 1977.

Lewis, C.S. "Donne and Love Poetry in the Seventeenth Century." *Seventeenth Century English Poetry*. Ed. W.J. Keast. New York: Oxford University Press, 1962.

Lifton, Robert Jay. "Death and History: Ideological Totalism: Victim-ization and Violence." *Totalitarianism Reconsidered*. Ed. Ernest Menze. Port Washington, New York: Free Press, 1981.

Loewenthal, Karl. *Hitler's Germany*. New York: Macmillan, 1939.

Lottman, Herbert. *Albert Camus: A Biography*. New York: Double-day, 1979.

Mann, Golo. *"1984."* *Frankfurter Rundschau* 5 Nov. 1949, p. 6.

Mann, Thomas. "Mario and the Magician." *Death in Venice and Other Works*. Trans. H.T. Lowe-Porter. London: Secker and War-burg, 1979.

Marcuse, Herbert. *Eros and Civilization*. New York: Vintage, 1955.

May, Rollo. *Love and Will*. New York: Norton, 1969.

McGill, Arthur. "Structure of Inhumanity." *Disguises of the De-monic*. Ed. A.M. Olson. New York: Association Press, 1975.

Menze, Ernest, ed. *Totalitarianism Reconsidered*. Port Washington, New York: Free Press, 1981.

Meyers, Jeffrey, and Valerie Meyers. *George Orwell: An Annotated Bibliography of Criticism*. New York: Garland Publishing, 1977.

Mills, Wright. *The Marxists*. New York: Dell, 1962.

Milosz, Czeslaw, quoted by Edward M. Thomas in *Orwell*. Edin-burgh: Oliver and Boyd, 1965.

More, Thomas. *Utopia*. Trans. Paul Turner. Harmondsworth: Pen-guin, 1961.

Moreno, Antonio. *Jung, Gods and Modern Man*. London: Notre Dame Press, 1970.

Muggeridge, Malcolm. "Muggeridge's Diaries." *Orwell Remembered*. Ed. Audrey Coppard and Bernard Crick. London: B.B.C. Ariel Books, 1984.

Nasty Girl. Dir. Michael Verhoeven. With Lena Stolz. 1989.

Nelson, John. "Orwell's Political Myths and Ours." *The Orwellian Moment.* Ed. Robert Savage, James Coombs, and Dan Nimmo. Fayetteville: The University of Arkansas Press, 1989.

1984. Dir. Michael Anderson. With Edmund O'Brien, Jan Sterling, and Michael Redgrave. 1955.

1984. Dir. Michael Radford. With John Hurt and Richard Burton. 1984.

Novack, George, ed. *Existentialism versus Humanism: Conflicting Views on Humanism.* New York: Dell, 1966.

Novoe Vremya, 1 Jan. 1984.

Olson, A.M., ed. *Disguises of the Demonic: Contemporary Perspectives on the Power of Evil.* New York: Association Press, 1975.

Olson, Robert G. *An Introduction to Existentialism.* New York: Dover, 1962.

Otto, Rudolf. *The Idea of the Holy.* Trans. J.W. Harvey. London: Oxford, 1923.

Patai, Daphne. "Gamesmanship and Androcentism in Orwell's *Nineteen Eighty-Four*." *PMLA* 97 (1982), 856–870.

——— . *The Orwell Mystique: A Study in Male Ideology.* Amherst: University of Massachusetts Press, 1984.

Price, Robert, and Kenneth Noble. *Damascus and the Bodhi Tree: Ancient Wisdom and Modern Thought.* Toronto: Thistle Printing, 1981.

Rahv, Philip. "The Unfuture of Utopia." *Partisan Review* (16 July 1949), 743–749.

Rai, Alok. *Orwell and the Politics of Despair.* Cambridge: Cambridge University Press, 1988.

Rees, Richard. *Fugitive from the Camp of Victory.* London: Secker and Warburg, 1961.

——— . "George Orwell." *Scots Chronicle* 26 (1951), 11 (quoted by Rodden 401).

Reich, Wilhelm. *The Mass Psychology of Fascism.* Trans. V.R. Carfagno. New York: Farrar, Strauss and Giroux, 1970.

Reilly, Patrick. *George Orwell: The Age's Adversary.* London: Macmillan, 1986.

Repentance (Pokayaniye). Dir. Tengiz Abuladze. With Avlandi Makhaladze. 1984.

Rieff, Philip. *Freud — The Mind of the Moralist.* Garden City, New York: Doubleday Anchor Books, 1961.

Roazan, Paul. "Orwell, Freud and *1984*." *Virginia Quarterly Review* 54 (1978), 675–695.

Robbins, R.H. *The Encyclopedia of Witchcraft and Demonology*. New York: Crown, 1960.

Roberts, Stephen. *The House that Hitler Built*. London: Methuen, 1937.

Rodden, John. *The Politics of Literary Reputation: The Making and Claiming of 'St. George' Orwell*. New York: Oxford University Press, 1989.

Rohatyn, Dennis. "Triplethink." Delivered at the American Historical Association Conference, Orwell Session, Honolulu, Aug. 14, 1986.

Roubiczek, Paul. *Existentialism: For and Against*. Cambridge: Cambridge University Press, 1966.

Russell, Bertrand. [George Orwell] *World Review* Jan. 1950, 5–7.

Russell, Francis. *Three Studies in Twentieth Century Obscurity*. London: Dufour Editions, 1959.

Sandison, Alan. *The Last Man of Europe: An Essay on George Orwell*. London: Macmillan, 1974.

Sartre, Jean-Paul. "Existentialism is a Humanism." *Existentialism versus Marxism: Conflicting Views on Humanism*. Ed. George Novack. New York: Dell, 1966.

———. "The Wall." *The Best Short Stories of the Modern Age*. Ed. D. Angus. Greenwich, Conn.: Fawcett, 1962.

Savage, Robert, James Coombs, and Dan Nimmo, eds. *The Orwellian Moment*. Fayetteville: University of Arkansas Press, 1989.

Schapiro, Leonard. *Totalitarianism*. New York: Praeger, 1972.

Schuman, Frederic. *The Nazi Dictatorship*. New York: Knopf, 1935.

Seligman, Kurt. *The History of Magic and the Occult*. New York: Harmony Books, 1948.

Shelden, Michael. *Orwell: The Authorized Biography*. London: Heinemann, 1991.

Simecka, Milan. "Introduction to the Czech Samizdat Edition of *1984*." Published by *Index on Censorship*, quoted by Labedz in "Will George Orwell Survive 1984?" *Encounter* 63 (July/Aug. 1984), 30.

Simms, Valerie J. "A Reconsideration of Orwell's *1984*: The Moral Implications of Despair." *Ethics* 84 (1973–74), 292–306.

Sinyard, Neil. *Filming Literature: The Art of Screen Adaptations*. London: Croom Helm, 1986.

Slater, Ian. *Orwell: The Road to Airstrip One*. New York: Norton, 1985.

Small, Christopher. *The Road to Miniluv: George Orwell, the State and God*. London: Gollancz, 1975.

Smith, Marcus. "The Wall of Blackness." *Modern Fiction Studies* 14 (1968–69), 423–433.

Smyer, Richard. *Primal Dream and Primal Crime: Orwell's Development as a Psychological Novelist.* Columbia: University of Missouri Press, 1979.

Solzhenitsyn, Aleksandr. *The Gulag Archipelago.* New York: Harper and Row, 1973.

Sperber, Murray. "Gazing into the Glass Paperweight: The Structure and Philosophy of Orwell's *Nineteen Eighty-Four*." *Modern Fiction Studies* 26 (1980), 213–216.

Stansky, Peter, ed. *On 1984*. New York: Freeman, 1983.

Stansky, Peter, and William Abrahams. *Orwell: The Transformation.* London: Constable, 1979.

Steiner, George. *Portage to San Cristobal.* New York: Simon and Schuster, 1979.

Steinhoff, William. *George Orwell and the Origins of 1984.* Ann Arbor: University of Michigan Press, 1975.

Sterny, Vincent. "George Orwell and T.S. Eliot: The Sense of the Past." *College Literature* 14 (Spring 1987), 85–100.

Stunia, Melor. *Izvestiya* 15 January 1984.

Swift, Jonathan. *Gulliver's Travels.* Ed. Louis A. Landa. Riverside Editions. Cambridge, Mass.: Houghton Mifflin, 1960.

Talmon, J.L. *The Origins of Totalitarian Democracy.* London: Secker and Warburg, 1955.

Thomas, Edward M. *Orwell.* Writers and Critics Series. Edinburgh: Oliver and Boyd, 1965.

Thomas, Norman. *Socialism Re-examined.* New York: Norton, 1963.

Tolstoy, Nikolai. *Stalin's Secret War.* London: Cape, 1981.

Trilling, Diana. *Nation* 25 June 1949.

Trilling, Lionel. *New Yorker* 16 June 1949.

——. "Introduction to *Homage to Catalonia*." *Homage to Catalonia.* By Orwell. Boston: Beacon Press, 1952.

Ulanov, Ann B. "The Psychological Reality of the Demonic." *Disguises of the Demonic.* Ed. A.M. Olson. New York: Association Press, 1975.

Underhill, Evelyn. *Mysticism.* London: Methuen, 1930.

Wain, John. "Del diagnostical la pesadilla." *Revista de Occidente* 33–34 (1984), 95–109.

——. "The Last of George Orwell." *20th Century* 155 (Jan. 1954), 71.

Warnock, Mary. *Existentialism.* London: Oxford University Press, 1970.

Weintraub, Stanley. "Homage to Utopia." *The Last Great Cause: The Intellectuals and the Spanish Civil War.* New York: 1968.

Wemyss, Courtney, and Alexej Ugrinski, eds. *George Orwell.* Contributions to Study of World Literature #23. Westport: Greenwood, 1987.

Williams, Raymond. *George Orwell.* Modern Masters Series. London: Fontana, 1970.

Wilson, Edmund. "Grade-A Essays: Orwell, Sartre and Highet." *New Yorker* 26 (13 Jan. 1951), 76.

Woodcock, George. *The Crystal Spirit: A Study of George Orwell.* New York: Shocken, 1982.

Zamiatin, Yevgeny. *We.* Tr. Mirra Ginsburg. New York: Avon, 1972.

Zwerdling, Alex. *Orwell and the Left.* New Haven: Yale University Press, 1974.

INDEX